THE BABY RESOURCE GUIDE

I'm Expecting is a division of Hazen Publishing Inc.

Publisher: Kari E. Hazen
Editor-in-Chief: Troy M. Smith
Layout Production: Troy M. Smith and Jude Lowell
Cover and Illustrations: Karen Olson
Proofreader: Carol J. Hazen
Baby Pages Representative: Kari E. Hazen
Local Editors: Boston: Allison Aley, Felice Lopez, Kelly O'Toole
                Los Angeles contributors: Anne Dullaghan, Connie Hurston,
                    Juliana Rose Meyers
                Portland: Deanna Nihill
                Sacramento: Kari MacDonald, Mary J. Patt
                Seattle: Andrea Rowe, Karen Wilkinson

Disclaimer: The authors have made every reasonable effort to provide the most accurate and updated information at the time Portland Baby Resource Guide went to print. The authors have not solicited or accepted payments or consideration of any kind from any person as an inducement to exclude or include material in this book, or to influence its content. However, the reader should bear in mind that the very nature of this book required that the authors receive their information from sources who may have had a bias or who may have been mistaken and that much of the material in this book is based entirely on the personal opinions of the authors and their sources and thus may be inaccurate. Therefore, the readers should make their independent evaluations of any product, service, or course of conduct mentioned herein prior to buying, using or engaging in the same and should not rely on this book as being authoritative in any respect. The authors strongly recommend that the reader discuss all health related issues, services and products with their medical professional and not rely on any health related "advice," suggestions, or information contained in this book. This book is simply intended to provide its readers with a starting point in their quest for information and, hopefully, a certain degree of entertainment.

Copyright © 1998 by I'm Expecting.

All rights reserved. No part of this book may be reproduced or transmitted by any means, electronic or mechanical, including photocopying, recording or by any information retrieval system, without permission in writing from the publisher. Brands and names are the property of their respective owners.

Published by Hazen Publishing Inc. dba I'm Expecting, Auburn, CA. Phone: (530) 823-3659; E-mail address: Karihzn@aol.com. For information regarding custom editions or for information on reproducing The Baby Resource Guide in another city or for The Baby Pages contact Kari Hazen at (530) 823-3659. To be listed in the next Baby Resource Guide, phone (530) 823-3659.

Visit our web site at www.thebabyguide.com
Baby Resource Guides are published in Boston, Los Angeles, Portland, Sacramento, and Seattle.

Manufactured in the United States of America.

HEAR WHAT PEOPLE ARE SAYING ABOUT THE BABY RESOURCE GUIDE...

"The Baby Resource Guide was by far the most helpful item I bought during my entire pregnancy. The product reviews and hospital comparisons were used when I was buying my merchandise and in selecting a hospital. The 'Where to Shop' section was a lifesaver for making purchases. This is a book that is used, cover to cover, and I'm sure it will be a big help when my baby is born."

—Vickie Blocker

"When I became pregnant, we didn't know where to start to prepare for our baby. The Baby Resource Guide gave us valuable insight into baby products, provided information on my maternity leave rights, and helped us save money with all the coupons in the back of the book. Preparing for a baby can be complicated but by the time Grant was born, with the help of The Baby Resource Guide, we were ready for everything, except the lack of sleep!"

—Christy, Rob and Grant Solorio

"The Baby Resource Guide really saved me during my pregnancy! Since this was my first baby, I didn't know where to shop for maternity clothing or baby products. And I knew nothing about the many classes available in town. I keep the guide with me in my car at all times for quick and concise information!"

—Lori Sacco

"The Baby Resource Guide was a godsend. I became pregnant shortly after moving to the area and was not familiar with local resources. Your guide covered every area where I had questions and needed product information. I carry it around with me in my purse whenever I am out. The guide is complete, clear, and accurate. I can't say enough about how wonderful and essential your guide is. Thanks!"

—Lori Bainton

"The Baby Resource Guide has been an invaluable source of information. We are new to Seattle and it really helped me to familiarize myself with the area as well as find the answers to some important questions. I have two of the guides: one for the house, highlighted with notes in the margins, and one in the car, so if I need an address or phone number, or have questions I can call from the cell phone, plus the coupons are on hand. It is so comprehensive and I love learning about other families from their testimonials. I don't feel alone with the obstacles that we have come to. This guide is the perfect gift for baby showers and expectant parents. Thanks for saving my sanity. This book is really a life saver!"

—Stefanie Leigh Grife

ACKNOWLEDGMENTS

The Baby Resource Guide is a collaborative effort of many people who believed in the need for such a book for new and expectant parents. We are thankful to the more than 100 people who made suggestions, contributed ideas, researched, wrote articles, shared their Life Experiences, reviewed articles, checked chapters, double-checked resources, proofread, and helped guide the project all along the way.

We are especially grateful to the medical and marketing staffs at the following health systems who helped us shape the book you have before you now:
- Glendale Memorial Hospital, Glendale, California
- Mercy Healthcare, Sacramento, California
- Northwest Hospital, Seattle, Washington
- Providence Health System, Portland, Oregon
- UC Davis Medical Group, Sacramento, California

Special thanks go to these dedicated health care professionals who gave freely of their time to review the book prior to publication: Kenneth Frank, M.D.; Nanci Newell, R.N.C.; Phillip Patton, M.D.; Carmen Rezak, R.N.P., and Carl Warsowe, M.D. Thanks to our other reviewers: Robin Song of the Placer County Office of Education Child Care Services, Cathy Morris of the Placer County (CA) Buckle Up Baby Car Seat Project, Sherri Martin and Janis Grusz of Safety for Toddlers of Kirkland (WA), Adrienne Disbrow, Linda Fraguglia, Dawn Malicoat, R.N., Kerry Breeler, Anthony Urquiza, Ph.D., Adrianne Westlake and Lisa Yount.

Contributing articles new to this edition are Ignacio Valdes, M.D.; Carmen Rezak, R.N.P.; Dawn Frankwick, M.D.; Adrienne Disbrow, ICCE, CMT; Sally Ellsworth, R.N., ICCE; Donna Hudson-Bryant, R.N.; Joseph Antognini, M.D.; Kari MacDonald; Dianne Neilson, R.N.; John Kuhn, M.D.; Charles F. Simmons, Jr., M.D.; Sharon D. Simmons, R.N., B.S.N.; Michael Lucien, M.D.

Thanks to those organizations allowing us to reprint articles: the American Sudden Infant Death Syndrome Institute, Child Care Resources of Seattle (WA), Fairview Press, the North American Registry of Midwives, the Pregnancy and Infant Loss Center, Providence Health System of Portland (OR), Northwest Hospital of Seattle (WA), and Washington State's Safety and Health Assessment and Research Program.

Special thanks go to the local editors and researchers who enthusiastically embraced this project and made each city's book special. Thank you, Allison Aley, Felice Lopez, Kelly O'Toole, Lindy Forrester, Sandy Lima, Juliana Rose Meyers, Deanna Nihill, Kari MacDonald, Mary J. Patt, Andrea Rowe and Karen Wilkinson. Thank you to Cheryl Deamas of Work at Home Moms (www.WAHM.com) and the moms who helped pull the Los Angeles book together.

We are grateful to all of the parents who shared their life experiences. Thanks to those who helped complete the guide and make it comprehensive and accurate.

To the business community, book stores, and childbirth organizations—your support shows the need for this guide. We salute you!

TABLE OF CONTENTS

INTRODUCTION 1

HOW TO USE THIS BOOK 2

SO YOU'RE HAVING A BABY! 3
Life Experiences: "Letter From a Dad, With Love" 4
Preconceptional Health Assessment 6
   Reviewing medical history before pregnancy.
Pregnancy Nutrition 9
   Eat right to keep you and baby healthy.
Choosing Your Practitioner 11
   There are a lot of choices; what's right for you?
Using a Labor Doula 16
   Information on professional childbirth assistants.
Ensuring Your Baby's Health 19
   Positive steps you can take during pregnancy.
Questions and Answers: Your Insurance Provider 22
   Insights on medical coverage during pregnancy.
Hospital Choices 24
   Comprehensive overview of hospital facilities.
Life Experiences: "Souvenir Pregnancy" 28
Your Hospital Stay: One Day or More? 30
   What you can expect and how to be prepared.
Staying In Shape 33
   Exercise for the pregnant woman.
Childbirth Education 36
   Explanation of the various childbirth methods.
Labor Pain Relief 40
   Low-tech ways to help you through labor.
Medical Pain Relief in Childbirth 43
   An overview of medical pain relief methods.
Life Experiences: "My Cesarean Birth" 46
Hints for Avoiding a Cesarean Section 49
   Proactive steps you can take to avoid a C-section.
Questions and Answers: Cesarean Births 51
   An ob-gyn explains emergency Cesareans.

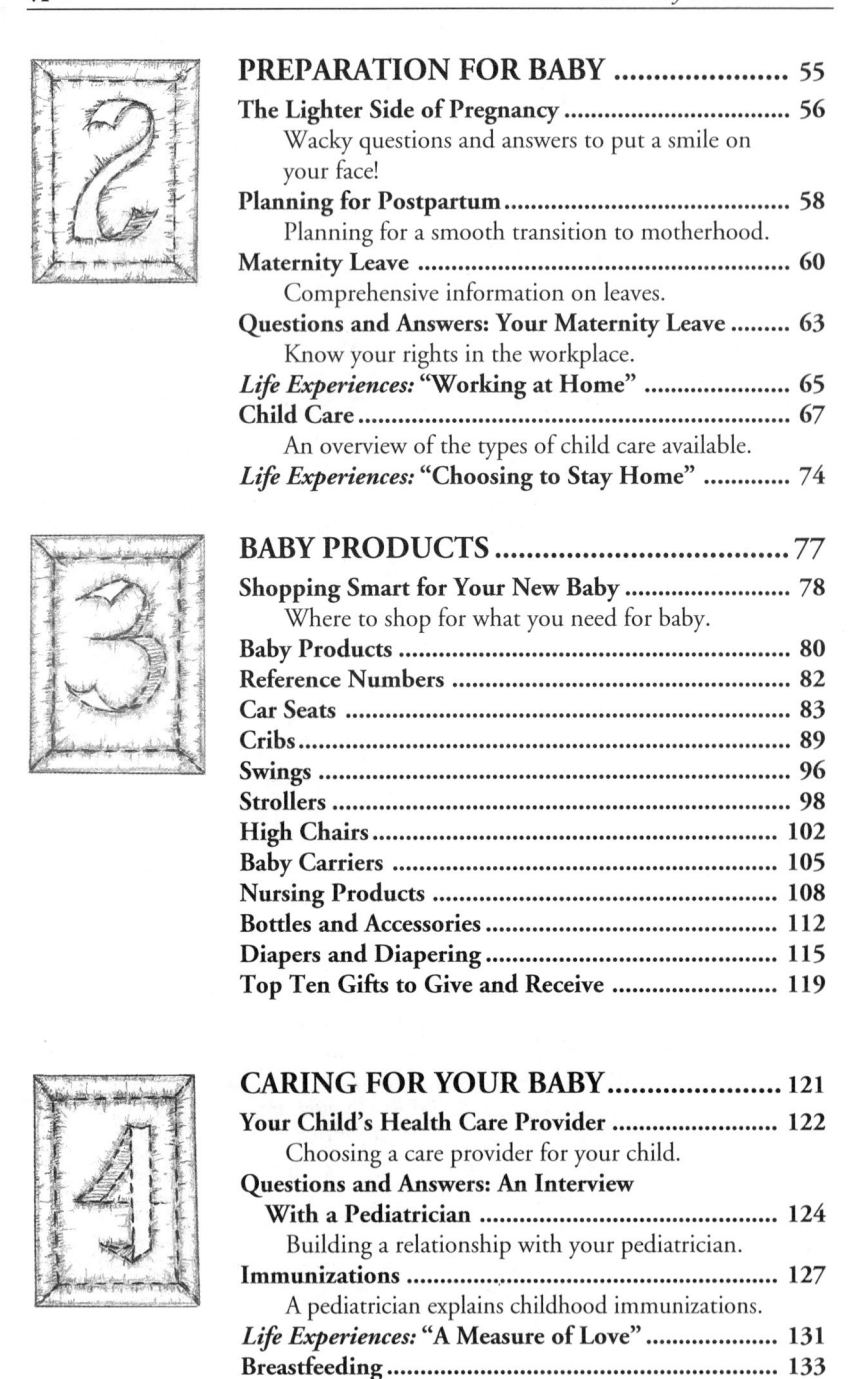

PREPARATION FOR BABY 55
The Lighter Side of Pregnancy 56
  Wacky questions and answers to put a smile on your face!
Planning for Postpartum 58
  Planning for a smooth transition to motherhood.
Maternity Leave 60
  Comprehensive information on leaves.
Questions and Answers: Your Maternity Leave 63
  Know your rights in the workplace.
Life Experiences: "Working at Home" 65
Child Care 67
  An overview of the types of child care available.
Life Experiences: "Choosing to Stay Home" 74

BABY PRODUCTS 77
Shopping Smart for Your New Baby 78
  Where to shop for what you need for baby.
Baby Products 80
Reference Numbers 82
Car Seats 83
Cribs 89
Swings 96
Strollers 98
High Chairs 102
Baby Carriers 105
Nursing Products 108
Bottles and Accessories 112
Diapers and Diapering 115
Top Ten Gifts to Give and Receive 119

CARING FOR YOUR BABY 121
Your Child's Health Care Provider 122
  Choosing a care provider for your child.
**Questions and Answers: An Interview
  With a Pediatrician** 124
  Building a relationship with your pediatrician.
Immunizations 127
  A pediatrician explains childhood immunizations.
Life Experiences: "A Measure of Love" 131
Breastfeeding 133
  Information and resources for nursing moms.

Table of Contents

Life Experiences: "You Can Work and Breastfeed" . 139
Questions and Answers: Sleep—Getting a
    Full Night's Rest 142
        Setting good sleep habits should begin early.
Pacifier Pros and Cons 144
        Read this before putting a pacifier in your baby's mouth!
Life Experiences: "Pacifier Pointers" 145
Feeding Baby 147
        Information on formula and baby food.
Child Safety 150
        Is your home safe for your baby?

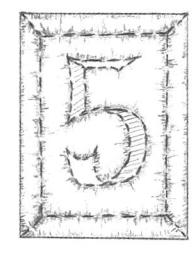

SPECIAL CONCERN RESOURCES 155

Life Experiences: "Alicia" 156
Children With Special Needs 158
        An overview of special needs conditions and listings of resources for parents.
Life Experiences: "Yes, I'm Pregnant" 166
Infertility 169
        The latest in fertility treatments.
Coping With Grief 173
        Coming to terms with a baby's death.
Life Experiences: "In Remembrance of Sara" 176
Pregnancy and Child Loss Resources 178
        An extensive listing of helpful resources.
SIDS Prevention Strategies 179
        What you can do to minimize SIDS risks.
Life Experiences: "My Baby's Premature Birth" 182
Questions and Answers: Premature Infants 184
        A neonatologist presents current information.
Life Experiences: "Bedrest Blues . . . and Triumphs" 189
Bedrest: A Prescription, Not A Sentence 192
        Tips for coping with bedrest.
Life Experiences: "You Are My Sunshine" 194
Multiple Birth Resources 196
        Having twins or more? Here's help.
Life Experiences: "Life as a Teen Parent" 197
Maternal Age Factors 199
        For teens and women over 40, pregnancy can be a challenge.
Child Abuse 201
        Important information about physical abuse—including shaken baby syndrome—and neglect.

TAKING CARE OF YOURSELF AND YOUR FAMILY 203

Keeping Your Relationship Alive 204
Your relationship can flourish even after the birth of a child . . . here's one mother's advice.
Life Experiences: "Camaraderie Makes the Difference" 206
Support Groups 208
Information on a variety of support groups.
Online Support 212
With a computer, modem and phone line, you can be in touch with many great resources.
Life Experiences: "Real Life With Baby" 214
Questions and Answers: Postpartum Depression 216
Valuable information for mothers who are battling more than the "baby blues."
Life Experiences: "More Than Blues" 220
Getting to Know Your Baby 222
Spending time getting to know your infant.
Infant Massage 227
Create a special bond with a soothing touch.
Life Experiences: "Zen and the Art of Mothering" .. 229
The Vast Advantages of Parenthood 231
Final thoughts from award-winning author Joyce Armor on the joys and struggles of parenthood.

LOCAL SECTION 233

Includes resources and information written just for your local area. The local section is followed by an index which covers the entire book. Finally you'll find The Baby Pages and coupons to help keep your expenses down while preparing for your new baby!

INTRODUCTION

Every day is a miracle. Nothing is more true than when you think about the birth of a child.

Think about it. It all starts with two people coming together, creating two cells that offer the blueprint of a human being. These cells multiply to create a heart, a mind and a soul. Every day a fetus is in its mother's womb, it gains strength to face this miracle... life.

As a parent, there are times when you will sit back and look with amazement at your child, overcome with awe that you created this special human being. It is frightening to think of the new responsibilities given to you, all with no instructions and no exam by which to validate your proficiency as a parent.

There are so many questions that come with the birth of a new baby. In today's complex society it may be difficult to find the answers you need. We may find ourselves living thousands of miles away from our families with no support network and possibly working through pregnancy and beyond, while at the same time wanting to be an involved and educated parent.

Because of this, a company named *I'm Expecting* was born. Its mission was to compile a resource guide for area parents. It started as a simple idea, yet grew as many area parents and experts contributed their thoughts and experiences to our endeavor, all with the hope of helping you in your new parenting role. And now, through the support of the baby business community and parents, The Baby Resource Guide is in print.

The Baby Resource Guide is meant to be many things, none of which is to replace medical advice or treatment, or to take the place of Consumer Reports. Please take care of yourself and your baby. Cherish these special days. As a soon-to-be parent, you are experiencing our greatest miracle... life!

> *In today's complex society it may be difficult to find the answers you need.*

HOW TO USE THIS BOOK

The Baby Resource Guide has been providing vital information for new parents for six years. The book has grown from a 200 page local guide to the 400+ page compendium before you now. Beginning with this issue, all resources and articles specific to your local area are located in the back of the book. Check both the national and local sections to find all relevant information on any topic. Convenient tabs help you find both the national and local listings within the book's six chapters. In the front section, you'll find national resources following most articles, plus the guide's irreplaceable slice-of-life stories we call "Life Experiences." Chapter topics include:

- **So You're Having a Baby!** From choosing the right practitioner and information about preconception counseling to ways to help you through your baby's delivery, this chapter prepares you for what you need to know about staying healthy through pregnancy, finding a childbirth educator, and both avoiding and preparing for a possible Cesarean birth.
- **Preparation for Baby.** Planning for postpartum should begin well before your baby's birth. Included is information about maternity leave, with the latest on the Family Medical Leave Act and the Pregnancy Discrimination Act. You'll also learn about child care options.
- **Baby Products.** Confused about available baby products? We've done the homework; just read our reviews to make the best choices on everything from car seats and cribs to swings, baby carriers, high chairs and breastfeeding accessories. Then go to stores to try out equipment and make your own decision. The local section of this chapter has reviews of stores in your area. Make sure you call ahead to verify locations. Businesses do occasionally change and we know your time is valuable.
- **Caring for Your Baby.** The nitty-gritty of caring for that new little one is here. A pediatrician answers parents' questions about doctor visits, and another pediatrician fills you in on immunizations. There's a great introduction to breastfeeding and a section on child safety.
- **Special Concerns.** Life doesn't always run smoothly. We present information for parents of children with special needs and articles on infertility, premature infants, and multiple births. There is an important article on coping with grief.
- **Taking Care of Yourself and Your Family.** Your family life is changed forever once your baby is born. Here's help for you to cope with the stress a new baby brings. Support groups are a way for new moms to connect with others. You'll find a primer on postpartum depression, then ideas for everyday life with baby. The local section includes a great many ideas for family activities in your area.

This isn't a book you read in one sitting. But dip into it here and there, use the index, which combines both the national and local sections, and you're on your way to learning more and more about having a baby—your special baby. And if you have a Life Experience you'd like to share, or know of a helpful resource we should add, drop us a line—we know that parents are the greatest resource of all.

SO, YOU'RE HAVING A BABY!

"Letter From A Dad, With Love"

A Life Experience by Bruce Patt

A few weeks before our baby's due date . . .
Dear baby girl,

You're ready now, and waiting, and this might be the first of very many times of patience in your life. Nothing I've read suggests that you're actually thinking yet, but something in you must sense, innately, that it's time to move on. But prevailing conditions can conspire against our instincts, and that's when we have to just do our best, have faith in the process, and be patient. I'm writing this to you, but I mean it for me as well; I probably need the advice even more.

Today, you live in the most exquisite harmony, awash in love and sustenance within your mother's womb. You don't have an idea of you, yet, and you haven't met any of the rest of us. There's no balance to seek, no conflict, no worry. But once you're born, harmony will be something which you will probably be striving for. At least that's been true for me. While I wasn't looking for it here, through my letters to you I have begun to find that sense of balance within my own life. Although you are an entirely separate human being, you, my little girl, are irreversibly a part of who I am. Whenever I introduce myself to people, if I simply say I am Bruce Patt I will be omitting the most important part: I am your father.

It's hard to be patient, even when you're feeling pretty well balanced. You know it's time to get on with it. But other people have their say, too; this time, it's your mother, whose body has not received your signal to begin opening your gateway to life. I could imagine you in there, bags packed, ready to travel, but the bus hasn't arrived. Although this isn't an issue for you now, by the time you read this letter you will have already experienced many times how waiting can be an opportunity. One time several years ago I was traveling to a seminar out of town and went outside at five in the morning to be picked up for a ride to the airport. For several minutes I paced and fretted and looked at my watch. Then I happened to look up, and I saw thousands of stars through the gently swaying branches of a big tree. Standing out there, with my bags on the pavement and my face to the sky, it struck me that so many times I have rushed out of the house, and then back in, and hardly ever stopped to look upward for some perspective. Patience is easy to forget about in a world in which having things, or being places now, seems more important than any of the reasons why.

Well, it's been a long wait for you, and every few minutes now I feel myself becoming, if not impatient, then excited and apprehensive about your coming. While I wait I am reminded to look upward; the view brings me closer to you, whether it's through these words or through the trees.

Your mom is in the study transcribing an interview for a story she hopes to write before you're born. The chicken soup she made today is simmering on the stove. I've been nibbling pretzels and sipping soda, and I'm listening to George Winston's album, "Summer," on the headphones while I write to you. Felix is asleep on the living room floor on a spot where the sun was about an hour ago. Your room is ready for you; we'll hang the window valance today and proclaim it done, for now.

Life is made of a lot of little things. Notice them, and try not to expect greatness to always be apparent. The little things are there, and somehow, magically, they combine to form your picture of the world and, in a way, yourself. I guess that you and I are really just little things in the big picture, but that will never mean that you are ever less than greatness.

Love, Dad

PRECONCEPTIONAL HEALTH ASSESSMENT

By Ignacio Valdes, M.D., and Carmen Rezak, R.N.P.

Seeking counseling with a physician and other health care practitioners prior to pregnancy is vital and can decrease maternal anxiety, risks of congenital birth defects and maternal and fetal complications in pregnancy and delivery. During this preconception visit a complete history and physical examination will take place, in addition to certain laboratory tests. Any anxieties and concerns may be expressed and questions answered during this visit. The following areas are of particular importance:

MEDICAL HISTORY

Certain health problems need to be identified and treated prior to becoming pregnant. Diabetes significantly increases the risks of birth defects if not treated prior to pregnancy. Hypertension, epilepsy, asthma, thyroid disorder and lupus erythematosis should be well controlled before pregnancy, labor and delivery. Other pertinent information to identify is a history of deep vein thrombosis, kidney disease or heart disease. Your health care provider will also ask you about your menstrual history, contraceptive methods used, previous sexually transmitted infections, allergies, surgical history, and rubella (German measles) status. Screening for rubella and receiving the appropriate vaccination will prevent congenital rubella syndrome. It is recommended to wait three months prior to getting pregnant after being vaccinated.

FAMILY AND GENETIC HISTORY

Emphasis is placed on the mother's health because it is crucial to give the baby a healthy environment in which to develop. But the health of the father is important, too. The provider will ask questions about family members (both mother's and father's) with any history of birth defects, mental retardation, Down syndrome, diabetes, anemia, twins or any possibly inheritable disease. Testing for inheritable diseases such as Tay-Sachs, sickle cell anemia, cystic fibrosis or thalassemia may be needed as well. On rare occasions substances in the environment or workplace may be harmful to a pregnant woman or fetus. It is important to offer information on exposure to toxic chemicals, radiation, lead, insecticides or other substances.

Depending on the history obtained, the provider will counsel the patient on its significance, or in some cases, refer the patient to a geneticist or genetic counselor. The goal of preconception counseling, relative to family and genetic history, is to provide the prospective parents sufficient information to make informed decisions.

MATERNAL AGE

Today more women are investing time in their careers and opting to delay starting a family. Most women in their 30s and early 40s have uncomplicated pregnancies. If a woman is in good health, there is no reason why she cannot have a healthy baby. The risks for miscarriage, diabetes, hypertension and chromosomal abnormalities—such as Down syndrome —increase with advancing maternal age. After the age of 35, the risks of chromosomal abnormalities are significant and many women elect to undergo amniocentesis after receiving counseling.

It is important to be informed about potential problems and discuss plans with the provider to ensure a woman gets the proper medical attention.

OBSTETRICAL HISTORY

Although it is uncommon for most complications of pregnancies to recur, it is nevertheless important to go over the significant details of all previous pregnancies. Questions regarding previous miscarriages, tubal pregnancies, abortions, stillbirths, neonatal deaths, preterm labor, vaginal bleeding and high blood pressure (hypertension or preeclampsia) are asked.

Specific information regarding labor and delivery may also be important. This would include: length of labor, complications of labor such as bleeding or fetal distress, mode of delivery (Cesarean section or vaginal), infant's weight and any post-delivery complications.

Preconception counseling can relieve a couple's anxiety by discussing any previous complications and exploring beliefs about previous losses. Counseling is a good time to encourage a couple to express fears, show support and to prepare for future pregnancies with optimism.

NUTRITIONAL NEEDS

It is important to follow a well-balanced diet, not only during pregnancy, but also during the time of preconception. A good prepregnancy diet is the best way to ensure that a woman and future baby get a healthy start.

Dietary habits are discussed and may be altered to optimize the development of the fetus. Vegetarians may need to make certain changes to increase protein consumption. Eating disorders and obesity may impact pregnancy and should be investigated prior to conception, as well.

Folic acid has been shown to significantly decrease the incidence of neural tube defects in infants, when taken at the time of conception. Although significant quantities of folic acid can be found in several foods (broccoli, beets, orange juice, green peas, avocado, romaine lettuce, spinach, various types of beans, wheat germ, fortified cereals), it is recommended that all women of childbearing age take a multivitamin containing at least 0.4 mg of folic acid.

GENERAL HEALTH AND LIFESTYLE

Good general health before pregnancy can help a woman cope with the stress of pregnancy, labor and delivery. It can also ensure that neither mom nor baby is exposed to things that can be harmful.

Only a few medications are known to cause birth defects; however, all medications (prescription and nonprescription) should be reported to the provider and certain changes may be necessary prior to conception. Oral contraceptives are not known to cause birth defects, but it is generally recommended to discontinue the pill approximately three months prior to conception.

Alcohol, tobacco and mood-altering drugs pose certain risks to the fetus and should be avoided. Low birth weight, placental irregularities and infant mortality, as well as long-term effects on the physical, emotional and intellectual development of children born to women who use these substances during pregnancy, have been reported. Testing for HIV and hepatitis B may be appropriate. These viruses can be passed to the fetus during pregnancy.

The importance of preconception counseling cannot be overemphasized. Seeking education and guidance, as well as a physical examination and review of the medical history, from a physician and other health care practitioners, can assist a woman and her partner in making informed decisions about future reproduction. Planning for a healthy baby should begin prior to conception.

PREGNANCY NUTRITION

By Dawn Frankwick, M.D.

While your body is busy preparing and nurturing your new child, you may tend to overestimate your nutritional needs. In reality, you should only add an additional 300 calories a day (equivalent to a glass of whole milk) while pregnant. You do not need to eat for two! By understanding what your body needs on a daily basis, you can be sure to choose those foods that provide the most benefit to you and your growing baby.

DIETARY RECOMMENDATIONS

The United States Department of Agriculture's food pyramid recommends lots of fruits and vegetables, breads and whole grains, and limiting the amount of fat, oil, and sugar. Specific recommendations include:

- **Grains: 6-11 servings a day.** Some sample servings are a slice of whole-grain bread, 1/2 cup of hot cereal, a pancake or waffle, 1/2 cup rice or noodles, a muffin, biscuit, or two tortillas. Emphasize whole grains to increase your fiber intake. Limit white flour and processed grains due to limited nutritional content.
- **Vegetables: 3-5 servings per day, and fruit: 3-5 servings per day.** Vegetables and fruits are important for their abundance of vitamins and minerals. Fresh is best, followed by frozen, then canned. To keep the vitamin content high, don't overcook vegetables. Consider buying organic produce.
- **Dairy products: 4 servings per day.** These foods can be very high in fat content so you may wish to choose low-fat versions of these items. Sample servings include one cup of milk, cheese (2"x1"x1" cube), or a cup each of yogurt, cottage cheese or frozen yogurt. These dairy products are high in calcium, which helps calcify baby's bones and minimize your risk of future osteoporosis.
- **Proteins: 2-3 servings per day.** Protein foods are important to build strong muscles and blood. Cut back on red meat, and emphasize skinless poultry as a good low fat choice for protein consumption. Don't forget about other protein sources—fresh fish, eggs, beans, tofu, peanut butter, and nuts. Cut back on processed meats such as hot dogs, sausage and bacon.

You should only add an additional 300 calories a day while pregnant. You do not need to eat for two!

Discuss weight gain goals with your provider. The American College of Obstetrics and Gynecology (ACOG) currently recommends a weight gain of 30-35 pounds for women of normal prepregnancy weight. Special attention should be paid to the needs of vegetarian women, those carrying twins, or those with allergies or medical needs that may affect nutrition. If you take any prescribed or over-the-counter medications, vitamin supplements, laxatives or diet aids, tell your provider.

Taking a good multivitamin, with your provider's approval, can be a good way to ensure adequate vitamin intake. Extra supplementation of iron is frequently necessary since the average diet doesn't meet minimum nutritional needs. ACOG recommends taking iron supplements between meals or at bedtime with water to maximize absorption. Iron may cause your stool to turn darker in color, or cause constipation. You can minimize these effects by drinking lots of fluids and eating high fiber foods. Beware: with vitamin supplementation, more is not better. Too much vitamin A can lead to bone, urinary tract, and central nervous system defects.

Don't forget water! Drinking two quarts of water each day can lessen your hunger and reduce constipation. Consider keeping a sports bottle with you and setting a goal of drinking two or three bottles of fluids each day.

HEALTHY SNACK OPTIONS

- Cheese, whole grain crackers, and grapes
- Frozen yogurt, fruit, and nuts
- Pita bread with cheese, tomato, and avocado
- Unbuttered air-popped popcorn
- Whole grain muffin with raisins
- Baked potato topped with low-fat cheese and broccoli
- Sliced vegetables or fruit with a yogurt dip
- Brown rice cakes with cottage cheese, scallions and tomato

KICK THE JUNK FOOD HABIT

- Switch to low-salt variety of pretzels, snack chips or crackers.
- Bake your own treats and reduce the amount of sugar and fats.
- Save candy for special occasions rather than an everyday indulgence.
- Choose unbuttered popcorn instead of potato chips for a quick snack.
- Avoid deep-fried foods such as French fries, potato chips and fried fish.
- Mix 1/2 cup fruit juice with 1/2 cup plain carbonated water or seltzer instead of soda pop.
- Choose low fat frozen yogurt or a frozen fruit juice popsicle for dessert.
- Have vegetable pizza and eliminate high-fat, high-salt meat toppings.

Nutrition hints courtesy of Northwest Hospital in Seattle, Washington.

CHOOSING YOUR PRACTITIONER

If you're thinking about becoming pregnant, or are pregnant, your very first step should be to get prenatal care; it is important for you and the unborn life that depends on you. It is equally crucial that you not wait for your initial prenatal visit to begin preparing your body for the birth of your child. If possible, meet with your practitioner before you are pregnant to discuss any issues you may have.

Your health care practitioner is the expert on prenatal care; listen to his or her instructions and establish an open and honest relationship. Your practitioner's goal, as well as yours, is to bring a new, healthy life into this world.

You may have questions about finding a practitioner. Many expectant mothers may already be completely satisfied with their present obstetrician, midwife or general practitioner. Others may choose to "shop around" or simply do not have a provider at all.

There are a variety of providers and referral agencies that can help you locate prenatal care. A good place to start is with your medical insurance or the state medical program to find out if you can select a provider of your choice, or if you must use a plan's specific provider. Ask friends or relatives for their recommendations. Keep in mind the personality, needs, and communication style of the person referring you. Her provider may have met her needs, but may not be right for you.

What you will probably find is that practitioners vary considerably in their philosophy, training, experience and expertise. The following information on providers' qualifications may help you make your choice.

Your practitioner's goal, as well as yours, is to bring a new, healthy life into this world.

FAMILY PHYSICIANS

A family physician has been trained to care for a broad variety of patients—from pediatrics to obstetrics to geriatrics. This allows you to have one physician overseeing not only your medical treatment, but also your family members'. Check to see if your family physician delivers babies. Family physicians have completed their undergraduate degree, four years of medical training, followed by three years of specialty training in family medicine that includes obstetrics and pediatrics. Family physicians who have successfully passed an oral and written examination given by the American Board of Family Practice are known as "Board Certified." The initials ABFP will follow their name and title. In case of a pregnancy complication, a family physician will have an obstetrician as a backup.

NURSE PRACTITIONERS/ PHYSICIAN'S ASSISTANTS

Some physicians' offices have either a nurse practitioner or physician's assistant. Depending on your physician, they may do some or most of your prenatal office visit. They are not licensed to deliver babies. A nurse practitioner has a bachelor's degree in nursing and then attends graduate school and completes an internship before practicing. In most states, a master's degree in nursing is also required. Registered nurse practitioners may be primary care providers and work in close collaboration with medical doctors. A physician's assistant has graduated from a rigorous specialized medical program, although it may not necessarily be in obstetrics, and cannot practice independently.

OBSTETRICIANS

An obstetrician has completed college, four years of medical school, and four years of specialty training in obstetrics and gynecology. Obstetricians are trained specifically in pregnancy and are acknowledged experts in their field. Obstetricians are able to identify pregnancy risks and perform surgical procedures as needed. Obstetricians who have successfully passed an oral and written examination given by the American Board of Obstetrics are known as "Board Certified." The initials FACOG verify that they have completed this training and joined the American College of Obstetrics and Gynecology.

PERINATOLOGISTS

A perinatologist is a doctor who specializes in the care of high-risk problems of pregnancy. These include conditions such as diabetes, heart disease, and preterm birth. Perinatologists' training is the same as an obstetrician's, plus an additional two to three years of subspecialty training.

MIDWIVES

For women who have a normal, low-risk pregnancy, a midwife can offer everything from prenatal care to the baby's delivery. Midwives tend to view birth as a normal, healthy event which, in most cases, works best with as little medical intervention as possible. Midwives are trained to watch for and identify potential or actual complications and, if necessary, can provide emergency treatment until additional medical assistance is available. Licensed midwives work with a physician backup. Although regulated individually by states, the following categories of midwives are recognized in the United States:

Certified Nurse Midwives. Certified nurse midwives practice most often in hospitals and birth centers. They are registered nurses who have a graduate degree in midwifery, and must attend an educational program and pass a follow-up examination to become accredited by

Choosing Your Practitioner

the American College of Nurse-Midwives Certification Council. They can be licensed in the individual states in which they practice.

Certified Professional Midwives. These midwives are certified through the North American Registry of Midwives (NARM), and have passed a written examination and skills assessment test. Certified Professional Midwives' credentials are not accepted in every state.

Direct-Entry Midwives. "Direct-entry" midwives are licensed in some states. They are not required to become nurses before training to be midwives, and most often practice in birth centers and homes.

Midwife definitions courtesy of the North American Registry of Midwives.

NATUROPATHIC PHYSICIANS

In Arizona, Arkansas, Connecticut, Hawaii, Maine, Montana, New Hampshire, Oregon, Utah and Washington, naturopathic physicians may be licensed to provide maternal care and attend births, generally in home or birthing center deliveries. The naturopathic physician, a graduate of one of the U.S.'s three four-year postgraduate naturopathic medical schools, practices holistic health care, treating patients with homeopathy, clinical nutrition and botanical medicine. High-risk deliveries are referred to an obstetrician.

INTERVIEWING A HEALTH CARE PROVIDER

The determining factor in choosing a practitioner is often your medical insurance. Your insurer will likely give you names of providers for you to choose from. Once you have a number of possibilities, call their offices to see if they are accepting new patients, verify that they accept your insurance carrier, and ask if an interview is available. Some providers provide a free, short consultation in person or by telephone, but others charge for an interview and many are too busy with patients. In the latter case, the only way to know if the provider is right for you is during or after your first prenatal visit. Some practices have an informational session open to prospective clients.

After the interview or first visit, ask yourself if you and your partner will feel comfortable with the qualifications and communication style of the practitioner. Also, consider how comfortable you feel with your provider's office staff. You probably will have more encounters with the office staff during your pregnancy than with the actual provider. Therefore, a friendly, open and available office staff may make a difference about how you feel about your provider.

Only your own circumstances and criteria can determine your provider-patient relationship. Use your judgment and trust your intuition when making your decision. Finding a provider that you can work with and trust completely will make for a happier, less stressful pregnancy, labor and birth.

~ RESOURCES ~

■ **AMERICAN COLLEGE OF NURSE MIDWIVES**
888-MIDWIFE
818 Connecticut Ave. N.W. #900
Washington, DC 20006
Web site: www.midwife.org
E-mail: info@acnm.org
The American College of Nurse Midwives offers information about nurse midwifery services and accredited university affiliated nurse-midwifery education programs. They will provide a list of midwives affiliated with their organization.

■ **HEALTHY MOTHERS, HEALTHY BABIES (HMHB)**
(202) 863-2458
409 21th St., S.W., Ste. 309
Washington, DC 20024
Backed by more than 100 national member organizations, Healthy Mothers, Healthy Babies coordinates services that foster healthy families. State coalitions work in their communities to promote maternal and infant health. Individuals can write for resource lists on topics such as pregnancy, breastfeeding and nutrition, adolescent pregnancy, and immunization, and to find out more about their local HMHB programs.

■ **INFORMED HOMEBIRTH/ INFORMED BIRTH AND PARENTING (IH/IBP)**
(313) 662-6857
P.O. Box 3675
Ann Arbor, MI 48106
Minimal intervention at birth is the focus of this organization, founded in 1977. Originally focusing on home birth, IH/IBP has since expanded to provide information on alternatives in birth and parenting, and referrals to childbirth educators, birth assistants, and midwives. A 14-page pamphlet, priced at $1.50 (plus 50 cents postage), introduces advantages and disadvantages of home birth, information about safety, and state midwifery organizations. Several books and videos are offered through IH/IBP, and each spring the group hosts a conference in Michigan for parents and early childhood educators, emphasizing Waldorf education from birth through the early grades.

■ **INTERNATIONAL ASSOCIATION OF PARENTS AND PROFESSIONALS FOR SAFE ALTERNATIVES IN CHILDBIRTH (NAPSAC)**
(573) 238-2010
Rt. 1, Box 646
Marble Hill, MO 63764
If you're interested in family-centered maternity care and childbirth alternatives, NAPSAC is a great place to find information. The organization offers a wide variety of pregnancy and parenting books and pamphlets, including the NAPSAC *Directory of Alternative Birth Services* for $7.95. A $20 yearly membership will pay for their quarterly newsletter, discounts on publications, and information on becoming a local NAPSAC leader to promote safe alternatives in childbirth.

■ MIDWIFERY TODAY
(541) 344-7438
P.O. Box 2672-708
Eugene, OR 97402
Web site: members.aol.com/midwifery/index.html
E-mail: midwifery@aol.com
Midwifery Today will provide pamphlets on topics such as home births and questions to ask your midwife. They make referrals to midwifery organizations. For an annual membership fee of $67, members receive a quarterly magazine subscription and "The Birth Kit," a quarterly newsletter, and the opportunity to attend the group's conventions. "The Birth Kit" subscription alone is $20.

■ MIDWIVES ALLIANCE OF NORTH AMERICA (MANA)
(316) 283-4543
P.O. Box 175
Newton, KS 67114
E-mail: MANAinfo@aol.com
MANA works with the North American Registry of Midwives and the Midwifery Education and Accreditation Council to establish independent midwifery as a viable health care option for women. They support a woman's right to choose her care provider and place of birth—home, birth center, or hospital. MANA promotes the "midwifery model of care" which is based on the fact that pregnancy and birth are normal life events. For referrals to local midwives, you must request information by mail. You can also request the brochures "What is a Midwife?," "Expecting a Baby? Consider a Midwife," and further information about the positive aspects of midwifery from this organization or from Carol Nelson, 107 The Farm, Summertown, TN 38483.

■ NATIONAL ASSOCIATION OF CHILDBEARING CENTERS (NACC)
(215) 234-8068
3123 Gottschall Rd.
Perkiomenville, PA 18074
E-mail: birthctr@midwives.org
A not-for-profit membership organization, NACC is the nation's most comprehensive resource on birth centers. NACC is dedicated to developing quality, holistic services for families that promote self-reliance and confidence in birth and parenting. NACC sets national standards for birth center operation, promotes state regulations for licensure, and national accreditation by the Commission for the Accreditation of Birth Centers. If you are interested in finding out more about birthing centers, write to NACC, including a $1 donation, and the organization will send you information about birth centers in your area and information on how to select a birth center.

■ NATIONAL MATERNAL AND CHILD HEALTH CLEARINGHOUSE
(703) 356-1964
2070 Chain Bridge Rd., Ste. 450
Vienna, VA 22182
E-mail: nmchc@circsol.com
A sister organization to the National Center for Education in Maternal and Child Health, the Clearinghouse provides consumer education materials on maternal and child health topics such as prenatal care, nutrition, infant care, breastfeeding, child health and dental care. You may request a free publication catalog by mail.

USING A LABOR DOULA

By Adrienne Disbrow, CIMI, Doula, CMT, ICCE

A doula is a professional experienced in childbirth who provides continuous physical, emotional, and informational support to the mother and expecting family before, during and just after childbirth. She understands the natural process of pregnancy, labor and birth, and the emotional needs of expecting families. A doula recognizes childbirth as a life-changing experience and understands her role as a member of the family's perinatal team during this experience.

Doulas come in all shapes and sizes with different philosophies, personalities, and experiences. Most importantly, you must be comfortable with and confident in your doula. Following are some general characteristics to look for in a doula.

- She should be flexible and in general good health, with good communication skills—and be an especially good listener.
- Because she is going to support you during your baby's birth, she should be able to put aside her personal beliefs and support you in your informed decisions.
- She should be professional, responsible, warm, compassionate, and enthusiastic.

CHOOSING A DOULA

Feel free to ask questions to help you determine if the doula is right for you and your family. Some good questions to ask when interviewing doulas:

- What is your training and experience?
- What services do you provide (i.e. in-home prenatal visits, in-home labor support, postpartum visits, etc.), and when do your services start?
- Are you available prenatally by phone?
- Do you have a backup doula?
- What are your fees?
- What do you consider the most important elements of care when working as a doula?

A doula understands the natural process of pregnancy, labor and birth, and the emotional needs of expecting families.

WHAT CAN A DOULA DO FOR YOU?

- **During pregnancy:** A doula can help your family prepare your birth plan and clarify your goals and perceptions of birth. She can also answer general childbirth questions. Your doula may also have videos and a lending library available for your use. You will probably meet with a doula several times before the birth to go over your birth plan and to discuss and practice comfort measures.

  If you are placed on bedrest, a doula may offer services to help with day-to-day needs. Examples would be light housekeeping, running errands, grocery shopping, etc. (There may be an extra charge for these services.)

- **During labor:** Depending on your desires, your doula may be present during early labor in your home or may meet you at your chosen birth location. She provides emotional and physical support to the laboring mother and her husband or support person. She will suggest comfort measures and can provide information and support if medical intervention becomes necessary. She does not make decisions for you, but can aid the family in decision making. She is also a constant companion during an unfamiliar experience and in unfamiliar surroundings. Doctors and nurses cannot be with the laboring woman continuously. Having a doula professional is a reassuring factor.

  Recent studies indicate that the presence of a doula during the birth decreases the need for forceps by 40%, reduces the need for epidurals by 60%, reduces oxytocin use 40%, shortens first time labor by an average of two hours, and decreases the chance of Cesarean section by 50%.

  A doula does not replace the partner or other support person during labor. Rather, she enhances the experience for both laboring mom and her support person by instilling confidence in both. A doula can be particularly valuable for moms without a labor companion.

- **During the early postpartum period:** Your doula can help your family make the adjustment to a new member. She may offer breastfeeding help and referrals if necessary. She makes at least one follow-up visit to check on and talk with mom and admire baby, of course. She may offer additional services of in-home help for an added fee.

Doula fees are not generally covered by insurance. Although fees nationwide average around $250, costs for doula services, including birth support and both a prenatal and postpartum appointment, may range from no-cost to $500, depending on special skills offered by individual doulas.

RESOURCES

■ **ASSOCIATION OF LABOR ASSISTANTS AND CHILDBIRTH EDUCATORS (ALACE)**
(617) 441-2500
P.O. Box 382724
Cambridge, MA 02238
E-mail: alacehq@aol.com
Web site: www.alace.org
ALACE is a national nonprofit organization dedicated to supporting women's choices in childbirth, and provides training and certification for childbirth educators and labor assistants/doulas. ALACE can refer parents to labor assistants across North America. "Professional Labor Support—Your Newest Option in Childbirth" is an ALACE brochure which articulates the benefits of using a labor doula. A quarterly magazine, *Special Delivery*, covers pregnancy, birth, midwifery, and labor assisting topics, and is available with ALACE membership ($20/year).

■ **DOULAS OF NORTH AMERICA (DONA)**
(206) 324-5440
1100 23rd Ave. East
Seattle, WA 98112
Web site: www.dona.com/
E-mail: AskDONA@aol.com
Doulas certified through DONA have passed a certification process that ensures their competence and adherence to the organization's code of ethics and standards of practice. Most of their members assist women and couples through labor and childbirth, although they do have postpartum doulas, who specialize in providing care and support to families with newborn babies. DONA publishes a referral directory, free for the asking, which lists their members nationwide.

■ **INTERNATIONAL CHILDBIRTH EDUCATION ASSOCIATION (ICEA)**
(612) 854-8660
P.O. Box 20048
Minneapolis, MN 55420-0048
Web site: www.icea.org
This international organization certifies birth doulas, postpartum doulas, childbirth educators, and postnatal educators. They offer references, referrals and resources for parents, as well as an extensive mail order catalog, called "Bookmarks," of books and materials related to childbirth and parenting.

■ **NATIONAL ASSOCIATION OF CHILDBIRTH ASSISTANTS**
(707) 939-0543
P.O. Box 1537
Boyes Hot Springs, CA 95416
The oldest national certifying organization of childbirth assistants, NACA trains doulas through a variety of courses, workshops and publications nationwide, and will refer expectant parents to a local NACA-trained doula. NACA doulas focus on facilitating an expectant woman's understanding of pregnancy, birth and postpartum, and reports shorter, more relaxed labors with less fear and tension before, during and after labor. Their doulas encourage active participation in decision-making by parents before and during childbirth.

ENSURING YOUR BABY'S HEALTH

Ideally, a woman would plan to become pregnant in six months time, stop all oral contraceptives, quit smoking and drinking, avoid x-rays, aspirin, and antacids. She would begin taking folic acid to reduce the risk of neural tube birth defects. She would reach her ideal not-too-heavy, not-too-thin weight, and exercise regularly.

In real life, however, pregnancy is often a delightful surprise that necessitates some quick changes in a pregnant woman's lifestyle. The first and foremost consideration is to do all you can to ensure your baby's health.

First, disclose to your health care provider any information about previous pregnancies, especially those ending in miscarriage or termination. Also, let your practitioner know if you've experienced any past sexually transmitted disease (STD).

Most providers recommend that pregnant women consume no alcohol. There is no known "safe" amount to drink, so it is in your baby's best interests to abstain during your pregnancy. Fetal alcohol syndrome (FAS) is often present in the children of heavy drinkers, with symptoms ranging from low birth weight to heart defects and mental retardation. Even women who drink moderately may give birth to children with hyperactivity and learning disabilities.

Another way you can improve your baby's chances of good health, and your own, is to quit smoking. Babies of smokers are smaller and shorter, and more likely to die of Sudden Infant Death Syndrome (SIDS) than children of nonsmokers. According to the American College of Obstetrics and Gynecology, other effects linked to maternal smoking are an increased risk for ectopic pregnancy, miscarriage and stillbirth, premature birth and vaginal bleeding. Many women quit smoking for good when they are pregnant. It is a time of change and reprioritization; quitting smoking can be a positive way to welcome your baby.

Illegal drugs are harmful to the fetus. Drugs cross the placenta, and their toxic effects can affect the baby's development. It just isn't worth the risk to your baby to use drugs. If you have any trouble quitting, ask your physician for a referral

In real life, pregnancy is often a delightful surprise that necessitates some quick changes in a pregnant woman's lifestyle.

CHEMICALS WHICH MAY AFFECT THE FETUS

Chemicals can enter your body through the air you breathe, through contact with your skin or through your digestive system if you accidentally swallow them. The fetus is exposed if the chemical passes from the mother's blood through the placenta to the fetus. These are among those chemicals harmful to the fetus:

- anesthetic gases
- benzene, tuolene
- cancer chemotherapy drugs
- carbon disulfide
- carbon monoxide
- ethanol (alcohol)
- ethylene oxide
- glycol ethers
- lead
- mercury

Strong irritants react with the first tissue they contact—usually the eyes, nose, throat or skin. Common irritants are ammonia, chlorine, bleach, and acids—hydrochloric, nitric and sulfuric. Very little of these chemicals enters the bloodstream, so they are unlikely to affect the fetus.

You can ask your employer for the Material Safety Data Sheets (MSDA) for products you use. Forms include information on hazards to childbearing. Further questions can be answered by your state's Department of Labor or your practitioner.

Information from the Washington State Safety and Health Assessment and Research Program.

---

to a treatment facility or rehabilitation program.

Medications prescribed before your pregnancy, and some over-the-counter drugs, can be harmful to your fetus. Even antacids, with their high concentration of sodium, can affect your pregnancy. Tell your health care practitioner what medications you take; call before starting a new over-the-counter medication to make sure it is safe for you and your baby.

Research is unclear as to whether caffeine intake is harmful. Caffeine enters the fetal bloodstream, and some believe it may increase the risk of miscarriage. Caffeine intake can also increase heartburn, which some women experience during pregnancy. To be safe, it's best to cut back to a minimal amount. That means to curb coffee, tea and cola consumption, and (unfortunately) avoid too much chocolate.

There is no hard and fast evidence that aspartame (NutraSweet), taken in reasonable amounts, is harmful to the fetus, although the phenylalanine in aspartame is transmitted to the fetus through the placenta.

If relaxing at the end of the day means some time in a hot tub or sauna, that's another habit you'll have to stop for the duration of your pregnancy. Very warm water can raise the fetus' temperature to dangerous levels within just a short time, increasing the risk of neural tube defects.

While home improvement is hardly a bad habit, it's wise to avoid paints, paint thinner, insecticides and fertilizers during pregnancy. If you are in contact with

Ensuring Your Baby's Health

these materials or other teratogens (harmful agents which can cause birth defects) at your workplace, discuss with your employer the possibility of switching jobs for the duration of your pregnancy. A good place to find current information on teratogen dangers is online with Genetic Drift's Teratogen Update, published semiannually by the Mountain States Regional Genetic Services Network, found at http://www.MSRGSNet/Genetic Drift/Teratogen Update.

Toxoplasmosis is a mild disease caused by a parasite found in raw meat and cat feces. If you are infected during pregnancy, your child may have mental retardation or vision problems. To avoid the disease, wash thoroughly with antibacterial soap after handling raw meat or vegetables, and have someone else change your cat's litter box. Keep the cat off your bedding.

Most physicians recommend a vitamin supplement rich in folic acid for women planning to become pregnant, to be continued for the duration of pregnancy and while breastfeeding. When taken daily before conception and during the first three months of pregnancy, 0.4 mg of folic acid reduces the risk of neural tube defects such as spina bifida, caused by incomplete fusion of the spinal cord, and anencephaly, an incompletely developed brain. Foods rich in folic acid include leafy vegetables, beans, citrus fruits and cereals. Follow your practitioner's guidelines for vitamin supplements carefully, as overly large doses of some vitamins can cause problems for your baby.

On a more positive and proactive note, eating a healthy diet and drinking plenty of fluids is a good way to give your baby a good start in life. Find an exercise program you can stick with, and make it part of your daily routine. Get adequate rest. Check with your provider if you are over- or underweight for specific recommendations. All women, especially those on vegetarian diets, should consult with their health care provider to ensure adequate protein intake.

As a pregnant mother-to-be, you have a great responsibility to your child. This is the time to break bad habits and make a clean start for your family.

HOW MUCH CAFFEINE IS IN . . .?

Coffee	7 oz.	80-175 mg.
Espresso	1 oz.	100 mg.
Tea	7 oz.	40 mg.
Iced tea	12 oz.	70 mg.
Cola drinks	12 oz.	35-45 mg.
Citrus drinks, i.e. Mountain Dew	12 oz.	55 mg.
Milk chocolate	1 oz.	15 mg.
Unsweetened baking chocolate	1 oz.	25 mg.
Chocolate chips	1/4 cup	13 mg.

QUESTIONS AND ANSWERS
Your Insurance Provider

Medical insurance coverage during pregnancy is a financial necessity today. If you do have coverage when you become pregnant, don't do anything that may risk the loss of that coverage. If you don't have, or can't acquire, insurance that covers a pregnancy, at least make sure that you have medical coverage that will guarantee to cover your newborn. The major financial risk parents face at the time of birth is the cost of care for medical problems of a newborn infant.

But what if you are already pregnant and don't have insurance? You can always negotiate with the hospital for a special uninsured early release delivery. This will reduce the hospital expense significantly and minimize your obligation. The other option if you are uninsured is a public assistance program. Qualifications vary from state to state for coverage associated with pregnancy.

Whatever you do, with or without insurance, at least opt for a prenatal program. Don't be tempted to cut corners by skipping this important care.

To help you understand the ins and outs of maternity insurance coverage, a private insurance broker discusses different aspects of insurance coverage.

Q. *If I do not have insurance and plan to become pregnant, what options are available to me?*

A. There are two options that you should consider. First are individual health insurance programs, such as Blue Cross/Blue Shield and any local HMO plan sponsors that offer individual coverage in your area. A woman under 30 applying for medical coverage can usually find coverage for about $100 per month. Consult with a qualified health insurance broker in your area (look in the Yellow Pages under Insurance) for the options available to you.

The second option is an employer-sponsored health insurance program. Check to see what benefits are available to you, and consider health insurance benefits as important as salary when looking for employment.

Q. *What questions should I ask my insurance company about maternity coverage?*

A. Here are a few to consider:
- What is the cost per provider visit?
- Does the insurance offer a co-payment plan or pay a percentage of each visit?
- What is the calendar year deductible that you must fulfill before coverage begins?
- Is the maternity deductible separate from a general services one?
- Will my newborn baby incur a separate deductible for its share of hospital charges following a healthy birth?

Questions and Answers: Your Insurance Provider

- What hospitals accept your insurance plan?
- What coverage is provided if complications arise?
- Is there a difference in coverage for a Cesarean or vaginal birth?
- How are laboratory charges handled and which labs may you go to and still receive coverage?
- Are twins or other multiple births handled any differently?
- Is the newborn child covered for the first 72 hours automatically or do you need to immediately enroll the child as a dependent?
- Do you have to pay provider and hospital bills up front and then be reimbursed by your insurance company? Are claim forms necessary?
- Who should you contact if you have questions about your policy?

Q. What questions should I ask my insurance provider regarding well-baby care for my new baby?

A. Well-baby care is defined as general checkups, immunizations, and other preventive care office visits when your infant is not ill. The checklist below provides questions to ask your insurance provider.
- Is well-baby care covered?
- What specifically is included?
- What amount will insurance pay toward each office visit?
- When the baby is born, does well-baby care cover any hospital visits?
- Are immunizations included?
- Is there a yearly dollar limit on well-baby coverage?

Q. How soon should I add my new child to my insurance plan?

A. The standard time is 30 days. This ensures that your new baby will be covered under the plan without any gap in coverage.

NEW FEDERAL HEALTH CARE REGULATIONS

Health coverage is more flexible than ever under the federal Health Insurance Portability and Accountability Act of 1996 (HIPPA). Now an individual leaving an employer's group coverage—even with a preexisting condition—cannot be denied coverage, as long as he or she was covered for the previous 18 months. The Act applies to those who meet the 18-month coverage test and are not eligible for most other coverages, including COBRA, Medicare and Medicaid, but not conversion policies. This provision of the law is due to take effect July 1, 1998.

As each state sets its own HIPPA guidelines, check carefully before switching insurers to make sure you won't end up with a gap in coverage.

For more detailed information on HIPPA or COBRA rights, consult a health insurance lawyer or research the Acts at your local library.

HOSPITAL CHOICES

Because mothers may spend such a short time in the hospital, educational and postpartum programs may be more of a consideration factor.

During your pregnancy you are faced with many choices. Deciding where to have your baby is probably one of your biggest decisions. Often, though, your insurance coverage dictates which hospital you must use to deliver. Delivery at your hospital of choice, if not covered by your insurance, may mean you'll be paying in cash for your hospital stay. Happily, almost all hospitals today offer expectant parents a wide array of services that make your stay comfortable and more "home-like" than ever before. Because mothers may spend a limited time in the hospital, the educational and postpartum programs may be more of a consideration factor. Here are some things you may want to consider when choosing your hospital:

- Where your health care provider delivers
- Hospital location
- The nursery facilities
- The number and type of labor and delivery rooms
- The hospital and nursing staff
- The quality of care
- Whether your insurance covers care at that hospital
- The types of educational programs offered
- Hospital policies on issues important to you, such as: electronic fetal monitoring, number of people allowed in the delivery room, eating and drinking during labor, rooming in with your baby, whether accommodations are made for partners to stay overnight, whether postpartum rooms have private showers
- Postpartum care
- Your overall feelings about the hospital

Before making your choice, try to obtain as much objective information as possible. Tour the local hospitals; ask friends, relatives, and coworkers for referrals; and ask questions to ensure the hospital meets your needs.

When talking to others about their birth experiences, you'll find patients who have received exceptional care at one hospital and others who were not completely satisfied at the same facility. The nurses and hospital staff make the personal difference and depending upon who cares for you, experiences may vary.

TYPES OF HOSPITALS

Some expectant parents are more comfortable with the smaller atmosphere of a community hospital while others prefer the comprehensive services a larger facility offers. Large hospitals often include nurseries equipped to handle most newborn emergencies, and may be more apt to offer extensive educational programs for expectant and new parents. Some large metropolitan areas may have a hospital which is a teaching facility affiliated with a medical school. Teaching hospitals generally have state-of-the-art equipment, and you may be seen by residents and interns as well as fully licensed physicians or midwives.

Some people are more comfortable surrounded by all the latest technology "just in case," while others feel that the presence of that technology makes it more likely that it gets used whether it's needed or not. It's important to think about these issues ahead of time.

CONSIDERATIONS

- **Cesarean delivery rates.** Nationwide, Cesareans account for over one-fifth of hospital births. The rate varies for many reasons, including the number of high-risk maternity patients and the patients' individual or medical needs. Expectant parents should discuss the possibility of a Cesarean delivery with their health care provider and find out under what circumstances the procedure would be done.

  Know that Cesarean delivery rates at hospitals are a sensitive issue. Also, realize the hospital does not perform the Cesarean; the physician does. Ask your provider about his or her personal Cesarean rate. Cesarean statistics are broken down by primary (number of first-time Cesarean deliveries) and secondary (repeat Cesarean deliveries).

- **Nursery levels.** The majority of newborn babies only need Level I care. Level II nurseries are equipped to handle most newborn emergencies. Most can care for premature infants who are at least 30-32 weeks gestation. Level III, the most sophisticated type of nurseries, are equipped with high-technology equipment and specialists who are capable of handling the most serious types of newborn emergencies. Level III nurses are trained in advanced life support. Each Level III nursery is equipped for long-term care of premature infants.

- **Fetal monitoring.** Nearly all U.S. hospitals require patients to receive an initial 20-minute fetal monitoring reading in accordance with the American College of Obstetrics and Gynecology (ACOG) guidelines. How long you will be monitored depends on your medical condition and the hospital's or your provider's policy. It is a good idea to explore the monitoring policy of your health care provider before labor begins.

- **Rooms.** Hospital rooms vary from the traditional to specially furnished private "homestyle" suites. The latter style of room is becoming increasingly common. Called Labor/Delivery/Recovery/Postpartum (LDRP) rooms, this concept was implemented nearly 20 years ago. The single-room suite offers the comfort and convenience of not being moved from room to room, as well as allowing more privacy and involvement by partners and other family members.

Labor/Delivery/Recovery (LDR) rooms offer patients the advantage of remaining in one room during labor, delivery, and recovery. Following recovery, mothers are moved to a "postpartum" room.

Most LDR and LDRP rooms offer the comforts of home with the sophistication of advanced medical technology. These rooms are equipped with all the necessary medical equipment, often stored out of sight, but readily available if needed. They also may offer such amenities as custom decor, whirlpool baths, televisions, VCRs and a hide-a-bed for your partner or guest.

- **Rooming-In.** The option to keep your baby in your room day and night, called "rooming-in," is generally encouraged. With short hospital stays as the norm, rooming-in gives mothers a better chance to observe and bond with their babies.
- **Lactation specialists.** While most hospitals support breastfeeding mothers with nursing information and assistance, many go one step further, with a lactation specialist on staff. Some hospitals charge for this service, while consultations are free at others. A lactation specialist

BIRTH CENTERS

Birth centers offer a viable option for low-risk maternity clients. Most women who give birth in a birth center find it to be a positive, empowering experience.

Moms and babies are seen by their birth center's midwives or physicians for their entire maternity care, including prenatal care, labor and delivery, postpartum, and early newborn care. Emergency medications and equipment are available at each birth center, including oxygen, resuscitative equipment, IV material, and certain medicines. Midwives perform deliveries with no anesthesia or instruments, such as forceps. Mothers who deliver at a birth center need to plan an unmedicated birth. If pain medication or pitocin become necessary, the mother will be transferred to a hospital, but the transfer rate of most birth centers is very low.

The setting for birth centers is similar to a bed and breakfast (without the breakfast), though families may bring foods of their choice, and design the atmosphere to include music, lighting, friends and loved ones. Because nonmedicated births generally result in quicker recoveries, the length of stay for a normal delivery in a birth center is a minimum of two to four hours after the birth, with a maximum stay of 24 hours.

Most major insurance companies cover birth center deliveries. Many insurance companies recognize the safety and cost effectiveness of this setting for birth.

is trained to give expert advice on breastfeeding techniques to new mothers.

- **Overnight guests.** Your primary support person stays with you during labor, delivery, and recovery. Support persons are generally allowed to stay overnight in postpartum rooms, except when you're sharing the room with another patient. Siblings are not usually allowed to stay overnight.
- **Visitors and visiting hours.** Most hospitals allow visitors, including non-immediate family members, during labor and delivery. Most also allow siblings to be present during a vaginal delivery with the supervision of an adult (other than the primary support person). Choose a supportive adult to supervise the child's experience.

  Most hospitals have open visiting hours and even those with structured hours do not restrict the support person or significant other. Given the relatively short postpartum stay for many mothers, hospitals usually advise that you limit the number of hospital visitors (other than support people and immediate family), so that you can focus on rest and recovery. Let your visitors know in advance what you would enjoy and ask all who plan to visit to be free of any illness. New moms and babies don't need to be exposed to colds or flu.
- **Safety precautions.** Extreme care and safety precautions are taken to secure your baby while in the hospital. Security personnel, video camera surveillance of all entries, staff identification, alarm systems, and patient education are the most common security measures. It is typical for hospitals to use the Identaband systems in which babies and parents/partners are banded at birth using the same numbers and names. Some hospitals have begun using a new computer chip identity tag system to ensure the safety of their patients. Most hospitals will not reveal details of their security programs until you are admitted into the hospital to protect you and your infant. The more informed you are about the hospital's security program, the more knowledgeable you will be in the rare case that a security issue arises.
- **Classes.** Childbirth and parenting classes are available through most hospitals. Many also offer exercise classes, support groups, and lending and resource libraries. In most cases, classes are available to the general public, whether or not you plan to deliver at that hospital. Nominal class fees are charged to participants.
- **Postpartum care.** Sometimes the time between the discharge from the hospital to the first visit with the pediatrician can be filled with questions and concerns, especially for first-time parents. Most hospitals have addressed this need by providing different options for postpartum follow-up soon after discharge, including a home health visit or free telephone consultation. Also, hospitals have lactation consultants and consulting nurses available by phone, and can refer you to a public health nurse or private lactation consultant if needed.

"Souvenir Pregnancy"

A Life Experience by Leanne Jordan

My husband and I had just returned from a glorious second honeymoon, happy that our 4- and 6-year-old daughters were old enough to spend a week being pampered by Grandma and Grandpa. I was hoping that the renewed passion we'd experienced would continue when we resumed our daily routines. Was I ever wrong.

The day after our return, the girls and I all came down with pneumonia. A week later we were all on the way to recovery, when I was struck by a severe cold, followed by a sinus infection. I was miserable. Gone were the feelings of carefree abandon, physical fitness and the tan I'd acquired on our vacation. I hardly noticed that my period hadn't begun. It must just be all the illness hitting, I thought. But once the sinus infection cleared up I was still tired all the time.

It should have been obvious. That wonderful honeymoon we took without the kids had given us an unexpected souvenir: I was pregnant. (Those high school family life teachers are right: you can get pregnant when you aren't mid-cycle!)

Although my husband was joyful, I couldn't bring myself to feel excited. Our daughters were finally out of babyhood and all the exhausting mom-work that entailed. The elder was in first grade, and her sister was due to start preschool. I was looking forward to going back to work part-time. Now my plans were in complete disarray.

I even dreaded telling my parents. One of two daughters, I knew my parents felt our family was already the perfect size. Avid population growth types, they had always let us know two children was plenty. Once I finally informed them, they were more bemused than upset. They checked our side of the family tree—in the past century, only one other family had more than two children.

Medically, the pregnancy was as easy as the other two. I was more tired due to the fact that there was more to do with two active girls already at home. "Three!" other people would say. "How are you going to manage it?" What could I tell them: "I'm not exactly thrilled about it myself"? Hardly. I felt ashamed of my own thoughts. How selfish of me to want the freedom from diapers, from sleepless nights, from the constant worry that babies bring.

Yet there were some positive aspects of this unexpected pregnancy. Maternity clothes were a lot cuter than they were several years ago! And I met some wonderful friends at our childbirth education refresher class. My mother instinctively realized my reluctance and comforted and reassured me throughout those difficult months. Our daughters were especially thrilled at the prospect of a new baby in the house.

As the delivery date grew closer, I began to come to grips with my own feelings. We hauled out the crib that had been packed away for our future grandchildren. I sorted through my remaining baby clothes (none, except for a few heirloom-type dresses) and baby blankets (three, currently used in the doll crib). I reread my dog-eared breastfeeding and infant care books, and agonized over the right kind of diapers to buy since there were even more bewildering choices than before.

And then, suddenly, I was in labor. A call to my folks, a quick trip to the hospital, one contraction that hurt, one push, and Ethan was born. My husband and I were so shocked to have given birth to a boy that we could hardly speak. He was blue as a blueberry and needed a pat on the behind and some good suctioning. Once I got to hold him, I looked into his deep blue eyes, and then, and only then, did I know without a single doubt that I would love him with all my heart. ❧

YOUR HOSPITAL STAY: ONE DAY OR MORE?

By Nanci J. Newell, B.S.N.

With recent and continuing changes in state and federal laws about maternity lengths of stay, this is no longer an easy question for anyone. Expectant parents may hear conflicting answers depending on who they ask and what they read. It is essential that parents are informed and ask the right questions to avoid unpleasant financial surprises late in pregnancy, or worse, when they get their bills following birth.

THE LAWS SAY:

Legislation in many states takes precedence over any federal legislation, but what it usually boils down to is that the decision regarding the length of stay following birth is up to the provider and you, based on your medical needs at the time. Medical need is the key phrase and does not necessarily mean the same thing to mothers as it does to providers. In general, medical necessity means blood loss, infection, or any other medical condition which would require continuing care in the hospital. The amount of rest needed or the number of other children or responsibility waiting for a new mother at home does not constitute medical necessity. Federal legislation is far from clear and defers to any state legislation at this time. Since the whole question of length of stay has became such a hot political topic, it is expected that several federal versions may be debated repeatedly during upcoming sessions of Congress before anything is finally passed at the national level. In the meantime, there are more questions to be asked.

INSURANCE COMPANIES SAY:

Most insurance companies have no incentive to limit a mother's length of stay in the hospital or birth center. They simply will not pay either the hospital or the doctor or midwife. Many contracts are negotiated with hospitals so that no matter what services are used by patients, a flat fee is paid per delivery. The same thing applies to many doctors, midwives and other providers. There are hundreds of insurance companies and

> *It is essential that parents are informed and ask the right questions to avoid unpleasant financial surprises.*

many variations of individual plans. Managed care is here to stay.

In areas without a state-mandated maternity length of stay regulation, nurses and case managers are reporting from many hospitals that many expectant parents are being told by their insurance companies that they can stay for two days following a normal vaginal delivery and three days following an uncomplicated Cesarean birth. What insurance companies are not telling expectant parents is that they can stay two days or three days providing there is medical necessity. So, when parents come to the hospital to have their baby, and are planning to stay two days, they are surprised to hear that they need to leave after 24 hours because it is not medically necessary for them to stay longer. This results in the provider giving the family the "bad news" that they must leave earlier than expected, and no one wants to be the bearer of that message.

The pediatrician or family practitioner is also responsible for determining whether or not a baby is medically stable and can be discharged from the hospital. The baby may be ready for discharge sooner or later than the mother is, and that potential difference may also create unexpected changes in plans for new parents. No new parent wants to feel rushed to leave the safety and comfort of the birth suite.

Clarify the following inquiries with your insurance company well in advance of your expected date of delivery:

- Exactly what is covered
- What "medical necessity" means
- How long a stay for new mothers and babies is covered following birth if there is no medical necessity
- Ask if there is anything not normally covered, such as circumcision
- Ask if hospital follow-up services such as support groups, classes, clinics, lactation services, and/or home visits are covered
- Ask if and how many provider follow-up office visits are covered
- Document the name of the person with whom you speak and ask for written confirmation

HOSPITALS SAY:

Make an appointment to see the admissions person or financial advisor at your hospital's birth center or obstetrical unit early in your pregnancy. Take all your insurance documents with you and have the hospital representative call your insurance company and verify with you what is covered.

Again, clarify what constitutes medical necessity. Ask how long most new mothers and babies stay following birth. Ask what normal charges can be expected and what your insurance company normally pays so that you can plan ahead for any deposits or differences in coverage. Ask if there are hours of the day or night by which discharge must take place in order to avoid further hourly or daily room rate charges. Some hospitals have specified checkout times; some do not.

Where public assistance is needed, an application can be made at this time with your financial advisor's help. Payment plans can be arranged so that when you come to the hospital there are no unpleasant surprises in either the charges or the length of stay. Ask for written confirmation of all arrangements made.

Ask what services are in place following discharge from the hospital for follow-up care. Some hospitals have extensive care services and support available for new parents and some do not. These services may include telephone hotlines or calls from a nurse, in-hospital clinic visits with a nurse, lactation services, doula services, home follow-up nursing visits, classes, and support groups. If available, ask what is included in the customary charges and what is not included in the charges.

PROVIDERS SAY:

Doctors and midwives do not want you to feel rushed in leaving the hospital or birth center. Neither do they want you to stay longer than is medically necessary. Ask how long most new mothers stay if they have an uncomplicated vaginal delivery and how long they stay if they have an uncomplicated Cesarean birth. Ask what constitutes a complication for either. Ask what follow-up arrangements are made for return visits to office or clinic following discharge from the hospital. Develop a "Plan A" with your provider for discharge based on your expected medical needs, in the event that all goes as you expect. Develop a "Plan B" in case it does not. Following birth, your doctor or midwife will be visiting you, following your post-delivery progress, and determine with you when you are stable and medically ready to be discharged.

THE PRENATAL PLAN

What can be done now to be prepared for a short length of stay in the hospital so that new parents can assume the care of themselves and their infants without feeling totally overwhelmed and exhausted? Actually, a great deal can be done in advance to make the transition to parenthood far more enjoyable.

- Determine what insurance coverage is available for pregnancy, birth and care of the newborn.
- Ask about home care coverage.
- Ask if lactation services are covered.
- What are the length of stay limitations? Do they differ with complications?
- Ask your practitioner what the usual length of stay is for patients.
- Tour your hospital.
- Attend early discharge, breastfeeding, and infant care classes.
- Develop a preliminary plan for child care if you plan to return to work.
- Talk to a financial counselor (usually located in admissions).
- If you have any unusual circumstances or additional needs, talk to the case manager or social worker at the hospital.
- Read as much material on prenatal and baby care as you can.

It is nearly impossible to absorb all of the new information about care for yourself and your newborn during a short hospital stay. It helps a lot to have attended some classes in advance, even if you don't have a baby with whom to practice.

STAYING IN SHAPE

By Lisa Yount, MSPT

Many different approaches and educational opportunities are available to assist you in preparing for the exciting event of birth and newborn care. Today, not only is exercise during pregnancy accepted by most providers, it is highly recommended. Even if you do not routinely exercise you can safely perform exercises that will make your pregnancy more comfortable. Because every pregnancy is different, an exercise program should be designed for the individual with special attention to both the pregnancy and postpartum periods.

During pregnancy, your balance, coordination, endurance and strength can be altered. Structural and hormonal changes cause the stretching or tightening of muscles, relaxing of ligaments and the loosening of joints. The curve in the lower back becomes more pronounced as the baby grows and the center of gravity moves forward. If adequate muscular support is lacking, the stress to the pelvis and back is increased, resulting in poor posture, fatigue and backache. It is important to exercise and maintain control of the voluntary muscles to help support the backbone and pelvis, which are put under significant stress. To be at your best during the pregnancy and to prevent future problems, it is essential to improve your physical condition. The important key muscle groups are the abdominal muscles, the pelvic floor and the postural muscles.

Be sure to talk to your health care provider before beginning an exercise program, and follow his or her instructions. This is not the time to start a vigorous program. The goals of prenatal exercise should include preventing discomfort, backache and fatigue. This is done by toning the essential muscle groups, stretching, relaxing, and performing proper body mechanics. Prenatal exercises strengthen the body and decrease the discomforts of pregnancy. You will have greater endurance for a long labor, and recovery is thought to be quicker. Feeling good physically also helps you to feel good mentally. Participants in exercise programs report decreased fatigue, decreased moodiness, wonderful peer support and shorter recovery periods.

Difficulties with present or previous pregnancies or general health problems may be contraindications to exercise during pregnancy. These concerns should be discussed with the physician.

> *The goals of prenatal exercise should include preventing discomfort, backache and fatigue.*

EXERCISE GUIDELINES

- Exercise regularly (three times a week).
- Avoid increasing the body core temperature; strenuous exercise should be limited to 15 minutes, and exercise should not be performed in hot, humid weather.
- Exercise heart rate should not exceed 140 beats per minute.
- Begin the exercise program with warm-ups and end with cool-downs.
- Repeat each exercise only a few times; change your body position to work the same muscle groups in different positions.
- Do not hold your breath during exercises. Avoid any exercise that causes you to do a Valsalva maneuver (bearing down).
- Exercises should be performed slowly; avoid bouncing motions.
- Avoid heavy resisted exercises overhead or with long leverage, for example, putting dishes in a high cupboard or lifting weights with straight arms.
- Avoid positions that increase the curve in your lower back.
- Drink plenty of fluids.
- Limit time spent exercising on your back, and stop if you feel any tingling or dizziness.

WARNING SIGNS

Although exercise during pregnancy is recommended, be aware of the signs indicating that exercise should cease or a physician be contacted:

- Bleeding
- Frequent uterine contractions during or after exercise
- Lower back or pubic pain
- Sciatic (lower back or leg) nerve numbness
- Pain, numbness or tingling in the wrist/hand
- A breathless, dizzy, light-headed feeling or fatigue
- Palpitations or rapid heart beat
- A noticeable decrease in the activity of the fetus

Inherent benefits to exercise can be appreciated during pregnancy and the postpartum period. The program should be individualized to provide the highest level of fitness without compromising the health or safety of the fetus or the pregnant mother.

PROPER POSTURE AND BODY MECHANICS

Proper posture and body mechanics are especially important during pregnancy and the postnatal period because of the structural (muscles, ligaments) and hormonal changes and increased possibility of injury.

- When walking for exercise, let your arms swing at your sides and don't put your hands in your pockets or hold them tight against your chest. Keeping your hands free helps to absorb shock as well as to keep your arms free to avoid loss of balance.
- When picking up objects (including children), bend at the hips and knees, not the lower back, putting one leg forward. Be sure the weight is held close to you and use your legs to return to a standing position.
- Avoid repetitive bending and twisting such as unloading the dishwasher or dryer. The proper unloading method for a dishwasher

would be to first unload everything to the counter, close the dishwasher, and then put the dishes away, a few items at a time. Use a laundry basket (only half full) to transfer clothes from the dryer to a table. Fold clothes at a dining table (or other furniture of similar height) to avoid bending to the dryer or floor.

- Push your vacuum cleaner like a lawn mower, walking behind it for long stretches, rather than using push-pull motions.
- For the care of newborns and infants, be sure to take advantage of high changing tables, and bathe the baby in a sink instead of a bathtub to avoid back strain.
- When nursing, bottle feeding, or cuddling with the baby, sit in a well-supported chair or rocker. Use pillows under your arms and under the baby to support and position the baby most comfortably.

SIMPLE EXERCISES

A complete prenatal exercise program includes stretching, strengthening, aerobics and relaxing. The following are a few basic exercises for all stages of pregnancy and the postnatal period. Perform a few repetitions several times daily:

- **Kegels.** Tighten the muscles of the pelvic floor (as if you were stopping the flow of urine). Hold five seconds; relax.
- **Pelvic tilts.** Tighten stomach and buttocks muscles to turn your pelvis as if to "put your tail between your legs"; relax.
- **Shoulder rolls.** Raise your shoulders to your ears, pull your shoulders back; relax.
- **Scapula pinches.** Squeeze your shoulder blades back together. Hold five seconds; relax.

STAYING COMFORTABLE AT WORK

If you sit for long periods of time at work, consider these guidelines for proper posture and comfort:

- Adjust the height of the chair to fit you to the desk. Be sure that you don't have to bend over to your desk (chair too high) or hold your shoulders up (chair too low).
- Adjust yourself to the chair. This may require bringing in a pillow for behind your back and a step stool or phone books for under your feet. Keep enough bend in your hips so that your knees are equal to or above your hips.
- Do not cross your legs or extend them straight out in front of you.
- Use a slant board or copy holder to avoid prolonged head-down positions.
- When using the phone, keep your head erect or neutral and avoid holding the phone between your ear and shoulder.
- It is very important to get out of your chair often. A good guideline is to get up every half hour, even just to fill up a water cup or to stretch.

CHILDBIRTH EDUCATION

By Sally Ellsworth, R.N., FACCE

Having a healthy baby is the goal of all expectant parents, and most expectant parents choose to take some form of childbirth preparation classes to help them toward reaching this goal. Since women carry vivid, powerful memories of their birth experiences for many years afterward, most childbirth preparation classes try to help women achieve not only a healthy outcome to their pregnancy but the most positive birth experience possible by providing information about labor, delivery, postpartum, birthing options and alternatives, and coping strategies. Classes also help the labor partner to learn many comfort measures and techniques to use to assist the laboring woman.

There are a number of factors to keep in mind when selecting a childbirth preparation course. Feel free to ask prospective class sources about any of the following:

- **Qualifications of the instructor.** Although in most states there is no law requiring licensure of childbirth educators, most are certified by one of several national or regional childbirth education organizations. These organizations also encourage their instructors to recertify on a regular basis to keep up to date on skills and knowledge.
- **Location of classes.** Most couples will probably prefer to take classes that are located close to home, although this is not always possible. Classes are taught in a variety of settings—hospital classrooms, public health departments and clinics, private doctors' offices, private homes, churches and community centers.
- **Size of classes.** Class size varies depending on where and with whom classes are taken with some as small as three couples or as large as 30 couples. Some instructors will teach private classes (for one couple only) and may even be willing to come to your home. This would be helpful for women who are on bedrest due to a pregnancy complication.
- **Timing.** Most programs suggest starting your classes some time within the last eight to ten weeks of your pregnancy, but of course you should try to sign up for classes much earlier to ensure the best chance of getting

Most childbirth preparation classes try to help women achieve . . . the most positive birth experience possible.

Childbirth Education

into the class series of your choice. Some programs, especially those offering instruction in the Bradley method, suggest starting your classes in the fifth month, so that nutrition, exercise and relaxation can be emphasized.

- **Length of class series.** Most childbirth education series are six classes in length although some are as short as three or as long as ten. Most classes are taught weekly with each class being two to three hours in length. In some locations, instructors offer a somewhat condensed weekend program, compacting as much as 15 hours of instruction into a Friday evening, Saturday, and Sunday format.

- **Price.** Again, this will vary according to location and instructor with some classes being free and others costing as much as $150. The average cost of most class series is $60-$75. The least expensive classes are offered at clinics, health departments and adult education programs. The most expensive classes are those taught one-on-one in a private setting.

- **Philosophy of instructor and program.** Bear in mind that some classes are designed to prepare couples for the health facility in which they plan to deliver and offer little information on choices and alternatives. Some classes are designed for couples planning a home birth and, as such, place much emphasis on birthing with few or no interventions; some classes place a great deal of emphasis on a nonmedicated birth. Some assume that all or most of the women in class will use medications or anesthesia. Yet other courses may be taught from a religious perspective.

- **Other classes offered.** Most instructors or organizations offering childbirth classes will also offer a variety of other classes and services that may include: early pregnancy classes, refresher classes (an abbreviated series for couples who have previously taken classes), breastfeeding classes, Cesarean preparation classes, VBAC classes, baby care classes, infant and child CPR classes, and labor support (doula) services.

As you can see, there are as many choices in childbirth classes as there are in hospitals, practitioners and insurance providers. Choose carefully to get the most out of your time and money and to optimize your chances of having a healthy, happy, fulfilling childbirth experience.

RESOURCES

ACADEMY OF CERTIFIED BIRTH EDUCATORS AND LABOR SUPPORT PROFESSIONALS
800-444-8223
2001 E. Prairie Cir., Ste. I
Olathe, KS 66062
The Academy of Certified Birth Educators trains and certifies both birth educators and labor support professionals. Their courses are approved by Doulas of North America. Birth educators pass a certification course and exam. The academy encourages women to incorporate breathing for pain relief during labor.

ACADEMY OF HUSBAND COACHED CHILDBIRTH (AAHCC)
800-4-A-BIRTH
P.O. Box 5224
Sherman Oaks, CA 91413
Web site: www.bradleybirth.com
This organization trains and certifies instructors in the Bradley method, the first method to emphasize the husband as labor coach. The Bradley method stresses proper nutrition, relaxation and slow abdominal breathing. There is also a strong emphasis on an unmedicated birth and breastfeeding as the optimal form of infant nutrition. Women are usually encouraged to start classes in the fifth or sixth month of pregnancy and Bradley class series are usually a bit longer than other methods. Contact AAHCC for a list of certified instructors.

AMERICAN SOCIETY OF PSYCHOPROPHYLAXIS IN OBSTETRICS/LAMAZE
800-368-4404
1200 19th St. NW, Ste. 300
Washington, DC 20036
Web site: www.lamaze-childbirth.com
E-mail: aspo@sba.com
ASPO promotes the Lamaze method of prepared childbirth and certifies and recertifies instructors (titled ACCEs or FACCEs) in this method, which emphasizes that birth is a natural and normal phenomenon and that most women can birth their babies with little or no medical interventions. Lamaze classes teach a variety of coping skills to the pregnant woman and her partner including relaxation, visualization, massage, and attention to breathing. ASPO/Lamaze has a mail order bookstore and will provide a list of local certified instructors.

ASSOCIATION OF LABOR ASSISTANTS AND CHILDBIRTH EDUCATORS (ALACE)
(617) 441-2500
P.O. Box 382724
Cambridge, MA 02238
E-mail: alacehq@aol.com
Web page: www.alace.org
ALACE is a national nonprofit organization dedicated to supporting women's choices in childbirth, and provides training and certification for childbirth educators and labor assistants/doulas. ALACE provides expectant parents with information to help them understand their options and make informed deci-

sions. They can help expectant parents find a childbirth educator, labor assistant or midwife across North America. A quarterly magazine, *Special Delivery*, covers pregnancy, birth, midwifery, and teaching/labor assisting topics, and is available with ALACE membership ($20/year).

■ BIRTHWORKS
(609) 953-9380
P.O. Box 2045
Medford, NJ 08055
Web site: members.aol.com/birthwks CD/bw.html
E-mail: birthwksCD@aol.com
Birthworks defines itself as an innovative and experiential organization that believes every woman has the knowledge to give birth. Believing that birth is an instinctive process, no specific breathing patterns are taught in Birthworks classes, and instructors help each woman find the best way to breathe during labor. They offer a referral service for education classes.

■ CHILDBIRTH EDUCATION FOUNDATION
(717) 529-2561
P.O. Box 251
Oxford, PA 19363
E-mail: jperon@delphi.com
The Childbirth Education Foundation provides information to discourage unnecessary medical intervention. The group publishes and distributes a large selection of childbirth, newborn care, and parenting education literature. Call or write for a complete list. The majority of the organization's literature focuses on circumcision with several publications supporting the decision not to circumcise.

■ GLOBAL MATERNAL CHILD HEALTH ASSOCIATION
(503) 682-3600
P.O. Box 1400
Wilsonville, OR 97070
This nonprofit corporation promotes preserving, protecting and enhancing the well-being of women and children during pregnancy, birth, infancy and childhood. Their education workshops focus on natural childbirth and midwifery. Topics include "Gentle Birth Choices" and "Water Birth: Gimmick or Godsend?" They offer educational videos, a "Gentle Birth" information booklet, referrals and sources for birth tub rentals and sales. You might want to check out Barbara Harper's book, *Gentle Birth Choices*, promoting the Global Maternal Child Health Association's philosophy ($16.95, Healing Arts Press).

■ INTERNATIONAL CHILDBIRTH EDUCATION ASSOCIATION (ICEA)
(612) 854-8660
P.O. Box 20048
Minneapolis, MN 55420
Web site: www.icea.org
E-mail: info@icea.org
This organization does not promote any specific method of childbirth but instead stresses "freedom of choice based on knowledge of alternatives." ICEA trains and certifies instructors (titled ICCEs) in a method that incorporates both Bradley and Lamaze techniques. ICEA instructors are often also ASPO/Lamaze- or AAHCC-certified. This organization has an extensive mail order bookstore and will provide names of instructors in your area.

LABOR PAIN RELIEF

By Donna Hudson-Bryant, R.N., C.C.E., C.D. (DONA)

Labor hurts. Because of this, we focus much of our energy in preparing for birth. Why does it hurt? How much will it hurt? How long will the pain last? Will I be able to take it? Will there be any help for me? These are the questions we ask ourselves whenever we are in pain. Pain frightens us at a very primitive level, because of its unknowns. But we know a lot about the labor process and can learn from that.

Most women fear the pain of labor. Fear is very powerful. It creates a rush of adrenalin which makes the heart race and quickens breathing. Blood flow shifts to the vital organs and large muscles of the legs and arms. Since the uterus is not a vital organ, when in this "fight or flight" state in labor, the working uterine muscle does not get normal blood or oxygen flow. This causes a painful build-up of lactic acid in the muscle. Contractions become less coordinated so, though they still come and they still hurt, the cervix is slow to open and the baby slow to descend. In other words, you have a more painful labor, which proceeds very slowly. This in itself is frightening, and feeds back into the cycle.

Grantly Dick-Read first described this fear-tension-pain cycle in the 1930s. He felt if women were prepared and approached birth without fear, their pain would be relieved. This is the basis for current methods of nonmedical pain relief in childbirth. In the 1950s, Ferdinand Lamaze introduced the concept of painless childbirth through a kind of Pavlovian training in breathing techniques. Other methods of "prepared childbirth" followed, all involving education and practice for giving birth, promoting a state of relaxation and decreasing fear. While no amount of preparation really makes labor pain-free, there are many safe alternatives for making labor pain more manageable.

UNMEDICATED BIRTH STRATEGIES

Pain is a signal, a protective mechanism. Labor pain and sensations are messages to us from our bodies. They show us how to help labor along. It is no coincidence that positions that reduce pain also help labor progress more quickly. Perhaps the pain is relieved by moving your body in a certain way. Maybe

Uterine contractions work to pull open the stretchy muscles of the cervix and the birth canal. This stretching hurts.

Labor Pain Relief

your stamina improves by drinking and eating. Every woman, every baby, and every labor is unique. Each woman must find what works for her in each labor. Here are some suggestions:

- **Feed your body for the work it must do.** If your provider permits, drink water or juice every hour or eat lightly if you feel hungry. Try popsicles, sweetened tea, cereals, rice, beans, soups, toast or crackers, peanut butter, and yogurt.
- **What goes in must come out.** Urinate every hour or two while you are awake. A full bladder can hold the baby back and make labor more painful.
- **Use natural forces to help your body do its work.** Use gravity, motion, heat, cold, and water to lessen pain and make the work easier for your body. Try standing, kneeling or sitting leaning forward onto something higher—your partner, a wall, or piece of furniture. Take walks, squat on a low stool, get on your hands and knees, or rock in a chair. Take relaxing showers or baths, or use hot or cold compresses
- **Your breathing can help you relax.** There is no one right way to breathe, as long as you do not hold your breath or hyperventilate. Slow, rhythmic breathing is relaxing and conserves energy. Making noise with your breath releases tension. Sighing, moaning, or groaning are helpful, as long as your jaw and throat are loose and open.
- **Set a mood in the labor room.** Certain sights, sounds, and smells can make it easier to relax. Dim the overhead lights. Music is soothing and can help shut out distracting or frightening sounds. Use music with a special meaning or that music which you used for relaxation during pregnancy. Certain aromas promote relaxation, decrease pain, and mask unpleasant odors. Clary sage and lavender may be helpful; consult an aromatherapist for instruction.
- **Set a mood for your mind.** Use visualization, meditation, and imagery to help maintain a sense of calm. Repeat a word, "open" or "baby," each time you breathe out, or try counting your breaths.
- **Being connected to other people can really help.** Get support from someone strong who will stay with you throughout the entire labor—your partner, mother, friend, doula, or midwife. This person shouldn't be afraid to see you in pain.
- **Touch can feel great in labor.** Whether you do it yourself or someone does it for you, massage can help labor pain a lot. Try massage that is firm and deep, smooth and light, or just as pressure. Massage your belly, shoulders and neck, breasts/nipples, hands, lower back, thighs, and feet. Hugs, kisses, and even holding hands can feel great.
- **Try to save your strength as you go.** Rest if you feel tired, because you do not want to burn yourself out. Find restful positions, such as sitting supported in bed or side-lying. Use lots of pillows. Try slow, deep breathing and relaxation exercises to get your body quieted down. A catnap between contractions can be very refreshing.

- **Use moderation and balance.** Change what you are doing every hour while you are awake. If it is night, try to sleep, or simply rest. If you have been sitting, get up and walk. After you go to the bathroom, grab something to drink or eat, then go to a different place and try something new.

Women who remain alert, active participants in their labors often describe feeling more powerful after the experience, and draw on these feelings as a source of strength as they face the challenges of mothering a new baby.

Keep an open mind about the use of pain medications in labor. Pain medications and anesthesia can promote relaxation and rest. No remedy or medication will relieve pain for the entire labor.

Take the time to understand your options for medical pain relief, then wait to see how your labor unfolds. Pain in giving birth is inevitable. Sooner or later, each woman must come to terms with her feelings about that.

COPING WITH BACK LABOR

Some labors are more painful than others. This is particularly true of what is known as back labor. This means that pain is felt almost entirely in the woman's lower back. The pain may be constant, intensifying tremendously during contractions. Often this means the baby's head is in a posterior position, so that the back of her head presses against the lower spine with each contraction. Back labors are often longer, since the baby must turn herself around to face the other way. There are some additional tricks to ease the special pain of back labor. In addition to relieving back pain, these things also encourage your baby to turn:

- Walk between contractions and stand during them.
- Lean forward whenever possible. Never lie on your back.
- Lie on your side where the baby's back is, opposite where you feel the most kicks.
- Rock, tilt, or gently sway your pelvis while leaning forward.
- Use heat on your lower back. After 20-30 minutes, switch to cold. Try a warm bath or shower.
- Gently but firmly stroke your belly. Start where the baby's back is and stroke towards the middle.
- Have your partner press hard on the painful spot with a fist or heel of a hand, or massage your lower spine with something hard, like a ball or rolling pin.
- Stand facing forward, with one foot on a chair beside you. Lunge towards the chair during contractions. Lunge towards the side where the baby's back is, or whichever side feels best.
- Have your partner stand behind you while you lean forward. Your partner places the heel of each hand on the middle of each buttock with fingers pointing toward the spine. As your partner presses down and in towards your spine (double hip squeeze), give feedback as to hand placement and how hard to press.

MEDICAL PAIN RELIEF IN CHILDBIRTH

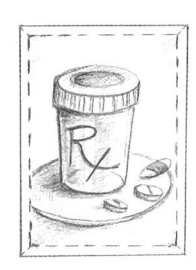

By Joseph F. Antognini, M.D., University of California, Davis

With childbirth comes pain. Some women experience small amounts of pain. For others, the pain of labor detracts from a positive labor experience. Fortunately for women today there are numerous medical methods available to diminish labor pain. Nationwide about 70% of births are medicated, with variations depending on specific geographic areas. Medicated births include epidural analgesia, spinal analgesia, pudendal blocks and "walking epidurals." Also, labor pain may be relieved by traditional methods including intravenous and intramuscular opiates, such as morphine and Demerol.

Labor pain relief may be administrated through an anesthesiologist who attends four years of college, four years of medical school and an additional three to five years of specialty training. Hospitals may also have nurse anesthetists perform obstetrical anesthesia. These nurses have received two years of training on top of a nursing degree.

EPIDURALS

An epidural is a technique in which local anesthetic and/or opiates are injected into the epidural space and bathe the spinal nerve roots after they've left the spinal fluid and spinal cord. The goal is to relieve a significant amount of the pain of labor without disrupting the natural progress of labor and the mother's ability to move and push during the delivery.

The procedure for epidural placement is straightforward. After a discussion between the laboring mother and the anesthetist, the patient's lower back is cleansed and a small amount of local anesthetic is then injected into the skin, which permits placement of the needle through the ligaments of the back, and then into the epidural space. Once that space is reached, a small catheter—which looks very much like a fishing line—is inserted through the needle and the needle is then removed and the small flexible catheter left in place. Sometimes the catheter will touch one of the nerves in the lower part of the back which will cause a sensation of electricity in the leg or into the buttocks, very similar to the sensation of

Numerous medical methods have been developed to diminish labor pain.

hitting your funny bone. This is usually not long-lasting and is present for a split second.

Small test doses of the anesthetic are then given to insure proper placement and functioning of the catheter, followed by the full dose or continuous infusion as required for either epidural analgesia or epidural anesthesia. Urinary catheterization is often needed with both epidurals and spinals. Common side effects include a decrease in blood pressure and itching. On very rare occasions reactions from an inadvertant injection into a blood vessel or the spinal fluid could result in seizures and heart irregularities or excessive numbness. However, these side effects, while very rare, are also easily recognized and treated so that the technique is quite safe. Backaches may occur after an epidural but appear to be no more common than those occurring after a general anesthetic. A spinal headache can occur if the epidural inadvertently goes into the spinal fluid.

One of the benefits of an epidural is that if the mother requires a Cesarean section, more anesthetic can be administered which will then numb the mother from the middle of the chest down. This allows the procedure to be performed with the mother awake but pain-free so she is then able to enjoy the experience of her child's birth.

SPINAL ANALGESIA

In some patients, instead of injecting in the epidural space, an injection of local anesthetic and/or opiate is made into the subarachnoid space which is closer to the nerves and therefore less anesthetic is required. This technique is called spinal analgesia. In some patients spinal opiates can be administered, either morphine or fentanyl which help relieve labor pain. These are often given with a local anesthetic and help to decrease the required amount of local anesthetic. A disadvantage is that only one injection can be made whereas with an epidural catheter injections can be made periodically or an infusion performed. Spinal analgesia also has the risks of developing a spinal headache, lowering the mother's blood pressure and causing mild itching.

"WALKING EPIDURALS"

Walking epidurals (or spinals) are so named because the patient is able to walk while receiving pain relief. This is because only an opiate—drugs such as morphine or fentanyl—is injected, not a local anesthetic which can weaken the muscles, therefore preventing walking or making it dangerous. In some patients opiates are sufficient to relieve pain and, because they do not affect the nerves to muscles, patients are able to walk around during labor (walking epidural).

PUDENDAL BLOCK

A pudendal block also can be used to relieve labor pain. This involves injecting a small amount of local anesthetic through the vaginal wall near the cervix.

GENERAL ANESTHESIA

In some patients the epidural catheter, which is otherwise apparently placed properly, does not relieve all of the mother's pain. This sometimes occurs because of some peculiarities of the patient's anatomy which prevents the local anesthetic from reaching all the

Medical Pain Relief in Childbirth

nerves that carry the pain. Sometimes this requires additional anesthetics including intravenous medications or, in the situation of a Cesarean section, may require administration of a general anesthetic. Although general anesthesia is considered safe for the mother and baby, this is usually the last choice for a medicated birth and attempts are made to avoid general anesthesia. General anesthesia renders the mother unconscious and therefore makes her unable to experience the birth of her child.

Patients who require a general anesthetic will be brought to the operating room and placed on the table and appropriate monitors will be placed including a heart monitor, blood pressure monitor and oxygen monitor. After breathing oxygen, the patient receives intravenous medications to induce general anesthesia and is unconscious for the duration of the operation. After the patient is unconscious, a small plastic tube is placed into the windpipe through the mouth; this protects the mother's lungs and makes it easier for her to breathe during the surgery. The anesthetic is maintained with inhaled anesthetics like nitrous oxide (laughing gas) and isoflurane. Luckily, only a small amount of these anesthetics get to the baby.

REACTIONS TO ANESTHESIA

It is unusual to develop an allergic reaction to the medications that are administered to the mother, but it is possible to have a rare reaction to the local anesthetics or opiates. More commonly patients will develop side effects such as backaches or headaches which are not true allergic reactions. In general the more drugs the mother receives, the more possible effects on the mother and the infant. However this is probably most important for the newborn in the setting of a general anesthetic, and even then, if the baby is removed quickly, there is usually not a problem. Some patients also develop itching as a result of opiate administration.

Mothers may experience shaking with a spinal or epidural. It is thought to be due to the disruption of the body's temperature regulation. The spinal or epidural lowers the body's core temperature and you shiver in order to raise your temperature.

Consider talking to your health care provider about the risks and reactions of different types of anesthesia before laboring. Many hospitals and organizations offer an education session on anesthesia prior to birth or as a part of a childbirth education series.

INSURANCE CONSIDERATIONS

Epidurals, general anesthesia and all the medical services performed are usually covered by insurance programs. Check with your individual plan, talk with an insurance representative and make notes about who you spoke with and when, to ensure maximum financial benefits. If you are receiving federal or state assistance, talk with your case worker to see what type of medicated options are available. It is better to know ahead of time the costs involved, than to be hit with a large bill after the birth.

"My Cesarean Birth"

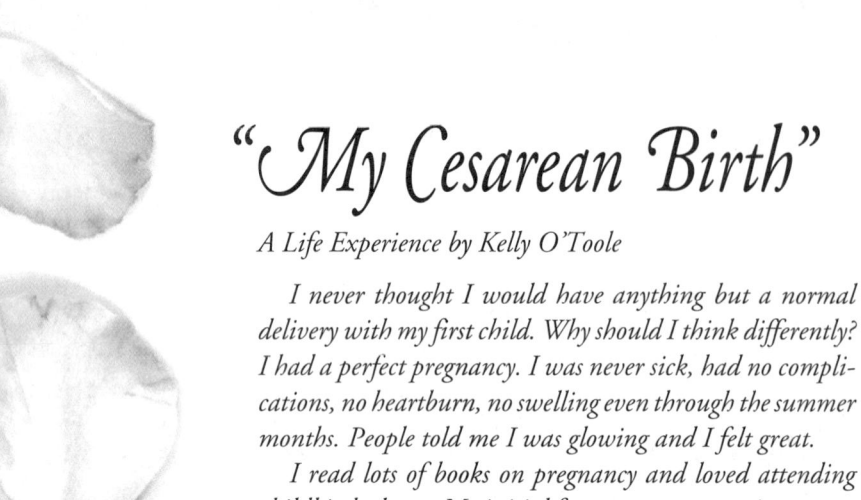

A Life Experience by Kelly O'Toole

I never thought I would have anything but a normal delivery with my first child. Why should I think differently? I had a perfect pregnancy. I was never sick, had no complications, no heartburn, no swelling even through the summer months. People told me I was glowing and I felt great.

I read lots of books on pregnancy and loved attending childbirth classes. My initial fear gave way to excitement as my due date approached. Cesarean birth never crossed my mind. I didn't read those chapters in the pregnancy books and frankly didn't pay close attention to the childbirth class on Cesareans. That is not going to happen to me, I thought.

During my eighth month my husband Michael kept insisting that the baby's head was up near my ribs, not low where it should be. I asked about the baby's position at every visit. Either my doctor didn't want to worry me or simply thought the baby would eventually turn. A few visits later, she finally ordered an ultrasound to check. A week later the ultrasound technician confirmed that the baby was breech, buttocks down. Less than four weeks to go and my whole plan for childbirth had been literally turned on its head.

My doctor recommended a version—she would attempt to turn the baby from the outside. It would require going to the hospital and being hooked up to an IV in case of fetal distress, which could mean an emergency Cesarean. We discussed the risks as well as the chance that the baby couldn't be turned. Even if successful, there was always the chance the baby would flip back to the original position. We decided to try the version and scheduled it for the following week. By this time I was 38 weeks, but everyone, including my doctor, told me not to worry about a Cesarean. At the visit before the version, I asked my doctor lots of questions about Cesarean births. She answered my questions but told me to wait and see how the version would go. I went home with some answers and lots of fear, nervousness and anxiety.

The next night, six days before the scheduled version and ten days before my due date, my water broke. We were going to the hospital to have our baby by Cesarean birth! I felt extremely nervous. I didn't know what to expect. I was also excited because our baby would be born within a few hours.

When I got to the hospital they hooked me up to a monitor. I was apparently having small contractions that I couldn't even feel. They took a sample of the fluid leaking from my cervix to confirm that my water had in fact broken. They wheeled me off to the operating room and my husband was whisked away to change into scrubs. He wasn't allowed to join me until I was prepped for surgery.

Finally, with an IV and monitors attached to my arms, a surgical screen placed in front of me and a room full of nurses, doctors, a pediatrician, an anesthesiologist, a med student and finally my husband—looking very funny in scrubs and a blue surgical hat—we were ready to begin. After a short time, my husband could see the doctor pull out first one foot and then the other, both shoulders and finally the head of our newborn baby Matthew. "It's a boy and he is poohing and peeing all over the place!" I heard the doctor say.

Matthew was carried to a table by the pediatrician where she suctioned out his breathing passages. Not having passed through the birth canal, he needed lots of fluid suctioned out of him. With Michael watching, she initially examined, washed and swaddled him. I couldn't see any of this as I was still flat on my back in the middle of surgery. Michael held Matthew and brought him over to show me. I saw a bright red face peering out of a bundle of blankets, his wide eyes looking at me. He was beautiful and I wanted to reach out, but I was in the middle of surgery and unable to hold him.

At this point the anesthesia was beginning to affect my stomach and the large meal I had eaten a few hours earlier. I was feeling incredibly nauseous and uncomfortable. I felt horrible and had to motion several times for that hospital blue vomit dish. In recovery, I shook uncontrollably from the anesthesia while Matthew was in the nursery. It was hours before I could hold and nurse him.

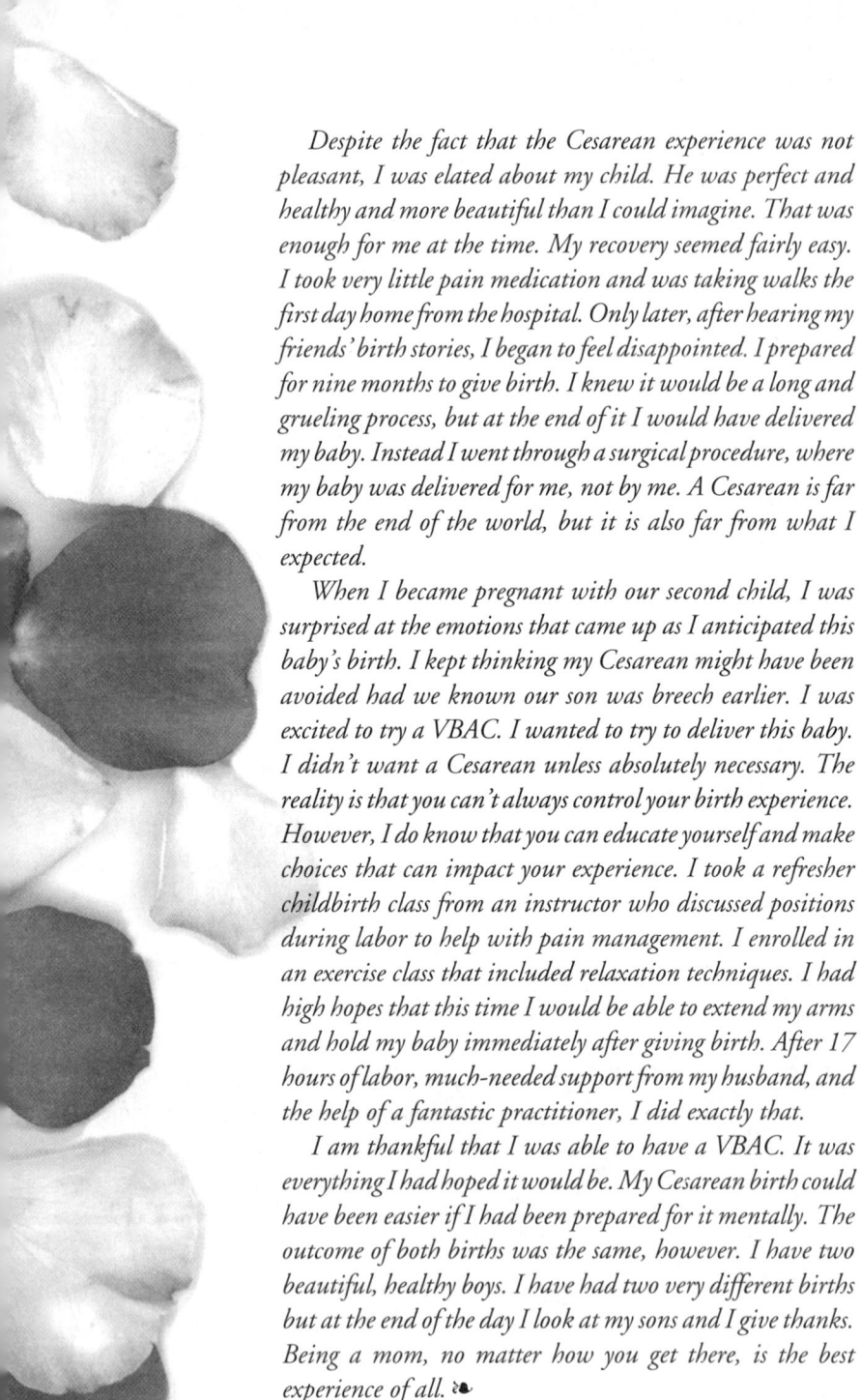

Despite the fact that the Cesarean experience was not pleasant, I was elated about my child. He was perfect and healthy and more beautiful than I could imagine. That was enough for me at the time. My recovery seemed fairly easy. I took very little pain medication and was taking walks the first day home from the hospital. Only later, after hearing my friends' birth stories, I began to feel disappointed. I prepared for nine months to give birth. I knew it would be a long and grueling process, but at the end of it I would have delivered my baby. Instead I went through a surgical procedure, where my baby was delivered for me, not by me. A Cesarean is far from the end of the world, but it is also far from what I expected.

When I became pregnant with our second child, I was surprised at the emotions that came up as I anticipated this baby's birth. I kept thinking my Cesarean might have been avoided had we known our son was breech earlier. I was excited to try a VBAC. I wanted to try to deliver this baby. I didn't want a Cesarean unless absolutely necessary. The reality is that you can't always control your birth experience. However, I do know that you can educate yourself and make choices that can impact your experience. I took a refresher childbirth class from an instructor who discussed positions during labor to help with pain management. I enrolled in an exercise class that included relaxation techniques. I had high hopes that this time I would be able to extend my arms and hold my baby immediately after giving birth. After 17 hours of labor, much-needed support from my husband, and the help of a fantastic practitioner, I did exactly that.

I am thankful that I was able to have a VBAC. It was everything I had hoped it would be. My Cesarean birth could have been easier if I had been prepared for it mentally. The outcome of both births was the same, however. I have two beautiful, healthy boys. I have had two very different births but at the end of the day I look at my sons and I give thanks. Being a mom, no matter how you get there, is the best experience of all.

HINTS FOR AVOIDING A CESAREAN SECTION

While Cesarean sections are safer than they used to be, they are still major surgical procedures. For babies, the outcomes of C-sections are about the same as for vaginal deliveries, but for mothers, C-sections pose higher risks of complications. In addition, the recovery time is much longer after a Cesarean: ten days, as opposed to two or three for a vaginal delivery, and six weeks before you can pick up that heavy diaper bag.

Still, over a fifth of births are by Cesarean section. In 1995, 20.8% of U.S. births were by Cesarean, compared to 10.4% in 1975. Cesarean rates do vary considerably by individual hospitals and providers.

In order to reduce the possibility of a Cesarean delivery, there are some proactive steps women can take. "At least 40% of all C-sections could be avoided with proper management of pregnancy, labor and delivery," says Cristin Babcock, M.D., a Portland, Oregon, obstetrician.

The first thing you can do is to talk with your provider early in your pregnancy and stress that a vaginal delivery is a priority for you. After that, there are five key things you can do to help reduce the likelihood that you'll need a C-section.

- **Prepare for childbirth.** You'll be better able to handle the stress of labor if you take a thorough childbirth preparation course—six weeks, if possible. After the course, you'll be more confident about labor and delivery.
- **Stay active in labor.** During labor, remain upright and active as long as you can to help your body along. Physical activity, warm showers and baths will help gravity work to bring the baby's head down into the pelvis.

Taking an active role in your labor also means taking childbirth preparation classes and learning as much as possible about what to realistically expect during labor. "Many women expect a pain-free delivery, but that's not realistic," says Dr. Babcock. "Having an epidural too early, to stop the pain, may also stop your labor and make a C-section necessary. If you need pain relief, one of the most important things you can do is to hold out until your cervix is dilated at least five centimeters."

> *"One of the most important things you can do is to hold out until your cervix is dilated at least five centimeters."*

- **Actively manage labor.** If labor is not progressing, talk with your provider about what can be done to stimulate labor so it doesn't go on too long or put unnecessary stress on the baby.
- **Don't induce labor unless medically necessary.** Although it may be tempting to "schedule" your baby's delivery by inducing labor, you may pay for that convenience with a C-section. Inducing labor often prevents the cervix from dilating enough or keeps the baby from moving into the correct position for delivery. Instead of taking that risk, be patient and work with your body.
- **If you've had a previous C-section, ask for a trial of labor.** Most women assume that if their first baby was born by Cesarean, the next one will be, too. That's not necessarily the way it has to be. Many women can deliver their second child vaginally. If you'd like to try, let your physician know that you would like a "trial of labor"—trying labor first, before resorting to C-section.

Not every C-section can or should be avoided. In come circumstances, a physician may recommend inducing labor or performing a C-section as the best way to protect mother and child. In other cases, a mother may try all of the suggestions listed above and still end up delivering by C-section.

Every delivery is different, and if a Cesarean becomes necessary for you to delivery a healthy baby or to protect your own health, don't view it as any kind of failure—rather, be thankful that such options exist.

Reprinted with permission from Providence Health System's "Good Health" magazine, Summer/Fall 1997.

RESOURCES

■ INTERNATIONAL CESAREAN AWARENESS NETWORK (ICAN)
(310) 542-6400
1304 Kingsdale Ave.
Redondo Beach, CA 90278
E-mail: icaninc@aol.com
Web site: http://www.childbirth.org/section/ican.html
ICAN has a threefold purpose: to lower the rising Cesarean rate through education, to provide a forum where women and men can express their thoughts and concerns about birth, and to provide a support network for women who are healing from past birth experiences and for those who are preparing for future births. ICAN has grown from one chapter in 1982 to the current 30 chapters nationwide. Contact the organization to receive the free brochures "Working for the Birth You Want" and "Things You Can Do to Avoid an Unnecessary Cesarean" and a free copy of "The Clarion," an informative newsletter which contains Cesarean news updates, book reviews, birth stories, and encouragement from families around the world. A one-year subscription is $25.

Questions and Answers: Cesarean Births

QUESTIONS AND ANSWERS
Cesarean Births

According to the American College of Obstetricians and Gynecologists, the percentage of Cesarean births have decreased from a high of 24.7% in 1988 to 20.8% in 1995. VBAC rates, just 12.6% in 1988, were 27.5% in 1995.

The following answers regarding Cesarean births were provided by Larry Veltman, M.D., who practices obstetrics and gynecology with Women's Healthcare Associates in Portland, Oregon, and is the Medical Director of the Women's and Children's Program for Providence Health Systems.

Q. Under what circumstances might a Cesarean be necessary?

A. The most common reasons for a Cesarean delivery are: the inability for the cervix to dilate or the baby to descend through the birth canal, some type of fetal distress, a problem with the presentation of the baby, the placenta covering the opening of the cervix (placenta previa), or when the placenta begins to separate from the uterus before the birth (placental abruption). These are not the only reasons that a Cesarean birth may result. In fact, sometimes a vaginal delivery can actually occur even with some of these conditions present. Good communication with your health care provider is essential to understand why a Cesarean delivery is necessary in your case.

Q. What can be done to avoid a Cesarean birth?

A. Some Cesarean births are mandatory. For example, if the placenta covers the cervix (placenta previa), vaginal birth is impossible without a possible fatal hemorrhage. On the other hand, when a baby is breech, sometimes it can be turned prior to labor (a procedure called version). It is also important during early labor to try to walk and to delay epidural anesthesia. The lack of walking in early labor and early epidural anesthesia have recently been associated with a higher chance of a Cesarean birth. Women who have experienced a Cesarean birth should thoroughly explore the option of a VBAC before deciding on a repeat Cesarean birth.

Q. What kind of anesthesia is used for a Cesarean birth?

A. A Cesarean delivery is usually performed using epidural or spinal anesthesia. This allows the mother to be awake during the operation and is usually safer for the mother and baby. On occasion, under emergency circumstances, a general anesthetic (putting the mother to sleep) might be required. In any instance the operation should not be painful to the woman undergoing the delivery.

Q. If I have a Cesarean delivery, who will be in the delivery room?

A. In addition to the surgical nurse, obstetrician, and anesthesiologist, there is usually a circulating nurse (who can get needed supplies), a surgical assistant who helps the obstetrician, and one or more individuals who are trained in newborn resuscitation. These individuals may be nurses, respiratory therapists, and/or physicians.

Pediatricians, or family physicians trained in newborn resuscitation, are usually present for most high-risk Cesarean deliveries but may not be present in the operating room at low-risk deliveries (such as repeat Cesarean deliveries). This will vary from hospital to hospital depending upon the training of support personnel. Most hospitals will also allow a support person into the operating room unless general anesthesia is required.

Q. Can my partner be present during a Cesarean birth?

A. In most instances, yes. It is very comforting to have a support person present during a Cesarean birth, but not essential. Usually a partner is allowed to be by the mother to give her moral support. The operative area is covered and it is not necessary to observe the actual procedure. The anesthesiologist will also be at the head of the operating table and gives a great deal of support. In the case of a general anesthetic, the woman's partner may be asked to leave during the delivery.

Q. What type of recovery is expected from a Cesarean birth?

A. With a Cesarean delivery you undergo both recovery from the pregnancy as well as recovery from a surgical operation. Therefore, there will be a longer hospital stay (usually two to four days), and more time needed for recovery once at home. There should be thorough instructions concerning when to call the doctor (fever of above 100.4, hemorrhaging, unusual pain, or any redness, swelling or opening of the incision). Driving, heavy lifting, and exercise is usually not recommended for two to four weeks. After about six weeks most women can return to normal activities.

Q. If a woman has a Cesarean birth can she have a vaginal delivery with a subsequent pregnancy?

A. In most cases, a woman will be encouraged to have a vaginal birth after a previous Cesarean. This is called a VBAC (pronounced vee-back). This issue should be discussed at the time of the Cesarean birth and again at your prenatal visits during the next pregnancy. There are certain indications for high success rates in achieving a VBAC. There are also a few reasons why a VBAC should not be attempted.

It is important to know about the type of uterine incision (not the skin incision, but the actual incision in the uterus). There is also a rare chance that the previous uterine incision could separate during a subsequent labor. A vertical uterine

Questions and Answers: Cesarean Births

incision (which is quite rare today) as opposed to a horizontal uterine incision is usually a reason not to attempt a VBAC.

Overall, however, vaginal birth after a Cesarean holds less risk for the mother and the baby than just repeating the Cesarean because it was done before.

Q. What is important about a physician's or a hospital's Cesarean birth rate?

A. Cesarean rates vary from physician to physician, from hospital to hospital, and from community to community. It is important, however, that the rate itself is not the only factor considered in choosing a provider. For example, if a physician refers all high-risk pregnancies to other practices, that physician will have a lower Cesarean rate. Conversely, if a hospital or a provider cares for an unusual number of high-risk pregnancies, this will be reflected in a higher Cesarean rate (sometimes in the range of 30%). The important issue is to have confidence that all birthing options will be considered for both the mother and the baby. If the best outcome is achieved by a Cesarean, then the mother should proceed with that option.

STAGES OF LABOR

Unless your birth is a scheduled Cesarean section, you should experience some of the following stages of labor. Also, this chart may be helpful for subsequent VBAC (Vaginal Birth after Cesarean) births.

STAGE	DILATION	CONTRACTIONS	WHAT TO DO
FIRST STAGE			
Early Labor	0-4 cm	20-5 min. apart; 30-60 seconds duration	Take a walk; relax; bathe or shower
Active Labor	5-8 cm	3-4 min. apart; 45-60 seconds duration	Use relaxation and breathing methods; walk if possible
Transition	8-10 cm	2-3 min. apart; 60 seconds duration	Pant, don't push; suck on ice chips
SECOND STAGE	10 cm	2-5 min. apart; 60-90 seconds	Work with coach to push for baby's birth!
THIRD STAGE		Very mild	Push when instructed to expel placenta

PREPARATION FOR BABY

THE LIGHTER SIDE OF PREGNANCY

A dear friend, Claire Voyant, who has had experience dealing with over six pregnant couples, has graciously agreed to answer the most often asked questions about pregnancy, childbirth and babies, no matter how ridiculous they may be (the questions, not the babies).

By Joyce Armor

Q. **Is it true that I'm more likely to get pregnant if my husband wears boxer shorts rather than jockey shorts?**

A. Yes, but you'd be most likely to get pregnant if he were wearing no shorts.

Q. **How can I be sure I'm really pregnant?**

A. Time your contractions.

Q. **I wear a size 34C bra (when I wear one) and have never needed much support. Why should I start wearing a bra now that I'm pregnant?**

A. No reason if you don't mind switching in the future to a size 34 long.

Q. **Does pregnancy cause dandruff?**

A. Pregnancy causes anything you want to blame it for.

Q: **My wife is six months pregnant and so moody that she overreacts to the simplest problem. Sometimes she's borderline irrational.**

A: So? What's the question?

Q. **What's the most common pregnancy craving?**

A. For men to be the ones who get pregnant.

The Lighter Side of Pregnancy

Q. *Now that I'm pregnant, my breasts and rear end are huge and even my feet have grown. Isn't there anything that gets smaller during pregnancy?*

A. Of course. Your bladder.

Q: *All the expectant women I know seem so sure of themselves. Am I the only pregnant woman who has ever had second thoughts about becoming a mother?*

A: Yes.

Q. *Is there anything that will alleviate the nausea I've been feeling during my pregnancy?*

A. Yes. Vomiting.

Q. *Both my husband and I are extremely good looking, and I know our baby will be too. I think he (or she) should be in commercials right away or even a TV series. Whom should I talk to about this?*

A. Your therapist.

Q. *The more pregnant I get, the more often complete strangers smile at me. Why?*

A. Because you're fatter than they are.

Q. *What position should the baby be in during my ninth month of pregnancy?*

A. Head down, pressing firmly on your bladder.

Q. *I hate baby showers. Is there any way to avoid them?*

A. Yes, change the baby's diapers very quickly.

Q: *My childbirth instructor says that it's not pain you feel during labor, but pressure. Is she right?*

A: Yes, in the same way that a tornado might be called an air current.

Q. *Who had the longest labor in recorded history?*

A. Whoever your most boring acquaintance is.

Q. *Can a sterilization operation be performed during a Cesarean?*

A. Only if it's on your wife. Schedule your vasectomy on your own time.

Q: *Please settle an argument I'm having with my sister. Can a mother get pregnant while nursing her baby?*

A: Yes, but it's much easier if she removes the baby from her breast and puts him down for a nap first.

Q: *Do newborns have a sense of taste?*

A: Apparently not, or why would so many of them wear those shapeless sacques and washed-out colors?

Q. *I'm pregnant for the first time, and I'm already worried about how far apart I should space my children. What do the experts say?*

A. Most experienced parents space their children at least six feet apart.

PLANNING FOR POSTPARTUM

Many women spend their pregnancies reading about their baby's prenatal development. They plan nurseries and consider names. They choose a layette and birth announcements. But often little thought goes toward their own postpartum planning. Nothing can fully prepare you for the emotions and physical elation and discomforts you'll feel, unless you've had a baby before. But just as each pregnancy is different, so is each postpartum period. Take a little time to mentally prepare for the days and weeks after your child's birth.

THE FIRST DAY

Plan to be euphoric, tired, anxious and extremely hungry! This is prime bonding time, so spend as much time as possible with your newborn. Ask your nurse to help you with nursing your baby, within the first hour postpartum if possible.

- Have a phone list ready so you or your partner can make calls from the hospital. Visitors may come to see you and the baby, but limit the visits so you don't get overly tired.
- If you have older children, consider giving a "big brother" or "big sister" gift when they meet their new sibling.
- Besides taking vital signs, a nurse will visit you often to massage your uterus until it firms up and to verify that the lochia (post-birth blood flow) is moderate.
- You may be given an ice pack, pain medication or anesthetic spray for your tender perineal area.

THE FIRST WEEK

Your lochia will still be flowing rather heavily, and there may be blood clots. Over the next couple weeks, it will turn pink, then whitish. It is recommended that you use sanitary pads rather than tampons. Have a box of heavy-flow pads on hand for your first week home.

- When you read about milk coming in, it may not prepare you for the actual event. Two to four days after delivery, your milk changes from the thick, yellowish colostrum to a thinner milk. Your breasts may become very full and sore, making it difficult for baby to latch on. This will

Take a little time to mentally prepare for the days and weeks after your child's birth.

- subside when you get into a regular nursing pattern.
- If you plan to bottle feed, you must avoid stimulating milk production in order to dry up the milk supply. A firm support bra worn 24 hours a day will help, as will ice packs and cold compresses.
- Nursing your baby may stimulate afterbirth pains for a week or so. The pains are stronger with second and subsequent children, and are caused by your uterus working to return to its prepregnancy size.
- Urination and bowel movements may be difficult for a few days. Nervousness about tearing episiotomy stitches can inhibit urine flow. Plan to drink plenty of fluids. To make bowel movements less painful, a diet rich in fiber and a stool softener will ease discomfort.
- A few repetitions of Kegel exercises several times a day will help you regain perineal muscle tone. These should be worked into your daily routine to prevent stress incontinence when you get older.
- Hemorrhoids are a side effect of pregnancy, labor and delivery. Sprays, dry heat, or witch hazel compresses will be soothing.
- Watch for danger signs. ACOG recommends you call your practitioner if you experience any of these problems: fever over 100.4 degrees, heavy bleeding, nausea or vomiting, urinary difficulties or perineal pain, swelling or pain in legs, chest pain or cough, or hot or tender breasts.

THE FIRST MONTHS

- Depression after childbirth is common and can range from "the baby blues" to serious depression. Read about PPD in Chapter 6.
- Your menstrual periods will resume about six to eight weeks after childbirth if you are not breastfeeding. Nursing mothers may not have a period for several months or more.
- Check with your obstetrician about the best birth control method to use postpartum. If you wait until your period starts to resume using birth control, you may be too late!
- Your obstetrical checkup, generally four to six weeks postpartum, is often the go-ahead signal for resuming your sexual relations. Others may feel ready a few weeks earlier, but be sure to think "gentle." You may need a vaginal lubricant if you experience dryness. Some breastfeeding mothers experience menopausal-type changes vaginally due to hormone fluctuation that can increase discomfort. If lubricant isn't helping, ask your provider; treatment is available.
- When you find some time alone, you and your partner may want to reconnect with some snuggling and talking. New dads may feel left out. Make sure your partner knows he is loved and appreciated.
- Exercise can increase your strength and energy level, and help you get back into shape.
- Rest is essential but not often possible. Ask your partner to take over as much of the household duties as possible, so you are ensured as much sleep as you can.

MATERNITY LEAVE

For women who work, planning ahead for your maternity leave is the key to making a smooth transition from leaving your job to enjoying your time at home with your new baby. The more informed you are about your rights in the workplace, the better you can maximize your options.

This section of the resource guide focuses both on the laws that protect pregnant women and on the "gray" areas that surround maternity leave. This section is not intended to replace legal advice. It should also be noted that the laws change often in this area, so use the resources given to fully understand the most current information.

One resource we found very helpful is a book entitled *Everything A Working Mother Needs To Know* by Anne C. Weisberg and Carol A. Buckler. The book offers both a legal and logistical approach to maternity leave.

THE FAMILY AND MEDICAL LEAVE ACT

In 1993, President Bill Clinton signed the Family and Medical Leave Act of 1993 (FMLA). If your state has its own family leave act, compare the state and federal regulations. You are generally allowed to use the more generous guidelines in planning your leave. The FMLA requires employers with 50 or more employees to permit most personnel to take up to three months of unpaid leave. This leave can be for the birth or adoption of a child, to care for a parent, spouse, or child, or personal leave if that individual has a serious health condition.

This Act prohibits employers with 50 or more employees from denying most employees' requests for a family care leave of absence. (The 50 employees is limited to worksites with 50 or more persons employed within 75 miles of the worksite.) The Act also requires employers to guarantee re-employment in the same or equivalent position to workers who return from family leave. Employers must also pay for employees' existing health benefits while they are on leave. However, an employer is not required to pay for health benefits if the woman is on pregnancy disability. If the employee does not return to work at the end of the leave, the employer may collect the cost of the premium.

The more informed you are about your rights in the workplace, the better you can maximize your options.

WHO IS ELIGIBLE FOR FAMILY LEAVE?

All employees with more than a year of service and at least 1,250 hours worked in the last 12 months with the employer are covered by this Act. Both spouses may take the full amount of the leave, as long as they do not work for the same company. The employer may limit the family leave for birth or adoption, not to exceed a total of 12 weeks between both spouses working at the same company.

Another provision in eligibility for the FMLA is the "Key Employee Exception." This means if you are a salaried employee among the highest paid 10% in a company and if restoration or taking the leave would lead to substantial and grievous economic harm to the employer, you may be refused the leave. This places a heavy burden on the employer to justify exempting an employee. If your employer does refuse your leave based on the "Key Employee Exception" it would be to your benefit to contact the U.S. Department of Labor, Wage and Hour Division, to clarify this clause.

HOW ARE THE TWELVE WEEKS DEFINED?

In accordance with the Family Medical Leave Act, you may take 12 unpaid work weeks in a 12-month period. This 12-month period does not have to be in one calendar year.

Employers may require, or an employee may elect, to substitute paid vacation or any other accrued time off for a portion of an employee's available unpaid leave. An employee may only substitute accrued sick time for a portion of the unpaid family care leave if the reason for the leave would otherwise entitle the employee to use sick leave.

THE PREGNANCY DISCRIMINATION ACT

All women who work in companies with 15 or more employees are protected against discrimination under federal law by the Pregnancy Discrimination Act of 1978. In effect, this 20-year-old law equates pregnancy discrimination with sex discrimination.

It is generally agreed that a woman is disabled by pregnancy at least two to four weeks before her due date and four to six weeks after a vaginal birth. The period is a bit longer for recovery from a Cesarean birth. These disability periods are, however, up to each health care provider. You are only entitled to the full four-month leave under the Pregnancy Discrimination Act if your provider certifies you to be disabled for that length of time. If you are medically able to return to work, but choose not to, you are not covered by the Pregnancy Discrimination Act.

Check with your state's disability leave regulations; they may be more lenient than the national requirements.

To receive a free Equal Employment Opportunity Commission brochure titled "Facts About Pregnancy Discrimination," call 800-669-3362.

ARE YOU PAID DURING YOUR LEAVE?

The employer does not need to provide any salary unless the employee uses vacation time or other paid time off during the period of family leave.

During your leave, you can not be forced to sacrifice any seniority or benefits. When you return from the family care leave, you will have the same seniority and benefits as before your leave. Your employer also cannot consider your leave a break in service for purposes of a layoff, promotion, job assignment, employee benefits (including vacation) and for any seniority provision under a collective bargaining agreement. Your employer, however, does not need to pay into your pension or retirement plan during your leave. You must be allowed to make contributions to your retirement plan.

WHEN TO NOTIFY YOUR EMPLOYER

You should give your employer at least 30 days advance notice in writing or as soon as possible when taking your leave for birth or adoption. Longer notice is always appreciated. If your leave is an unanticipated emergency, you must verbally notify your employer within 24 hours and provide written notice within three days of taking your leave.

RESOURCES

■ **9 TO 5 NATIONAL ASSOCIATION OF WORKING WOMEN JOB SURVIVAL HOTLINE**
800-522-0925
Hours: M-F (EST) 10:00 a.m.-2:50 p.m.
This is a hotline devoted to answering questions about the National Family Medical Leave Act (FMLA), and all other employment-related topics. They can provide a fact sheet highlighting the legal language of the Act. The 9 to 5 staff can also help you if you have questions about maternity leave, health and safety on the job, or sexual harassment. The hotline operator will make referrals specific to your state's employment policies.

■ **U.S. DEPARTMENT OF LABOR EMPLOYMENT STANDARDS ADMINISTRATION, WAGE-HOUR DIVISION, FAMILY MEDICAL LEAVE ACT OFFICE**
(202) 219-8412
200 Constitution Ave., N.W.
Room S3502
Washington, DC 20210
This department's staff are the experts on the federal FMLA, and can send you a complete copy of the Act.

QUESTIONS AND ANSWERS
Your Maternity Leave

The following interview with the Microsoft Corporation Benefits Department answers commonly asked questions about maternity leave. The information below should not take the place of legal advice or information from your company's human resources professional.

Q: When should I notify my employer about my pregnancy?

A: At Microsoft, we encourage our employees to notify their manager regarding their estimated leave of absence dates as soon as possible. This enables the manager to arrange for contingent staffing and/or time to determine what duties will need to be temporarily reassigned.

Q: Although the law provides guidelines for maternity leave, is there room for negotiating a flexible or longer leave than what the law or current company policy stipulates?

A: It's important that the employee be familiar with her company's leave of absence policies. In some cases, employers may allow you to extend your leave by using your floating holidays or accrued vacation. Additionally, based on the type of work you do, in rare instances some employers may be open to allowing you to take your leave of absence on an intermittent basis.

Q: What is the benefit of a short term disability plan?

A: If your physician determines that you will not be able to work up until the time you deliver, short term disability plans allow the expectant mother time off prior to her delivery and maternity leave. Some short term disability plans provide benefits only after sick leave benefits are exhausted.

Q: Once my employer knows of my pregnancy, should I expect to be treated any differently and will my responsibilities change?

A: Based on the type of work that you do, your health care provider may indicate that some of your job duties may need to be modified until after you return from maternity leave. It is best to discuss this with your health care provider and your employer, so that your employer can determine the feasibility of your request for this temporary accommodation.

Q: After I've had my baby, should I call my employer? And what should I say?

A: Employers and co-workers are usually anxious to hear if you had a boy or girl, how you are feeling, and information about your new family. Additionally, if your employer h care plan that your ... will be a part of, this is a good time to enroll your baby in the plan.

Q: Can a man take advantage of a parental leave?

A: New fathers are eligible for leave under the provisions and in accordance with the 1993 FMLA unless both spouses work at the same company. In this case, they may choose to share the allotted time allowed by the Act.

Q: What if my maternity leave is up and I decide I really don't want to return to work?

A: If, at the end of your leave, you decide not to return to work, it is best to inform your employer right away so that they can hire someone to replace you. Also, under the FMLA of 1993, the employer may require you to pay back the health benefits that were paid for during your family leave.

PLANNING YOUR LEAVE

Here is a checklist that may be helpful while planning your maternity leave.
- Consult your library and review the Family Medical Leave Act of 1993.
- Review your state's maternity leave laws.
- If your employer does not qualify for the FMLA, review the Pregnancy Disability Act.
- Write a letter to your employer regarding your pregnancy and anticipated leave.
- Discuss the following questions with your human resources department:
  - Will I receive any income during my leave?
  - Does the company provide short-term disability insurance?
  - Does the company allow the use of vacation and sick days during a maternity leave?
  - Will my current position, or a comparable one, be held open for me?
  - What expenses does the company medical plan cover, and what expenses should I expect to pay?
  - Is health plan coverage available for my new baby, and how soon must I enroll the baby?

"Working at Home"

A Life Experience by Mavis Heyward

How did my journey toward working from home begin? I've really made a round-trip visit and picked up some priceless treasures along the way. In June 1986 I left a $38,000 a year job at an aerospace company to start my own tax, accounting and auditing firm from home. Eleven years ago, clients and society alike believed that if you operated a business from home, you were more likely to be a fly-by-night company; my home-based business lasted only three months. I moved to a small office downtown, then a larger office, then once more to an even larger office.

As the years went on I dropped the employees, and gave birth to three lovely, adorable, talented and mischievous gifts from God (otherwise known as children). Just before the birth of our first child, my husband quit his job as a controller at an auto dealership and joined my firm to allow me more time with our baby. We briefly discussed operating out of the home, but at that time we lived in a two-bedroom condo, so the discussion was short and sweet. A few years later I again brought up the subject of operating out of the home. This time I had some fuel. We had two more children and had moved to a larger home. The time was right: a year ago we began operating out of our home and haven't looked back since then.

Now I have peace of mind that can't be matched by any corporate office. It may not be as plush, but I know that it is my domain and in it I am as relaxed as I could possibly be. I also get to watch my children grow and mature. The challenges of operating a business and mothering are multiplied, but the opportunities for learning are too. The children get real life lessons of business at an early age so they see the importance of ABCs and 123s.

From a business point of view, the main overhead expense-rent-has been cut. I could expect my office rent to increase at least 5% every three years. Now we are able to maintain our clients' fees at a reasonable level. (That's the tax lady talking.) Also, I can now work at my peak hours: very early in the morning. My husband's peak hours are after noon and after 10 p.m. It works well for him also.

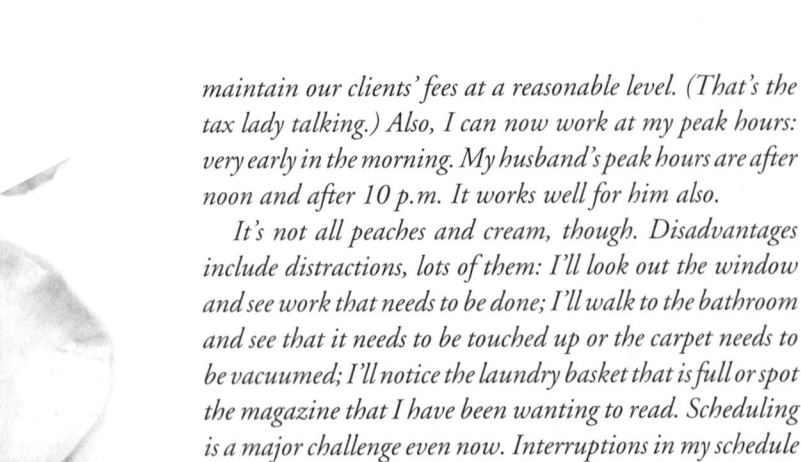

It's not all peaches and cream, though. Disadvantages include distractions, lots of them: I'll look out the window and see work that needs to be done; I'll walk to the bathroom and see that it needs to be touched up or the carpet needs to be vacuumed; I'll notice the laundry basket that is full or spot the magazine that I have been wanting to read. Scheduling is a major challenge even now. Interruptions in my schedule drive me crazy, but they cannot be avoided. While the two oldest children go to Grammy and Papa's house three days out of the week, the baby stays home everyday.

My personality tug-of-war is an issue that is not unique to home-based businesses as much as it is to a working mom. My personalities consist of being a Mom, a Wife and a Professional Woman. Sometimes I have to remind myself that I am a professional woman who has a "secular job" that needs to be done daily, especially when the distractions are bombarding me. Other times, I don't want to stop working even to feed myself, let alone the rest of the family.

Sometimes I feel I could easily transition into a non-working stay-at-home mom, but then I think of the skills I've acquired and the clients that I'd be leaving behind. I don't really want to stop working. This focused attitude is actually a form of selfishness that my husband has helped me to see. We are continually working on this trait.

As a mom, I cherish every moment with my children. I love to teach them, nurture them, cuddle them and play with them whenever the opportunity arises. During the tax season, a busier than normal time, the one who has paid the highest price is our oldest child. As she leans on the front of my desk, her big brown eyes beg me to spend time with her now that I am home. She doesn't fully understand yet that although Mommy is at home, she is working. But, I'd still rather be in a home-based office situation to see her mature and to nurture her along this way.

CHILD CARE

Whether you work full-time, part-time or stay at home with your child, quality child care is a necessity. Although child care facilities must meet certain state standards, you should have your own list of preferences and expectations. Listen to your parental instincts when making your selection. Leaving your child is difficult anyway, but to do so with a child care arrangement that you are not completely satisfied with is even more stressful.

To begin your child care search, it is important to examine the options available to you. Below is a brief description of the most common child care choices, including registered family child care homes, child care centers, and live-in child care.

FAMILY CHILD CARE HOMES

Licensed family child care refers to child care in the private home of a licensed individual. The number of children a single provider may watch is regulated by each state, and may depend on the age range of the children. Typical is a maximum enrollment of six children (12 if the care provider has a full-time aide). To obtain licensing, most states require an initial visit to the child care site to ensure the safety of the children in the home and a criminal and child abuse record check, in addition to a certificate of completion from an approved infant safety and CPR course. If you have questions, contact your state's child care licensing agency.

Family child care homes vary widely, from the neighborhood mom who takes in a few children to help earn extra money to professionally-run businesses. There are some definite advantages of working with group child care homes:

- The provider is licensed and therefore must follow certain guidelines provided to retain licensing.
- A small, family-like environment.
- Can be less expensive than other forms of child care.
- Social interaction with other children.
- May be more flexible. Some home care providers offer weekend and evening care.

Disadvantages may include:

- Since you're often dealing with only one provider, if he or she becomes ill or takes a vacation, you must work around that person's schedule.

Although child care facilities must meet certain state standards, you should have your own list of preferences and expectations.

...y be treated more ...se the provider is in ... home and not directly ...pervised.
- If the provider is caring for her own children, there is the possibility that her child could be favored.
- The provider may not stay in business for the length of time your child needs care, i.e., may stop providing services if economics or family needs change.

CHILD CARE CENTERS

Child care centers are licensed for the care of more than 12 children. Staffing requirements ensure that children are cared for by qualified teachers. Caregiver to child ratios are 1:4 for infants, and ratios for toddlers range from 1:7 to 1:12, depending on state law. Typical ratios for toddlers are 1:12 and, for age 5 and up, one adult to every 15 children.

Besides following an adult-to-child ratio, child care centers are expected to fulfill educational requirements and provide more than a baby-sitting environment. Many child care centers will give you written reports that include everything from the number of diaper changes to the achievements of special milestones, such as a first step. Child care centers must also follow specific fire, building, and zoning codes.

Some child care centers go beyond minimum requirements to gain accreditation by the National Association for the Education of Young Children (NAEYC). This requires meeting nationally recognized quality standards and includes a site evaluation by a NAEYC staff member.

Some advantages of choosing a child care center may be:
- Convenient location for parents.
- Licensing of the center's caregivers.

STEPS FOR CHOOSING CHILD CARE

- List things you feel are important for you and your child.
- Screen potential caregivers on the phone to see if they meet your basic requirements and make appointments with those you would like to visit.
- During your visits, use a checklist to evaluate programs. Visit more than once and at different times of the day.
- Count the number of children and staff at each of your visits.
- Ask about the provider's experience and education.
- Check references by talking to parents with children in the program and calling the child care licensor of the program.
- Read the caregiver's written policies and procedures carefully.
- Consider substitute plans in case your child is ill or your child's care provider or the child care center is on vacation or closed.

The above information is reprinted with permission from "Choosing Child Care," provided by Child Care Resources in Seattle, Washington.

ble between 18
ience caring

included in the pro-
are based on arrival in
, and do not include air fare to
ty. Au Pair Care determines the
mestic portion of airfare which is due
30 days prior to the flight.

A host family application is filled out and returned with a $100 application fee and $125 interview fee. A confidential reference form should be provided directly from the friend or other personal reference used. The program fees of $4,070 cover screening and selection, English language testing, proper family matching, visa forms, travel to New York, health insurance while in the U.S., orientations for au pairs and families, community counselor's services and cultural and social activities for au pairs. A program fee deposit of $1,200 is required upon matching and the balance of the fees are due 30 days prior to arrival. They do have a payment plan if you prefer to spread out the payments.

Telephone calls and free time should be arranged in the beginning and car insurance added if the au pair is to use the family car. Repeat families do not need to submit an application or interview fee.

■ AU PAIR HOMESTAY
800-479-0907
1015 15th St. N.W., Ste. 750
Washington, DC 20005

The Au Pair Homestay program has been operating since 1986 to provide caregivers from around the globe. It is part of World Learning Inc., a nonprofit organization founded in 1932 as "The Experiment in International Living." This organization is the oldest of its kind and invented the homestay concept. A 20-minute video is available to further explain their program. Au Pair Homestay participants, now numbering over 2,000, presently come from over 20 countries.

Families seeking an au pair are considered on a first-come, first-served basis. You must qualify as a host family by completing a family application kit, providing two character references, and a check for $250. Prematched or returning families submit a $175 deposit.

After your application is reviewed, an interview in your home with the community coordinator is set up.

A program fee of $3,950 covers health and accident insurance, orientation, seminars, year-long support, counseling/advising from community coordinators, educational materials, local and special occasion activities and round-trip airfare from Washington, D.C. There will be an additional cost to bring the au pair to your city. Automobile insurance will need to be adjusted if the au pair is expected to use the family car. An au pair works approximately 45 hours per week with two weeks off per year.

■ AU PAIR IN AMERICA
800-928-7247
102 Greenwich Ave.
Greenwich, CT 06830

For more than 10 years, Au Pair in America has been helping families with child care. Most au pairs are from western Europe and the United Kingdom. Au Pair in America has a four-day training program which includes child safety and child development. The screening process includes reference verification, child care when my daughter was eight months old. F[...] one caregiver-to-infant ratios appear reasonable on p[...] but when I observed them firsthand, I felt they were woef[...] inadequate. The caregivers I observed ranged from lovi[...] but harried women, to inexperienced teenagers, to retired women helping out to fill their time. I have no doubt that most teachers love the children and do the best they can. But "the best they can" was still not good enough for me. I wanted my daughter to have all of someone's time, attention and energy. Most of all, I wanted that someone to be me.

I won't lie and say that staying at home with my daughter is easy. We are living on a strict budget with no room for extras. We have no savings and a ridiculously high Visa bill. We tear fabric softener sheets and paper towels in half to extend their use. We make our own cleaning solutions and I've taken to washing my hair every other day to save shampoo. I shop at the cheapest pack-your-own grocery store and buy all store-brand foods. No snacks, chips, ice cream, frozen food or individually packaged convenience foods are allowed. All of my daughter's clothes and toys are hand-me-downs or are purchased at resale shops. When my husband needs a haircut, it sends us scrambling to make room in the budget somewhere. I haven't bought myself anything in more than two years, and my underwear sorely need replacing.

Despite these lifestyle adjustments, I've never been more at peace with my decision. I realize that the choice is clear: "things," like name-brand foods, toys and Windex, versus time spent with my daughter laughing, playing, and learning during these few crucial developmental years. As long as we can, we will continue to scrimp and save and sacrifice, because she is worth it all, and even more.

I constantly battle with myself and others over this decision to stay home. Most of my co-workers are incredulous. "You're not the type," they say. "You'll be bored stiff." Internally, I wonder if I shouldn't be contributing somehow to society, being an educated, able-bodied adult. I keep reminding myself that raising a kind, moral, educated, and happy child is a great contribution.

BABY PRODUCTS

CHAPTER THREE

SHOPPING SMART FOR YOUR NEW BABY

Even veteran shoppers may be overwhelmed by the tasks of purchasing maternity and baby clothing, a crib, car seat, stroller, diapering equipment, special linens and toiletries, and nursing or bottle feeding accessories. (And that's just the bare minimum!)

Matching the bewildering array of items to purchase are the number of places where such purchases can be made. Expectant parents must choose between shopping at discount stores, department stores, warehouse stores, baby specialty stores, resale shops, or staying at home and buying through catalogs or over the World Wide Web. Here is a little information to help you choose where to shop for those purchases designed to help you welcome a new person into your home.

- **Baby specialty stores.** Often thought of as top-of-the-line, exclusive stores, specialty stores are often the best place to shop for baby furnishings. Staff is usually very knowledgeable about each line and model, and is willing to spend time to discuss which items will suit your needs. Prices are often not that much higher than at discount stores, and the personal service may more than make up for the markup.

- **Department stores.** People often have a favorite department store, which may be a good place to investigate for baby items, even though department stores may have limited baby furnishings departments. Sales can bring prices down to the discount store range. Staff is usually helpful, and returns are often handled with little problem.

- **Discount stores.** You won't find much in the way of helpful staff at discount stores, and often car seats and strollers are displayed up high, where they are difficult to examine. But discount stores do carry familiar brand names and enough variety to make you feel you're making an informed product decision. Pricing is generally low, with occasional sales that bring prices down even more.

Matching the bewildering array of items to purchase are the number of places where such purchases can be made.

- **Warehouse stores.** For low prices, warehouse stores can't be beat. But sales help is nonexistent, and displays are limited. You may find only one or two models available of only a couple of products. However, if you like what you see, buy it! Prices don't get much lower than at huge warehouse stores.

- **Catalog shopping.** A pleasure for those who just can't bear the thought of trudging through store after store searching for just the right thing, catalogs offer a wide variety of merchandise for expectant and new parents. From the upscale full-color catalog to the mimeographed type stapled at the catalog owner's kitchen table, you will find a variety of merchandise advertised in a wide variety of ways. Be sure to check return policies, and make sure that the shipping and handling charges don't overwhelm your purchase price. Otherwise, shopping by catalog—especially for nursing clothes and diapering products—can be a quick way to find marvelous things. (Also, you can't beat getting packages in the mail for a real day-brightener!) You may also want to check the Internet for a wide variety of products prior to shopping. Manufacturers' and retail stores' web sites generally list products, prices, and information.

- **Resale shops.** Some people are hesitant to shop at resale stores. There is a wide range, from the decidedly upscale resale store to jumbled thrift shops. If you plan your shopping trips wisely, you'll find that most resale shops carry top-quality, gently used merchandise that is very affordable. Remember resale shops when you no longer need your baby equipment and clothing—resale shop owners generally offer you about half the selling price either on consignment or will purchase outright.

- **Garage sales.** You can find baby equipment and clothing at rock-bottom prices at local garage sales, but you must check items over carefully—there is no returning a garage sale item. Be especially cautious about baby furnishings offered without manufacturer's directions and product information.

BABY PRODUCTS

It can be difficult to choose baby products that meet your needs and budget. This section includes information on a variety of baby products, including their features and benefits. It is not meant to take the place of *Consumer Reports* or other scientific baby product reviews but rather to give you a starting point on baby product purchases.

Products included in this chapter are: strollers, car seats, cribs, swings, child carriers, nursing accessories and bottle feeding products, and great gift ideas. We hope this information will prove helpful as you evaluate your upcoming purchases. We do not endorse any one brand or product, nor do we validate the safety of any product. Readers should make their own choices based on personal preference and on the safety of each item. With that in mind...read on!

PURCHASING DECISIONS

How do you find products that best meet your needs and your budget? Start by asking yourself the following questions:
- Are you looking for products that will last through more than one child?
- Do you care about added convenience features, or do you want to purchase products for the lowest possible price?
- How informed are you about baby products on the market?
- Does your partner have an opinion on the baby products you purchase?

This section includes information on a variety of baby products, including their features and benefits.

BABY PRODUCT TIPS

Once you've answered these questions regarding your purchasing decision, consider the following general tips which can help you decide where to shop and what to look for.

DURABILITY AND CONVENIENCE

If you are looking for products that will last beyond one child, you may want to consider purchasing a higher quality product that offers durability and convenience. Consider a duo stroller, a high-quality mattress or a crib that converts into a toddler's bed, and colors that will work as well for a boy as they do for a girl.

PRICING

Although some department stores and discount stores offer low-priced baby products, you will probably not find available staff in these stores to assist and inform you about the individual items. You may be left to make your product decisions and choices alone. For those of you who know little about baby products, this may prove to be a frustrating experience. However, once you know what you are looking for, you may want to shop around for the best price.

PRODUCT INFORMATION

We found baby specialty stores more responsive to parents' needs since they can be a valuable source of information. The staff at most baby specialty stores is well-trained and available to assist you and answer your questions.

Several publications review baby products that will help you become more informed. *Baby Bargains*, written by Allen and Denise Fields, is an excellent source of information on baby products. Another useful resource is *Consumer Reports*. This magazine periodically reviews baby products. They also have a book entitled *Consumer Reports Guide to Baby Products*, which is updated almost every two years. It evaluates the safety, convenience and durability of hundreds of baby products. It also includes buying advice, price guidelines for products and recall information. Also check out manufacturers' web sites for specific product information. Becoming informed before you make a purchase may save you time and money, as well as aggravation.

OPINION

Check with your significant other before shopping. You may be surprised by your partner's opinions and besides, it is fun to shop for baby items together.

SOME GENERAL SUGGESTIONS

In case you don't have time to read the entire baby product chapter, here are some "biased" random opinions regarding products.

- Double check the buckle and harness system on your car seat. Make sure it is easy to get the baby in and out of the car seat without fumbling with buckles.
- Buying a stroller that is lightweight and has the features you want, although it may be more expensive, is well worth the purchase. For families on the go, a stroller is a lifesaver.
- Consider a swing with a bassinet feature. The bassinet can be used when the infant is newborn and placed directly in the crib, alleviating a separate bassinet purchase. Swings with this feature are only about $30 more than the swing-only seat.
- If you don't have a walker, it is probably the one purchase you should skip. The American Academy of Pediatrics recommends that children not use walkers due to the high rate of walker-related injuries.

REFERENCE NUMBERS

Here are some quick references to product information and car seat recall numbers.

CUSTOMER SERVICE AND CONSUMER INFO

Juvenile Products Manufacturers Association	609-231-8500
Aprica	310-639-6387
Baby Jogger	800-241-1848
Britax	888-4-BRITAX
Century	800-837-4044
Combi	800-992-6624
Cosco	800-544-1108
Emmaljunga	800-848-3864
Evenflo	800-837-9201
First Years	800-533-6708
Fisher Price	800-828-4000
Gerber	800-443-7237
Gerry	800-525-2472
Graco	800-345-4109
Infantino	800-365-8182
Johnson & Johnson	800-526-3967
Kelty	800-423-2320
Kolcraft	800-453-7673
Little Miss Liberty	800-RND-CRIB
Little Tikes	800-321-0183
Medela	800-435-8316
Nojo	800-854-8760
Peg Perego	219-482-8191
Playskool	800-PLAYSKL

CAR SEAT SAFETY/PRODUCT RECALL NUMBERS

D.O.T. Auto Safety Hotline	888-327-4236
National Highway and Traffic Safety Administration	202-366-2768
Child Safety Seat Resource	800-772-1315
Consumer Product Safety Commission	800-638-2772

CAR SEATS

By Cathy Morris
Placer County (CA) Buckle Up Baby Car Seat Project Coordinator

Vehicle crashes are the number one preventable cause of unintentional death and injury to children. When used correctly, child car seats hold a child securely, spread the crash forces over a wide area of the child's body, and keep the child from striking the interior of the vehicle in a sudden stop or crash.

A common question asked by new parents is: "What is the best car seat?" Initially, the answer seems simple. The best car seat is the seat that fits your child, fits in your

WHAT TO LOOK FOR

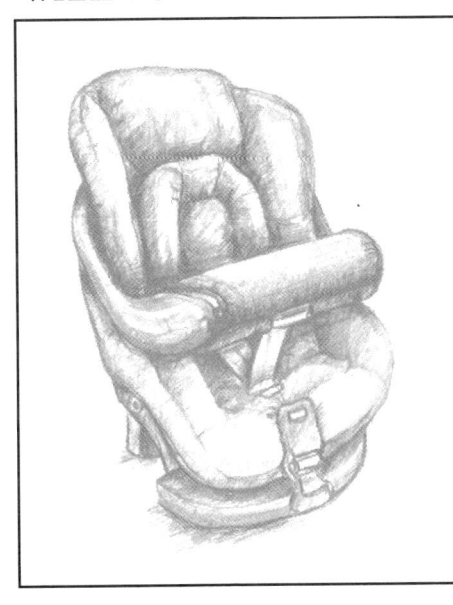

WHAT PARENTS LIKE
- ✓ STURDY AND SAFE
- ✓ EASY TO GET BABY IN AND OUT
- ✓ ALSO A CARRIER

WHAT PARENTS DON'T LIKE
- ✓ TOO HEAVY, BIG AND BULKY
- ✓ HARD TO BUCKLE AND UNBUCKLE
- ✓ HARD TO PUT IN THE CAR
- ✓ UNCOMFORTABLE FOR A NEWBORN

vehicle, and one that you will use correctly and consistently. However, once some parents start shopping for the "best" car seat, they can find it to be a frustrating experience. This is because vehicles are designed for the safety and comfort of "non-car seat" passengers. Be aware that safety belts are designed differently—types of belts, locking mechanisms and insertion points. Also remember that vehicles seats are designed differently as well, with fabric, plushness, pull-down armrests, and slope of the seat all factors that can affect the fit of a car seat.

When parents begin trying different child car seats they may find that a particular brand does not fit their particular vehicle, while another brand may fit perfectly. The following tips may help you when choosing your child's car seat:

First, decide the type of child car seat you need:

- **Infant-only,** from newborns to 18-22 pounds or 26 inches in length. If your baby's head reaches the top of the seat before the weight limit, you must move your baby to a rear-facing convertible seat. Most infant seats are rear-facing only and are designed to recline to around a 45-degree angle. Sometimes a rolled towel must be added beneath the base of the seat to maintain the angle. Some infant seats have a removable base. The base is belted in the car, and seat can be lifted in and out of the base. These seats can also be installed without the base.
- **Convertible car seats** fit babies from about seven pounds to 40 pounds. The seats convert from the infant rear-facing position to the toddler forward-facing position. Economically, this seat is the best choice. However, if this type of seat is used for a newborn, it's important that a five-point harness be chosen. This type of harness provides a snugger fit for the small newborn. When trying this seat in your vehicle, remember to try it in the rear-facing position as well as the forward-facing position.
- **Forward-facing car seats** are for children from 1 year old and at least 20 pounds and up to 40 pounds. These seats are designed to face forward. You cannot place this seat in the rear-facing position.
- **Booster seats** are for children who have outgrown their convertible car seats. You'll need to check manufacturer's information for specific weight and age requirements. Some boosters use the car's own three-point buckling system, while others use a shield or harness system integrated into the booster seat.

FITTING YOUR CAR SEAT

Before making a purchase, try adjusting the shoulder harnesses. Is it something you'll take the time to adjust every time? Consider whether the harness adjustment is easy for you to reach after the car seat is in the vehicle. A snug shoulder

---

TETHERS: HOLDING CAR SEATS FIRM

Some car seats have a tendency to move about, and not be completely secure in a car. Tethers are an excellent way to prevent any movement. Car seat manufacturers may recommend a tether, depending on the type of seat belt, but you may choose to install one to keep your baby more secure. The tether strap attaches to the car seat and is bolted into a predrilled anchor point, usually covered with a plastic rivet, in your car's back deck or van's floor. Cars built before 1987 will need a hole drilled; do not do this yourself. Take your vehicle to your dealership or certified auto mechanic.

Several manufacturers, including Evenflo, Gerry, Cosco and Century, will supply a tether on request; Britax and Fisher-Price car seats include tethers. Britax's seat even has a tether for a rear-facing infant. Visit your local baby specialty store to see car seat tethers and discuss this important car seat option.

harness is crucial—it's what holds your baby inside the car seat. How do you know if the shoulder harness is tight enough? There should only be room for one of your fingers between the shoulder harness and your child's collar bone.

Try the seat in your vehicle. The safest place is in the back seat. Put your body weight into the car seat while you fasten the safety belt. Pull all slack out of the safety belt to make it tight. Next, try to move the seat—there should be no more than an inch of movement side to side or an inch forward. If rear-facing, check the angle of the seat. You may need to add towels under the front of the seat to maintain an angle of around 45 degrees. If the seat is forward facing, make sure the seat is fully upright. You may need to move the car seat to a different location to achieve a tight fit. You may have to add a locking clip to the safety belt to lock the safety belt in place. The locking clip will be located somewhere on your new car seat. The car seat instructions tell you when you need to use the clip, and explain how to use it.

AIR BAGS

Air bags are effective in saving lives. However, babies and young children can be at risk if seated next to one. Air bags inflate quickly and forcibly, and a child's small body may not tolerate the force. Therefore, when there is a passenger side air bag in the vehicle, babies and children (12 and under) should be restrained in the back seat. Never place a rear-facing car seat in the front seat if the vehicle is equipped with a passenger side air bag.

If your car seat has been in a crash, it must be replaced. A crash can cause unseen structural damage to the car seat and it may not restrain your child in a subsequent crash. Do not use a second-hand car seat unless you know the history of the seat. If you've used your car seat consistently for five years, safety experts recommend replacing the seat.

CORRECT USE OF CAR SEATS

Many parents use car seats incorrectly. It's critical to read the car seat instructions and the vehicle instructions. The car seat's instructions will tell you how to properly secure your baby in the seat and will show you the correct path for the safety belt. The vehicle instructions will tell you how to use a car seat in your vehicle and if you need any additional attachments to make your car seat secure.

If your child is taken to child care by one parent and picked up by another, consider buying two car seats. This will help cut down on installation errors.

Remember to fill out the registration card that came with your car seat. Mail it to the manufacturer. You will be contacted if the seat goes on recall. If you think your car seat has a defect, call the manufacturer, and report it to the Auto Safety Hotline at 800-424-9393.

Laws vary from state to state regarding car seat usage. But common sense and the desire to keep children safe dictates that children should use a child restraint until they reach 4 years old or 40 pounds and, depending on the child's size, booster seats or seat belts after that. Even if your state does not require car seat usage, buckle your children!

FOR OLDER CHILDREN

For children old enough and heavy enough to ride without a car seat or booster, you must teach proper use of safety belts. The lap belt should fit low over a child's upper thighs. Make sure the child sits straight against the vehicle seat back. Keep the belt snug. If the lap belt rides up onto the tummy, it could cause serious injuries in a crash. The shoulder belt should stay on the shoulder with less than an inch of slack across the chest. If the shoulder belt rubs against the neck, but not across it, it may be uncomfortable for the child but is not harmful. You can fold a soft cloth over the belt to reduce discomfort. If the shoulder belt goes across the child's neck or face, raise the child with a belt positioning booster. Never put the belt under the child's arm or below the back. Either of these kinds of misuse could cause serious injury in a crash.

POPULAR BRANDS

BRITAX

Britax is new to the U.S., but has been in business in Europe and Australia for more than 30 years. The company has gained international recognition for their excellent products and commitment to safety. Britax car seats are sold exclusively in children's specialty stores. All stores that carry Britax seats must attend training sessions on the installation of their car seats, and be fully prepared to educate customers in the installation and proper use of the seat.

Britax car seats are designed with cars in mind, taking into account that many back seats now have shoulder/lap belts rather than lap belts, and bucket rather than bench seats. They also offer tethers and tether kits for most models.

The five-point restraint Freeway seat is designed for children 20-40 pounds. It has a patented lock-off clamp that

INFANT CAR SEAT

locks the shoulder belt in place, eliminating the need for a locking clip. The forward-facing reclining seat has deep side panels that not only protect against impact, but catch the child's head if he falls asleep.

Britax also carries a rear-facing infant seat, the Rock-a-Tot, and the Cruiser, a transitional seat for children 30-60 pounds. All Britax seats have beautiful cloth covers and are well-padded. The seats are more expensive than most, ranging from $80-$200, but the additional safety features and education are well worth it.

CENTURY

Century offers a wide variety of car seats from infant to toddler sizes. The infant car seats are the 565, 590 and 4525 models. The 565 is a basic model without a canopy, but it does have a handle. The 590 model has a canopy and detachable base. The 4525 models are called "SmartFIT." They have a stay-in car base that is sculpted to fit today's cars, and a curved handle for easier carrying. They also have a level indicator near the handle to determine if the seat is properly installed. If the ball is under the arrow, the seat is correctly installed; if not, the seat is tipped too far forward or backward. Century's infant car seats run from $50 to $80.

Century's convertible car seats begin with the 1000 series. Their least expensive model costs about $60 and has a five-point harness with no shield. The top of the line model runs about $160, and offers a wide variety of luxury features including a pillow, shield and extra padding. Century also offers a car seat named Smart Move, designed to let infants ride in a more reclined position, at a 47-degree angle rather than current infant car seats' more upright angle. The car seat is designed to meet the needs of both infants and toddlers. It costs around $140.

Century also offers an infant car seat/stroller combination named the 4-in-1 System. It can be used as a car seat, an infant/car seat stroller, a carrier and a toddler's stroller. This product runs around $150. We found it at baby specialty stores.

COSCO

Cosco is the only car seat company to offer all five types of child restraints: car bed/car seat, infant-only, convertible, auto booster, and travel vest. The Dream Ride is the only car bed available, allowing premature or other special-needs babies to lie flat. If parents can't find this model in their area, call Cosco at 800-544-1108. It can convert later to a car seat, and costs around $55. They also offer three infant car seats: TLC, Arriva and Turnabout, which has a 360-degree rotating handle grip for ease of carrying. Their convertible car seats—Touriva, Regal Ride and Olympian—feature five-point harnesses, T-shields or overhead shield designs, and have comfortable pads. Some models add an infant insert or removable pillow. Prices range from $30-$75 for infant seats and $40-$100 for convertibles.

One of Cosco's newest products in the Travel Vest, designed for use by children from 25-40 pounds. Just four pounds, the vest can be used with either a lap or shoulder belt. The child wears the five-point harness while seated directly on the car's seat. It is perfect for those times when you don't want to lug your car seat around—for traveling, carpooling and to use at Grandma's. This vest costs $30 to $35, and is available at Toys R Us and major department and discount stores.

FISHER-PRICE

Fisher-Price is back in the car seat market, with a simple line featuring both infant and convertible models. Their infant seat has a five-point harness and built-in locking clip. Its uniquely engineered sliding track system allows you to adjust the car seat's belts with the touch of a button, and costs approximately $70.

Fisher-Price's "Safe Embrace" convertible car seat retails for around $140, and includes a built-in tether strap to secure the seat into your car. Its five-point harness has two buckles for greater adjustability. The car seat's unique color-coding system shows parents where the car seat and auto restraint straps should be placed for both rear- and forward-

> **POINTS TO CONSIDER**
> - Try out your infant car seat's handle. Many of the handles used to carry the car seat are extremely difficult to move from front-to-back or vice-versa.
> - The advantage of car seats with a detachable base is that the seat is removable from the car without undoing the seat belt each time.
> - Consider purchasing a car seat with a built-in locking clip and/or tether system. These devices provide the most secure fit in your car.
> - If you can't afford a car seat, you may want to check with your hospital or community agency to see if any programs are available. Midas Muffler and Easter Seals also have special low-cost car seat programs.

facing positions. These seats are available at major retailers.

EVENFLO

Evenflo is a large manufacturer of a variety of juvenile products. In their car seat selection alone, they offer more than 15 styles. Their infant car seat offers cloth padding, a handle and canopy. The seat can also be used as a baby carrier, and in some cases a rocker. The seats have a base that is permanently installed in the car, enabling you to snap the car seat in and out without adjusting the belts. They are also designed to be used without the base, but *Consumer Reports* recommends using the base for additional safety. The Joy Ride car seat can be installed directly into the car, using the lap belt, or can be used with the Travel Tandem Base. Prices begin at $50 for the basic Joy Ride, a little higher for the Travel Tandem. The On My Way car seat comes with the base and an ergonomic curved handle, making it easy to carry the baby. The seats cost about 10% more than the Joy Ride. Both the Joy Ride and On My Way also have the option of the Travel System, which includes a stroller. The car seat snaps into the stroller, which has a large storage basket, and can be used as a toddler stroller when the baby gets older. The Travel Systems cost about $150.

Evenflo makes three styles of convertible car seats: the five-point harness, the T-shield and the overhead shield. The five-point harness offers the advantage of having a buckle that attaches to the harness rather than the base of the car seat, making it easily accessible. The five-point harness car seats run from $60 to $120, depending on the features you choose. In reviewing Evenflo's car seats, we found only one T-shield model which buckles at the base of the car seat, costing about $60. Evenflo sells a large selection of car seats with overhead shields. A large plastic shield is pulled down in front of your child's body. You buckle the child in through the base of the car seat. The overhead shield model costs between $80 and $120. Evenflo's convertible car seats cost more for additional padding, additional places to adjust the harness, and headrests.

CRIBS

Expectant parents generally decide on their child's crib based on its looks. There are, however, safety features to be considered. Most were mandated by the CPSC in 1973. Major manufacturers also follow voluntary standards as developed by the Juvenile Products Manufacturers Association (JPMA). Products that meet these standards usually carry a JPMA certification sticker, but a crib without a sticker doesn't necessarily mean that it does not meet the safety standards. What all this

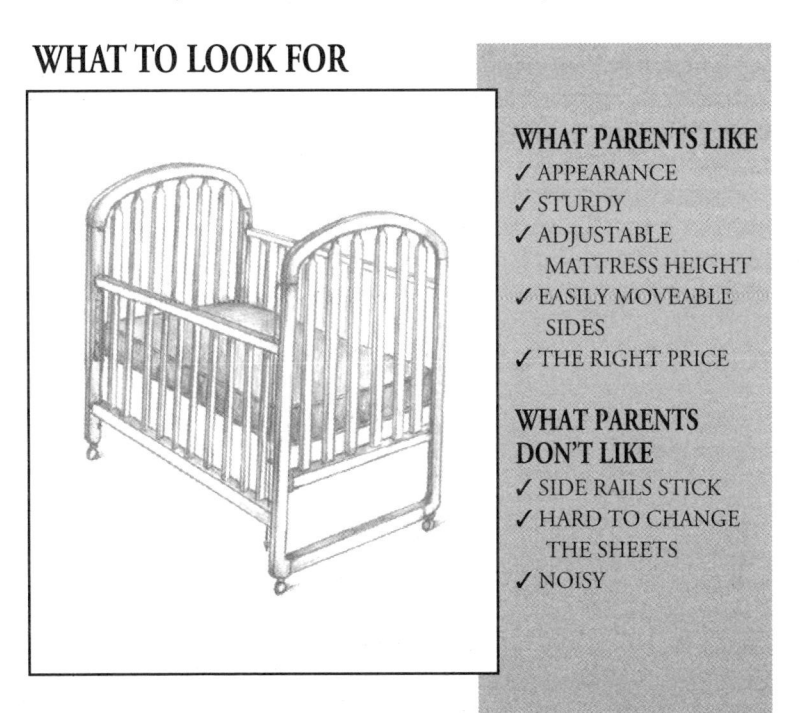

WHAT TO LOOK FOR

WHAT PARENTS LIKE
✓ APPEARANCE
✓ STURDY
✓ ADJUSTABLE MATTRESS HEIGHT
✓ EASILY MOVEABLE SIDES
✓ THE RIGHT PRICE

WHAT PARENTS DON'T LIKE
✓ SIDE RAILS STICK
✓ HARD TO CHANGE THE SHEETS
✓ NOISY

means, basically, is that if you purchase a new crib, you can safely base your choice on convenience, price and looks. The rest has been taken care of for you. The federal government came up with the following requirements that are still in effect today:

- Crib slats must be no further apart than 2-3/8".
- A lowered dropside must be 9" above the mattress support at its highest setting. The raised dropside must be at least 26" above the support at its lowest position.
- A dropside must take at least two separate actions to activate. If it is too easy to drop, an older baby could activate it.
- The mattress must fit snugly. You should be able to fit no more than two fingers between the crib interior side and the mattress.

Voluntary standards cover aspects such as corner posts and mattress supports. Corner posts should be either practically flush with the top of the end panels or very tall, such as on a four poster bed. If they are not completely flush, they should be no more than 1/16" above it. Mattress supports should be firmly secured to the brackets at the end panels. Also, the end panels should extend lower than the mattress support at its lowest position. This prevents accidents caused by a child becoming trapped between the end panel and the support.

There are a few features of convenience that you may consider when choosing a crib. Wheels make a crib easier to move. Round, ball casters move better, especially on carpet, than narrow, disk-shaped wheels. The dropside release mechanisms vary from model to model, and some are easier to work than others. Try them out at the store when shopping. Keep in mind that you may be holding an infant when putting the side down. A mechanism that can be worked with one hand is preferable.

Cribs are available with either one or two dropsides. A one dropside model is less expensive; if your crib is going to sit against a wall, it may be a better choice. The extra money isn't worth it if you aren't going to use both sides.

Ease of assembly is also a consideration. Some cribs require only a screwdriver to put together while others are more complicated. Some stores offer the option of having the crib assembled at your home when it is delivered. There is an extra fee for this service, but it may be worth it.

To help you choose a crib, you can write to the CSPC for their free brochures called "Tips for your Baby's Safety" and "Nursery Equipment Buyer's Guide." Their address is U.S. Consumer Product Safety Commission, Nursery Equipment Buyer's Guide, Washington, DC 20207. Specify which brochures you want and send along a self-addressed stamped business-size envelope.

MATTRESSES

Crib mattresses need to be purchased separately, and there are a few things to look for. Mattresses are either foam or inner-spring. It is just a matter of preference which you choose. Inner-spring models may keep their shape better, although a high-density foam can be just as good. There are many variations of inner-spring models, which contain anywhere from 60 to 360 coils. A large number of coils doesn't guarantee firmness. You will want to purchase as firm a mattress as you can afford, and the only way to measure firmness is by giving it a "squeeze" test.

Squeeze the mattress in the center and around the edges to test firmness. Vent holes in the sides are also good to have. They help keep the mattress fresher and reduce pressure on the seams. New mattresses on the market are firmer on one side than the other. The softer side is for infants up to 20 pounds. The other side is firmer and more durable for older infants and toddlers. Whichever mattress you choose, it should fit snugly in your crib.

CRIB SAFETY

Even with the current safety regulations, *Consumer Reports* magazine reports that more infants die each year in accidents involving cribs than any other child product. General consensus is that most of these involve older model cribs that were manufactured before 1978. If you are purchasing a used crib or using a family hand-me-down, you'll need a tape measure to check to see if it meets the CPSC requirements. Also check to see that there are not cutouts or decorative items attached to the head or footboards. These can pose a choking or strangulation hazard. All bolts and screws should be present and fit tightly. Another thing to check for, especially on cribs manufactured before 1970, is that they may be coated with paint that contains lead. If the used crib you are considering does not meet the current safety requirements, don't use it. Special note: If your infant is in child care and is using a crib there, check the crib to see if it meets the safety standards.

There are a few things to remember so that you use your crib safely. First, position it away from windows, heating elements, lamps, wall decorations, cords, and climbable furniture. When your baby is alone in the crib, keep the dropside up and locked. Hanging toys and mobiles should be out of the baby's reach, and as soon as the child can pull herself up on hands and knees, remove any toy that goes across the top of the crib. Don't leave pillows, stuffed animals or large toys in the crib. A tiny infant could smother in them, and an older child can use them as steps to climb out. Also, as soon as your child can stand in the crib, you should remove the bumper pads. They can also be used as steps to climb out. A rule of thumb is that when your child either reaches a height of 26" or can climb out of the crib, it's time to make the move to a regular bed.

When considering bedding, be aware of a warning issued by the CPSC in 1994 which strongly discourages soft bedding because they found it could cause asphyxiation in small infants. The warning is based on research done at Washington University in St. Louis. They have found that soft bedding may be responsible for up to 25% of infant deaths from SIDS. The infant can become wrapped in the bedding, which leads to re-breathing of exhaled air that can eventually lead to death from carbon monoxide poisoning. To avoid this the CPSC recommends:

- Putting the baby to sleep on his or her back on a flat, firm mattress without any plush, fuzzy bedding.

- Don't use soft, fluffy products such as pillows, sheepskins or toys under the infant as he or she sleeps.

To check on a particular model for recall information, call the CPSC at 800-638-2772. Many manufacturers also have consumer information hotlines, which are listed in the reference numbers section in this chapter.

ARM'S REACH

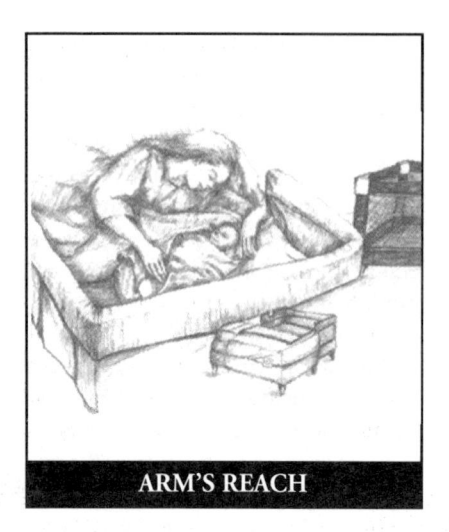

SPECIAL CRIBS

ARM'S REACH CO-SLEEPING SYSTEM

Invented by a mom and endorsed by Dr. William Sears, the Arm's Reach patented system links its special bassinet right to your bed mattress. Arm's Reach is a dream come true for new parents who want to sleep close to their infants but may be afraid of rolling over on them. It is also perfect for nursing moms or those recovering from C-sections. Available for under $200, the system folds into a travel bag, and can be converted to a changing table or play yard. Current information can be found on their web site, www.armsreach.com. The Arm's Reach system is available through specialty stores and catalogs.

THE BUMPA BED

The Bumpa Bed is a crib mattress with built-in bumpers. It is manufactured by the same company that makes the Baby Jogger. It's formed from a solid piece of breathable foam and fits right into the crib. Having built-in bumpers eliminates the dangers of tie-on strings and sagging bumpers. It also comes with custom made, quilted cotton sheets that velcro right onto the mattress. This saves the parents the hassle of lifting the mattress in and out of the crib and retying bumpers when changing sheets. After the child has outgrown the crib, the Bumpa Bed can be placed on a toddler frame or on the floor. The bumper sides prevent rolling out of bed. The bed also had a foam insert that makes it usable as a guest bed or a juvenile couch. The bed is very light, and has a carrying case which makes it ideal for travel. Retailing at around $140, the Bumpa Bed is available from the factory, 800-241-1848, and at some baby specialty stores.

THE DURA-CRIB™

An alternative to the rectangular crib is finally here! Little Miss Liberty Round Crib Company, created by actress Jean Kasem (wife of LA disc jockey Casey Kasem) and named after their daughter Liberty, offers Dura-Crib, a very attractive round crib. While researching the history of cribs, Jean learned that the first cribs were round or oval-shaped.

With safety as its primary feature, Dura-Crib is made of stress-resistant polyplastic components that will not flake, yellow, peel or blister. There are no small, breakable parts or corners, and the crib uses less floor space than traditional models. The round crib also offers easy, two-sided access and increased visibility for baby. The canopy model, with its beautiful coordinating bedding, is the ultimate crib for the parent who simply must have the best of everything for baby. Each crib comes with a custom

THE DURA-CRIB

round mattress. Suggested retail prices begin at $300 with prices exceeding $1000 when you include custom bedding on a higher-end model.

NATURE'S CRADLE

After more than five years of extensive research, development and testing in the hospitals, Infant Advantage brings Nature's Cradle into the home. This patented FDA-approved sleeping environment is designed to ease baby's transition into the world by simulating the sounds and motions experienced in utero. Nature's Cradle is a complete crib mattress, sheet and "sleeping environment" kit. It actually moves and produces sounds that change during the first 16 weeks of using the product. Each week the movement and sounds lessen until about four months when the child sleeps on the mattress without the simulation technology.

According to its manufacturer, Nature's Cradle infants sleep longer at night, cry less, and sleep through the night sooner than babies who sleep in a traditional crib or bassinet. Parents with premature or colicky babies may want to contact the company for their research and the benefits this cradle may specifically offer your family. This is a truly remarkable product with solid information backing it. Suggested retail price is about $359. Contact Infant Advantage at 800-272-3538 for a retailer near you.

CONVERTIBLE CRIBS

Both Child Craft and Gerry have introduced cribs which convert into youth beds. Child Craft's new "Crib 'N' Double Bed, retailing at about $349, goes from crib to day bed to double bed. It may be the only bed you need to purchase for your child. It also has coordinating furniture pieces to complete your child's nursery. Gerry's "Room to Grow" is similar as its crib converts to a twin bed. It also has a changing table which becomes a bench/toy chest. Both manufacturers offer their products in gorgeous wood with a classic look.

A smaller furniture manufacturer named Pflop House Pfurniture offers a unique crib which sits on the floor and converts to a toddler bed and, with a full-sized mattress, becomes a platform bed. Quality and safety come first with this company. As a newcomer to the baby market, you may need to contact Pflop House directly at (303) 964-9608 to find their crib and other products, including a two-drawer chest/changing table/travel cradle and a rocking chair with a "sidecar" for baby to rock gently along with you.

PORTABLE CRIBS

Portable cribs are very popular items with parents. The new portable cribs are also playpens, but are easier to set up, and they fold up into a small bundle. Portable cribs are great for the babysitter, grandparents and for travel.

POINTS TO CONSIDER

- There are no separate Consumer Product Safety Commission (CPSC) standards for portable cribs. Most of the new models, however, meet voluntary safety standards set by the manufacturer.
- The most important thing to consider when shopping is that a portable crib should be portable! They should set up quickly (within a few minutes) and fold up into a convenient carrying size. The best ones come with a travel/carry bag.
- They are rectangular like a crib, instead of square.
- They can be used either as a temporary bed or play area for babies up to 30 pounds or under 34 inches in height. When used as a playpen, the play area is slightly smaller than in a conventional playpen.
- Portable cribs should not be used in place of a regular crib for everyday use.

POPULAR BRANDS

Most portable cribs are made with a plastic or metal frame with woven fabric and mesh sides, and include a mattress and fitted sheet. Basic models have two mesh sides and two fabric sides, while more deluxe models may have four mesh sides and/or roll-down flaps that can be secured when the child sleeps. Some also have sun shades for outside use and attached bags for toys. One feature you might consider is a portable crib with a bassinet that fits in the top of the crib. It's a nice way to get three products in one, and the bassinet can also be used as a changing area.

COSCO

Cosco's three Zip 'N Go travel play yards set up in less than a minute. The deluxe models have lockable wheels, canopies, side bags to hold toys and accessories, and side shades. Manufacturers' suggested retail prices range from $50-$80.

EVENFLO

The Evenflo Happy Cabana is easy to put together and affordable. It has a removable cover for indoor or outdoor use, lockable wheels on one side, which makes moving the crib easier, a toy bag, and a mattress with a stylish fitted sheet.

PORTABLE CRIB

The mesh sides have pull-down flaps and the top rail is padded. They also have the Happy Cabana Bassinet with all of the above features, plus a removable bassinet. The Happy Camper line includes the basic Happy Camper without the toy bag, bassinet, wheels, or flaps and the Happy Camper Bassinet which has all of the deluxe features except for the sunshade. Evenflo notes that all of their cribs set up in less than a minute.

FISHER PRICE

Fisher Price's Travel Tender with Soothing Bassinet has some interesting features. It's a lightweight, compact portable crib with four mesh sides, and wheels on one side for easier moving. It also has a bassinet that vibrates to simulate the motion of a car, to help soothe a fussy baby. The bassinet can be switched on and off, and uses a D battery. Fisher Price portable cribs now come in three colors, and cost about $120.

GRACO

Graco's Pack'n'Play portable cribs are popular and easy to use. For around $60, Graco's basic Pack'n'Play has four mesh sides, is lightweight, and very easy to assemble. Other models have the options of wheels on one side, sunshades, bassinets, bug netting and cargo bags with individual pockets. They also make one extra-large model that is 36 inches square, instead of the standard rectangular style. The most deluxe model is about $160. All Graco portable cribs have padded mattresses with fitted sheets and come in a wide variety of colors.

GERRY

Gerry portable cribs are not like other brands, in that they are wooden like a real crib. Their wheeled Fold-Away Crib folds to fit through doorways, but in general the crib is not light or compact. It has a fold-down side for putting in and taking out the baby, and a lightweight foam mattress. This crib is a good option for a grandparent's house, or other place the baby visits frequently. Because the other styles of portable cribs are so popular, it can be difficult to find sheets to fit the Gerry crib. It does have the advantage of having the "feel" of a real crib, with the option of attaching bumpers or mobiles, which might make the baby feel more at home while sleeping at the sitter's or Grandma's house, while still portable enough to wheel away into the closet when not in use.

MORE PRODUCT INFORMATION . . .

Want a comprehensive look at all juvenile products on the market today? The national best-seller *Baby Bargains* takes you through the maze of your baby product purchases, including recommendations by the authors, Denise and Alan Fields, who are new parents themselves.

Another excellent resource is the *Consumer Products Guide to Baby Products*, which includes reviews and product testing results of the most popular baby purchases. Both books are available at bookstores nationwide.

SWINGS

An infant swing is a product that isn't absolutely necessary to have, but many parents swear by them. It can be used to stimulate a baby's senses, rock a tired baby to sleep or soothe a colicky baby when nothing else can. Early swings were crank operated with vinyl seats. Most have been changed over the years to make them more convenient, accessible and comfortable for the infant. Most models are battery operated, with seats that can be removed from the swing to be used as a separate baby seat. The trays now swing away to make it much easier to take the infant in and out.

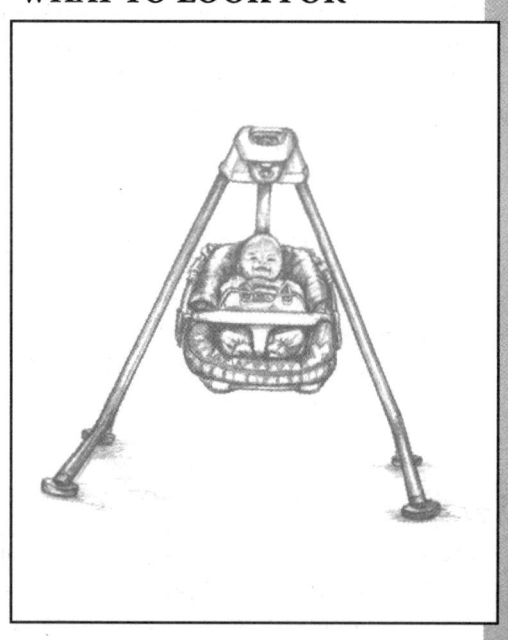

WHAT TO LOOK FOR

WHAT PARENTS LIKE
- ✓ AUTOMATIC
- ✓ THE BABY LOVES IT!
- ✓ QUIET
- ✓ SEAT RECLINES
- ✓ PORTABLE
- ✓ EASY TO PUT BABY IN AND OUT

WHAT PARENTS DON'T LIKE
- ✓ DOESN'T SWING LONG ENOUGH
- ✓ DIFFICULT TO PUT BABY IN AND OUT
- ✓ TOO LOUD
- ✓ NOT STURDY

One thing to keep in mind is that not all infants like swings. Before purchasing one, it might be wise to borrow one to see how your baby reacts to the swing.

POINTS TO CONSIDER

- If space is limited, look for a swing with detachable legs for easier storage.
- Parents mentioned that they liked swings that detach for use as a carrier.
- Some swings are vinyl; others have removable, washable covers. Parents again commented that they preferred the cloth removable covers over vinyl. They are easier to clean, and parents felt their babies looked more comfortable.

POPULAR BRANDS

CENTURY

Century swings are only available as battery operated. The motor runs on two D batteries for up to 100 hours. All their patterns coordinate with other Century products such as their strollers and car seats. For the fashion-concerned parent, this is an advantage. Each Century swing model also comes with a machine-washable pad and detachable links and toys, which give your baby something to look at and to play with. All models offer at least a two-position posture seat that reclines for your baby's naps. Their most expensive model offers a four-position angle and rocking base. These swings range from $75 to $100.

COSCO

All Cosco swings are wind-up models, with whisper-quiet winding that gives 30 minutes of swing time. Their Quiet Time Elite, for babies up to 25 pounds, has a push-button T-bar/tray that rotates out of the way to make it easy to get baby in and out of the swing. The Dream Ride Plus is multipurpose: a car bed/car seat, swing and cradle swing all in one for babies up to 20 pounds.

FISHER PRICE

Fisher Price recently began offering its 3-in-1 Cradle Swing. This swing has the option of swinging side to side like a cradle, or forward and back like a traditional swing. The frame isn't open-top, like Graco's, but it is designed to be very accessible and give the baby an unobstructed view. The seat reclines in two positions, has a soft cloth cover, and removes from the base so it can be used as a carrier, and a rocker if placed on the floor. The 3-in-1 Cradle Swing also has a flip-top tray with detachable activity bar. This swing folds compactly for storage as well. We saw the swing offered for about $100.

GERRY

Gerry offers an open-top glider as its alternative to the traditional swing. The glider is smaller than traditional swings and makes less noise as it glides. It has a padded, two-position seat with a tray that lifts and pivots for loading and unloading. Gerry claims the glider will run for 100 hours on its four batteries.

GRACO

Depending upon the model, all of the swings recline to two or more positions. Nearly all models feature a flip-open tray that makes it easy to get the baby in and out, and removable cloth seat covers. Graco's low-end swings have a closed top and crank winding mechanisms that have been recently improved to be more quiet, with a run-time indicator. Their battery-operated swings have an open top, which makes it much easier to get the child in and out, especially when he's asleep. Parents have the choice of two or three speeds, toy bars for the tray, or music with some models. One of the most practical Graco swings is their Three-in-One Swing. This style features a removable cradle—a lifesaver during the early weeks—and a swing that can also be used as a baby carrier. If parents choose this model, they can use the cradle as a bassinet and eliminate the need for one additional purchase. The cradle also fits easily into a crib. Graco swings generally run $60-$100.

STROLLERS

A stroller will probably be one of your most useful baby products. It is also one of your most important, as you will use a stroller for a longer period of time than almost any other baby product (depending on the brand). There are a variety of brands and styles of strollers on the market. You'll find everything from umbrella strollers to old-fashioned buggies to double strollers. This is one of the products that you may consider buying what you really want, if it is in your budget. Sometimes, for a little extra money, you receive more features and a stroller that will last (and that you want to last) for more than one child.

WHAT TO LOOK FOR

WHAT PARENTS LIKE
- ✓ FOLDS EASILY
- ✓ MANEUVERS EASILY
- ✓ RECLINES, SO INFANT MAY LIE DOWN
- ✓ HANDLE IS REVERSIBLE
- ✓ DURABLE

WHAT PARENTS DON'T LIKE
- ✓ HARD TO MANEUVER
- ✓ TOO LARGE AND HEAVY
- ✓ THE WHEELS STICK
- ✓ TOO BULKY
- ✓ DIFFICULT TO CLEAN

POINTS TO CONSIDER
- Check out the storage availability. The larger the basket, the better.
- Strollers with removable, washable pads are a real plus.
- Up-and-down adjustable handles come in handy, especially if one parent is much taller than the other.
- Since many parents want to take their newborns out for a stroll, finding a stroller that completely reclines makes this possible. Remember, babies don't sit up until about five months old.

- Good quality wheels can make all the difference in a stroller. Large, sturdy wheels can make for a more enjoyable ride for you and baby.
- Practice opening and folding strollers before you buy. Some are difficult or awkward to use.
- Umbrella strollers are very affordable and make an excellent investment, as you can use them as your child grows. They are also very convenient to use when traveling.

POPULAR BRANDS

BABYJOGGER

Light and easy to push up hills and on rugged terrain, jogging strollers offer one of the smoothest, lightest rides available. They are suitable for walking, running, hiking, or even on sandy beaches. The tripod base makes them very easy to steer. These strollers are not always widely available; call BabyJogger at 800-241-1848 to find the nearest retailer.

Babyjogger is a well-known maker of jogging strollers. Their strollers have light aluminum frames that fold easily. The tires are large and have thorn-resistant inner tubes for use on all surfaces. The brakes are hand-operated caliper brakes, similar to bicycles. Babyjogger also offers many stroller accessories including sunshades, baskets, and a trailer conversion kit so that it can become a bike trailer. There are even models for twins and triplets! Babyjoggers are available in many colors and start at about $250 for a single and $350 for a double.

CENTURY

Century offers several stroller styles, but the one they are best known for is the 4-in-1 System. Century was the first to develop this system which includes a car seat, infant carrier and stroller. The car seat snaps into the stroller base or the base that remains in the car. When in the stroller, the baby faces the parent and rides high up for easier viewing. These strollers fold easily, and recline in two positions. The type of handle and wheels vary from model to model. The 4-in-1 System is about $150.

Century also offers compact-folding lightweight umbrella strollers with large baskets, and the Adventure stroller, with oversize knobby wheels, suspension, and an large canopy.

COMBI

Combi makes one of the lightest, most durable strollers available. Their lightest stroller weighs just seven pounds, and their heaviest is only 18 pounds. By contrast, the typical Graco stroller is about 17 pounds. Combi strollers are well built and very portable. Most have a foot release, fold very compactly, and self-stand when folded up. All Combi

JOGGING STROLLER

strollers have aluminum frames, shock absorbers, and ventilated seats. Most models' seats recline to some degree. They also all have a large storage basket. Except for the umbrella stroller, all Combi strollers are also height adjustable. Combi also offers a double stroller that weighs only 20 pounds, but is fully adjustable, and each seat reclines independently. Basic Combi strollers start at $170, and go up to about $270 for the double stroller.

COSCO

Cosco's Rock n Roller strollers feature rocking and gliding movements which help calm fussy riders. With a seat that can be removed for use as a bassinet as well as adjusted to four seating positions, a canopy, large market basket, and forward- and rear-facing positioning, this is a versatile stroller you can use for years to come. The Rock n Roller is also available as a double stroller. There's even a model that includes a car seat for babies to 22 pounds. These models range from $50 to $170.

Cosco's carriage stroller can be used with newborns, and sits up for older babies and children. Their market stroller is a snazzy model with a huge basket and machine-washable toss-in pad, with a see-through window in its canopy.

EMMALJUNGA

Emmaljunga strollers were originally manufactured in Sweden. A very popular European brand, the Emmaljunga stroller offers old-fashioned high quality—many parents save their strollers as heirlooms. These classic, high-performance strollers are not cheap, but are well worth the cost. Emmaljunga strollers are classic buggies with oversize, shock-absorbing wheels that have a lifetime warranty. They have large, collapsible hoods, and extra-long sure-grip handles. Their five-point harness restraints are the type touted by *Consumer Reports* as the safest stroller restraints.

All of their strollers have washable, removable pads made of a material that allows fresh air to come in and moisture to evaporate quickly. They are Scotchguarded for stain control. The frames have an antimicrobial finish that prevents mold and rust. Emmaljunga strollers start at about $250, and are sold primarily through baby specialty stores.

EVENFLO

Evenflo offers several unique styles of strollers. Their Fresh Air Gear line of outdoor products includes the Hike 'n'Roll—a baby carrier that becomes a stroller—and the Tri-Wheel Stroller. This all-terrain stroller has three extra-large, rugged wheels, plus a two-position handle and a large canopy. The storage basket is moderately sized. When folded, this stroller will stand on its own.

Evenflo also offers the On My Way Travel System, a combination car seat/stroller. The rear-facing infant seat snaps into the stroller or the car base. Without the car seat, the stroller is lightweight, has an enormous carrying basket, and is reclinable. The handle is ergonomically designed for comfort. This system has a wide wheel base for extra stability. The combination system is also available with Evenflo's Joy Ride car seat, which is similar to the On My Way, but has a less comfortable handle. The On My Way Travel System costs about $150.

GERRY

If you are looking for a stroller that makes it easy for the parent, check out Gerry's Convenience Stroller. It features one-hand steering, cupholder, and trays for both the adult and child. Add in an extra-large basket, side storage pockets, and infant bolsters on the deluxe model, and you've got a stroller that is a pleasure to use. Prices range from $80-$100.

Gerry's carriage stroller models recline fully and include a big storage basket. The higher-end model has side storage baskets. Prices are $100-$120.

GRACO

Graco offers many types of strollers including basic strollers, full-size carriages, double and triple strollers, and umbrella strollers, all with washable pads and easy folding capability.

Graco's basic full-size strollers have extra head support, four sets of swivel wheels, and a storage basket. Depending on the model, you can also get adjustable-height handles, reversible handles, and larger storage baskets. All of the strollers have a rain/sun canopy with a viewing window, and reclining seats.

Two double canopy stroller styles with reclining seats are available, including side-by-side and one-in-front-of-the-other. Double strollers start at $90.

Graco's popular LiteRiders have several styles from a basic umbrella stroller to a nearly full-size lightweight stroller. All have extra large storage baskets and ergonomic handles. Deluxe models have adjustable handles and extra large wheels, plus suspension for a smoother ride. At around $80, they are among the most durable, least expensive strollers.

The Outrider is a rugged sport stroller with sturdy frame, oversize, knobby tires, extra storage, and a comfortable handle. They also offer a jogging stroller with a single wheel in front.

PEG PEREGO

Made in Italy, Peg Perego strollers are beautifully designed. Their rust-resistant, aluminum frame strollers are just 16 to 22 pounds. The washable pads come in several attractive patterns. Peg Perego strollers have extra large metal wheels and large storage baskets. They also feature a "remote control" device in the handle that opens and closes the stroller with one hand.

The full-size stroller carriages have European styling, with adjustable and reversible handles. They come with an apron for cold days. The large, removable basket can hold a full grocery bag.

Peg Perego also offers double and triple strollers in various styles, in side by side and facing styles. The seats individually recline on all of these strollers, and the strollers are still quite portable. Peg Perego strollers start at $150.

HIGH CHAIRS

High chairs are essential for your baby once he or she is ready to eat solid foods and can sit up easily. This usually occurs during the fifth or sixth month. Parents have a wide selection of types of high chairs—from the basic to the sophisticated.

Basic high chairs are plastic with vinyl seats. They may require one or two hands to adjust the high chair. Most models today offer the one-hand option, which makes it much simpler for the busy parent. You can also purchase a "no frills" wooden high chair for your child. Although these chairs look beautiful, they may be more difficult to clean, and they also take up a little more room because they don't fold. There are

WHAT TO LOOK FOR

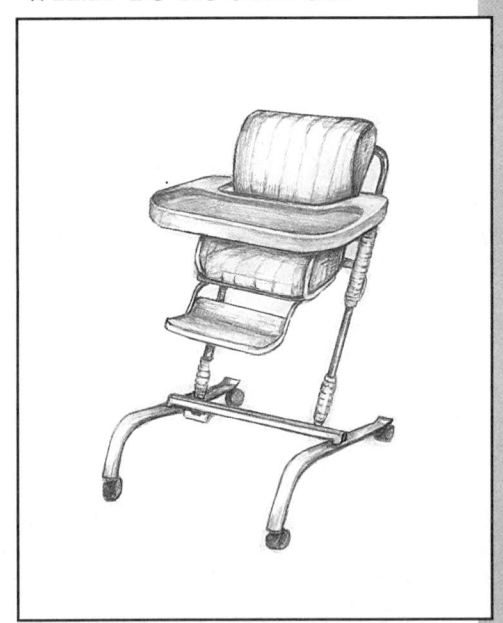

WHAT PARENTS LIKE
- ✔ LARGE TRAY
- ✔ EASY TO CLEAN
- ✔ ONLY NEEDS ONE HAND
- ✔ STURDY
- ✔ APPEARANCE
- ✔ ADJUSTABLE
- ✔ WHEELS

WHAT PARENTS DON'T LIKE
- ✔ HARD TO CLEAN
- ✔ TRAY STICKS
- ✔ SEATBELT STRAP IS DIFFICULT TO USE

also high chairs available that will "grow" or adjust to your child. Many baby product manufacturers offer this option. The advantage of these high chairs is that they may be used as a high chair, youth chair and also a play chair. They may be placed in several positions, extending the life of the high chair. The adjustable models also come with the convenience features of a large tray, non-splash sides and one hand adjustments. Many also come with wheels! You'll pay more for this type of high chair, but it will also last longer.

The final type of high chair is a portable high chair. Portable high chairs may either be strapped onto one of your chairs or placed directly on the table (it hangs on your table). If you travel or visit friends and family, a portable high chair is great.

One safety feature that is a must on any high chair purchase is the waist belt to secure your infant. According to CSPC, falls from high chairs are a leading cause of childhood injuries. Make sure you buckle your child in every single time you put him in the high chair.

ADJUSTABLE HIGH CHAIR

POPULAR BRANDS

CENTURY

Century has two models of high chairs. The basic high chair has a wrap-around tray, and is adjustable and foldable. The pad is vinyl and easy to clean. The more deluxe model has a thick, textured cloth pad and a six-position height adjustment. The restraint incorporates a crotch buckle for additional safety. This model has locking wheels for portability.

COSCO

Cosco manufactures both the basic model of high chair as well as others which are height-adjustable or convertible. Their Sit 'n Gro 3-in-1 Chair doubles as a youth chair for dining and converts to a junior chair for kids up to 8 years old. Cosco's Rise & Dine chairs include four-position reclining backs for use while feeding, napping and playing and three height adjustments. The seat's rotation T-bar secures baby to minimize slippage. The one-hand, wrap-around tray snaps into the last adjustment position and most models include locking casters. Options is five chairs in one—infant feeding seat, high chair, youth chair, booster seat and play seat.

EVENFLO

Evenflo's Right Height high chair can be adjusted to six different levels, and can be used as a high chair, play chair and youth chair. The tray can be adjusted into eight positions, all with one hand. This chair has a vinyl pad, a tri-buckle restraint system, and comes with locking wheels. The Phases high chair is even more versatile. A car seat or carrier can be locked into its base for an infant feeding chair; it can be used as a regular high chair; the tray can snap off and the chair can be pulled up to the table as a booster seat, and the entire unit can be broken down to become a table and chair set for a toddler. The tray has high anti-splash sides, and is one-hand adjustable. This chair also has a vinyl seat and tri-buckle restraint system. The Phases chair costs about $70.

FISHER-PRICE HIGH CHAIRS

Fisher-Price offers a high chair that can be adjusted to six different heights. It can also be used as a youth chair for sitting at the table. The tray has a splash guard in back, to protect the baby's clothes, and can be operated with one hand. This seat doesn't have wheels and isn't collapsible. The Fisher Price high chair costs about $70.

GRACO HIGH CHAIRS

Graco offers a wide variety of basic high chairs. Almost all of its models fold and have the one-hand entry-and-release feature. Most are height-adjustable, and have a T-bar restraint for additional security. Graco high chairs come in a wide variety of colors and patterns. Prices range from $60 to $80. Graco also makes a portable high chair, which sits directly on the dining room table and costs around $30.

GERRY

Gerry's Adjust-A-Height Chair is three chairs in one: a high chair, youth chair and play chair. It has six adjustable positions and a tray that can be adjusted and removed with one hand. The Play Top High Chair is really unique. It is a high chair that converts into a table and chair set. The high chair is made of sturdy wood, and has a large, one-hand release tray. The chair lifts out of the base to be used as a wooden table and chair. The play table has two surfaces, one smooth side for coloring, and a building block side. The low price, around $60, is a bargain for three pieces in one.

PEG PEREGO

Peg Perego was one of the first manufacturers to offer an adjustable high chair. The high chairs are about $175, but loaded with features that make them a worthwhile purchase. All models have swivel wheels and spacious trays. The Prima Pappa chair can be used from infancy and is reclinable in four positions. This chair has seven height positions. The chair also folds up very compactly. The well padded cloth cover comes in two patterns. Peg Perego also has deluxe high chairs that are adjustable and compact. These chairs are upholstered, and have push-button release restraining belts. They even have a handle on the back of the tray, to make it easier to move around on the wheels. There is also an optional toy tray that fits onto the regular tray.

BABY CARRIERS

Baby carriers are a nice item to have for situations when a stroller isn't practical, or you need to have your hands free, yet keep the baby close to you. Young babies really seem to enjoy them. Carriers come in a variety of styles. The classic front pouch keeps the baby close to your chest—very soothing to babies in the early weeks. Most have the option of having the baby face in or out. Slings are growing in popularity. They keep the baby more horizontal, but still close to the body. They can make it easier for babies to sleep, and provide a private and convenient way to breastfeed.

WHAT TO LOOK FOR

WHAT PARENTS LIKE
✓ EASY TO GET BABY IN AND OUT
✓ THE BABY LOVES IT!
✓ HANDS-FREE CARRYING
✓ ADJUSTABLE FOR BOTH PARENTS

WHAT PARENTS DON'T LIKE
✓ STRAPS THAT SLIP
✓ DIFFICULT TO PUT BABY IN AND OUT

Backpacks are for babies who are sitting up well. Most styles have an external aluminum frame, and are designed to rest the baby's weight on a parent's hips rather than the shoulders and back, which is much easier with an older, heavier baby.

POINTS TO CONSIDER

- Try out the baby carrier before you buy, if possible. Some are difficult to get on and off, especially once a baby is in them. With backpacks, pay attention to where your baby's knees and feet are in relation to your back. It is very uncomfortable to be constantly kicked!

- If you're very short or very tall, fitting a backpack frame can be problematic. It is very important that the weight rest on your hips or you may injure your back. Be sure to adjust the straps properly.
- Examine the seat when buying backpacks. Some packs are all one piece, while others have an adjustable seat. While adjustability is a nice feature for a growing baby, the seats are often adjusted with straps. Unless the straps are of equal length, the seat will tilt your baby to one side, or the baby may even start to fall out of a leg hole.
- Check that the straps on slings and carriers have a locking mechanism. Some people have had accidents when they placed the baby in the carrier and the weight of the baby caused the straps to slip out.

POPULAR BRANDS

BABY BJORN

The Baby Bjorn is a little more expensive than many front pouch carriers, at about $70, but parents feel it is well worth it. This carrier has clips on the side, enabling the carrier to be completely open on one side for loading and unloading. The clips also allow you to detach the carrier from the straps and lay the baby down without removing the baby first. It has a safety tab to prevent the straps from slipping. The straps are well padded and are designed to fit your back snugly, keeping weight distributed evenly and preventing back strain. They also have a model made especially for taller people to ensure a comfortable fit.

EVENFLO

Evenflo offers two carriers as part of their Fresh Air line. The About Face dual facing baby carrier is a front pouch where the baby can face in or out. It has extra padding in the seat and legs, and a zipper for easy nursing. The Hike'n'Roll system is unique—it's a backpack that converts into a lightweight stroller, with adjustable padded straps and a chest strap for additional support. The frame has a kickstand which provides a stable base to load the baby, and folds to become the stroller handle. There are also molded fenders on the wheels, which protects the backpack wearer from dirty wheels. The Hike'n'Roll costs about $80.

FISHER PRICE

Fisher Price's Perfect Support Carrier is a classic front pouch that gives the option of having the baby face in or out. It has a soft padded shell that offers additional head support and makes it easier to get the baby in and out of the carrier. This carrier has a removable bib and is washable. The Deluxe Perfect Support Carrier has all the features of the regular carrier with the added option of a sling. The carrier also comes with a removable weather protector. The deluxe carriers cost about $40, and the basic model slightly less.

GERRY

Gerry Snugli carriers are a favorite with many parents. Gerry carriers are affordable, ranging from $15 to $50. The Snugli Double Take is a soft front carrier with padded straps. The baby can face in or away from the parent. This carrier is only designed for infants 0-12 months. The better-equipped model adds the option of using the carrier as a backpack as well as a frontpack. Suitable for children up to 20 months old, it has built-in pillows to support the child's head and an adjustable seat. The Gerry Trailtech is a backpack with a loading stand, lightweight frame, and a storage bag. The backpack has five hip positions to fit adults from 5'-6'2". This carrier can be used until your child weighs 40 pounds. The Trailtech costs about $50.

INFANTINO

Infantino is famous for its 6-in-1 carrier, which fits into a car seat, attaches to a grocery cart, and converts to a backpack. The carrier costs about $20, comes in many attractive colors, and includes a free video to instruct parents in the proper use of the carrier. Infantino also offers the Side Traveler, in which the baby faces in towards the parent, but rests on the parent's hip, rather than the chest. Some of their carriers have other features as well, including large storage capacity, breathable mesh seats and a weather protector that keeps the baby warm in winter, but can be zipped out for summer. All Infantino carriers have padded leg openings, removable terry bibs, and high-back headrests.

KELTY

Kelty is well known for its infant carriers among recreational backpackers. They offer five different carriers suitable for use on light day trips up to several day backcountry hikes. The Kangaroo is a front carrier with the option of having the baby face in or out. It has a clip-on carrier that attaches to a jog-bra harness. It also has a built-in hood that protects against weather and provides some privacy for nursing. The other four Kelty styles are backpacks intended for older babies. The lower end models are for use on short trips, while the deluxe models are for serious hiking. All are very lightweight, with an ergonomic curved aluminum frame, stable kickstand base and adjustable shoulder and waist straps for both the child and adult. The carriers are all a striking spruce color with purple trim, and have reflective piping. A Kelty carrier costs about $130.

NOJO

Nojo is the maker of the original Babysling, created by Dr. William Sears. The sling can be worn in several positions including classic cradle hold, snuggle hold in which the baby faces the mother, hip carry where the baby rests on the parent's hip, and kangaroo carry where the baby faces out. The Babysling is adjustable and has a patented "stopper" which secures the tail of the sling and prevents slipping. Nojo also makes the Suburban 3-in-1 carrier which holds babies up to 30 pounds. This is a classic front carrier with the option of having the baby face in or out, and a backpack.

OVER THE SHOULDER BABY HOLDER

The only sling to be awarded the National Parenting Center's seal of approval, the Over The Shoulder Baby Holder is a deep sling with generous padding. A special feature is the patented nylon rod sewn into the bottom portion of the strap's tail which keeps the strap from slipping. The OTSBH, in three sizes for ease of carrying, is available in nearly 50 fabrics. You'll find these $39 slings at specialty stores or order from the manufacturer at (714) 361-1089.

NURSING PRODUCTS

Feeding your baby is probably one of your most important responsibilities as a parent. Experts agree that breastfeeding is ideal for babies, and there are many products that can make it easier to breastfeed longer, even if you are a working mother. This section discusses breast pumps, breast pillows and other nursing accessories.

BREAST PUMPS

Breast pumps can make it convenient to continue breastfeeding. By storing and freezing the pumped milk, your baby can receive the benefits of breast milk in a bottle, even when you can't be there. Many hospitals sell and rent breast pumps, as do local maternity/nursing stores and lactation consultants. Make sure to choose a breast pump that will meet your needs and maintain your milk supply. Consult a lactation consultant if you have any questions or concerns.

MEDELA

Medela, the largest and best known of breast pump manufacturers, makes high-quality electric pumps, handheld battery/electric pumps, and manual pumps. Most are available for purchase or to rent. Medela pumps are lightweight and portable, are available in models suitable for light, occasional use, or long-term separations. Many models have an option to double pump both breasts at once, to save time. A Medela pump has a built-in vacuum release, designed to simulate the way a baby would breastfeed.

The Lactina pump comes in two models: the Select and the Plus, both of which can also be used as a double pump. The only difference between the two is the speed. The pump has autocycle pumping action, which simulates the action of a baby's mouth. This pump can be used either an electrical outlet or the PowerPak battery accessory, which is a rechargeable battery and has an adapter for use on the go, or in a car.

The Pump-in-Style is a high performance professional breast pump with an insulated storage area that fits the pump, four milk storage bags or bottles and a cooling unit, all in a sophisticated carrying bag. This pump offers double pumping, a double pump kit, the collection bottle and cooling elements to chill the expressed milk. It has adjustable suction and Autocycle pumping action and, like any other Medela pump, you can pump directly into milk storage bags. A PowerPak is also available for this model.

The Mini-Electric is a lightweight, portable pump, designed for short-term separations. A battery adapter is available. In addition to autocycle pumping and adjustable suction, it has universal threads, allowing it to be attached to any standard baby bottle, and is small enough to fit in a purse. A new double mini pump is also available.

The SpringExpress is a manual pump for occasional pumping. It has a spring inside the piston to create suction more easily. These pumps are dishwasher-safe, and can be used with any standard baby bottle. They are useful for a night out, or during illness, but are quite labor-intensive for everyday use.

AMEDA-EGNELL

Ameda-Egnell is another large manufacturer of breast pumps. For over 50 years, their pumps have been used in hospitals and through rental stations. The Egnell Elite is a lightweight, quiet, efficient pump. It offers variable suction, and a cycle that imitates a baby's natural sucking. It also comes with HygieniKits for hygienic pumping. The Elite also comes with an adapter so the pump can be used in a car.

The One-Hand Breast Pump is a unique and convenient way to pump milk. The pump is small enough to fit in a purse. The amount of suction and cycling are controlled by a hand squeeze. Because it is one-handed, a mother can pump one breast while nursing on the other.

AVENT

Avent makes two styles of breast pumps: manual and battery powered. The manual breast pump is operated one-handed with a lever. You can pump directly into a storage liner to be frozen, or into an Avent bottle. The battery breast pump has an AC adapter for traveling. It features adjustable suction and a suction release button for added control. A special valve prevents splash back. Avent pumps are designed primarily for occasional pumping.

NURTURE III

The Nurture III is an electric pump with cycling action controlled by lifting a finger on and off a valve. The suction has four adjustments. The Nurture III also has the option of pumping both breasts at once. The pump is lighter than the Elite, and more economical.

WHITE RIVER

White River manufactures two styles of breast pumps. The Model 9050 features variable vacuum control, automatic cycling, and a patented Soft-Cup system that simulates a baby's suckling. The easy-to-clean pump comes with a carrying case.

The Model 0500D is a manual pump with the Soft-Cup system. This is a more labor intensive, but more economical choice. The pump can also be converted to an electric pump with White River accessories. Conversion kits are available for all White River pumps, as well as attachments for double pumping.

BREASTFEEDING ACCESSORIES

There are a number of accessories available to make nursing more comfortable and convenient. Doctors have noted that mothers nurse their babies longer and have a more positive experience when they use these products.

NURSING PILLOWS

Breastfeeding pillows provide back, arm and elbow support during nursing. They elevate the baby to get the baby in the proper position for nursing. They can also help mothers recover from a Cesarean section by lifting the baby off of the incision.

My Brest Friend is a nursing pillow that wraps around the mother's waist. It comfortably fits most body types, and doesn't slip out of place easily. It can be used for classic cradle hold nursing, or shifted to the side for football hold nursing. The contoured cover is washable soft cotton-flannel. When your child is older, it can also be used as a travel pillow, or for supporting a baby learning to sit. My Brest Friend costs about $40 and is sold at many maternity and nursing specialty stores.

The Nurse Mate Nursing Pillow is specially designed to make nursing twins easier. It has extra-wide cushions, a washable cover, and adjusts to many positions. The Nurse Mate for Twins costs about $50.

Nojo's Deluxe Nursing Pillow is a thick C-shaped pillow that rests on the mother's lap. The pillow was developed by a nursing mother and helps to prevent backache by raising the baby closer to the mother. The pillow is filled with non-allergenic fibers and is washable.

SLINGS

Slings are a useful nursing accessory both at home and away. Slings are designed to keep baby close to the body in a variety of positions, while providing excellent back support for the parent. The wide span of fabric also provides privacy during nursing. Nojo, Over the Shoulder Baby Holder, Gerry, Parenting Concepts and Fisher Price are just some of the popular sling manufacturers. For in-depth descriptions of slings, refer to the Baby Carriers section of this chapter.

NURSING STOOLS

Elevating the feet may alleviate back, shoulder, leg and arm strain by lifting the lap and the baby closer to the breast. The Medela footstool comes in oak or white finish and costs about $35. It can also be used as a computer stool, to alleviate back pain while working.

BREAST PADS/BREAST SHELLS

Breast pads are designed to absorb leaks. Breast pads come in disposable or washable styles.

Johnson's and Evenflo are well-known makers of disposable breast pads. The pads adhere to the inside of your bra with an adhesive strip. They are multi-layered to keep skin dry, and can be thrown away in the trash. A box of 36 costs around $5.

Medela's Washable Bra Pads are seamless pads designed to keep moisture away and allow air to circulate. A package of four pads costs about $8.

BREAST PUMP

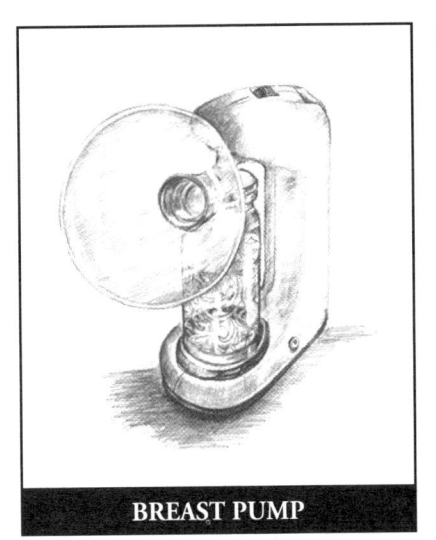

Ameda-Egnell sells 100% cotton reusable nursing pads that are contoured to conform to breast shape for a natural look. They absorb milk well, to let skin breathe. A package of six pads costs about $10.

Milk Diaper nursing pads are also 100% cotton, washable and reusable. They have eight layers of cotton for maximum absorbency. A pack of two pairs is about $6, and a five-pair pack is $14.

Breast shells treat sore, flat or inverted nipples. They keep fabric away from the breast to allow air circulation which improves sore nipples. Medela, Ameda-Egnell and Blis make various styles of breast shells.

MILK STORAGE BAGS

When expressing, it is crucial to store the milk properly to prevent bacteria growth. Milk storage bags are specially designed for expressed milk. They are presterilized and close tightly to prevent freezer burn. The bags are of high quality to prevent splitting and cracking during freezing. Many are designed to hook directly to a breast pump; the bag can then immediately be closed and refrigerated or frozen. Many are printed with measurements, so you can determine how many ounces you've pumped.

Medela makes collection, storage and freezing (CSF) bags that attach to any Medela breast shield so you can pump directly into the bag, and then immediately freeze the milk. A pack of 50 bags is about $18.95.

One of the most popular storage bags is manufactured by Mother's Milk. The bags last for four to six months, have a built-in twist tie, and a place to write the date. You can buy 25 in a pouch for under $8.

Avent's breast milk storage bags are safe for use in the freezer up to three months, and can be fitted directly into a disposable bottle for use. The bags are closed with sealing clips and come with date labels.

SUPPLEMENTAL NURSING SYSTEM

The Medela Supplemental Nursing System is for adoptive and nursing mothers. A plastic bottle hangs around the mother's neck with two thin feeding tubes that carry expressed breast milk or formula to the baby, who "nurses" from the mother. This system can help an adoptive mother to bond with her child, or help a nursing mother to continue breastfeeding while she builds her milk supply. The system costs about $40.

BOTTLES AND ACCESSORIES

Bottles and nipples come in many shapes and sizes, and it can be difficult to choose between them. Many times, it's best to try a few different styles of bottles and nipples to see which works best. Some of the major brands of bottles and bottle accessories are Playtex, Gerber, Johnson's, Evenflo, the First Years, and Avent.

Bottles generally come in four- and eight-ounce sizes. Three styles of bottles dominate the market: the standard, plastic bottle; the disposable bottle, and the angled bottle.

Disposable bottles have a plastic shell that is reused, and disposable plastic liners that are inserted inside the shell. The liners are sterile, which assures a hygienic feeding. The disadvantage of disposable liners is that while they are graded by ounces, it can be difficult to determine how much liquid you've added, or how much a baby drank. Playtex, Evenflo and Avent are the available choices in disposable bottles. Playtex and Evenflo liners, shells and nipples are interchangeable.

Angled bottles are built like a standard bottle, but at the nipple end they are bent at an angle. Manufacturers claim these bottles reduce gas in babies because the nipple remains full of liquid due to the angle. It makes it easier to feed the baby in an upright position, while still tilting the bottle. They reduce a parent's arm strain because you don't have to lift your arm to tilt the bottle. Evenflo and Johnson's were the first to come out with this system, but now most major bottle manufacturers make an angled bottle.

NIPPLES

Nipples are a very individual choice among babies. It is impossible to predict which a baby will like, and it is usually best to try several. Nipples comes in rubber and silicone. Rubber nipples are orange, and silicone nipples are clear. Silicone is preferred by many babies because it is softer in the mouth. Silicone doesn't collapse as often during feeding, and the size of the hole is not affected by heat or cold. It is usually a good choice for formula or milk feeding. Rubber nipples are often used for juice, but some babies like them for milk as well. The holes can be adjusted to increase or decrease flow by manually enlarging the hole, or boiling the nipple to tighten the hole.

Nipples also come in many shapes. Each shape claims to simulate a breast, but again, nipple shape is an individual choice among babies. All shapes come in rubber and silicone. Most brands offer slower flow for younger babies, and faster flow for older babies, by varying the size of the hole.

Babies often have an easy time grasping the nipple on disposable bottles without gagging. Many breastfeeding mothers have had good luck with this nipple shape, but some breastfed babies have a difficult time alternating between rubber nipples and their mother's.

Johnson's makes an infant nipple that is narrow and elongated. This nipple is believed to be better for premature babies because there is a smaller tip at the end to grasp, and a slower flow.

The standard nipple is the one most often seen attached to a bottle. These are made by Johnson's, Gerber, Evenflo, First Years, and Playtex. The best thing about these nipples are that they are so easily attainable and interchangeable. Many babies, especially those that are exclusively bottlefed, use these nipples without a problem.

Gerber Nuk nipples are unique in that they have a round top and flat bottom. Again, this is supposed to simulate a human nipple, and the shape the nipple takes on during suckling. The nipple is designed to fit comfortably inside a baby's mouth and help reduce gas.

THE AVENT SYSTEM

The Avent System combines breastfeeding and bottlefeeding, which is ideal for the working mother, or to allow the father or other person to participate in feeding. The system includes breast pump, reusable bottles, disposable bottles, several styles of silicone nipples, cups, pacifiers, and accessories.

Avent bottles come in four- and eight-ounce sizes. They offer reusable bottles as well as disposables with special sterile liners. The disposables have a unique base that allows the bottle to hold either size liner, and provides support during the filling of the liner.

The natural-shaped nipples have an anti-collapsible tip, and are designed to make it easier for a baby to alternate between breast and bottle. The reusable bottle nipples have an anti-vacuum skirt with an air valve to prevent gas. Avent offers several nipple options including the newborn nipple with one hole; the Slow, Medium, and Fast Flow nipples, with increasing numbers of holes; and the unique Variable Flow Nipple with slots instead of holes. By turning the bottle, you can vary the flow to suit the baby's needs.

Avent offers several other bottle accessories. A steam sterilizer uses the power of the microwave oven to sterilize up to four bottles, nipples and caps in under ten minutes. The electric steam sterilizer can hold up to six standard bottles, nipples and caps. The Bottle and Baby Food Warmer is a convenient way to heat foods, and is safe for disposable bottle liners. Avent also offers a training cup set with interchangeable spouts and a straw adapter to transition a baby to cup drinking. All Avent products can be purchased singly or in sets.

BOTTLE ACCESSORIES

There are a host of products to make bottle feeding easier. Drying racks have many posts to rest bottles, nipples and caps. Allowing these products to air dry helps resist bacteria growth. Bottle warmers are a convenient, safe way to heat bottles. Microwaves are not recommended because they can cause heat spots which may burn a baby's mouth. You can safely place a bottle in a warmer and have it ready for the middle of the night feeding as well.

One crucial accessory for bottle feeding is a dishwasher basket, available in most drug stores, which keeps nipples, rings and caps from falling to the bottom of the dishwasher.

Insulated bags are designed to keep bottles warm or cool while traveling. They can also be used to store pumped breast milk. There are also special bottle caps for powdered formula used for mixing formula on the road. You fill the bottle with sterile water, and the cap with pre-measured powdered formula. When you're ready to mix, you open the valve and shake.

All major bottle manufacturers make these products for their bottles and nipples. Most are very reasonably priced.

WHAT YOU NEED TO KNOW ABOUT JPMA

The Juvenile Products Manufacturers Association (JPMA) wants all parents to be confident that the juvenile products they purchase are designed and built with baby safety in mind. For this reason, JPMA initiated a voluntary Safety Certification program. This program is in effect for high chairs, play yards, walkers, strollers, gates full-size cribs and portable hook-on chairs. The program is being expanded to include non-full size cribs, toddler beds, bath seats and bedding products.

JPMA's seal is available to manufacturers who voluntarily submit products for testing. Only after the product passes rigorous testing can it display the certification seal.

Parents can learn more about safe use of their baby products by requesting a free copy of Safe and Sound For Baby, by including a self-addressed, stamped envelope to: JPMA Safety Brochure, 236 Route 38 West, Suite 100, Moorestown, NJ 08057.

The brochure is also available in Spanish.

DIAPERS AND DIAPERING

Seven thousand. That's the minimum number of diapers you should expect to change before your baby becomes a fully toilet-trained child. While not always a pleasant experience, keeping your baby dry and clean is a necessary parenting task that expresses caring and love.

DISPOSABLE DIAPERS

Disposables are undoubtedly one of the greatest inventions ever for busy parents. They are easy to put on, fit well, and keep baby dry. There are even disposables especially made for newborns with a cutout area to avoid rubbing on the baby's umbilical cord stump.

One caveat: the newer disposables are so absorbent that the baby may not feel wet even when the diaper is soaked. The rules are the same, even for disposables—you must change the baby every time he wets in order to avoid a diaper rash.

Proponents of disposables point out that the savings by not washing and using energy to run washers and dryers make up for the landfill problems caused by disposables. The fabric diaper boosters point out that disposables in landfills can cause contamination of groundwater and rodent-borne disease from the feces often left in diapers. Disposable manufacturers recommend that all fecal matter be flushed before the diaper is tossed out, but all parents know that isn't always practical.

CLOTH DIAPERS

Cloth diapering has benefitted by new diapers and diaper covers which make leaky cloth diapers and stiff plastic pants a thing of the past. A cottage industry of mail-order cloth diapering suppliers has grown to fill the demand for high-quality cotton diapers, often with terrycloth linings, and diaper wraps and pants of soft, breathable fabrics that still provide leakage protection. All-in-one cloth diapers, while more expensive, are convenient and great for parents nervous about diaper pins.

Less expensive cloth diapers, in flat and prefolded styles, are available in most baby stores, discount and drug stores. Pull-on pants in nylon are less apt to crack and stiffen and are usually a better choice than plastic.

Keeping your baby dry and clean is a necessary parenting task that expresses caring and love.

DIAPER SERVICES

The greatest luxury of all is using a diaper service. Your baby's diapers are picked up and a new batch of sanitized diapers are brought right to your door. Especially during the first few months, when your days may seem to be an endless round of diapering, a service can be invaluable. Compare prices and features of your local diaper services before making your decision.

Most services require that you order diapers one month before your baby's due date. Diapers should be delivered a week ahead of time. Most diaper companies require a minimum service period and need notification of at least one week before cancelling the service.

RESOURCES

■ BABY BUNZ & CO.
800-676-4559
P.O. Box 113
Lynden, WA 98264

Since 1982, Baby Bunz has offered Nikky diaper covers, diapering products, and baby clothes and toys. Their beautiful catalog features cotton, polyester, and lambswool felt diaper covers from $12.50 to $18.95. The aptly named "Cottonclouds," "Heavenly Bottoms," and Spoil Me! Snugglebottoms" are cotton diapers in styles to suit your baby's needs. Unique offerings include a 25" x 31" pure wool "puddle pad" for $22. Baby Bunz's product line also includes Hyland's homeopathic remedies and the Weleda natural baby care products.

■ BABYWORKS
800-422-2910
(503) 645-4349
11725 N.W. West Rd.
Portland, OR 97229
E-mail: Bbworks@aol.com

Babyworks' catalog is a pleasure to read. Besides offering a wide array of cloth diapers and accessories, you'll also find cloth diapering tips, washing suggestions, "trouble shooting" hints, and an essay about the environmental importance of using cloth diapers. Babyworks offers the Nikky line, wool diaper covers, nylon waterproof pants, and Bumkins all-in-one diaper-plus-covers, as well as many varieties of cloth diapers and diaper doublers. There's even a swim diaper, diaper pack, baby blankets, bibs and capes.

■ BIOBOTTOMS
800-766-1254
617-C 2nd St.
Petaluma, CA 94952
Web site: www.biotottoms.com/
children@biotottoms.com

Biobottoms' 60-page color catalog is filled with rugged, comfortable clothes and shoes for children. One page is devoted to diapering products, including Biobottoms' exclusive felted lambswool diaper covers with velcro tabs, available in white or with rainbow stitching at the edges ($18-$18.50). Their "Cottonbottom" is a all-in-one, cotton lined with a polyester moisture shield, available in white or pastels for $15.50-$16). They carry Gerber prefolded six-

Diapers and Diapering

layer diapers (per dozen: $19/infants; $25/toddler) and Happy Me diapers with extra thickness in front for boys and in back for girls (per six: $21-$25).

■ DIAPER BUNNY
(607) 276-6755
11 Angelica St.
Almond, NY 14804

Owner Jonna Statt includes washing instructions and easy hints with each purchase. Chinese cotton prefolded diapers are $20.95/dozen (infant size) and $24.95 (regular size). The catalog also includes Di-D Klips for pinless diapering. Other products carried include MotherEase fitted diapers with snap covers, snap-in diaper doublers, and Prorap diaper cover. Diaper Bunny's own pull-on diaper cover is made of lightweight, waterproof Ultrex. These covers are available in watermelon or jade colors, and cost just $3.95 each.

■ ECOBABY
800-596-7450
9319 Northview Terrace
Santee, CA 92071
Web site: www.ecobaby.com

Founded by a mother seeking natural products for her infant son, Ecobaby is a full-color catalog that offers children's and nursing clothing, toys, books, bedding and diapers. Kushies ($8.95/infant, $11.95/toddler) and Bumkins ($11.95) are convenient all-in-one diaper-wraps. Ecobaby carries a variety of cloth diapers and wraps, both wool and nylon. The catalog includes a section on setting up a cloth system and reasons to choose cloth.

■ THE HEALTHY BABY SUPPLY COMPANY
(612) 225-8535
323 W. Morton St.
St. Paul, MN 55107
E-mail: MKostohr@netcom.com

For those interested in natural health care, this is a wonderful catalog, as it includes a host of natural baby and bath care products, herbs and herbal oils, vitamin supplements, and books. Two pages are devoted to cloth diapers—prefolded, contour, and fitted with snaps. You'll find Prorap diaper covers ($6.95), the nylon/polyester EZ Cover ($4.95), and a 100% cotton wrap ideal for sensitive skin ($8.50). There's even a "recipe" for making baby wipes from paper towels.

■ MOMMY'S LITTLE HELPERS
800-859-3559
9250 Watson Rd.
St. Louis, MO 63126
E-mail: MommysLH@aol.com

A bare-bones catalog jam-packed with advice and information, Mommy's Little Helpers offers a plethora of diapers, covers, liners, and all-in-ones. Unique offerings such as the $9.30 all-organic "snap-to-fit" diaper, with velcro waist closures that fit newborns to 35-pounders, make this a special catalog. Mommy's Little Helpers stocks eight different kinds of diapers and eight wrap models, including the Biobaby wrap, with a "belt" that holds the diaper in place. The catalog includes a full page each on folding techniques, washing hints and "number crunching" to help you decide how many diapers you'll need to purchase.

■ MOUNTAIN AIR NATURALS
(406) 388-1056
113 North Davis
Belgrade, MT 59714
E-mail: mtnair@aol.com

A homegrown catalog that features hand-drawn illustrations, diapering hints and "mom-made" products, Mountain Air Naturals is a great find. For $20, their "Trial/Gift Set" includes three newborn diapers, a diaper cover, two wash cloths, a nylon tote bag and five note cards. The catalog includes flannel, terry/flannel and birdseye diapers; diaper clips (a pin alternative); a variety of diaper covers; washable nursing pads, and "dolly diapers" for your older sibling's favorite dolls.

■ SIMPLE ALTERNATIVES
800-735-2082
10513 S.E. 30th St.
Bellevue, WA 98004

Simple Alternatives presents a small selection of top-quality products. Included is "Diapering Details"—a great read if you're uncertain about which type of diapers to use. Made of 100% cotton flannel and thick terrycloth, their "Barefoot Baby" diapers are durable and absorbent. Their sampler pack includes a Barefoot Baby diaper, a Snugglup diaper cover, a Bumkins all-in-one diaper/cover, a Bumkins vented diaper cover, a Nikky diaper cover, six Barefoot Baby wash cloths, a package of baby wipes, and a small container of Nature's Second Skin baby ointment for $45.

■ TUSHIES
800-344-6379
675 Industrial Blvd.
Delta, CO 81416

An environmentally-friendly disposable diaper? That's right. Tushies' diapers are free of any gels, perfumes or dyes, with a cloth-like cover and cotton padding. If Tushies are not carried in a store near you, you can join the Tushies Club, and get regularly scheduled delivery of Tushies to your home. Club prices for Tushies are $42.95/case (270 newborn, 160 small, 120 medium, 88 large). You can also order Weleda, Earth Friendly, and Healthy Times baby products from Tushies.

■ WEE BEES
(303) 794-0966
P.O. Box 712
Littleton, CO 80160
E-mail: webees9@mail.idt.net

The Wee Bees catalog opens with five pages on the owner's good-natured diapering hints (and Rhonda Wiebe, with six children, knows diapers!). Inventory is small but well-chosen, and includes diaper service diapers with four cotton layers on the sides and eight in the center ($18/12 newborn; $25/12 regular; $31/12 toddler). Their nylon pants with snaps on both sides won't crack or harden and are economical at $8 for a pack of two ($10 for toddler size). Pull-on pants are $6.25 for two ($7.50 for toddlers). They also carry Mother-Ease snap-to-fit and Aplix (heavy duty velcro-type closure) diaper covers. The catalog closes with washing and diapering instructions, and several commonly asked questions.

TOP TEN GIFTS TO GIVE AND RECEIVE

Most of these gift suggestions may not seem like necessities, but we found them extremely helpful. Also, the recommendations are biased as they are products we ourselves, or parents we know, really appreciated. Take a look:

❶ **The Diaper Genie.** The Diaper Genie is now the number one best-selling individual juvenile product. It's easy to see why! For parents who use disposable diapers, this product removes odors from your home. Newly improved, it now can store more diapers, making it easier to use. It costs about $29 and is available at baby and discount stores.

❷ **Baby Bits computer software.** For any parent who has a computer and wants to make recording their baby's milestones simple, Baby Bits is a must! Baby Bits software allows parents to easily document everything from the first breath to the first step. Parents can even physically "record" their baby's cry or words with this software. The software comes with an expandable binder and 50 sheets of acid-free archive-quality paper. Suggested retail price is $40, with a portion of each sale going towards the SIDS Alliance. There is also a junior version which runs only about $18. Available only for Windows systems, Baby Bits can be purchased at specialty stores.

❸ **A locking clip.** Retailing at about $3, this is probably the most useful and inexpensive item you can purchase. A locking clip is to be used with a car seat to hold the seatbelt in place. It keeps your baby and the car seat secure. You can find a metal locking clip in the plastic bag attached to the back of almost all new car seats. It should be used at all times. We found this item at discount stores and local baby stores.

❹ **A Kelty Kids diaper bag or back pack.** We were especially excited about the Kelty Kids line of products as they seemed durable, functional, yet stylish in a '90s way. For parents on the go, the diaper bag should keep you organized. And, the Kelty backpack is one of the best-selling items at specialty stores nationwide.

...there are also some great items to consider buying as a gift or simply to pamper yourself.

DIAPER GENIE

❺ **A gift certificate for a cleaning service.** What all new parents need is time and order. Surprise yourself or a friend with a cleaning service gift certificate.

❻ **Books, books and more books!** One of our favorites is *What to Expect the First Year*. In our opinion, this is by far the best, easiest-to-read book for your baby's first year. Other books such as Dr. Berry Brazelton's *Touchpoints* and Dr. Jane Healy's *Your Child's Growing Mind* are wonderful also. Gift and baby books are also nice to receive.

❼ **A night of baby-sitting.** Offer your time and your care. It is probably the least expensive and most appreciated gift you could give to tired new parents.

❽ **A nightgown.** Between nursing, sleepless nights, and wanting your old body back, a mother needs pampering. A silky or brushed flannel button-down nightshirt or pajamas just may make the perfect pick-me-up every mother needs.

❾ **A car seat with a built-in locking clip and/or tether.** Safety comes first in every parent's mind. A car seat which has a built-in locking clip and/or tether helps the baby stay secure in a vehicle. Although these car seats may cost a little more than other models, it seems the benefits far outweigh the cost.

❿ **The Arm's Reach co-sleeping unit.** Sleeping near baby during the first months of life may be important to parents-to-be. The Arm's Reach co-sleeping unit makes it easy for parents to sleep near baby without fearing they may roll over on baby. Its own separate unit, the crib easily fits on any bed. It can also be used as a portable crib and/or bassinet when parents decide not to co-sleep with their baby. Available through the Right Start catalog and specialty stores, the Arm's Reach system costs under $200.

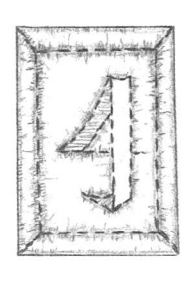

CARING FOR YOUR BABY

CHAPTER FOUR

YOUR CHILD'S HEALTH CARE PROVIDER

Your most important, fundamental goal is to keep your children healthy. Your child's well-being must come first, which means:
- Get regular well-child checkups and immunizations.
- Be aware of symptoms that can contribute to illnesses.
- Make sure your child receives proper care when he is ill.

Choosing your child's health care provider is an important decision. You should feel comfortable with the provider's communication style, office hours, staff, credentials, and medical background. Parents may choose between pediatricians or family practitioners when looking for a medically trained primary care physician.

You should feel comfortable with the provider's communication style, office hours, staff, credentials, and medical background.

PEDIATRICIANS

Pediatricians don't just see small children. A child can see a pediatrician until she is out of high school. To become a pediatrician, a doctor must graduate from a four-year medical school and then serve three additional years of residency training in pediatrics. Pediatricians who pass the written examination given by the American Board of Pediatrics are issued a special certificate, and use the initials "FAAP" following their names. Choosing a physician within a "network" allows you access to specialists affiliated within the primary health system.

FAMILY PRACTITIONERS

Another choice for your child's doctor is a family practitioner. The benefit is that this health care provider can treat everyone in the family. So, when your child comes down with strep throat and you do too, one provider is aware and can treat your entire family. A family physician must graduate from medical school and then serve three years of residency training. Family physicians who have successfully passed an oral and written examination given by the American Board of Family Practice are known as Board Certified and the initials "ABFP" follow their name and title.

HEALTH INSURANCE

Once you've decided on your physician, evaluate your health insurance opportunities. If at all possible, choose your health insurance based on your provider. If you do not have a choice, you may find yourself limited to the physicians your insurance company contracts with. Most insurance companies have a booklet which lists the providers covered. You can also speak to your physician or the office staff to explore the possibility of adding another insurance carrier. Also, keep in mind that open enrollment takes place at many organizations annually, so you can switch insurance carriers if your health needs change.

If you are not covered by insurance, you can either seek public assistance, free or low-cost state or local government-sponsored clinics, private health insurance policies, or pay-as-you go for your children. While counties or community health centers typically sponsor well-child clinics, it may be more difficult to find clinics that treat ill children. Physicians accepting new patients should be willing to see you on a pay-as-you go basis with an office visit running generally around $60 to $75. It may be recommended to visit the health care provider's office ahead of time, interviewing the pediatrician at no cost, and getting the child registered, so if treatment is necessary the system is in place.

CHOOSING A CARE PROVIDER: A CHECKLIST

From a practical point of view, here are some other questions you may want to consider when choosing a provider:

- What is your provider's educational background and experience? Does she have any area of specialty?
- Are specialists available with a referral from your physician?
- Is there a large network of specialists if your child needs special care?
- Is your provider near your home or office? Proximity is key when dealing with sick children.
- How accessible is your provider? Ask about the provider's days off and the backup plan for when he or she is away. What are the provider's office hours?
- At what hospital(s) does your physician have admitting privileges?
- How open and friendly is the office staff?
- How well does the provider listen and respond to your questions?
- What is the provider's off-hours policy?

QUESTIONS AND ANSWERS
An Interview With a Pediatrician

All pediatricians are not alike, and your challenge is to find one who relates well to both you and your child.

Every pediatrician is committed to helping parents raise healthy children; however, individual pediatricians take different approaches so you may want to interview several doctors before selecting the one who best meets your needs. A pediatrician should be selected before your baby is born. This will allow the pediatrician the opportunity of giving your newborn her very first examination. The information below was obtained through an interview with Peter Wang M.D., a pediatrician practicing in Sacramento, California.

Q: How do I choose a pediatrician?

A: One way to choose a pediatrician is to ask your friends and neighbors about their pediatricians. You can also ask your obstetrician for a recommendation. Before your baby is born, it is possible to interview different pediatricians until you find one with whom you are comfortable.

Here are some things to look for in a doctor:

- Someone who will explain things clearly, including diseases, development, anticipated problems, and behavioral issues.
- He or she should be available and accessible most of the time; find out about backup procedures when the doctor is unavailable.
- Experience.
- A doctor who likes and works well with children.
- Someone who shares your basic philosophies on baby care, feed-ing/nursing, and medication.

Q: What type of relationship should I expect to establish with my child's pediatrician?

A: You definitely should be able to discuss any of your concerns with your doctor. The doctor should explain your child's sickness—why it has developed, what symptoms to expect and when. However, parents need to also understand that some illnesses are difficult to diagnose or predict. They should be willing to accept a sincere, "I don't know what is going to happen in the next few days. We just have to observe the child closely." Part of the doctor's job is to alleviate the parents' fears and worries, but at the same time to be completely honest.

Q: May I call the pediatrician during non-office hours?

A: Yes! Doctors and their associates should be available at all times for emergency situations. Most doctors try to educate their parents during regular office visits to explain the situations in which they should call, and those in which they should wait. If a parent has a real concern, however, he/she should not feel guilty for calling during non-office hours.

Q: Are there times when an appointment is not necessary and I can call for additional advice over the telephone?

A: There are times when you may want to call and speak with the nurse or leave a message for the doctor to call you back. When you call the office because your child is sick, you should be prepared to give the following information:

- Your child's age and approximate weight.
- Your child's temperature, when appropriate.
- The duration of the illness, and what measures have been taken so far.
- Whether your child has an underlying condition, such as diabetes, or takes medication on a regular basis.
- Have the phone number of your pharmacy on hand in case a prescription is needed.
- Have a pencil and paper ready so that you can write down the instructions.

Q: What happens during the doctor's first visit with a newborn?

A: The doctor has two main purposes in checking the newborn:
❶ To make sure the child is capable of meeting the challenges of life outside the womb.
❷ To screen out possible birth defects.

When a totally dependent fetus becomes an independent newborn, dramatic physiological changes occur. For more than 95% of newborns, the doctor will inform the parents that their newborn is healthy and normal. Most newborns develop normally; however, 5% of newborns need some kind of medical intervention to help them survive this critical period. There is a 3% to 5% chance that a newborn will have a birth defect or irregularity. Sometimes this situation can be life-threatening. If you had complications during pregnancy or delivery, your baby should be examined at birth. If your pregnancy was trouble-free, the exam can take place anytime during the first 24 hours of the child's life.

Before you leave the hospital, a blood sample is drawn from the baby for a blood count. Thyroid function tests are also administered, and enzyme tests are run to detect PKU (phenylketonuria), galactosemia, and sickle-cell anemia. Other tests for disorders such as congenital hypothyroidism and congenital adrenal hyperplasia may be run as well, depending on your area's newborn screening guidelines.

Q: What else should I expect during this first visit?

A: Your doctor will examine your baby every day during your hospital stay and discuss with you the baby's current condition and symptoms that babies normally develop later. These may include:
- jaundice
- molding of the skull
- cephalohematoma (bleeding under the scalp)
- forceps marks
- puffy eyelids
- subconjunctival hemorrhage (bleeding in the white of the eye)
- hemangioma (birthmark made by blood vessels)
- mongolian spots (bluish spots on the buttocks)

Q: Once we leave the hospital, what are some of the things I may notice with my infant?

A: Some of the more common occurrences are:
- frequent hiccupping
- spitting up
- sneezing
- initial weight loss
- vaginal discharge or blood
- transient hair loss

In addition, your baby may experience these common skin conditions:
- heat rash
- neonatal acne
- diaper rash
- skin peeling
- other infant rashes

Q: What are some issues I should discuss with the doctor and/or nursing staff before leaving the hospital?

A: You should ask for information and advice on the following:
- feeding: breast or bottle
- burping techniques
- clearance of air passages if baby gags or chokes
- care of umbilical cord
- crying
- sleeping patterns
- infection protection
- postpartum adjustment
- bathing techniques

IMMUNIZATIONS

By Kenneth A. Frank, M.D.

All normal and healthy children should be immunized against diseases which may be crippling or fatal. Benefits of immunization are partial or complete protection against the consequences of disease, which range from trivial and inconvenient symptoms to paralysis and death. No immunization is completely effective or completely safe. Minor reactions to immunizations are frequent; severe reactions are extremely rare. It is more likely a child will have severe health problems from serious illnesses than to have significant problems from the immunization against the illnesses. Minor illnesses, even those with some fever, are usually not sufficient reason to postpone immunization, but you should discuss any illness with your pediatrician. Immunizations should not be given if an individual is hypersensitive to a vaccine component or has altered immune response. "Vaccine Information Sheets," prepared by the Communicable Disease Center for each vaccine, are designed to inform parents of the benefits and risks of the immunizations. If you have any questions, ask your provider.

Most states require that children be immunized before enrolling in school, preschool, child care centers or family home day care, unless exempt for medical or religious reasons. As a parent or guardian, you will be required to complete a certificate showing proof of this. Below is information about the different diseases for which your child may be immunized.

The American Academy of Pediatrics recommends that all normal, healthy children in the United States receive immunizations.

DTAP/DPT IMMUNIZATION:
DIPHTHERIA, PERTUSSIS, TETANUS

Diphtheria occurs primarily in children. This throat infection produces a toxin which damages the heart, kidneys and nerves, and may cause death.

Pertussis (whooping cough) is most severe in young infants. The illness produces protracted coughing, and may cause lung damage, seizures, brain damage and death. Immunization protection wanes in adulthood so adults can be a reservoir for the disease. It is always present.

Tetanus (lockjaw) is caused by a toxin produced by a wound infection. The toxin may cause severe, painful muscle spasms, breathing problems and death.

There are two vaccine types available:
- **DTWP** (or more commonly **DTP**). In addition to containing diphtheria and tetanus toxoid, this vaccine also contains inactivated "whole cell" pertussis organisms.
- **DTaP** contains diphtheria and tetanus toxoid, as well as more purified cellular components of pertussis, not the whole organism. It is believed that DTaP has fewer adverse side effects, such as fever, than DTWP.

POLIO IMMUNIZATION:

Polio is a viral infection of the nervous system which may produce extensive paralysis and death. The polio vaccine has been very successful; wild polio virus is no longer causing disease in the Western Hemisphere. There are two types of polio vaccine:
- **Oral Polio Vaccine (OPV)** is an attenuated live virus vaccine. In addition to protecting the recipient against paralytic polio, it also induces intestinal immunity.
- **Enhanced Inactivated Polio Vaccine (eIPV)** is a killed polio virus vaccine. It protects the recipient against paralytic polio but does not induce intestinal immunity.

MMR IMMUNIZATION:
MEASLES, MUMPS, RUBELLA

Red measles or "rubeola" is the most serious common childhood illness. The illness lasts ten days, with a high fever and generalized rash. Complications are pneumonia and encephalitis, which can produce deafness, blindness, retardation and death.

The mumps virus causes painful swelling of the salivary glands. It may cause inflammation of the pancreas. Fortunately, complications are rare. Infection in adult males may cause sterility.

Rubella, also called "German measles" or "three-day measles," is usually a mild illness with fever and rash. Infection in a pregnant woman can result in disastrous defects in the fetus.

HIB IMMUNIZATION:
HEMOPHILUS INFLUENZA TYPE B

Invasive hemophilus influenza type B disease is one of the most serious bacterial infections in the young child. This bacterium causes meningitis, which has a high mortality rate. There is a high rate of residual neurological effects among survivors. HIB may also cause serious infections of the throat (epiglottis), lungs, bones and joints. This vaccine has dramatically reduced infections from this organism.

HBV IMMUNIZATION:
HEPATITIS TYPE B

Hepatitis is a liver disease caused by several types of viruses. The serious forms can result in chronic liver damage, liver cancer and death. Vaccines are available for two types of hepatitis.

Hepatitis B Vaccines (HBV) protect against hepatitis B which is transmitted through blood and body fluids. Hepatitis B is the leading cause of liver cancer in the world. Infected mothers may pass the virus to their infants at birth. The risk can be greatly reduced by giving the newborn infant a dose of hepatitis B immune globulin (HBIG) on the day of birth and then vaccinating the infant with the hepatitis B vaccine series. This vaccine series has recently been added to the list of required vaccines for those children entering school for the first time.

CHICKEN POX IMMUNIZATION:
VARICELLA VACCINE LIVE (VVL)

Chicken pox is a highly contagious, common childhood illness with fever and a blistery rash as the primary symptoms. The complication rate of this disease is low; yet 25 children die each year in the U.S. due to chicken pox, and many more may end up with brain damage. More commonly, chicken pox causes significant economic problems with disruption of child care and school attendance. Shingles at an older age is a long term complication of chicken pox. Talk with your pediatrician about the pros and cons of this vaccine.

OTHER VACCINES

- **Hepatitis A Vaccine (HAV)** protects against infectious hepatitis (hepatitis A) which is spread via ingestion of fecally contaminated material. Symptoms include fever, malaise, jaundice, decreased appetite, and nausea. Although not recommended for routine use, it is advised for those traveling to Mexico and third world countries.

- **Influenza Vaccine** is given yearly in the fall to high-risk individuals to prevent influenza. This includes those with asthma and other chronic lung diseases, major heart disease, sickle cell anemia, diabetes, chronic renal or metabolic disease, and immunosuppressed individuals including those with HIV infection. Influenza spreads in epidemics during the winter time. Symptoms vary but usually include fever, chills, headache, malaise, muscle aches, cough, and stomachaches. Since the influenza virus mutates frequently, a yearly shot is needed to build resistance to newer strains.

- **Pneumococcal Vaccine** is recommended for children 2 and older with increased risk of acquiring systemic pneumococcal infections—those with sickle-cell disease, functional or anatomical absence of the spleen, nephrotic syndrome or chronic renal failure, HIV infection and conditions associated with immunosuppression. Pneumococcus is a bacterium which can cause bacteremia, meningitis, otitis media (ear infection), pneumonia, and sinusitis. Some doctors recommend vaccination in older children with recurrent ear infections.

- **Meningococcal Vaccine** is currently recommended for children 2 and over who have functional or anatomical absence of the spleen and those with complement component deficiencies. Meningococcus is a bacterium which causes meningococcemia and meningitis. Shock, coma, and death are common.

RESOURCES

■ AMERICAN ACADEMY OF PEDIATRICS
800-433-9016
(847) 228-5005
P.O. Box 927, Dept. C
Elk Grove, IL 60009-0927
Send a self-stamped envelope to request information on immunizations from the medical perspective. This resource also offers the most current recommendations in the immunization schedule.

■ CENTERS FOR DISEASE CONTROL AND PREVENTION (CDC)
800-CDC-SHOT
Web site: www.cdc.gov/nip
Through this free service of the National Immunization Program, you can request information by fax, mail or recorded information on hundreds of topics—everything from the theory of immunizations to specific information about each vaccine, including disease and immunity information, statistics, and side effects. You may request up to five documents at any one time. We found this to be the most comprehensive resource available on immunizations.

■ CENTERS FOR DISEASE CONTROL AND PREVENTION NATIONAL IMMUNIZATION HOTLINE
800-CDC-2522
If you have questions about vaccinations, the hotline puts you directly in touch with a knowledgeable operator who can fill you in on recommended vaccinations, answer questions about side effects, and refer you to free or low-cost immunization clinics nearby. CDC will mail out free brochures including a parent guide to immunizations, common misconceptions, and recommended vaccination schedules. The hotline is staffed from Monday through Friday, 8:00 a.m. until 11:00 p.m., Eastern Standard Time.

■ NATIONAL VACCINE INFORMATION CENTER
800-909-SHOT
512 W. Maple Ave., Ste. 206
Vienna, VA 22180
Web site: www.909shot.com
This is a nonprofit center founded by parents whose children responded negatively to immunizations. They represent the small number of children who have had significant reactions, and offer several packets of information regarding immunization reactions. The group's toll-free number can also help you access their six-minute tape on preventing vaccine reactions ($12).

■ VACCINE ADVERSE EVENT REPORTING SYSTEM (VAERS)
800-338-2382
If your child has suffered a serious reaction to a vaccination, call for a report form. You can do this yourself. Your child's physician is also required by law to report the reaction.

"A Measure of Love"

A Life Experience by Mary J. Patt

It's 11:00 p.m., and I am sitting on the carpet beside the white wooden crib that has been shrinking steadily for 23 months. My daughter's porcelain face, framed by golden ringlets, lies so close to mine that I can see her eyes dancing beneath the lids as she slips into REM sleep. Her right hand, poking out between two slats, is closed tightly around my left index finger. She squeezes it involuntarily the way she did as a newborn, when her hand was one-third this size. She is wearing her favorite vegetable pajamas, which are getting tighter by the week. With each warm breath, a garden of carrots and peas and tomatoes and corn and radishes rises and falls across her chest.

I am so in love with this child that my heart hurts. I can't let go of the moment. I want her to fit in the crib and remain my baby forever. But her body, mind and spirit have their own agendas, as they should. In a few days she'll be moving on to a toddler bed, just as she has moved on to toddler aspirations. Her favorite phrases this week ("All by self....Show Julie....Julie do it...") suggest that my husband and I have been doing our job of helping her to grow into a confident and purposeful human being. But only years and years of trial and error, on all our parts, will tell.

Since the beginning we have been torn between comparing her to other children (to assure ourselves that she is "normal") and not comparing her to other children (because each one develops so differently). Numbers cannot describe the unfolding of a unique soul. How could I possibly quantify the questioning light that has been shining in my daughter's eyes since the first moment I took her in my arms? How could I tally the myriad expressions that shaped and reshaped this beautiful face long before she had words to describe pleasure, pain, amusement, fear, anger, curiosity, and surprise?

A baby is a constant reminder to stop analyzing life and just immerse oneself in it. While we have wasted precious time worrying about how much self-esteem Julie will have as a teenager, or how we'll afford a great college education, or whether the world will be destroyed by pollution and overpopulation during her lifetime, she has been busy finding joy and awe in each bug, book, and bird that has come her way. When she was tiny, so many parents of older children stared wistfully at her and sighed, "It all goes so fast. Cherish the baby days." Suddenly we find ourselves in their place, looking at newborns and wondering how she could ever have been that featherweight and fragile.

In several hours she will stand up and call out from this crib: "Momma. Dadda. Ooouuuuut!" She will hit the ground running, demanding juice, a book, a song, a hug from Big Bird and several more from us. We will embrace her as she embraces life, as she begins her daily dance with the essence of all things. And we will renew our trust in her to find her own path, to come up with her own definition of success.

There are so many things I cannot know about her future. All I do know is that she loves her life now. She loves her Mom and Dad and Grandmas and Grandpa and other children and, of course, some furry friends—alive and stuffed. Tonight, as she tucked several animals into some pretend beds she had made out of old cloth diapers, she whispered to them what she usually hears from me. "Good night. Sweet dreams," she told them as she gently patted them on the back.

What she doesn't know is that her Dad and I never go to bed without creeping back into her room, separately, to whisper our hopes and dreams into her sleeping ears. Tonight I kiss her soft hand before letting go with a silent prayer I have repeated many times: "God bless your soul, tonight and always, Julianne. Know that your father and I love you and we always will. Sleep long and deeply and sweetly. Count your blessings, and we'll see you in the morning for another wonderful day."

BREASTFEEDING

By Dianne Neilson, R.N., I.B.C.L.C.

Breastfeeding is the most special gift you can give your baby. Although it is natural, nursing is really a learned skill that you acquire together with both time and patience. Breastfeeding provides frequent, close physical contact that helps to promote feelings of security and increasing health for you both.

The ideal first food, breast milk has immune properties that increase your baby's resistance to infections such as respiratory viruses and ear infections, as well as diseases that occur later in life—diabetes, lymphoma, Crohn's disease, and ulcerative colitis. Breast milk is associated with less constipation, stomach upset, and diarrhea. Many breastfed babies experience fewer or delayed allergies and research has shown the incidence of SIDS in breastfeeding babies is significantly reduced.

Exclusive breastfeeding for a minimum of four to six months is recommended by the American Academy of Pediatrics, the U.S. Surgeon General, and the World Health Organization. These three influential organizations recommend continuing breastfeeding, supplemented with solids, through the baby's first year of life.

Conveniently, breast milk is always ready, warm and fresh. There is nothing to mix, measure, heat or carry, no added cost or product waste. The hormones stimulated during nursing promote feelings of relaxation and well-being and help the uterus to contract after birth, minimizing blood loss and improving recovery. Also, the milk production process utilizes the nursing mother's calories, helping her to return to her prepregnant weight more quickly and easily. New research indicates breastfeeding may have a beneficial effect in reducing risks of breast and uterine cancer and osteoporosis. The benefits are many and the experience too wonderful to miss.

PREPARATION FOR BREASTFEEDING

Prior to the birth of your baby there are a few things you can do to get off to a good start. It is recommended that you not stimulate or even wash your nipples with soap in the last few weeks of pregnancy as your body is naturally preparing them for breastfeeding.

Attend a breastfeeding preparation class to get basic information, especially on latch-on and positioning. Having a

Although it is natural, nursing is really a learned skill that you acquire together with both time and patience.

current breastfeeding book purchased prior to the baby's birth is also recommended. During their last trimester, many mothers also purchase two to three supportive bras designed for nursing.

Other than that there is little to do. Attending a La Leche meeting, talking with friends who have successfully breastfed, or speaking with health professionals who are knowledgeable and supportive about breastfeeding can be helpful.

GETTING STARTED

Once your baby arrives it helps to be patient. Offer your baby an opportunity to breastfeed as soon as possible after delivery—within the first hour is ideal. Breastfeed skin-to-skin with your baby—your body will keep your baby warm. Colostrum is the valuable first milk your body produces for your baby's first days. Present in small quantities, colostrum has antibodies which give your baby early protection against germs. It also has a laxative effect and helps to move the first dark, tarry stools. This also helps to minimize jaundice.

Most often mothers notice increasing breast fullness by the third or fourth day postpartum. By this time babies are ready for more milk. Some mothers' breasts will feel warm and lumpy and a low-grade fever may be present while milk volume increases. On this day nurse often (up to 10 times a day, or every one and one-half to two hours), keeping baby awake to nurse longer than five to 10 minutes. Continue frequent nursing for 48 hours. The swelling normally lessens within this time.

Babies need to nurse a minimum of eight times a day after that. Babies nurse for different lengths of time so watch your baby, not the clock. If your baby falls asleep after nursing for five minutes, and wants to nurse again within an hour, you may find it easier to keep him awake the first time so he feeds 15 minutes or longer. Then he may sleep two to three hours before waking to nurse again. Most mothers like to use both breasts at each feeding, starting on the last breast nursed.

Most importantly, parents need to know that their baby is getting enough milk. You don't need to see it or measure it—you will know. You will learn to recognize the sounds of your baby swallowing, especially after your milk increases. The most reassuring sign is frequent soiled diapers. By the fifth day it is important that your baby is having three or more soft yellow bowel movements in a 24-hour period, as well as six or more wet diapers. At checkups, reassurance comes from the baby's weight measurements. After losing 5% to 7% of their weight in the first few days of life, babies begin to put the weight back on at approximately an ounce a day, regaining or passing their birth weight by 10-14 days old.

THE COMFORT FACTOR

Breastfeeding needs to be comfortable. Often mothers feel tender when baby first latches on. If the tenderness disappears after slowly counting to 10, then it is usually a sign that baby has latched on well. If the tenderness continues, baby needs to be relatched. Babies need to have more than just the nipple in their mouths—they need to mouth enough areola to compress the pockets under the areola that hold the milk in the breast. Their lips need to be flanged out around the breast with their noses and chins touching the breast at all times. Mothers find it helpful to relax and lean back once baby is latched on, which helps the baby to stay on the breast fully.

Pillows are important to support baby and mother's arm as they relax while nursing. Many mothers find putting their feet up on a short stool can help baby to stay up on the breast. With good latch-on and positioning you are not only comfortable and can enjoy nursing your baby, but your baby also nurses more effectively, getting more milk in a shorter amount of time. Massaging your breasts while nursing also helps increase the amount of milk your baby drinks.

If you experience pain, are unsure if baby is getting enough milk, or have questions and concerns about what you are experiencing it is best to contact a breastfeeding/lactation specialist who can provide you with individualized guidance and support.

LACTATION CONSULTANTS

Lactation consultants are specially trained in breastfeeding education, management and support. Their goal is to help you breastfeed successfully and to help you work through any problem. Most lactation consultants are International Board Certified Lactation Consultants (IBCLC), which means they have met the necessary qualifications set by the International Board of Lactation Consultant Examiners and meet continuing education requirements. Fees for private lactation consultants vary yet usually start at $45-$60 per hour depending on the services you need. Most lactation consultants also sell and rent electric pumps and related supplies.

Some insurance companies may reimburse lactation consultant fees, breastfeeding supplies or breast pump rentals; be sure to ask your provider. If you are a WIC recipient, you may qualify for a breast pump or other supplies.

DISCREET NURSING IN PUBLIC PLACES

After the first couple of weeks, most moms are more comfortable with nursing but may have concerns about nursing in public. Often new parents are more concerned about making someone else uncomfortable even though they feel good about what they are doing. You might practice in front of a mirror to see what others will see. You can always wear your baby in a sling, handy for both carrying and nursing, or toss a sweater or baby blanket over your shoulder. Many mothers just pull their T-shirt up and rest the edges against their breast, covering it but not the baby. There are also beautiful nursing shawls and aprons and a variety of styles of nursing tops and dresses designed for easy access and discreet nursing. Often just finding a location like rest room lounges, dressing rooms, or even sitting in your car will be more comfortable than nursing in a crowded area. Most times mothers who nurse simply look like they are cuddling their babies. It really is simple to take baby anywhere.

WHAT TO WATCH

All things you ingest may affect your milk, your milk supply, or your baby. Some things can reduce the amount of milk your body will produce. Others can cause fussiness in babies or may harm your child. You do have choices.

Regular alcohol intake will often decrease a mother's milk supply and readily passes into breast milk. If you do drink an alcoholic beverage, always nurse first prior to drinking and wait two to three hours before nursing again.

Current recommendations for caffeine intake is a two-cup limit of caffeinated coffee (300mg) per day. Most medications are safe but always remind your prescribing physician that you are nursing. If you are unsure about the medication's safety, contact a lactation consultant or another health professional who keeps up with current information on drug and medication effects on lactation and the breastfed baby.

NURSING AND WORK

Dedication and planning can help nursing moms overcome challenges when returning to work. Waiting until your milk supply is fully established (six weeks or longer) increases your chances of successfully combining breastfeeding and work. Breast pumps allow you to save milk for later bottle feeding by your child's caregiver. It's best to begin pumping and saving milk a good two weeks before returning to work. Not only does this help you create a backup milk supply but it also familiarizes you with your pump and your body's response to pumping. (See the Products chapter for a review of breast pumps.) Breast milk can be stored in the refrigerator for three to five days or in the freezer for three to six months, if stored in glass or plastic bottles or milk storage bags.

Often the best time to pump is in the morning right after your baby has nursed. At this time most mothers' breasts are more full so there is usually extra milk. Pumping right after the baby nurses won't interfere with baby's next nursing time. Most mothers like the advantage of a double pump collection kit which minimizes pumping time, often draining both breasts in 10-15 minutes.

INVOLVING THE NEW FATHER

Fathers' support of breastfeeding is the most influential factor in mothers' feeling successful about their nursing experiences. Some dads claim to feel left out of the breastfeeding experience. Of course, not much can be done about sharing the actual act of breastfeeding but knowing that their baby is getting the best food available anywhere usually makes both parents feel good. Fathers can participate in so many other activities with their babies when they are not nursing—babies also need to be cuddled, sung to, rocked, burped, bathed. Babies especially love to sleep on their fathers' chests and have preferences for skin to skin contact.

Breastfeeding Resources

At work, plan to pump and then nurse evenings, mornings, and on your days off. Pumping at the times your baby would nurse is ideal but you often need to coordinate with work times that are available to you. It's wonderful if you can visit and nurse your baby on your lunch break.

When you pump and save your breast milk, it can be used to provide breast milk exclusively for your baby, or your baby can have formula while you're at work and nurse while at home. In either case, make sure the baby will take a bottle when the time comes to return to work. Introducing your three- to four-week-old baby to a bottle assures acceptance. Offer a bottle once or twice a week to keep your baby familiar and to help with the adjustment between breast and bottle.

Before returning to work it is usually a good idea to inform your employer of your plans to pump. Hopefully, your employer can help you locate a private, comfortable area for pumping.

Finding supportive child care is essential. When you feel more confident with your care provider, the easier it is for you to leave your baby, the less anxiety you will have, you'll be able to express more milk, and your baby will be happier to nurse on your return. The key is to be flexible and creative, and trust your intuition in trying to create a balance between work and motherhood.

RESOURCES

■ HOLLISTER/AMEDA EGNELL
800-323-8750
755 Industrial Dr.
Cary, IL 60013

Ameda Egnell, now part of the Hollister pharmaceutical firm, has been manufacturing breast pumps for over 50 years. Their "Breastfeeding Answers" covers everything from what a breastfeeding mother should eat to how to manage breastfeeding and working. You can request a free subscription to the "Circle of Caring" newsletter, which covers topics of interest to lactation consultants and nursing moms. The company's Elite breast pump is the only one on the market controlled by a microprocessor, allowing the user to find just the right combination of suction and cycling. Many other pumps and accessories for purchase and rental are available.

■ LA LECHE LEAGUE INTERNATIONAL
800-LA-LECHE (525-3243)
1400 N. Meacham Rd.
Schaumburg, IL 60173

La Leche is the world's largest source of information on breastfeeding and related topics. It is a nonprofit organization founded in 1957 that offers support groups, monthly meetings, breast pump rentals, a catalog and educational materials. A $30 membership includes six issues of the newsletter "New Beginnings" and a 10% discount on most purchases. Their book, *The Womanly Art of Breastfeeding*, is a comprehensive guide to nursing your baby.

■ **MEDELA BREAST PUMP RENTALS AND ACCESSORIES**
800-TELL-YOU (835-5968)
4610 Prime Pkwy.
McHenry, IL 60050
Medela's Breastfeeding National Network is a 24-hour, seven-day-a-week warmline. Staffers provide information on where to buy or rent Medela breast pumps, accessories or nursing bras, and lactation consultants in your area.

Most local Medela outlets carry the "Pump in Style" breast pump that looks like a purse but comes with everything needed for double pumping. Medela also has a line of specialty feeding products for babies with special feeding problems. Local Medela dealers offer a free breastfeeding information guide and a catalog of the full product line.

■ **NURSING MOTHERS COUNSEL**
(415) 599-3669
P.O. Box 50063
Palo Alto, CA 94303
Web site: www.nursingmothers.org
This network offers information and support for nursing mothers. The Nursing Mothers Counsel will mail a free breastfeeding informational packet, including recommended reading. The group offers phone counseling and referral to Medela breast pump rentals. The nonprofit group is made up of women volunteers who have had firsthand experience with breastfeeding. The organization is also a source of support for combining nursing and returning to work.

■ **WOMEN, INFANTS AND CHILDREN (W.I.C.)**
This federal supplemental food program helps pregnant women up to six months after delivery, nursing mothers up to 12 months after delivery and children from birth to age 5, who have a nutritional or medical need and low income (up to 180% of the poverty level). They also provide education and assistance with breastfeeding. Eligibility is determined at the first clinic visit. Classes, counseling, nutritious foods and referral to health care are offered. Your local health department, hospital or care provider can refer you to the nearest WIC agency.

BECOMING A HUMAN MILK DONOR

Though the days of the wet nurse are long gone, one satisfying way a mother can share her breast milk is by participating in the Human Milk Banking Association of North America's donation project.

For babies unable to tolerate formula whose mothers cannot nurse, donor milk can be lifesaving. Donors may choose to express daily over weeks or months, or may make a one-time donation of stored milk. Before donating, women are screened and tested to rule out blood-borne diseases.

For more information about milk banking, contact the Human Milk Banking Association of North America, Inc. toll-free at 888-232-8809. Their address is 8 Jan Sebastian Way #13, Sandwich, MA 02563.

"You Can Work and Breastfeed"

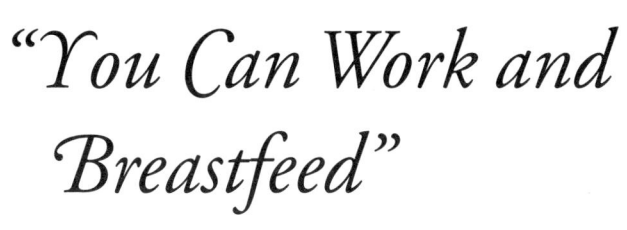

A Life Experience by Mary E. Kessler

With a little planning and support, you don't need to give up breastfeeding when you go back to work. I was able to exclusively breastfeed my son, Paul, until he was almost a year old while working full-time. Whether you rely on breast milk alone, or supplement with formula, you and your child can reap the many benefits that breastfeeding provides.

One of the biggest benefits breastfeeding provides is to prolong and preserve the close relationship you enjoyed with your baby while on maternity leave. Noted pediatrician T. Berry Brazelton states, "I think breastfeeding is of extra importance to a working mother in maintaining the attachment between her and her baby."

My experience was that continuing to breastfeed reduced my guilt of leaving my child when returning to work. Even though I couldn't be with him all day, I knew he was getting optimal nutrition and protection against illness. Sitting down to nurse in the evening helped me to unwind and reconnect with my son. I was fortunate to find child care near my office and so was able to nurse at lunch time—a delightful break which also afforded an opportunity to tune into my child's daily activities. When I was unable to go to his child care center, I booked a locked conference room and pumped for 20 minutes which helped me maintain my milk supply.

I also got more rest! With no formula to mix or bottle to warm, I could nurse Paul during the night while I was half asleep and catch another 40 winks during his morning feeding, snuggled in bed.

One question people often ask me is how I was able to continue to breastfeed without worrying about juggling work and pumping. My answer is I didn't concern myself with caring about what people thought, nor did I tell very many people what I was doing. As the regional vice president of a bank, I found myself in a traditional environment and yet I found a way to balance my personal needs with my work expectations.

A good support team is essential. At home, my husband, Michael, cooked and cleaned up after many meals, giving me time to nurse the baby. My child care provider was knowledgeable about breastfeeding and did not sabotage my efforts. I also arranged for a long enough maternity leave that allowed me to establish my milk supply and energy level. I found that easing back into work with a flexible schedule allowed additional nursing time. Finally, I found that I really needed to rest as much as possible to maintain my milk supply.

Most important, I found it was essential to keep my priorities straight. Nursing a baby is one of life's greatest joys and it lasts for just a few short months. For me, making the commitment to breastfeed was worth every minute of the extra effort it took.

Mary's Tips for Fast, Easy and Effective Pumping:

To maintain your milk supply and provide milk for baby, pumping the breasts is important. Here are a few hints I found helpful:

- Rent a top-quality electric pump. Some insurance companies will reimburse part of the cost. With a double hookup, you may be able to pump six to eight ounces of milk during a typical coffee break.

- Find a private space at work so you can relax (an office with a door that locks, a conference room, seldom-used restrooms).

- Two piece suits work best for pumping and covering up an occasional leak.

- Assist your "let-down" reflex with your baby's picture or an item of clothing.

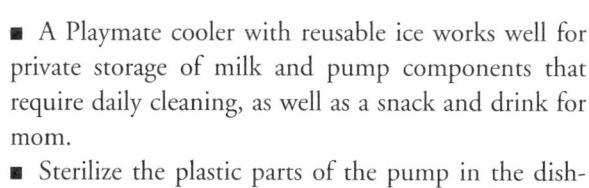

- A Playmate cooler with reusable ice works well for private storage of milk and pump components that require daily cleaning, as well as a snack and drink for mom.
- Sterilize the plastic parts of the pump in the dishwasher every night to save time.

To help you stay organized, here is a list I found helpful each morning:

Work Checklist
- Cooler
- Ice
- Pump kit (assembled to save time during pumping breaks)
- Empty bottles to store milk
- Snack and drink for mom
- Briefcase, purse, etc.

Child Care Checklist
- Breast milk pumped the previous day
- Baby food, juice for an older infant
- Baby's "lovey" and/or pacifier
- Mom's lunch (if nursing at lunchtime)
- Mom's "bib" for protecting work clothes from spit-up (made from an old towel)
- Weekly: diapers, wipes, clothes, etc.

After-Work Checklist
- Refrigerate and label pumped milk
- Sterilize pump kit and used bottles in dishwasher
- Refreeze ice
- Pack cooler for tomorrow!

QUESTIONS AND ANSWERS
Sleep: Getting a Full Night's Rest

For parents and children, sleep is essential. It is not until parents are faced with sleepless nights and children wake up haggard and grumpy that the true appreciation of a full, good night's sleep sets in. During pregnancy, we hear parents talk about sleepless nights. But what we may not hear is that the patterns we set for our infants can carry on into the toddler and school age years. Starting life with healthy sleep patterns makes an enormous difference in a child's and parent's life. To explore sleep needs and habits, we asked John Kuhn, M.D., some of the most common questions about sleep.

Q. How do you get your baby to sleep?

A. To start healthy sleep patterns, parents may consider keeping a normal, healthy baby out of close proximity once they are ready to move baby out of the parents' bedroom. Because parents are so in tune with a baby's sounds, every noise or movement can result in parents not sleeping fully or deeply. Also, as baby awakens and makes sounds in the morning, parents may rise immediately, rather than let the baby explore himself and his surroundings and perhaps return to sleep. Babies will let parents know when they need to get up.

Other culprits in forming poor sleep habits include pacifier use and/or using a parent as a prop to help baby get back to sleep. How you fall asleep is how you put yourself back to sleep. So, if a child falls asleep laying next to Dad with a pacifier in his mouth and wakes to find neither the pacifier nor Dad, a child may react by desiring both. Then, a parent wakes up to a screaming child and rushes to pop in the pacifier and hold the child again, and so the vicious cycle is formed. By putting the child to bed either awake or partially awake in his own bed, you are teaching the child to fall asleep alone, and when the child wakes he can put himself back to sleep alone.

Q. Are security blankets or special animals okay for children to use to sleep with?

A. Security blankets are a very good idea. Don't ever let your baby take a bottle to bed because it can become the "security blanket" and can be very harmful and difficult to stop. I definitely would encourage a "blanky" or soft animal. These are extensions of us, and make for a transference of the feeling of closeness. Of course that makes it difficult to take them away. We've all seen the 3-year-old carrying a special friend. Sooner or later they wear out and can be left behind. It's interesting that the memory of these items stays in the parents' minds so vividly—we know their importance.

Q. What about the family bed?

A. Years ago, in less sophisticated societies, families slept together. We needed warmth and huddled in the cave or in an unheated home. Now, with a more sophisticated society, sleeping together is not physically necessary. Many families sleep in the same bed by personal choice.

The only thing I stress is to be consistent in your choices. If you have a family bed, a child cannot sleep with you one night and then not be allowed another. You also need to think about when you will have your children sleep in their own room and about any sleep problems that may occur when making that transition. And, finally, you may want to consider your own sleep habits. Are you a light sleeper? Do you awaken every time your child does, or is it comforting for you to have your child next to you? These may all be factors in your sleep decision.

Q. How much sleep is necessary for my child?

A. This is a purely individual question. There is no hard rule for each age group. Sleep needs are dependent on your child's personality and your tolerance level. The biggest indication of whether your child is getting enough sleep is how she wakes up in the morning. Does she wake up on her own? Is she sluggish, sleepy, cranky? Look at the morning results and then base your child's bedtime generally around those criteria. Also, you can put your child to bed earlier than when she actually falls asleep. After following a bedtime routine, you can allow your child to play or read a book quietly in his room and then put himself to sleep when tired.

Q. Why is a bedtime routine so important?

A. Children thrive on routine and consistency. We all do better when we know what is going to happen. When it is time for bed, have a routine you follow—reading a story, brushing teeth, singing a quiet song, getting a drink of water, then going to bed. It is vital that you stick to the routine. Do not change the order of bedtime rituals or forget one of the steps, but instead go through the same routine every night. Then once you've done the final tuck-in, leave the child's room and do not go back. Children will always want one more story or one more drink, but what they really want is you. A parent provides a security blanket, and at bedtime a child is alone and senses a loss of control of his environment, so sleep can be scary. By making bedtime positive and consistent, a child learns good sleep patterns.

PACIFIER PROS AND CONS

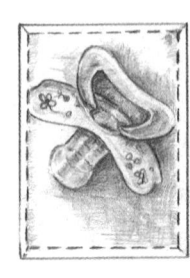

Before your baby is born, it is easy to decide not to use a pacifier. With a squalling infant who seems to need vast amounts of sucking time, however, you may change your mind rather quickly. For some, pacifiers are a magical device which instantly stop crying once they are popped in the baby's mouth.

Parents are cautioned against pacifier overuse, which causes babies and their families to become overdependent on the "plastic plug." A little experience will tell you if your baby's cries are for hunger, boredom, crankiness, or just a request for a little cuddling. Pacifiers are perfect for that cranky cry which sucking can soothe. Breastfeeding moms, especially until their milk supply is well established, should always try feeding a cranky baby before offering a pacifier.

Choose your baby's pacifier with safety foremost in mind. Don't use the nipple of a bottle as a pacifier. Choose one designed specifically for your baby's age. The pacifier should have shield vents and a sturdy design which will resist breakage. The orthodontic-type pacifiers have the disadvantage of only fitting in the right-side-up position. It's up to you (and your baby) to determine which shape is most comfortable.

Never tie a pacifier to a string around your baby's neck. To avoid possible strangulation, keep any ties attaching pacifier to clothes very short—6" or less. The makers of Mam pacifiers recommend replacing pacifiers every two months owing to the breakdown of the nipple due to baby's saliva, coupled with exposure to heat and sunlight. Pacifiers need to be washed either in the dishwasher or in hot, soapy water. It's best to have more than one pacifier so frequent cleaning is possible.

Some babies prefer the natural pacifier—thumbsucking. As it often starts well before birth, thumbsucking is a difficult habit to break. Parents can try to substitute a pacifier for thumb, but success is unlikely. Unless thumbsucking continues well into childhood, permanent malformation of teeth is unlikely. An advantage of thumbsucking is that the thumb is always available as baby requires, as parents who have spent many nights waking hourly to reinsert pacifiers will attest.

For those non-thumbsucking babies who refuse pacifiers altogether, parents are on their own as far as comforting techniques go. The old familiars of rocking and gentle motions are age-old methods to calm baby.

Parents are cautioned against pacifier overuse, which causes babies and their families to become overdependent on the "plastic plug."

"Pacifier Pointers"

A Life Experience by Kari Hazen

If anyone would have warned me about the instant attachment my newborn would have for that nice soft, plastic pacifier, it would not have entered our home. It was an instant love affair between baby and pacifier at about two weeks. Her constant desire to suck gave me two choices—a baby at the breast constantly or a pacifier. Although I loved breastfeeding, I also desired some independence—and the opportunity to go to the grocery store without a screaming infant. With one trip to the nearest pharmacy I came home with pacifiers galore. My life, or so I thought, would become quieter and simpler with a content baby.

My daughter became one of those children who constantly had a pacifier in her mouth. She slept with it, she played with it and used it for security. I was not quite sure of the "rules" of pacifier use, as my first child wanted nothing to do with the plastic security blanket. I had visions of my second-born starting kindergarten with a pacifier, or graduating from high school with a moldy piece of plastic in her mouth.

What I didn't realize was the impact the pacifier would have on my sleep habits. Night after night, as soon as my daughter would wake up "pacifier free," a loud shriek would be heard throughout our household followed by sobs. Once she began to talk, she shouted, "Binky! Binky!!" throughout the night. Almost on autopilot, I would make a zombie walk to her bedroom, place the pacifier in her mouth and return to bed exhausted. My husband and I concocted a plan—we would buy several binkies and place them in her crib. She would have so many to choose from, including "glow-in-the-dark" models, that she would not have to wake us up.

The night we put our plan into place, we snuggled in bed thinking "finally, a full night's sleep." To our despair, it became obvious that the habit of one of us placing the pacifier back in her mouth was already formed, so after 15 minutes of screaming I got up and gave her a pacifier.

There were other problems that arose from the pacifier. I'll never forgot the night my husband called me at an evening meeting: "Go to the store and buy a pacifier right away and come home." That was the entire conversation. When I arrived 30 minutes later, the furniture was rearranged in an attempt to find the lost pacifier. My husband wordlessly handed me a screaming child who instantly became content with a pacifier back in her mouth.

I am the first to admit we "enabled" our daughter's habit. One well-known parenting book suggests saying goodbye to the pacifier at age 1, as it may be very difficult after this time period. I read it, looked at my daughter, and decided I did not have the energy to remove it.

Once she turned 2, I began slowly weaning her from the pacifier. She didn't use it during the day unless she asked for it. I began to put it in a drawer after I brushed her teeth, so she knew where it was when nighttime arrived. During this time, I read an article that stated pacifier use contributed to a greater number of illnesses. Since my daughter had a dozen ear infections by the time she was 18 months old, I thought the sooner we said goodbye to the pacifier, the better. It's strange that after all my worrying, eventually it just went away. As she matured, she simply didn't need it as much.

We bought a Muppet board book entitled "Bye-Bye Pacifier" and it explained how great life is without a pacifier. There were, and still are, times my daughter asks for it and I explain it went bye-bye. The only downside is that she still does not typically sleep through the night. Those habits formed in her earlier days of waking, being comforted, and settling back to sleep, have stayed with her.

I know several other parents whose children used a pacifier without a problem. A friend who is a nurse told me the sucking reflex is very strong up to age 2. She explained that all children are different, and so are the parents' experiences. I wish, though, I had known some of the side effects of a using a pacifier. Maybe I would have tolerated more of the fussiness in her earlier months and would sleep better today.

FEEDING BABY

FORMULA

Scientifically, baby formulas are meant to imitate mother's milk. For women who cannot breastfeed, or for those who choose not to nurse, formula is a safe and appropriate choice. It is recommended that cow's milk not be used until a child is one year of age because of the high amount of sodium and protein it contains and its lack of other vital nutrients for infants. Most starter baby formulas are milk-based and allergies can occur.

Several brands and types of formula are on the market. Discuss with your baby's pediatrician the different choices available and ask for a recommendation.

If you decide to bottle-feed your infant, you should know which formulas are the most nutritionally balanced. No formula is identical in composition to breast milk; however, some are closer than others.

Commercial formulas are manufactured and available as:
- Single-serving bottles with sterilized nipples
- Ready-to-pour from a can into your own bottles
- Liquid concentrate to dilute with water in bottles
- Ready-to-mix from a powdered concentrate.

BABY FOOD

When should a parent introduce solids to the baby? The typical introduction period is when your baby is four to six months old. Discuss with your pediatrician any questions you may have regarding solids and what is best for your child.

When you're ready to introduce baby food, you may choose to pursue one of two avenues. One is to purchase commercial baby food from the grocery store; the other is to make the food yourself. The choice is an individual one.

COMMERCIAL BABY FOOD

Purchasing commercial baby food offers some great advantages, especially during your child's infancy. The texture is the perfect consistency for babies during this early stage. Single-ingredient foods make it easy to detect any food allergies.

The convenience of commercial baby food is undeniable. Most full-service grocery stores carry major brand-name baby

For women who cannot breastfeed, or for those who choose not to nurse, formula is a safe and appropriate choice.

BOTTLE FEEDING SAFETY

- Always check the expiration date on the formula.
- Follow the manufacturer's directions when preparing formula.
- Do not use leftover formula; bacteria which develops in formula may cause infection.
- Do not heat formula in a microwave oven. The formula may heat unevenly and burn the baby's mouth or throat.
- Do not use formula that has been frozen or shows white specks or streaks.
- Keep the bottles and nipples clean, and wash your hands before preparing formula.
- Refrigerate unused portion or prepared amount of formula until feeding.
- Follow manufacturer's guidelines for the refrigerator life for formula.

foods that offer a wide variety of single foods and combinations. Read labels carefully so that you can avoid ingredients such as added sugars, salt, modified food starch, MSG, preservatives and artificial colors and flavors. It is possible to buy commercial baby food that consists of only the food and water.

To minimize germs, portion baby food from the jar to a dish. Don't feed baby from the jar unless she will finish the entire contents. After opening, the unused portion of baby food fruits or juices will keep in the refrigerator for three days; vegetables may be safely stored for two days. If you warm your baby's food in a microwave oven, be sure to stir thoroughly and test the temperature before giving any to your child.

ORGANIC BABY FOOD

Many parents prefer to feed their baby certified organic baby food in order to avoid food treated with synthetic pesticides and fertilizers. Federal standards for production, processing and certification of organic foods, and independent certification that you will see noted on organic baby foods, such as Earth's Best, let consumers know the food is truly synthetic pesticide- and fertilizer-free. You can also make your own baby food with organic produce found at health food stores and farmer's markets.

HOMEMADE BABY FOOD

Taste some store-bought baby food and ask yourself, "Is this what I want for my child?" If taking food from a jar is not exactly your idea of a delicious, nutritious, satisfying meal, then read on.

For less then $15, you can purchase a baby-food grinder from most stores that carry baby products, including some grocery stores and pharmacies. Other than this, you need not invest more than a little time in order to offer your baby homemade food. Simply grind up the fresh vegetables, fruits, grains and meats you already have at home. Don't salt or sweeten baby food—babies' taste buds are different from adults'. Add a small amount of formula, breast milk or water if too thick. The easiest way to store homemade baby food is to prepare each food in bulk, freeze in ice cube trays, then store the cubes in plastic bags in the freezer. The cubes can be defrosted as needed for your baby. When on the go, instead of grabbing a few jars of baby food, go to your freezer.

Remember it is best to stick with one new food a week in case of allergies and for the purpose of identifying which food may be causing the problem. Once foods have been introduced, you can start mixing them.

If organic is what you want, you may want to shop at either a health food store or a natural food co-op for fruit and vegetables. Some grocery stores also sell organic foods.

FOODS TO AVOID

Certain foods are best avoided until your baby is one year old because they are either highly allergenic, contain too much fat or are difficult for a baby to digest.

Avoid:
- wheat: until 6 months
- corn: until 6-9 months
- citrus fruits and juices: until 1 year
- egg whites: until 1 year
- honey: until 1 year
- raw vegetables: until 1 year
- peanut butter: until 1 year
- pudding and fruit desserts: avoid at all ages since they contain excess sugars and empty calories.

BABY FOOD MANUFACTURERS' FREE OFFERS

■ GERBER PRODUCTS COMPANY
800-4-GERBER
The 24-hour toll-free number at Gerber will put you in touch with experts who can answer any questions you may have about feeding your baby. They will also send you a free packet with brochures about food safety, nutritional requirements, feeding your baby, and Gerber coupons.

■ BEECH-NUT NUTRITION CORPORATION
800-523-6633
Web site: www.beech-nut.com
Beech-Nut's representatives give advice on infant feeding and general baby care. Forty audio tapes are available over the phone on topics such as breastfeeding, colic, allergy, baby's nutritional needs, and discipline. The helpline is staffed Monday-Friday, 9:00 a.m. to 8:00 p.m., Eastern Time.

■ EARTH'S BEST BABY FOOD
800-442-4221
Web site: www.earthsbest.com
All Earth's Best baby foods are certified organically grown without synthetic pesticides. You can call to enroll in their Family Program, which includes three newsletters with information about infant feeding, Earth's Best products and coupons. It will take six weeks to receive your first newsletter, so plan to enroll before your child starts solids.

CHILD SAFETY

Accidents continue to be the leading cause of death among American children ages 1-5; however, up to 90% of accidents are adult-preventable. As a parent, be aware of situations in which accidents are likely to happen. Get down on the floor and see the world from your child's point of view. This will open your eyes to the potential disasters waiting to happen.

- Teach safety at an early age.
- Check every room of the house and eliminate hazards.
- Be aware of the increasing abilities of your child.
- Never leave a child in a home alone.
- Be prepared in the event an accident does occur.
- Learn infant CPR and first aid!

Children get into everything. From the moment they begin to scoot across the floor, everything within reach is fair game. Take time to review your environment and begin child-proofing before you bring your baby home from the hospital.

Auto safety: Use an approved, properly installed infant carrier or child's seat from birth to four years, or 40 pounds, and booster seat or seat belt thereafter. Auto deaths account for the largest group of fatal injuries among American children. The possibility of death or injury is reduced 70% when a child is in a safety seat. Never place an infant in a car seat or carrier on a counter or table top.

Changing tables: Never leave a baby unattended on a changing table. The day you turn your back will be the day your baby rolls over for the first time.

Choking: Avoid hard candy, hot dogs, grapes, nuts, popcorn, chips, and other small food items that your child could choke on. Learn CPR and know what steps you should take if your child chokes.

Cleaning supplies: Keep all cleaning supplies in a high, locked cupboard.

Cribs, strollers and walkers: Check current safety standards. Make sure equipment is sturdy and properly assembled. The American Academy of Pediatrics recommends foregoing the use of walkers because of the number of injuries they cause. Never use an infant carrier as a car seat. Do not place a crib near

Children get into everything. From the moment they begin to scoot across the floor, everything within reach is fair game.

Child Safety

draperies or blinds where a child could become entangled and strangle on the cords. Don't use pillows, and make sure the mattress fits snugly in the crib.

Cupboards: Put safety latches on all cupboards that contain items children should not get into, especially in the kitchen and the bathroom. Anything that could be considered a poison (Ask yourself: would I want to put this in my mouth? If not, treat it as poisonous.) must be in a high, locked cabinet.

Electrical outlets: Keep them all covered...even ones that are up high; children are great climbers. Consider using self-closing outlet covers that cover outlet holes automatically upon removal of appliance prongs.

Gates: All gates should be permanently mounted into wood or a wood stud. If you have plaster walls find the stud and mount a board to the wall and then mount the gate.

Hanging cords: Wrap up all cords from telephones, answering machines, lamps and appliances out of reach to avoid strangulation. Be sure any cords from draperies or blinds are tied up and out of reach.

Lead: If your home was built before 1978, it's quite possible that your walls are coated in lead paint, which can cause a wide range of problems in children. Contact the National Lead Information Center, 800-LEAD-FYI (532-3394), for a lead information packet. Old lead and chrome-plated water pipes in the home can cause lead poisoning in children. Call the Environmental Protection Agency's Water Safety Line at 800-426-4791 for more information. Non-glossy vinyl miniblinds contain lead which creates lead dust on the blinds. The Consumer Product Safety Commission advises replacement with blinds labeled "made without lead."

Medications: Keep all medications in a locked tool box or fishing tackle box and place the box out of reach of the child. Even vitamins can be deadly; the number one cause of poisoning deaths in young children is iron overdose. Just a few pills can cause deadly results.

POTENTIALLY DANGEROUS HOUSEHOLD SUBSTANCES

- alcohol, rubbing and drinking
- ammonia
- bleach
- detergent
- floor wax
- furniture wax
- gasoline
- lighter fluid
- lye
- medicines
- mouthwash
- oven cleaners
- paint thinners
- pesticides
- toilet cleaner
- turpentine

Contact your state's Poison Center for answers to your questions regarding these and other dangerous substances. If you have non-emergency questions about household chemical products, you may call the Chemical Manufacturers Association's Chemical Referral Center at 800-262-8200 weekdays 9:00 a.m.-6:00 p.m. EST.

Plants: Some plants are safe and some are toxic. Know the difference. You can ask your pediatrician for a list of poisonous plants.

Poisons: Always keep a bottle of syrup of ipecac on hand. It is available without a prescription and should be used to induce vomiting upon the advice of your area's Poison Center. Find the number and keep it near your telephone.

Pools: Pools should be fenced all the way around, and the doors leading to the pool should be locked. Never leave a baby or young child by the pool unattended.

Purses or pocketbooks: Always store up high since many contain medications, mace, pepper spray or weapons, and have straps that could cause a choking hazard.

Sleepwear: Since January 1997, infant and children's sleepwear is no longer required to be made of flame-resistant material. Now "longjohns" and rompers made of cotton can be labeled for sleepwear if tight fitting. If you buy cotton sleepwear, make sure the garment fits snugly, as that is the key to fire resistance.

Stairs: Keep a gate at both the top and bottom. If the posts are more than four inches apart, consider plexiglass or safety netting.

Stoves: Use only the back two burners or adhere a child stove guard. If burner knobs are accessible to a child, remove them and only use when cooking. Any freestanding stove should be secured to the floor or wall. Call the stove manufacturer for appropriate hardware.

Strings: To prevent strangulation, never put a pacifier or other items on a string around a baby's neck. Maximum length for any strings, ties, belts, etc. is seven inches.

Toys: Any toy can be unsafe if it is misused or given at an inappropriate age level. Keep older children's toys away from infants.

Water: More than 200 children have drowned in five-gallon buckets of water since 1984. Keep children away from buckets of water and use toilet latches to avoid accidents. Never leave an infant or young child alone in the bathtub. Babies can drown in less than two inches of water! Your home's hot water heater should be set to 120 degrees or lower to prevent scalding.

Windows: To keep your child from falling out of an open window, prevent windows from opening more than four inches with a window lock out of the child's reach. Window screens are for bugs only; they are not strong enough to keep children from falling.

RESOURCES

■ AMERICAN ACADEMY OF PEDIATRICS
800-433-9016
P.O. Box 927
Elk Grove Village, IL 60009
The American Academy of Pediatrics offers safe baby tags ($4.95/set) which can be easily attached to a diaper bag or stroller. The cards include first aid guidelines for emergencies and have room for you to list your infant's health information. Several safety-oriented videos are available, including "Baby Alive," "Child Safety Outdoors" and "Infant and Toddler Emergency First Aid."

■ AMERICAN TRAUMA SOCIETY
800-556-7890
(301) 420-4189
8903 Presidential Pkwy., Ste. 512
Upper Marlboro, MD 20772-2656
The American Trauma Society is an injury prevention advocate. The society provides posters, brochures and other materials showing common injuries, their prevention and treatment. It will also refer you to other resources, if necessary. It has materials suitable for schools, homes and public service organizations.

■ CHILD HEALTH ALERT
(617) 239-1762
P.O. Box 610228
Newton Highlands, MA 02161
Child Health Alert is a six-page newsletter containing summaries and evaluations of late-breaking reports from medical journals, meetings, and public health press releases. Topics covered include medications, product recalls, infections and other illnesses, environmental issues, immunizations, nutrition and parenting concerns. To maintain its independence, there are no advertisements. A one-year subscription (10 issues) costs $29; you can request a free sample issue.

■ CONSUMER PRODUCT SAFETY COMMISSION (CPSC)
800-638-CPSC
Washington, DC 20207
Web site: www.cpsc.gov.
This government commission reviews product safety. They offer free brochures such as "The Baby Safety Checklist" and "The Safe Nursery." All are available by sending a postcard with your name and address (call first to find out the names and numbers of publications you'd like to receive). Many are available over the Internet. This is the agency to report unsafe children's products, receive recent product recalls and general product safety information. To check on recalls and seasonal safety information, check their web site. CPSC regulates most mainstream products except for car seats.

■ THE DANNY FOUNDATION
800-83-DANNY
P.O. Box 680
Alamo, CA 94507
Web site: www.dannyfoundation.org
E-mail: dannycrib@earthlink.net
The Danny Foundation exists to educate the public about crib dangers. Call or write for your free brochure, "Is Your Crib Safe?" which discusses proper mattress fit, acceptable space between crib slats and appropriate corner post heights.

■ DEPARTMENT OF TRANSPORTATION AUTO SAFETY HOTLINE
800-424-9393
Web site: www.nhtsa.dot.gov
This federal government hotline is staffed by members who can tell you whether your safety seat has been recalled. Part of the National Highway Traffic Safety Administration, they can provide registration forms if you never registered with the manufacturer to be alerted of any future recalls. When you call, have the manufacturer name, model number and the date the seat was made.

■ JUVENILE PRODUCTS MANUFACTURERS ASSOCIATION (JPMA)
(609) 231-8500
236 Route 38-West, Ste. 100
Moorestown, NJ 08057
Web site: www.jpma.org
The Juvenile Products Manufacturers Association is a national trade association comprised of manufacturers of baby products. The JPMA logo appears on products which have been lab tested for safety. For information regarding JPMA, safety standards and a list of JPMA's Directory of Certified Products, send a self-addressed stamped business-size envelope to the address above.

■ NATIONAL LEAD INFORMATION CENTER
800-LEAD-FYI
Lead is an insidious poison that can be found in older homes' paint, water pipes, even miniblinds! Call the Lead Information Center to receive a free information packet about lead and how to go about minimizing your family's risk of exposure.

■ MIDAS MUFFLER SHOPS PROJECT SAFE BABY
800-868-0088
P.O. Box 92292
Libertyville, IL 60092
Under the "Project Safe Baby" program, Midas sponsors community education programs on car seat safety. When you purchase a car seat from Midas for $42, you are eligible to return it for $42 in services. Check with your local Midas dealer about the car seat program. Call Project Safe Baby for a free brochure or video ($2.50) entitled "Tips for Safer Travel with Children."

■ SAFETYBELTSAFE U.S.A.
800-745-SAFE
P.O. Box 553
Altadena, CA 91003
This nonprofit group provides information on safe car seat installation and use. A representative will call to answer your questions about car seats if you leave your name, phone number, city and state. Safetybeltsafe can also answer questions about an individual seat.

■ WINDOW COVERING SAFETY COUNCIL
800-506-4636
Long window-blind cords can be a strangulation hazard in the home. To prevent this, furniture should be moved away from windows, cords shortened or cut, and drapery cords anchored to the floor. This safety council is making available, at no charge, retrofit tassels or tie-downs to make existing cords safe. You can find them at participating retailers; more information can be obtained through the 800 number.

SPECIAL CONCERN RESOURCES

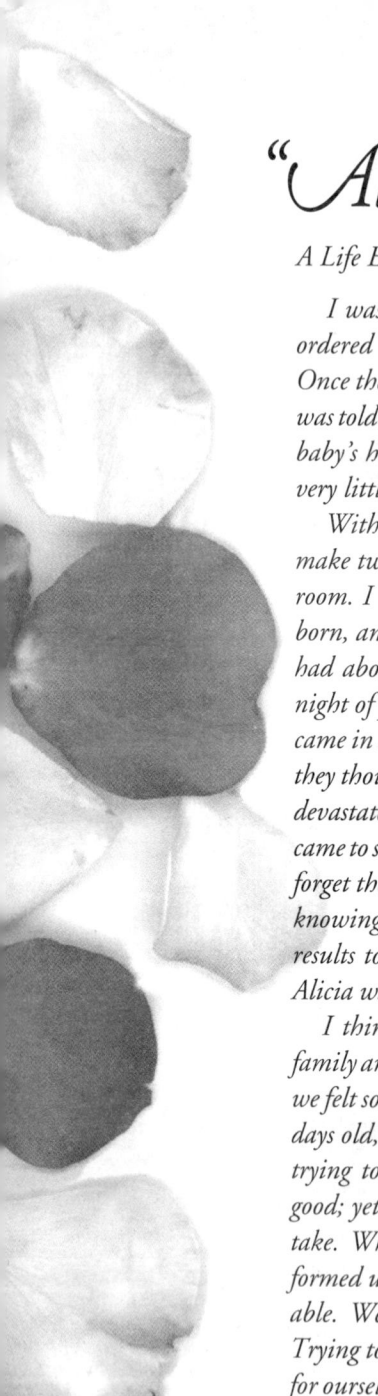

"Alicia"

A Life Experience by Carrie Camacho

I was ten days past my due date when my gynecologist ordered a non-stress test to make sure everything was okay. Once the test was completed, I had an ultrasound and then was told that an emergency C-section was needed because the baby's heartbeat was showing signs of stress and there was very little amniotic fluid left.

Within 30 minutes I was prepped for surgery, allowed to make two phone calls and then wheeled into the operating room. I was frightened, but also excited. Once Alicia was born, and seeing she had all her fingers and toes, the fears I had about the non-stress test were eased. After a difficult night of pain, nausea and very little sleep, the pediatrician came in and told me they were running genetic tests because they thought our new daughter had Down syndrome. I was devastated! I waited until that evening when my husband came to see us to tell him what the doctors suspected. I'll never forget the look on his face. We just stared at each other, not knowing what to do or say. We decided to wait for the test results to see if there was anything to worry about. When Alicia was four days old, the test results came back positive.

I think the most difficult part was having to tell our family and friends. We didn't want people to feel sorry for us; we felt sorry enough for ourselves. Then, when she was seven days old, we found that Alicia had a heart murmur. I was trying to be positive in thinking that Alicia was looking good; yet I didn't know how much more bad news I could take. When Alicia was ten days old, the cardiologist informed us that she had three heart defects that were repairable. We just cried! Such tragic news in ten short days. Trying to be there for each other when we were barely there for ourselves was so difficult, not knowing what to do or say.

For the next six months, Alicia went to the cardiologist once a week, then gradually every two weeks, then every three weeks. It was such a struggle for her to put on weight. Her *heart was working three to four times harder than it should, so her body was really burning off the calories. I attended a monthly support group for parents of children with heart defects. They helped me to understand that I wasn't the only one with an ill child. There were others who had much worse conditions than Alicia.*

At six months and one day, Alicia had open heart surgery. Nobody in either of our families had ever had any operation so critical. Family members rallied to our support and donated blood for Alicia. Her surgery went well with the exception that we were told she might have to wear a pacemaker. Seven days after surgery, Alicia was released from the hospital the day before Thanksgiving. Needless to say, Thanksgiving is a special time of year for us.

Alicia has steadily improved over the past two years. She has quite a personality. Alicia and I are learning sign language so we can better understand each other. Lacey, her younger sister, is a big help and an excellent role model for Alicia. Alicia is also Daddy's girl. She seems to melt everyone's heart.

I have received help from the community that I can't imagine being without. It was difficult having a handicapped child, especially our first. Professionals in the community helped us to help Alicia. They showed us methods we could use when playing with her. It's really neat to see her learn something from us through playing.

As I look back over the last two and a half years, the negatives have turned into positives. We have all learned so much and become better and stronger people. The struggle to learn, and to help Alicia, has enriched our lives. Everything she conquers also becomes a victory for us. Normal children will eventually learn to do things. Alicia has to be taught over and over until all of a sudden she catches on, and it is such a natural high. We tell everyone about her newest victory.

Once you work through the anger, denial, shock, depression and accept the fact you have a handicapped child, you can start healing yourself. That little bundle will open your eyes and your heart to a whole new way of life and an appreciation for the little things in life. ❧

CHILDREN WITH SPECIAL NEEDS

By Janet M. Hier

Soft lights, romantic music, maybe a nice bottle of wine...and *voila*! Forty weeks later a squalling little child is presented to the world. Obviously not every moonlit tryst creates another human being. All sorts of microscopic errors can occur between the candlelight and the cradle. Some fertilized eggs fail to implant in the uterus, while others have defects that cause them to be shed in the menstrual flow even before the woman may know she is pregnant. In fact, some statistics have shown that the awe-inspiring process that leads from conception to birth is so fraught with peril that as few as 25% of all successful conceptions actually end with the birth of an infant.

Although these numbers may make it seem as though the chances for ever having a baby are pretty overwhelming, a glance at the birth rate proves this simply isn't so. The vast majority of infants are born after having "beaten the odds" and come into this world in a healthy state. Unfortunately, though, not all are born this way. The number of newborns with some sort of congenital abnormality readily detected at birth has been estimated at 3% of the population, with another 3% being diagnosed within the first year of life.

According to statistics from the American Medical Association Encyclopedia of Medicine, the 12 most common birth defects in descending order are:

- **Heart Defects:** Range from minor heart murmurs to severe heart valve errors requiring immediate surgical repair.
- **Mental Retardation:** Includes cerebral palsy, a disorder that can be caused by developmental defects in the brain or trauma at birth. It also includes the effects of Fetal Alcohol Syndrome (FAS), which has been recognized as the most common cause of mental retardation in the United States. At first FAS was thought only to affect the babies of severely alcoholic mothers, but recent research has shown that even relatively small amounts of alcohol can cause birth defects.

Statistics seem pretty irrelevant when the child in question happens to be yours.

- **Pyloric Stenosis:** A narrowing of the muscle at the bottom of the stomach that causes vomiting and problems with eating. Surgical correction is necessary and curative. This condition is much more common in boys than girls.
- **Anencephaly:** The brain fails to fully develop. Often detected during prenatal testing, anencephalic babies carried to term die soon after delivery.
- **Spina Bifida:** The backbone does not fully fuse around the spinal cord. How severely a child will be affected depends upon the size of the opening and its location. Research shows a decrease in occurrence of spina bifida when the mother takes folic acid before and during pregnancy.
- **Down syndrome:** A chromosomal defect that causes a characteristic appearance, heart problems and often some degree of mental retardation.
- **Cleft palate and cleft lip:** Immediate surgery and intervention help these children to breathe and suck properly. Later operations minimize disfigurement.
- **Clubfoot:** One or both feet are turned in an abnormal direction. Clubfoot is often corrected with special braces and shoes while little bones are still soft. Sometimes babies' feet turn because of their position in the uterus before they are born. This is not true clubfoot and may require no special treatment.
- **Hypospadias:** A malformation that causes urine to flow from a displaced opening along the penis.
- **Congenital dislocation of the hip:** This malformation is possibly due to several genetic factors.
- **Congenital deafness:** Some children are now being fitted with electrical devices implanted into the inner ear that enable them to perceive sounds.
- **Cystic Fibrosis:** A disorder in which the lungs fill with sticky mucus; other severe health problems occur. Some genetic markers for CF have recently been found, although there is no cure as yet.

Statistics seem pretty irrelevant when the child in question happens to be yours. Although some prenatal tests can detect a few abnormalities in utero, and surgical intervention has been successful at reversing certain problems even before birth, most parents have no warning their child will not be born "perfect."

Adjusting to this situation will take family members through a series of stages similar to those of the grieving process. Mothers, fathers, grandparents, siblings and even extended family members will all experience the seven stages of reaction at different times and in different ways. These stages do not necessarily occur in order, but they can generally be considered as:

- **Shock:** A period of helplessness and numbness. It can be especially difficult to concentrate through this stage. Some parents have referred to it as "running on autopilot." Write down everything you need to remember, from questions to ask the neurologist to a reminder to feed the dog every day. Using a small hand-held tape recorder at the

physician's office will give you something to refer to when it all seems to blur.
- **Denial:** Disbelief; a sensation that it is all a bad dream, rationalizing a child's developmental patterns to "he'll (crawl, walk, roll over) when he's ready!"
- **Sadness:** This stage can overwhelm parents at awkward times, causing embarrassment or even paralyzing grief. It is of the utmost importance that you find non-judgmental help for this stage, either through a support group for parents of children with similar problems, or by seeking professional counseling.
- **Anger:** Hair-triggering nerves and a general feeling of rage. Many people find this stage affects their relationships with coworkers, family members and spouses. Very few marriages are truly seamless unions, and this stage can amplify the tiniest flaws into tremendous conflicts. Seek help and support if the crisis negatively affects your marriage.
- **Anxiety:** Nervousness, sleeplessness, lack of appetite. The sense of isolation at this time is very strong. It may be difficult for outsiders to understand why you haven't "gotten over it." Hard as it may be to comprehend, it is vital for parents to take a break from the strain of coping with their child's needs. Other siblings also need a chance to "get away" without feeling guilty.
- **Bargaining:** A faith in God may be restored at this point, although it may not resemble what it was prior to the birth of a special child. Many parents will find themselves trying any and all treatments they can find at this time, from the most conventional and aggressive to very non-traditional, alternative sources.
- **Acceptance:** The ability to pull all the above together and still cope with your life. There is no set time as to how long these stages can take to work through, and not everyone feels them in the same order. Additionally, unexpected events such as emergency surgery or milestones like entry into kindergarten can cause emotional relapse.

RESOURCES

■ **AMERICAN HEART ASSOCIATION**
(214) 373-6300
7272 Greenville Ave.
Dallas, TX 75231
Web site: www.amhrt.org
Founded in 1924, the American Heart Association promotes education, supports research into heart disease, and trains CPR instructors. For parents of children with congenital heart defects, the association provides information on feeding, dental care and general information about the condition. Information about other heart conditions such as rheumatic fever and heart murmurs is available.

■ AMERICAN LUNG ASSOCIATION
(212) 315-8700
1740 Broadway
New York, NY 10019
Many local chapters of the American Lung Association offer support for parents of children with pediatric asthma, including resource material and referral to support groups.

■ AMERICAN SOCIETY FOR DEAF CHILDREN (ASDC)
800-942-ASDC (2732)
(916) 482-0121
2848 Arden Way, Ste. 210
Sacramento, CA 95825
A nonprofit parent-helping-parent organization, ASDC provides support, encouragement and information to families of children who are deaf or hard of hearing. For a yearly $30 membership, families receive a quarterly publication with national news of interest to the deaf community, family profiles and children's activities. A convention is held every other year. The national office provides information on signing, language acquisition, special equipment, and advocacy issues.

■ AUTISM SOCIETY OF AMERICA
800-328-8476
7910 Woodmont Ave. #650
Bethesda, MD 20814
Web site: www.autism-society.org/
For over 30 years, the Autism Society of America has supported parents whose children have autism. Information and referral services are provided by phone. The society operates local support groups, and members receive the bimonthly "Advocate" newsletter. If you have questions, the society's "What Is Autism?" brochure, or one or more of the 21 packages of information on various autism-related topics, are sure to help you find answers.

■ BEACH CENTER ON FAMILIES AND DISABILITY
(913) 864-7600
3111 Haworth, University of Kansas
Lawrence, KS 66045
E-mail: Beach@dole.lsi.ukans.edu
The Beach Center supports families with special needs through research, training manuals, and a variety of reading materials. Their publications catalog includes booklets such as "Research Brief: Fathers, Their Children, and Disability," "Start Your Own Parent to Parent Program," and "Learn About the Laws That Impact Your Family's Life" for 50 cents each.

■ CLEFT PALATE FOUNDATION
800-24-CLEFT (242-5338)
1829 E. Franklin St., Ste. 1022
Chapel Hill, NC 27514
Web site: www.cleft.com
One of every 700 newborns has some form of cleft lip or palate. The Cleft Palate Foundation distributes pamphlets on the genetics of cleft lips and palates, feeding an infant with a cleft, and a basic introduction to cleft lip and cleft palate, and will send a bibliography of other books and pamphlets available. The foundation makes referrals to medical specialists and parent support groups.

The foundation is affiliated with AboutFace, a support and information organization. Networking with pen pals and by telephone, videotapes, newsletters and an annual conference are part of the support for families AboutFace offers. To contact AboutFace, call 800-225-FACE (3223) or e-mail: abtface@aol.com.

■ CYSTIC FIBROSIS FOUNDATION
800-FIGHT CF
6931 Arlington Rd., Rm. 200
Bethesda, MD 20814
Web site: www.cfs.org
Parent support, information and referrals to local centers and chapters are made by the Cystic Fibrosis Foundation. Brochures and other educational materials are mailed free of charge.

■ EASTER SEALS SOCIETY
(202) 387-4434
2800 13th St., N.W.
Washington, DC 20009
Through its local chapters, the Easter Seals Society offers a variety of programs for children with physical and mental disabilities. Some chapters offer therapeutic pools, respite programs, summer camps, and all offer referrals and written information on a variety of disabilities.

■ EXCEPTIONAL PARENT MAGAZINE
800-372-7368
555 Kinderkanack Rd.
Oradell, NJ 07649
Exceptional Parent is a monthly magazine devoted to parenting children and young adults with disabilities. Good articles on a variety of disabilities and how to deal with them are targeted to parents, professionals and educators. A resource guide is included in the magazine's January issue. Annual subscriptions are $32.

■ JUVENILE DIABETES FOUNDATION
800-223-1138
120 Wall St.
New York, NY 10005
Resources, brochures, and referrals for information and training are available through the national Juvenile Diabetes Foundation. The primary goal of this foundation is to raise funds for juvenile diabetes research. Informational pamphlets are available, as is the foundation's newsletter, "Countdown."

■ LEUKEMIA SOCIETY OF AMERICA, INC.
800-955-4572
600 3rd Ave., 4th Fl.
New York, NY 10016
This society has publications on most of the childhood leukemias. Financial assistance is also available to patients.

■ MARCH OF DIMES
888-MODIMES (663-4637)
TTY: (914) 997-4764
1275 Mamaroneck Ave.
White Plains, NY 10605
Web site: www.modimes.org
E-mail: Resourcecenter@modimes.org
March of Dimes' Resource Center offers free publications, brochures, and public health information sheets on general pregnancy issues and specific birth defects. The nonprofit organization, with 100-plus local chapters nationwide, can give referrals and information on pre-pregnancy, pregnancy, birth defects, genetics and drug and chemical exposure during pregnancy.

■ MEDIC ALERT
800-432-5378
2323 Colorado Ave.
Turlock, CA 95382
The MedicAlert emblem immediately identifies the wearer as needing special medical treatment during an emergency. A bracelet or necklace identifies the life-threatening allergy, critical medical condition, or impairment of 2.6 million Americans. The adjustable 6" stainless steel bracelet is suggested for children. For a $35 initial membership fee, and $15 each year thereafter, subscribers receive a bracelet with identifying information and MedicAlert's emergency response phone number.

■ MUMS NATIONAL PARENT-TO-PARENT NETWORK
(414) 336-5333
150 Custer Ct.
Green Bay, WI 54301
E-mail: MUMS@netnet.net
When a child is born with a medical condition or a child is diagnosed with a disorder, the family may have no one to turn to for support and sharing. MUMS matches families whose children have the same or similar conditions so they can provide mutual support, information, and education. Referrals are given, at your request, to local and national support groups, phone support, or matching with another family for phone and written contact. With one of the largest databases in the world (28 countries) of 8,600 families covering over 1,600 disorders, MUMS can match even the rarest conditions in many cases. A nonprofit organization, MUMS offers newsletter subscriptions for $10, and will send information about their organization at no charge (but donations are appreciated). If your child has a rare disorder or special need, it is well worth your while to contact MUMS.

■ MUSCULAR DYSTROPHY ASSOCIATION
800-572-1717
3300 E. Sunrise Dr.
Tucson, AZ 85718
Web site: www.mdusa.org
Clinics, physical and therapy evaluation and support groups are offered through local chapters of the Muscular Dystrophy Association. A wide variety of publications and videotapes are available.

■ NATIONAL ASSOCIATION FOR PARENTS OF THE VISUALLY IMPAIRED, INC. (NAPVI)
800-562-6265
P.O. Box 317
Watertown, MA 02272
NAPVI helps parents find information and resources for their blind and visually impaired children. The $20 yearly membership fee includes a quarterly newsletter, access to a national parent-to-parent network, information on legislation and conferences. NAPVI offers books, including *Children With Visual Impairments: A Parents Guide* at discounted prices to members.

■ **NATIONAL INFORMATION CENTER FOR CHILDREN AND YOUTH WITH DISABILITIES (NICHCY)**
800-695-0285
P.O. Box 1492
Washington, DC 20013
E-mail: nichcy@aed.org
Web site: www.aed.org/nichcy
NICHCY is a clearinghouse that provides information on disabilities and disability-related issues. Brochures such as "Parenting a Child With Special Needs: A Guide to Readings and Resources," "A Parent's Guide: Doctors, Disabilities, and the Family" and "Children With Disabilities: Understanding Sibling Issues" are available free or at nominal cost. In addition, NICHCY personally responds to disability questions, makes referrals to other organizations and agencies, and offers technical assistance to parent groups. NICHCY is a project of the Academy for Educational Development.

■ **NATIONAL INSTITUTE OF CHILD HEALTH AND HUMAN DEVELOPMENT (NICHD)**
(301) 496-5133
31 Center Dr.
Building 31, Rm. 2A32
Bethesda, MD 20892
Web site: www.nih.gov/nichd/
The Public Information and Communications Branch of the NICHD distributes research reports, fact sheets, and publications to health care providers and the general public on topics related to disease prevention in maternal and child health, congenital malformations, and vasectomy safety.

■ **NATIONAL ORGANIZATION FOR RARE DISORDERS (NORD)**
800-999-6673
P.O. Box 8923
New Fairfield, CT 06812
Web site: www.nord-rdb.com/~orphan
E-mail: orphan@nord-rdb.com
This is a clearinghouse for information on up to 5,000 rare disorders. NORD will send you information and articles and recommend other resources and networking possibilities. You may request articles for free; these contain files and medical literature. Reports are more in-depth, and include pertinent symptoms, causes, epidemiology, therapies, drugs, references and resources, all reviewed by a medical advisory board. The first report is free; there is a $5 fee for additional reports.

■ **NATIONAL ORGANIZATION OF PARENTS OF BLIND CHILDREN (NOPBC)**
(410) 659-9314
1800 Johnson St.
Baltimore, MD 21230
Web site: www.nfb.org
E-mail: nfb@acess.digex.net
Believing that, with proper training and opportunity, blindness can be reduced to a physical nuisance, NOPBC works to provide information and support to parents of blind children. An $8 annual membership entitles parents to *Future Reflections* magazine, informative literature, local resources, and a link to the National Federation of the Blind.

■ PATHWAYS AWARENESS FOUNDATION
800-955-2445
3633 West Lake Ave.
Glenview, IL 60025
Web site: www.pathwaysawareness.org
The goal of the Pathways Awareness Foundation is to assist families with concerns about their children's movement abilities. The foundation offers parents a free brochure regarding developmental milestones and early warning signs of physical, occupational and speech delays. If you have any questions about your baby's muscle control abilities, this brochure is an excellent first step towards answering your concerns. You can order other brochures and a video version of "Is My Baby Okay?" Pathways provides information and services for children with movement difficulties or physical challenges, with a strong commitment to early detection and intervention.

■ SHRINERS HOSPITAL
800-237-5055
International Shrine Headquarters
2900 Rocky Point Dr.
Tampa, FL 33607
Shriners Hospitals treat children ages 0 to 18 for orthopedic problems, burns, or plastic surgery (such as for cleft palate) in 19 orthopedic hospitals and burn institutes in the U.S., Mexico and Canada. A newly opened Sacramento, California, hospital treats both burn and orthopedic patients. Application forms, available by calling their national number, are reviewed for medical and financial eligibility. Since 1922, more than half a million children have been helped, completely free of charge, through the Shriners Hospitals.

■ SOCIAL SECURITY INCOME
800-772-1213
If your baby has a disability that is expected to last more than one year, you may be eligible for SSI. Eligibility and financial assistance depend upon income. Staffers can refer you to a local office, where you can set up an appointment. SSI will also make referrals to other assistance groups.

■ UNITED CEREBRAL PALSY ASSOCIATION
800-USA-5-UCP
1660 L St., Ste. 700
Washington, DC 20036
E-mail: ucpinfo@aol.com
Local branches of the United Cerebral Palsy Association offer families support, sibling workshops, activities, newsletters, information on funding and referrals, and respite care. The national group will get you in touch with one of the nation's 200-plus local affiliates, and provide cerebral palsy fact sheets and a publications catalog.

■ WOODBINE HOUSE PUBLISHERS
800-843-7323
6510 Bells Mill Rd.
Bethesda, MD 20817
Publisher Irv Shapell, who has a child with Down syndrome, offers more than 40 titles designed for parents of children with special needs. Considered a leader in disabilities publishing, Woodbine House aims to provide parents with a wide array of information. Book topics cover mental retardation, cerebral palsy, autism, deafness, epilepsy, Down syndrome, Tourette's and resource handbooks for parents of special needs kids.

"Yes, I'm Pregnant"

A Life Experience by Karen Bauman

All my life I have been perfectly healthy, or so I thought. At 35, I learned not everything in my body was in order.

My husband Tom and I had been trying for some time to have a baby, with no success. After two years of hoping and failing, I made an appointment with a specialist. More time passed, with tests and interminable waits, until the laparoscopy showed my tubes were badly scarred from an illness I hadn't even known I had. Our only hope to conceive was through in-vitro fertilization (IVF).

We interviewed three IVF clinics before deciding to use a well-known fertility center with a high success rate. Our chance of success was estimated to be 30% per try (cycle). We chose the "Option Three" plan, for three cycles (embryo implantations) to be performed within one year. Sometime during the coming year I would either conceive or be childless for life.

My first cycle (30 days) started with no exercise, no caffeine and no sex. Tom gave me daily intramuscular injections of fertility drugs, which were followed by two vaginal sonograms which monitored my egg follicle maturity and uterine lining. Three blood tests indicated my estradiol (hormone) level. According to the textbooks, I was a model case. Six egg follicles were surgically retrieved under general anesthesia. Eggs and sperm were then combined (in vitro) for two days. Four picture-perfect embryos were gently transferred vaginally into my uterus. I spent seven days in bed, waiting for the embryos to attach to my uterine lining.

I was filled with hope and fear. I pleaded, begged and bargained with God for a baby. Ten days after embryo transfer a blood draw indicates pregnancy. The results: no baby. But my embryos, estradiol levels, uterine lining, were all perfect. No complications. I was confused, angry and downright depressed. I felt I had lost control over my life. It seemed like a big broken promise. It just wasn't fair.

My driving sense of purpose escalated. I became single-minded, putting all my energy into making the dream of a baby a reality. I read every birthing, parenting and IVF book published. I was determined to do whatever it took. I tried again.

The staff at the fertility clinic was positive and supportive from start to finish. One of the three nurses always returned my call within the hour. They were there for me 100%.

Cycle Two—I knew what to expect from the physical procedures from the first cycle, the shots and surgery. The biggest challenge was the total loss of control. There was absolutely nothing I could do to ensure pregnancy. The wait was painfully exhausting.

The second cycle was another perfect cycle with quality embryos, uterine lining, estradiol level. Again seven days of bed rest was followed by a tenth-day blood draw—yes! I'm pregnant! Reproductive technology has blessed us with un-fathomable joy! We won! Sheer bliss!

I carried pictures of my six-week-old embryo and showed them to everyone, recounting my miracle to anyone who would listen. I welcomed with delight sore breasts and fatigue. I started buying maternity and baby clothing.

In my seventh week, I suddenly doubled over with severe cramps. Tom immediately rushed me to the hospital's emergency room. My IVF doctor diagnosed an ectopic pregnancy in my fallopian tube. He immediately removed both tubes. I recovered at home...waiting for seven days for a sonogram to see if the baby in my uterus was still alive. I had a one in 40,000 chance. Yes! Alive! This baby miraculously survived the ectopic pregnancy. The baby was the correct gestational size for eight weeks, with a normal heart beat. Two weeks later my IVF doctor released me to an obstetrician.

Three weeks later I woke up with an intuitive sickening feeling that something was seriously wrong. A sonogram that morning showed no heartbeat. There was no longer a miracle baby. I was in shock; I cried for days. This was the most horrible experience of my life, a heart-wrenching ordeal. I felt an unbearable loss, and was overwhelmed by my grief. The worst part was how fast everything was erased. After imagining the baby, talking with new moms, planning the years ahead, my life suddenly collapsed in one second. My place in the world, my identity, was no longer the same.

My obstetrician explained it was just nature taking care of an abnormality. One in four women miscarry and it was "no big deal." Well, it was a very big deal to me! I searched out, and had every test done, to try to determine why I miscarried. Still no explanation. I'll never know why. It's an unsettling feeling.

Sometimes it seemed almost too painful to risk letting myself hope for a new pregnancy, and to risk being crushed again. But gradually the courage to try again grew. I had more hope than fear.

I joined a women's IVF group for eight weeks. That helped me immensely. Finally I found I wasn't alone. It was comforting talking with women who were having the same physical and emotional challenges. We gave each other hope and strength and confirmed the insanity of it all.

My friends were as supportive as they could be. They liked the happy, enthusiastic, positive Karen. (I prefer her also.) But with so many disappointments, coupled with massive amounts of hormones raging through my body, my energy was spent working overtime (IVF is very expensive).

Cycle Three—My last chance. The pressure was intense. I was hopeful, because I did get pregnant before. I tried to be realistic, understanding that getting pregnant is just the beginning of a very long process. There are many hurdles, and anything can happen.

Once again perfect embryos, estradiol, lining, bedrest, ten-day wait for a blood draw, then a five-week wait to see the heart beating. Pregnant! Fraternal twins! Two separate placentas, two beating hearts.

We are beaming with happiness. I am going to be a mother. We are going to be a family. I praise medicine. As my story goes to print, I am now one week to delivery ...waiting...and enjoying every minute.

Editor's Note: *Karen and Tom delivered two healthy boys shortly after this essay was written.*

INFERTILITY

By Phillip Patton, M.D.

Raising a family is an expectation for most married couples. Unfortunately, 10% to 15% of all couples fail to conceive after one year and need to seek treatment from infertility specialists.

In the last decade the demand for infertility services has escalated tremendously, and the demand is expected to increase as more women enter the work force and delay childbearing. Most couples are shocked to learn that only one in four couples conceive each month of attempting pregnancy. Ultimately, 80% of young women (18-34) will conceive within one year, which is reassuring. Unfortunately, the prospects for older women are not as favorable. Less than 60% of women over 35 will conceive within the first year of attempting pregnancy. While only 4% of women in their early twenties suffer infertility problems, a staggering 30% of women over age 35 will have difficulties conceiving. A clear message emerges: women over 35 who want to have a baby cannot waste valuable time. Take charge, be assertive, and begin an aggressive program designed to start a family.

> *Most couples are shocked to learn that only one in four couples conceive each month of attempting pregnancy.*

WHAT CAN WE DO TO IMPROVE OUR CHANCES?

It is imperative that women under 35 seek an infertility evaluation after one year of attempting pregnancy. Women over 35 must be even more vigilant. A logical first step begins with a consultation with your gynecologist. A thorough infertility evaluation takes about an hour, reviewing your general health, risk factors for infertility, and physical objectives. First, you should leave the consultation with a clear understanding about the causes of your infertility. Second, you should have a game plan that outlines your future evaluation and treatment that fits you. Be sure that these simple, but critical, objectives are met before you leave your physician's office. It is wise to limit any treatment plan to a short interval because nearly 60% of couples conceive within the first three to four months of directed therapy. Longer treatment plans are often frustrating and unproductive. The best results occur when there is an organized and evolving treatment plan. Some couples may require the services of a reproductive endocrinologist who has additional specialized training in infertility.

Take charge of your emotional needs as well. Fighting infertility may be one of the most stressful events in your life. Support groups such as Resolve may be tremendously helpful in putting you back on track. At times, couples may feel the need for counseling. Ask your physician about therapists who have experience in dealing with infertility issues.

The basic infertility investigation can be concluded within one month of seeing your physician. Disorders of ovulation, fallopian tube or sperm abnormalities are factors that can be easily reviewed. Infertile couples often have multiple problems which must be identified quickly to obtain the best results.

DISORDERS OF OVULATION

Ovulation problems can often be identified during your initial consultation. Unusually short or long menstrual cycles or irregular and unpredictable cycles are hallmarks of an ovulation disorder. Subtle ovulation problems can be diagnosed using a variety of tests, including blood tests for progesterone and pelvic ultrasonography used to monitor aberrant follicle development.

Both oral and intramuscular drugs are used to treat ovulation disorders. Make sure you know how these drugs work, their potential side effects, and their success rates. Serious ovulation disorders may not respond to treatment. For women with poorly functioning or absent ovaries, ovum donation is becoming a popular and highly successful option. Donor eggs can be fertilized with a male partner's sperm and the resulting embryos are transferred into the recipient's uterus. Both known and anonymous donors can be used.

SPERM DISORDERS

Sperm problems are one of the most common disorders identified. Even small irregularities in sperm may be associated with subfertility, and a delay in the diagnosis of a male-related problem can cost you valuable time.

A variety of therapies exist for sperm disorders. One of the most popular techniques is intrauterine insemination (IUI), a relatively simple procedure where sperm, washed free of the ejaculate, are placed into the uterine cavity with the aid of small plastic tubing.

For couples with a severe male-related problem, intracytoplasmic sperm injection (ICSI) offers new hope. ICSI refers to the injection of a single sperm into an egg in conjunction with in vitro fertilization (IVF). The resulting embryos are then transferred into the uterus after three days of culture.

An alternate treatment for male related problems is donor sperm. Donor sperm can be purchased from a sperm bank, and nearly all samples now have been frozen and quarantined for a minimum of six months to reduce the risk of infection. Pregnancy rates using donor sperm are highly variable and the results depend on many factors.

ABNORMALITIES OF THE FALLOPIAN TUBE

Damage to the fallopian tube may prevent sperm from reaching the egg at the time of ovulation. Obvious damage to the fallopian tubes can be determined by a radiologic procedure known as a hysterosalpingogram (HSG). An HSG involves the injection of a clear media which can be seen by X-ray. In women with open fallopian tubes, the X-ray media passes from the uterine cavity into the fallopian tubes and then out into the abdominal cavity. More subtle forms of tubal disease require laparoscopy for diagnosis. This is an outpatient surgical procedure where an incision is made into the area of the belly button and a small telescope is passed into the abdominal cavity under general anesthesia. Many forms of tubal injury can now be treated through laparoscope, avoiding the more expensive and risky abdominal surgery.

In vitro fertilization involves removing eggs by passing a needle through the vaginal tissues. The eggs are then fertilized in the laboratory and transferred into the uterus two to three days later.

KEY INFERTILITY TESTS

Most cases of infertility do not require "high tech" treatment. In fact, using a simple, low tech approach, nearly 70% of infertility causes can be diagnosed and treated effectively. A review of a simple but productive strategy is presented as follows:

- **Basal body temperature (BBT) records.** The BBT record is a simple method to evaluate whether ovulation occurs. Basal temperatures are taken orally immediately after waking before arising, and recorded on a special chart that plots the temperature record against the day of the menstrual cycle. Ideally, the basal temperature will rise slightly after ovulation, due to progesterone production, and remain elevated until a few days before menses.

- **Hysterosalpingography (HSG) and saline infusion sonohysterogram (SIS).** The HSG is considered the gold standard in the diagnosis of tubal blockage or uterine abnormalities, but the test is somewhat invasive and costly. A less expensive test with emerging promise, SIS uses ultrasonography combined with saline infusion to evaluate the uterus and the fallopian tubes. One to two teaspoons of fluid is used to distend the uterus. Pelvic ultrasonography used at the time of saline

FERTILITY TREATMENTS ON THE HORIZON

The progress of infertility treatment in the last decade has been staggering. While once thought of as experimental, in vitro fertilization is now a widely practiced technique. In addition, most high-tech infertility centers now offer donor egg and sperm programs, male factor treatment with intracytoplasmic sperm injection (ICSI), and some forms of surrogacy. Selected sites can perform preimplantation genetic diagnosis that can be used to detect genetic abnormalities in embryos before embryo transfer. The future promises to be exciting. The development of protocols for in vitro maturation of immature eggs could radically reduce the cost of IVF. Human egg cryopreservation, now a reality, may see widespread use in women requiring cancer chemotherapy, and potentially in women who desire "egg banking" for future use.

injection can trace the path of fluid into the uterus and diagnose abnormalities.
- **Semen analysis.** A semen analysis should be performed early in the infertility investigation because 30%-40% of infertility is secondary to problems in sperm production or function.
- **Post-coital testing.** Occasionally cervical mucus obtained at the mid-cycle after intercourse may identify mucus problems. However, the timing of the test is critical. Ovulatory or sperm problems are also factors that may cause a poor mucus test.

A FINAL WORD

Winning against infertility requires dedication to an organized plan which meets both your medical and emotional needs, and uses your resources wisely. Also, consider your personal value system when deciding your treatment. Infertility care is often an evolving process where one form of treatment is replaced by another form. Remember that a proactive plan coordinated with your caregiver is the best method to achieve your goals.

Contributing author Phillip Patton, M.D., is a Board Certified Reproductive Endocrinologist and Obstetrician-Gynecologist in Portland, Oregon.

RESOURCES

■ INTERNATIONAL COUNCIL ON INFERTILITY INFORMATION DISSEMINATION (INCIID)
(703) 379-9178
P.O. Box 6836
Arlington, VA 22206
Web site: www.inciid.org
This nonprofit group educates the public as to the prevention and treatment of infertility and pregnancy loss. Their web site is a filled with comprehensive infertility information that covers cutting-edge technologies and treatments. INCIID Interactive provides a place for you to discuss your questions and concerns with others. On tap: a set of fertility drug fact sheets which explain fertility drug options in detail.

■ RESOLVE
(617) 623-0744
1310 Broadway
Somerville, MA 02144-1731
Resolve offers information and support for those touched by difficulties with infertility. Send a self-addressed stamped envelope to the national headquarters for an information packet, including referrals to the nearest local chapter. Local Resolve services include monthly support group meetings, information on fertility specialists, resources and help with adoption agencies.

COPING WITH GRIEF

Losing a baby can be the most painful and challenging event most parents will ever have to face. No parent can anticipate this type of loss and is usually unprepared for the psychological, social, and even physical turmoil that accompanies the death of a child.

A PARENT'S FIRST REACTION

Though everyone's course through bereavement is different and there is no particular "right" way to grieve, for most parents the period directly following the infant's death is the most distressing. Initial grief is typically marked by shock, a feeling of numbness or bewilderment, and difficulty in comprehending events surrounding the loss. This is followed by the profound and intense emotions associated with grief. In the beginning, parents may experience all or some of the following:

- Uncontrollable tearfulness, depression, or problems with work and concentration.
- Physical weakness, weight loss, loss of appetite, and difficulty breathing and talking.
- Problems getting to sleep and staying asleep. Parents may need to see their doctor regarding sleep medications. But a doctor may hesitate to prescribe medications to numb feelings, since those who deny and avoid all expressions of loss tend to fare considerably worse later.
- A constant, seemingly uncontrollable preoccupation with the child, accompanied by the tendency to withdraw from interest in the outside world. This can be a particularly difficult time for young children who don't have the capacity to understand their parents' withdrawal.
- Powerful guilt and self-reproach as they seek to come to terms with the death. At the same time, they may direct anger and rage at God, caregivers, and—most painfully—spouses and surviving children.
- Symptoms may become severe enough that parents doubt their sanity. They may imagine that they hear the cries or voice of their infant and even feel that they have caught a fleeting glimpse of him or her. These are not atypical manifestations of this type of loss and not a sign that the parent is losing his or her mind.

For most parents, feelings of depression and even despair will remain for varying lengths of time. This is normal.

As disturbing as these feelings are, the intensity of this initial period will pass and is followed by a transitional time of variable length marked by a generally less powerful sadness and attempts to cope with the loss.

MAKING PROGRESS

For most parents, feelings of depression and even despair will remain for varying lengths of time. This is normal. During this period, parents may feel isolated and frequently misunderstood. Previously supportive and caring friends and relatives may be uncomfortable talking about the infant, using his or her name, or reminiscing. There is a sense from them that it is now time to "get better and get on with life."

Parents should realize that mourning an infant can be lifelong in many ways and more acute feelings of depression may take a year or two to lessen significantly. Because of this, support groups can be useful for parents in giving them assurance that others know and have survived what they are going through.

Anniversaries such as birthdays, holidays and the date of death are powerful reminders of the lost infant. Parents will cope better when they discuss or plan for these events in some way rather than ignoring them.

SPOUSES GRIEVE IN DIFFERENT WAYS

Studies show that men and women grieve differently in our society. Men tend to be less expressive in their feelings of grief although they may feel them acutely. Women tend to be more open about the emotions they are experiencing and more easily find outlets to express them. Men also are more likely to concentrate on work as a way of getting through their feelings of loss. For instance, women may wish to talk about the loss and men may wish to completely avoid the subject. These and other individual differences can lead to considerable tension in relationships.

Generally, it is best not to be silent about these differences in coping. Couples who tolerate and accommodate them tend to manage their grief better.

SIBLING GRIEF

This can be a particularly difficult time for young children who don't have the capacity to understand their parents' mourning and possible withdrawal. Parents may wonder how to tell siblings about the death. The way a parent may approach this depends a great deal upon the parent's style and the age of the child. A reasonable rule of thumb, as in much of bereavement, is that excessive concealment is generally a poor approach. Parents should speak honestly in a language the child can understand.

RESOLVING THE LOSS

As time passes, both the vivid memories and the pain begin to fade. However, this dulling of memories can be frightening and sad for many since these memories are a way to keep alive connections with the infant. Nevertheless, this is just one way the mind has of healing itself over time.

Parents should not expect to be entirely without feelings of loss. It is not unusual for someone to return briefly to a support group after an extended period to talk about these feelings. Many parents who have been through the initial process of bereavement find it healing to help others through it.

COMPLICATED GRIEF

In rare instances grief is prolonged, and bereaved parents will find themselves unable to function as well as they might expect. They may continue to have very low self-esteem and significant physical symptoms of grief longer than the 12 months which can be expected. They may give up hope and have suicidal thoughts. Under these circumstances, professional help and medications for depression may be needed. A visit to a physician might help with this decision. Major depression can needlessly prolong suffering in those who are bereaved.

SUBSEQUENT CHILDREN

Though the next child is not—nor should ever be—a replacement for the lost infant, he or she can be a source of considerable hope and healing. However, parents who have lost an infant to SIDS generally raise a new infant with much apprehension, as the risk of SIDS for subsequent children is five to ten times greater than that of infants in the general population. Even so, the vast majority of subsequent children will not die of SIDS. Additionally, there are medical approaches that appear effective in reducing the SIDS risk in this group and provide some degree of control over the threat of another loss.

This article was provided by the American Sudden Infant Death Syndrome Institute from their brochure, "Coping With Infant Loss."

A MISCARRIAGE MEANS LOSING A BABY, TOO

By Troy Smith

Miscarriages are far more common than most people think. According to the American College of Obstetrics and Gynecology, 15%-20% of all pregnancies end in miscarriage. Yet each woman who is expecting a baby begins to plan and anticipate the birth of her child from the moment the pregnancy test comes back positive. Even a very early pregnancy loss can lead to feelings of grief and perhaps guilt.

The guidelines above for coping with the death of an infant hold true for dealing with loss from miscarriage. If it makes you feel better to talk about it with friends or relatives, do so. Your health care practitioner may be able to refer you to a local support group, or you can contact the MIDS Support Group, Pails of Hope, the Pregnancy and Infant Loss Center, or SHARE—national groups (resource listings follow) created to help couples through this difficult time. Most offer a newsletter, peer counseling, and brochures and other publications.

Most women who miscarry go on to carry subsequent babies to term. If you have any questions or concerns, don't hesitate to ask your practitioner.

"In Remembrance of Sara"

A Life Experience by Sherry Waldorf

I gave birth to a stillborn daughter, Sara Annette Waldorf, on a fall day two years ago. She is a beautiful, perfect angel who now lives in heaven and within our hearts forever. It is only after much grief and pain that I think of her in this way.

In the beginning, my husband and I allowed ourselves to feel any emotion that helped us to somewhat accept the death of our daughter. We experienced grief, sorrow, sadness, anger and unjustified guilt. My husband's emotions were much more under control than mine, because he wanted to stay strong for me. There were good days and bad days. Life was fragile and unpredictable.

Some people encouraged me to let my emotions out while others told me to get a hold of myself. Thankfully, I listened to those who cared enough to allow me to grieve in their presence. I chose for myself when it was time to move on.

I wrote in my journal daily. I had started to write when I found out I was pregnant with Sara. It had all of my feelings and anticipation about becoming a mother, my dreams about what our baby would look like and every detail of my doctor visits. It seemed only appropriate that I would finish the pregnancy story with my account of labor and delivery and how the ending was so different from what I had imagined. I had dreamed of the birth of my first baby even as a little girl. I wrote lots of poetry. My journal was a tribute to Sara.

Sometimes, I wrote letters to people who had hurt my feelings by things they had said. I never mailed these letters—they are still in my journal. It helped just to put my feelings down on paper.

My mother-in-law made me a beautiful shadowbox to display my keepsakes of Sara—her ashes, footprints, pictures and crib card. I realized that I had kept everything and the grandparents had nothing. After all, they had lost a grandchild.

I wrote a special poem for Sara's grandparents. I had the poem done in calligraphy, included a photocopy of Sara's footprints and framed it. Our parents proudly display it in their homes.

I planted a flower garden around the beautiful marble headstone my Dad had engraved for me. I worked many hours in that garden. It was, and still is, great therapy. I decorated it with lots of angels, birdbaths and wind chimes. Family and friends gave us gifts for our garden. When I felt like crying, I would walk down to her garden and talk to Sara and pray to God for strength.

After only three months of grieving, writing and planting, I became pregnant again. One year after Sara's birth and death, I gave birth to another beautiful daughter, Payton Brooke Waldorf.

Now, Payton and I work in Sara's garden. I swing her in the yard swing. When she is old enough to understand, I will tell her about her big sister and they will, we will, celebrate their birthdays together.

This article was first published in "Loving Arms," the quarterly newsletter of the Pregnancy and Infant Loss Center, Inc. in Wayzata, Minnesota.

RESOURCES

■ AMEND
(314) 487-7582
4324 Berrywick Terrace
St. Louis, MO 63128
AMEND (Aiding A Mother and Father Experiencing Neonatal Death) offers a free counseling service to parents who have experienced the loss of an infant. Volunteer counselors give neither medical advice nor information, but listen and share in order to help ease the pain of loss and suffering. A free brochure explains problems encountered by parents after the death of their baby.

■ AMERICAN SIDS INSTITUTE
(404) 843-1030
6065 Roswell Rd., Ste. 876
Atlanta, GA 30328
E-mail: prevent@sids.org
Web site: www.sids.org
The mission of the American SIDS Institute is to prevent and conquer SIDS and promote infant health through a national program of research, clinical services, professional education and family support. With regional offices in Washington, D.C. and El Paso, Texas, the Institute is an invaluable source of up-to-date information about SIDS. Their brochures provide advice for parents-to-be and parents concerned about SIDS. For those who have suffered a loss, the institute offers crisis phone counseling, literature and references. "Helping a Friend Cope with Infant Loss" is designed for friends who would like to know how to support a friend or relative experiencing a loss.

■ BEREAVEMENT SERVICES/ RTS
Gundersen Lutheran Medical Center
800-362-9567, ext. 4747
(608) 791-4747
1910 South Ave.
La Crosse, WI 54601
E-mail: berservs@lhl.gundluth.org
RTS is an international perinatal bereavement program which provides training and materials to professionals working with parents who have lost a baby. Parents who call will find compassionate staff who listen, provide written resources, and offer referrals to local support groups or RTS-trained health professionals. A free catalog includes materials for bereaved parents.

■ CENTER FOR LOSS IN MULTIPLE BIRTHS (CLIMB)
(907) 746-6123
Jean Kollantai
P.O. Box 1064
Palmer, AK 99645
CLIMB publishes a quarterly publication called "Our Newsletter" for families who have experienced the death of one or more, or all, of their children during a twin or higher multiple pregnancy. Several parents share their stories, poems and ideas to help with this unique kind of grief. Special issues feature parents who have lost a multiple to SIDS, and material for parents who learn during a pregnancy that one multiple will not live past birth. CLIMB keeps a list of national and international contacts for parents suffering similar losses.

SIDS PREVENTION STRATEGIES

Sudden Infant Death Syndrome is a terrifying thing to consider. New parents want nothing more than to protect their infant any way they can. For most families, that means taking all the precautions usually covered in infant care books:

- Pregnant moms should not smoke, nor should anyone smoke around a newborn.
- Babies should be put to sleep on their back or side, not on their stomachs, to lessen the risk of SIDS. "Back sleeping" is now considered the safest position for infants. Check with your doctor or call the national Back to Sleep campaign at 800-505-2742 for information on sleeping positions.
- When sleeping, newborns should not be overdressed, nor should their room be overheated.
- Avoid the use of sheepskin products in infant beds, which may lead to suffocation.
- Don't put your baby to sleep in a water bed or a beanbag-type chair.
- Don't use pillows in infant beds.

Premature and low birth weight babies are at higher risk for SIDS, as are those born to young mothers. SIDS may occur for no known reason. What it all boils down to is that it simply is not known exactly what causes SIDS. One possibility includes immature neural development. Another theory gaining respect is that SIDS babies do not rouse themselves when they stop breathing during sleep.

Some believe that one way to lessen the incidence of SIDS is co-sleeping, a traditional pattern of bed sharing between infant and mother, which causes a pattern of rousing and sleeping throughout the night.

Babies from two to four months old are beginning to experiment with both automatic and controlled breathing ("planned" breaths which enable humans to speak). Some babies may have difficulty with the transition. At this critical stage, having a parent close by, breathing rhythmically, may help the infant to keep on breathing when rousing.

By U.S. standards, neither parents nor infants "sleep well" in a shared bed. Both rouse more often, and movements of one affect the other. Yet the sleep may be better because a nursing mother can feed her baby during the night without fully waking up.

Some caveats do apply:

- Make sure there is no possibility of the child falling off the bed, or being caught between mattress, headboard or wall.
- Do not use a pillow, featherbed or heavy blankets near an infant.
- No shared sleeping in waterbeds.
- Never share a bed if you smoke, use drugs, or drink heavily.

One alternative is an "attached bed," which is similar to a crib pulled up to your bed. For special moments, there's no reason why a baby can't sometimes sleep in his own room.

■ **CENTERING CORPORATION**
(402) 553-1200
1531 N. Saddle Creek Rd.
Omaha, NE 68104
Web site: uikpage.com/C/centering
E-mail: j1200@aol.com
This company publishes a free "Creative Care Package" catalog that features several books and pamphlets on bereavement issues that deal with each facet of the death of a child. They also offer some of the best children's grief literature available.

■ **COMPASSIONATE FRIENDS**
(630) 990-0010
P.O. Box 3696
Oak Brook, IL 60522-3696
Compassionate Friends is a self-help organization offering friendship and understanding to bereaved parents. The group's purpose is to support and aid parents in the positive resolution of the grief experienced upon the death of a child. In all its literature and philosophy, Compassionate Friends promotes healing and fosters the physical and emotional health of parents and siblings. Upon your request, an information packet will be mailed which includes referrals to local support groups and information about joining. A subscription to the "We Need Not Walk Alone" quarterly newsletter for parents and grandparents is $20, and the group also publishes the quarterly *Stages*, written by and for siblings, for $10 per year.

■ **MIDS SUPPORT GROUP INC.**
(973) 263-6730
16 Crescent Dr.
Parsippany, NJ 07054
MIDS, which stands for miscarriage, infant death, and stillbirth, is a support group for parents suffering from all types of pregnancy or infant loss. Begun by Janet Tischler in New Jersey in 1982, the group has expanded to locations in many states. Besides offering understanding and support, group members are provided "telephone friends" who seek to provide a positive resolution to their loss. A quarterly newsletter is provided with the $18 annual membership fee to this helpful nonprofit group.

■ **NATIONAL SUDDEN INFANT DEATH SYNDROME RESOURCE CENTER (NSRC)**
(703) 821-8955, ext. 249
2070 Chain Bridge Rd., Ste. 450
Vienna, VA 22182
Part of the National Maternal and Child Health Clearinghouse, the NSRC produces and provides resources, referrals, and consumer education materials for families and medical professionals. A variety of materials are available free from NSRC on topics ranging from "What is SIDS?" to statistical research, bibliographies, and a variety of brochures. "Facing Anniversaries, Holidays and Special Events," "Parents and the Grieving Process," and "The Grief of Children After the Loss of a Sibling" are designed to help families deal with their loss.

■ PEN PARENTS
(702) 826-7332
P.O. Box 8738
Reno, NV 89507
E-mail: penparents@prodigy.com
Pen-Parents is an international referral network for parents, grandparents and siblings who have suffered the tragedy of pregnancy loss or the death of a child. Many bereaved parents find it healing to express their feelings through writing. Pen-Parents fills the need for support and validation through correspondence with others in similar situations.

Pails of Hope is a bimonthly publication, sponsored by Pen Parents, for parents who have battled infertility and/or experienced pregnancy or infant loss and are contemplating pregnancy, are pregnant or have given birth and/or adopted a baby subsequent to loss or infertility. A bimonthly newsletter (subscriptions, $15) includes articles, stories and poems.

■ PREGNANCY AND INFANT LOSS CENTER
(612) 473-9372
1421 E. Wayzata Blvd., Ste. 30
Wayzata, MN 55391

The Pregnancy and Infant Loss Center recognizes that the death of a baby can be one of life's greatest heartaches. The center provides information, education, and consultation services to both parents and professional caregivers. They can refer you to a support group in your local area. When you call, the center will send you a packet that includes Loving Arms, a quarterly newsletter filled with stories both sad and inspirational, poetry, and upcoming events nationwide. A descriptive order form lists a wide variety of books for parents, siblings and care providers, as well as books to guide families through subsequent pregnancies, and special remembrance items like birth certificates and memory books. Yearly membership in support of this nonprofit organization is $20 per year.

■ SHARE
800-821-6819
St. Joseph's Health Center
300 First Capitol Dr.
St. Charles, MO 63301
Web site: www.NationalSHAREOffice.com

The mission of SHARE (Pregnancy and Infant Loss Support Inc.) is to serve those who are troubled by a tragic death of a baby. Six times a year, they publish a newsletter with information and ideas from parents and professionals to support and provide a sense of friendship for bereaved parents. Subscriptions are free for one year, and $15 for each additional year.

■ SUDDEN INFANT DEATH SYNDROME ALLIANCE
800-221-7437
1314 Bedford Ave., Ste. 210
Baltimore, MD 21208

The National SIDS Alliance offers emotional and informational support to those who have experienced a baby's death due to SIDS. Publications, newsletters, and brochures are available from the national group. The alliance's 50-plus chapters offer peer counseling, personal visits, regular phone contact and assistance in funeral planning. They also offer support in future pregnancies and after the baby is born.

"My Baby's Premature Birth"

A Life Experience by Diane Hughes Valente

My first two children were born using natural childbirth and the guidance of a wonderful midwife. The thought of number three was a little sad because we had moved and felt the birth might not be quite the same. I investigated birth centers and midwives in the area and settled on one. Trying to help our little girls understand what was happening inside of me, I brought them to my ultrasound. With very little compassion I was told I had a complete placenta previa and would have to leave the birth center program. I would be seeing their affiliated doctors. I sat, wishing my husband was with me, and that my 2- and 3-year-olds were not. I switched practices the next day.

Approximately five weeks later, I felt something. I thought my water had broken, but it was not amniotic fluid; it was blood. There was no time for crying. Phone calls were made and we rushed to the hospital. The details are endless but they stopped the bleeding and sent me home a couple of days later. I was on bedrest with a husband who traveled, my own company to run in the height of the season, and two toddlers.

Life became surreal. I questioned everything—working, family relationships, my marriage and my friends. All of a sudden this third little baby was no longer a happy event but something that made me question all that I had.

One day I started to bleed again. I drove myself to the hospital. My blood count was very low and I was told my baby was going to be born then, in my seventh month. As we waited for the results of an amniocentesis to find out if the baby's lungs were developed, I felt like my life was at a standstill. We got the word that her lungs were good. My doctor was off-duty that weekend, and his partner had a dinner party to attend, but they both agreed that they would much rather be present for my daughter's birthday party.

They performed an emergency Cesarean section an hour later. Robin was born weighing three pounds, 12 ounces. Thank God we were where we were, with excellent doctors and emergency care.

Robin was placed in the special care nursery. I had to go home four days after her birth. Leaving her that day was the most painful experience of my life. The guilt on days I couldn't visit was unbearable. I pumped breast milk for Robin. She was tube-fed for a while until she was strong enough to bottle feed and nurse for short periods. We took her home the day she reached four pounds, around three weeks after her birth.

For me, having a premature baby was like having a first child all over again. I was not sure what to expect from her and I questioned my ability to care for this tiny little person. Looking back, I must say that I was just in shock all those months, both before she came and for a time after. I felt very alone and tired. It was very hard on my girls. I did everything I was not supposed to do with siblings—I would not let the other children touch her, I made them be quiet so she could sleep. It was not the ordinary beginning for a third child.

I realized a lot of things that I had planned would not now be possible. For instance, I was not going to be able to put this little girl in the home day care where her sisters spent three days a week. But we needed my income, so we decided to open a small photography studio near our home. Donald took two months off through the Family Medical Leave Act. Robin had made us realize that one moment can change your life forever. We found a wonderful nanny, and I was close enough to come home and nurse Robin at lunchtime.

Donald has left his job and joined our photography business full-time. Here we are, 13 months after our little one was born. She is behind other children her age physically but is catching up. She still is facing open heart surgery, but we feel very lucky to have her.

I must say I feel a bit like Dorothy in "The Wizard of Oz" for it was not the trip I intended to take. The experience has changed me forever, and I am glad to be home.

QUESTIONS AND ANSWERS
Premature Infants

Neonatologist Charles F. Simmons, Jr., M.D., and Sharon D. Simmons, R.N., B.S.N., of Children's Hospital in Boston, Massachusetts, share current information on prevention and treatment of premature babies.

Q. What are the reasons that babies are born prematurely?

A. Approximately half of preterm deliveries result from maternal conditions such as congenital anomalies of the female reproductive tract, anemia, pregnancy induced hypertension (also known as preeclampsia or toxemia), premature rupture of the fetal membranes, or infection of the fetal membranes and uterine environment. However, a significant fraction of women begin premature labor for unidentifiable reasons. The risk of premature delivery is severalfold higher in women who have previously delivered a premature infant.

Q. Is there anything that can be done to lessen the risk of having a premature infant?

A. Preconception counseling may reduce the risk of preterm delivery in selected instances. Timely prenatal care in the hands of a qualified professional will assure that all the modern approaches to monitoring the pregnancy will be appropriately considered and utilized. If premature labor occurs, certain therapies may decrease the frequency of premature contractions and, if indicated, accelerate maturity of the fetal lungs.

Q. What are the current statistics with regard to premature births and premature babies?

A. Modern advances in the practice of obstetrics and neonatology have resulted in steadily improving morbidity and mortality of premature infants. Up to 10% of pregnancies in the United States result in preterm delivery (less than 37 weeks gestation), accounting for up to 450,000 births per year. As one would expect, the smallest and most immature babies have the most significant challenge for survival and normal outcome. Despite this, in 1997, greater than 90% of infants weighing more than two pounds survive, and the majority experience good long-term outcomes. However, individual pregnancies vary greatly. A woman should consult a trained specialist in maternal fetal and/or newborn medicine to determine the likelihood of fetal survival and possible long-term problems in the case of threatened preterm delivery.

*Q. **What medical technologies are commonly used with premature infants?***

A. Major improvements in medical tests, treatments and medical devices have significantly contributed to the improvement in premature infant survival statistics over the past two decades. Examples include:

- **Isolettes and warming tables:** these devices maintain a newborn infant in a warm, neutral thermal environment, thus conserving calories otherwise expended to generate heat.
- **Cardiorespiratory monitoring:** these electronic devices continuously monitor both newborn heart and respiratory rates, and are equipped with alarms that alert nursing and medical staff to the presence of apnea (temporary cessation of breathing) or abnormalities of heart rate or rhythm;
- **Oximeters:** these monitors measure the oxygen saturation of hemoglobin in red blood cells in the bloodstream of the newborn infant. This relatively new approach allows noninvasive measurement of the efficiency of oxygen uptake in the lungs and delivery of oxygen to the baby's tissues.
- **Mechanical ventilators:** some premature infants experience temporary respiratory failure, and therefore require mechanical breaths administered via a ventilator or respirator. Conventional and high-frequency (or hi fi) ventilators increase the efficiency of oxygen exchange and carbon dioxide elimination by the lungs.
- **Arterial and venous catheterization:** the unstable mineral, fluid, and blood gas status of the extremely premature infant requires frequent tests performed on blood samples, which can be obtained through these catheters with minimal disturbance.
- **Laboratory micromethods:** the advent of new laboratory measurement technologies has resulted in drastic reductions in the amount of blood required for routine monitoring. An amazing number of tests can be performed on just a few drops of blood.

*Q. **What medical therapies are commonly used?***

A. Several effective new medical therapies have markedly improved the outcomes of premature infants. Examples include:

- **Prenatal glucocorticoid therapy:** steroid treatment of the mother can accelerate maturity of the fetal lungs. The combination of prenatal steroids and effective mechanical ventilation has reduced premature infant morbidity and mortality.
- **Surfactant therapy:** premature babies with immature lungs temporarily lack a natural substance called surfactant. Surfactant is composed of lipid and protein molecules that reduce the surface tension and thus the collapsibility of the air sacs that promote gas exchange in the lung. Adequate surfactant production allows easy inflation and deflation of the air sacs and thus promotes adequate

gas exchange and oxygenation. Up to four doses of surfactant are usually given at six to eight hour intervals to infants with persistent lung immaturity.
- **Phototherapy:** phototherapy lights can promote the excretion of the waste product bilirubin from the bloodstream into the urine. Since the formation of the yellow pigment bilirubin occurs at an accelerated rate in premature babies, and since the liver is relatively immature, serum bilirubin concentrations can rise to dangerous concentrations in the extremely premature infant. Phototherapy alters the bilirubin molecule in the skin and reduces the risk of neurologic damage.
- **Intravenous therapy:** major advances in understanding the nutritional requirements of the premature infant have resulted in the design of intravenous solutions that can provide sufficient quality and quantity of calories to promote growth of the premature infant. Intravenous nutrition is a temporary measure in most infants, followed by a transition to feedings with breast milk or formula.

Q. *What is apnea and how does it affect the premature infant?*

A. Apnea is the temporary cessation of breathing. In the premature infant, apnea can either be central or obstructive.
- **Central apnea:** the immature brain of the premature infant may not send regular breathing signals to the diaphragm and other respiratory muscles. This temporary immaturity of brain signalling to the respiratory muscles can be overcome through treatment with aminophylline or caffeine, two well-studied medications that increase the regularity of brain cell respiratory signals.
- **Obstructive apnea:** extremely immature infants frequently lack muscle tone of the upper airways that conduct air to the lungs. Obstructive apnea often requires extra positive airway pressure through a tube placed in the nose. This continuous positive airway pressure is administered by a ventilator, and may, in selected instances, need to be accompanied by actual intubation of the trachea and mechanical ventilation.

Q. *What about breastfeeding the premature baby?*

A. Breast milk is almost always the best form of nutrition for any baby, whether term or premature. Premature infants who are not able to coordinate their suck-and-swallow reflexes will need to ingest breast milk collected by their mothers via mechanical or electric breast pumps. Infants who can digest breast milk but cannot yet suck and swallow will require feeding through a soft plastic tube placed through the nose or mouth into the stomach.

Because of the special needs of premature infants, it may be necessary to supplement breast milk with mineral and vitamin additives that optimize the nutritional status of the preterm baby. In addition to the beneficial nutritional aspects, breastfeeding may improve the immune status of preterm infants and reduce the incidence of certain types of infection. In addition, the routine of expressing breast milk and later, actual nursing, offers many emotional benefits to both the mother and the premature infant.

Q. When can premature babies be released from the hospital?

A. Former premature infants may be ready for discharge anywhere after the equivalent of 35 weeks gestation period. Rather than a specific age or weight, the discharge is related to when important developmental milestones are achieved. The infant must demonstrate:

- **Adequate thermal regulation:** the former preterm infant must maintain body temperature with minimal wrapping.
- **Adequate nutrition:** good weight gain on a reasonable feeding regimen every three to four hours will ensure the family's ability to cope with the infant's feeding needs.
- **Adequate respiratory control:** former premature infants must demonstrate regular respirations with no episodes of apnea or heart rate slowing. Absence of such episodes for a period of up to five days prior to discharge is the standard of care in many institutions across the country.
- **Adequate parental education:** ongoing parental education regarding any special infant needs, cardiopulmonary resuscitation, and home resources are all part of routine discharge planning sessions that will precede discharge.

Q. Do you have any advice for parents of premature babies with regard to coping strategies?

A. "Hope for the best, but emotionally prepare for stressful times." This adage is useful for many parents and families who will experience euphoric highs and depressing lows during what can be a prolonged hospitalization. It is important to remember the support available from extended family, friends, and clergy in order to help cope with the uncertainties of hospital care and outcomes of premature infants.

Q. Do you have any advice for parents of premature babies with regard to working with insurance companies?

A. Although the value of a successful outcome for a premature infant is beyond measure, the associated financial costs of hospital care of the premature infant can be staggering. Several months of hospitalization can easily exceed $100,000. Families fortunate enough to have insurance should inform the insurance company of the birth of the premature infant as soon as feasible after delivery.

Irrespective of insurance, the financial aid office at your hospital should be contacted in order to determine whether any applicable local, state, or federal programs may help defray hospitalization expenses.

RESOURCES

■ INTENSIVE CARING UNLIMITED
(215) 629-0449
910 Bent Ln.
Philadelphia, PA 19118
Services to parents with a baby in intensive care are offered, including over-the-phone advice from parents who have had similar experiences with their babies. Volunteers are trained as counselors to help with crises. They publish a bimonthly newsletter on prematurity, developmental delays, grieving, and other parental issues.

■ IVH PARENTS
(305) 232-0381
P.O. Box 56-1111
Miami, FL 33156
IVH Parents offers support to parents whose babies have had an intraventricular hemorrhage—bleeding in the brain—that frequently occurs in babies born weighing less than three pounds. They provide caring counseling by phone and publish a newsletter.

■ LITTLE ANGEL FOUNDATION
(516) 736-2512
P.O. Box 510
Seldon, NY 11784
Founded to help parents of premature and seriously ill infants, the foundation offers support during and after neonatal intensive care. The group's information packet includes a telephone referral network, parent-to-parent listening program, high risk pregnancy and bereavement packages, video and book library and biannual newsletter.

■ PARENTCARE
800-808-2224
7910 Woodmont Ave., Ste. 300
Bethesda, MD 20814
Web site: www.look.net/acch
E-mail: acch@clark.net
Parentcare is part of the Association for the Care of Children's Health (ACCH), an international organization of parents and health professionals focusing on the unique needs of infants in health care settings. Parentcare provides information through publications, videos and conferences. Individual memberships range from $35-$65. ACCH's annual conference and twice-annual regional conferences address high-risk neonatal care issues.

■ SIDELINES
(714) 497-2265
P.O. Box 1808
Laguna Beach, CA 92652
Web site: www.earthlink.net\~sidelines
E-mail: sidelines@earthlink.net
Sidelines is a network of support groups across the country for women with complicated pregnancies and their families. Over 5,000 trained peer counselors can be matched to those who have had similar experiences. There is a lending library and an annual magazine covering a variety of issues such as how to cope with bedrest and dealing with various issues of difficult pregnancies.

"Bedrest Blues... and Triumphs"

A Life Experience by Krista Minard

Seven months along, my pregnancy had been a breeze so far. I had escaped morning sickness and major weight gain, and knew I was having a girl sometime in September. I expected to work at my job as a magazine editor right up until I had the baby.

The breezy part of my pregnancy ended on the way home from a seaside vacation with my husband, Mike, when I began having contractions every three minutes. A stop at the hospital landed me on a gurney with a fetal monitor and a comment from the nurse: "You're 26 weeks along? Oh, we've delivered them smaller than that...not much smaller, though."

The labor turned out to be false, but didn't stop until I'd received muscle relaxants and a syringe full of terbutaline (a contraction stopper). I was sent home with orders to rest quietly on my left side for the rest of the weekend, drink plenty of water and see my physician as soon as possible.

That Monday, my first day back at work after vacation, I left to see my obstetrician who examined me, discovered cervical effacement and ordered me to bedrest for at least the next six weeks. "We've got to get to at least 32 weeks," she said. No working at the office, no housework, no cooking, no walks, no gardening, no grocery shopping...the list of don'ts was endless. I could get up to use the bathroom, shower and drive to her office once a week for a checkup. She gave me a list of red flags that would require me to call no matter what time of day—contractions that are too frequent, too long, too strong or too different; bleeding; a gush of amniotic fluid. She also prescribed nifedipene, a medication that works on uterine contractions. The drug's side effects—light-headedness, vessel dilation, increased heart rate—were little compared to the risks of premature delivery.

When I got back in the car to drive the few blocks to the office, the contractions started up again. As my baby arched and kicked, I started crying—I knew I had to obey doctor's orders if I wanted my girl to be born healthy, but I wasn't prepared to quit work and lie around. I didn't have anything ready for the baby to arrive. Magazine deadline was looming. I was supposed to be a guest of honor at an out-of-town baby shower. The more I thought about it all, the more panicked I felt.

I got to the office and told my boss that I had to go home right away and lie down for the next two months. He offered me the use of the company laptop computer, and we concocted an arrangement that would allow me to continue to work from home, via e-mail, fax and phone. I called Mike and broke the news; he immediately pledged his willingness to pick up any household slack.

And so it went. Propped up on pillows, I had my computer, my files and my telephone within reach. A tremendously long cord stretched through the house from the laptop to the phone jack for modem access. The phone rang every five minutes—co-workers asking questions and expressing concern; friends and family members nagging me to take care of myself. I canceled the baby shower, a trip to my parents', a haircut appointment. I counted contractions. I drank my water. Mike fixed meals, fed the animals, ran errands, waited on me and kept the house clean—in addition to working 40 hours a week.

Every day at 6:00 p.m., I e-mailed to the office a contingency plan of what to do if I became unavailable. Then I unplugged the phone and broke the rules long enough to walk to the couch, where I watched reruns on TV. In July, I avidly followed the Summer Olympics, even the events I'd always hated, like heavyweight lifting and wrestling. I even endured the Dream Team and their squeaky shoes.

Friends and family visited. My sister brought a foot-high stack of books and magazines. Sisters-in-law Jody and Carrie transported the already-purchased baby shower gifts and set up my living room with so much pink, frilly stuff that my girl's arrival began to seem real.

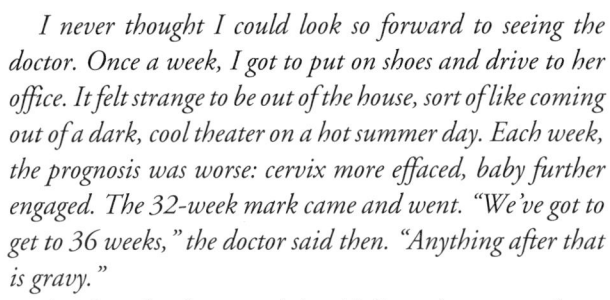

I never thought I could look so forward to seeing the doctor. Once a week, I got to put on shoes and drive to her office. It felt strange to be out of the house, sort of like coming out of a dark, cool theater on a hot summer day. Each week, the prognosis was worse: cervix more effaced, baby further engaged. The 32-week mark came and went. "We've got to get to 36 weeks," the doctor said then. "Anything after that is gravy."

At 35 weeks, she stopped the nifedipene because my heart rate was too fast. She told me she expected I'd go into labor within a week. The contractions continued at about the same rate they had for the past two months. At 36 weeks, the baby was getting to be a good-sized girl, according to the doctor, but I might take it easy for another week. At 37 weeks she shrugged and said I could get up and go back to work. She also suggested that we schedule a labor induction. She was a little worried that my labor would proceed extremely fast, and she estimated that the baby was at least six pounds—the size limit she felt I could deliver.

I returned to work for two weeks, and felt better than I had in months. I wore the same denim jumper almost every day—just put a different shirt beneath it. I prepared for my maternity leave. At home, I sewed crib bumpers and curtains. I washed all the newborn drawstring gowns in special soap, burying my nose in them because they smelled so sweet. In a burst of energy, I assembled the crib and changing table, despite Mike's protests that he'd do it over the weekend. I went out to dinner with friends, shopped for diapers, took phone calls from people who said, "Still pregnant?" I patted my daughter on the behind, felt her feet flex against my ribs, and gave thanks that she'd stayed indoors.

Then, one morning, I woke up with crampy contractions and an unrelenting urge to clean up the garage. Instead, we went to the hospital, where our daughter, Anna Marie, was born that evening at 7:50 p.m. She weighed seven pounds, 13 ounces and was 21 inches long.

We'd made it to 39 weeks. 🌿

BEDREST: A PRESCRIPTION, NOT A SENTENCE

You're at a routine obstetrical appointment. Expressing concern, your doctor recommends bedrest. "I can't be on bedrest!" you immediately think. But if you're like thousands of women each year, you won't have a choice. For the safety of your unborn child, a period of bedrest will decrease the chance of premature labor.

You will survive bedrest. We suggest calling Sidelines, a group dedicated to helping women through bedrest and complicated pregnancies, at (714) 497-2265. They will send you information to make this time easier for you and your family.

It is important to be equipped to cope with the stresses of bedrest. Be prepared to be totally dependent on others, and expect feelings of inadequacy. You can fight feelings of isolation by calling friends and relatives, and having people come and visit. People may tell you how "lucky" you are to "lay around all day." Know that bedrest is serious work for a confined mother, and the focus is on keeping you and the baby healthy through your pregnancy. Find friends who will be supportive and caring, and let them help you! Some suggestions:

- Be sure phone, phone book, television remote control, reading and writing materials and projects are within reach on the bed or next to it. Put everything into a laundry basket to set up your "nest."
- Have a small ice chest within reach, packed with the day's supply of drinks and snacks.
- Open your window—weather permitting—to let the outdoors in and get some fresh air.
- Make a list of things people can do for you, so that when they ask, you can easily respond and even give them a choice.
- Work on long-put-off projects: update photo albums, write letters, finish stitchery projects, mend clothes, update your phone book and holiday card list, reorganize files.
- Consider renting a sliding side table (similar to the ones used in hospitals) to make it easier to eat or write while in bed.
- Have a "date" with your husband—gourmet take-out food and candles.
- Invite another couple for a game of cards or trivia or to watch a video movie on Saturday night.

If you have other children in your household, find creative ways to interact with them. Play bed-basketball with rolled-up socks and a laundry basket. Keep building blocks, board games, coloring books and crayons, puzzles, play dough, children's books, paper, scissors, paste and old magazines in a laundry basket near your bed. Include paper towels for spills.

Sidelines provided information for this article.

"*You Are My Sunshine*"

A Life Experience by Michelle Holman

Little did I know when my husband and I carefully selected the pretty pink, yellow and blue hooked rug for our first sweet little nursery, that only 18 months and a set of twins later, what I would most appreciate about our purchase was how nicely splattered globs of lemon yogurt would blend in without serious compromise to its beauty.

When my husband Greg and I decided to get married we were both ready for family life. At 36 and 31, married for just eight months, we braved the prospect of having a child. What we got was "insta-family."

Anyone who has had naturally occurring twins can tell you about the feeling you have on that fateful, albeit routine, day when you go to see the first ultrasound of your baby. Nonchalantly the obstetrician says, "Here we have one baby and here we have another." I thought he had to be kidding, having triplets himself. I figured he just wanted to see my reaction. Could this be true? We were going to have twins. We were so excited. We laughed, we panicked and we went into shock. I immediately found the phone and called—who else—my mother.

No one likes to be the only one to emotionally shoulder the full brunt of such joyous calamity. We were no exception, so when my mother asked if the baby was a boy or a girl, my reply was, "Which one?" I was gratified when I heard her scream and cry all at once. I had never heard her so happy.

I know I'm not the first woman to have twins, or at least that is what they kept telling me. But I was the only one of my immediate acquaintances, family or friends to have twins, so from my point of view I was the only woman to have twins.

At first it was funny, but at 21 weeks reality struck. I was in premature labor and dangerously effaced to 70%. I had immediate surgery and full bedrest was prescribed for the next four months. Hardship overcome is one of the rites of passage to motherhood, and my mother was there for all of it. She flew in for the surgery and did not leave until the diabetes, toxemia, magnesium, terbutaline pump, two bouts in the hospital, bedrest, home monitoring and carefully adjusted diet were through. She waited on me nonstop for 135 days, day in and day out. Hardship or no, she was determined that I was going to have two healthy babies. I delivered Jacob William and Jessica Lynn at 38 weeks and both were, as my mother had willed, healthy.

Of course now the real circus began! Being a first time mom of two, I needed to learn and learn fast. Even before I began I was exhausted. After the first ten weeks of feeding, diapers, and laundry I wasn't sure which way I was going. Any mother of multiples will tell you it's not like having a second child in diapers, it's like nothing else one has ever experienced. The only advice that actually made any practical sense I received from a newly found friend with twins. She said, "Listen to your instincts. You are the mother of your two children and you will know the right thing to do for your children when the time comes." This was good advice, and with a little less panic as a result of her pep talk, most everything went smoothly.

We certainly should not forget about dealing with the adoring public. With the twins about three months old I got my nerve up to take them out in public and selected—the mall! It was revenge of the peekers. In just over an hour I had strolled no more than 50 feet. Don't get me wrong, I really do enjoy talking to people about our twins and I realize that people are naturally curious. I just couldn't believe how many times I was asked if my little girl dressed in pink and my boy dressed in blue were identical twins. This in itself is not so bad, but just try answering it 15 times in a single morning after about six hours of sleep in three days.

One of the most common comments I received was, "Oh, a boy and a girl—so...you're done." I often wondered if people were "telling" me I was done having children or asking me. My all-time favorite was from those who yelled in passing, "I'm glad it's you and not me." I simply responded, "So...am...I."

In a local Twins Club—a social support group for mothers of multiples—I found a haven. Only mothers of multiples truly understand what you are going through.

Now my sweet angels are nearly 2 and life is their playground. They can destroy the house in 15 minutes flat, outflank me in strategy, energy and resolve. They even communicate in their own secret language. I hear them jabbering to one another, laugh and scream, then run off to their next adventure. Sometimes I even feel left out, but as long as they are having a good time, life is good.

I've been lucky enough to wander across a wonderful poem which helps me puts my life in perspective now. It reminds me how blessed I am:

The Little Shadows
I saw a young mother with eyes full of laughter,
and two little shadows came following after.
Wherever she moved, they were always right there,
holding on to her skirts, hanging onto her chair,
before her, behind her—an adhesive pair.
"Don't you ever get weary as, day after day,
your two little tagalongs get in your way?"
She smiled as she shook her pretty young head,
and I'll always remember the words that she said:
"It's good to have shadows that run when you run;
that laugh when you're happy, and hum when you hum.
For you only have shadows when your life's filled with sun."
                                    —*Author Unknown*

As life would have it, unfortunately, my mother passed away suddenly when Jacob and Jessica were only four months old. She will never know them the way I dreamed she would and they will know her only through my memories. So my twins are destined to have a guardian angel. It is comforting to me that I knew theirs so intimately. When Mom used to touch my stomach, singing her favorite song, "You Are My Sunshine," it seemed silly. It seems entirely perfect now that Jacob and Jessica are truly the sunshines of my life. ❧

❧ RESOURCES ❧

■ MOTHERS OF SUPERTWINS (M.O.S.T.)
(516) 434-MOST
P.O. Box 951
Brentwood, NY 11717
This nonprofit organization provides resources, information, empathy, and support to families with triplets, quadruplets and higher number multiple births. Information about pregnancy issues, prematurity, development and family life is available.

■ NATIONAL ORGANIZATION OF MOTHERS OF TWINS CLUBS (NOMTC)
P.O. Box 23188
Albuquerque, NM 87192-1188
This organization was the brainchild of several mothers dealing with the stress of raising twins, and is now a network of 450 clubs. Its mission is to provide information to parents of twins and/or multiple births. Write for a free brochure, "Your Twins and You." If you're interested in starting your own local chapter, NOMTC can send you that information as well.

■ TWINS MAGAZINE
800-328-3211
(303) 290-8500
5350 S. Roslyn St., Ste. 400
Englewood, CO 80111
This national magazine offers support and caring for parents of multiples with a wide variety of articles and essays. It is printed bimonthly (six issues a year). An annual subscription runs about $24.

■ TWINS WORLD MAGAZINE
(219) 627-5414
11220 St. Joe Rd.
Fort Wayne, IN 46835-9737
Dr. Brandt publishes *Twins World* magazine. This magazine is for twins, parents of twins, and twinless twins. The magazine has sections on twin research studies, entertainment, social functions, and twin loss. The cost for the magazine is $20 per year.

■ TRIPLET CONNECTION
(209) 474-0885
P.O. Box 99571
Stockton, CA 95209
Web site: www.inreach.com\triplets
E-mail: triplets@inreach.com
The Triplet Connection maintains what is perhaps the world's largest data base of multiple births. Information packets include a copy of the organization's newsletter, information about strollers for multiples, and networking opportunities are available for parents who are expecting or who have had three or more babies. Other offerings include a quarterly newsletter (subscriptions are $20) and a resource list ($20).

■ TWIN SERVICES
(510) 524-0863
P. O. Box 10066
Berkeley, CA 94709
Twin Services has a complete listing of services including multiple birth information and referral, parenting publications, and consultations with multiple birth experts. This group operates a 900 number with information about caring for twins.

"Life as a Teen Parent"

By Cinderella Constant, age 17

Being a teen parent isn't all that it is cracked up to be. The reaction you first feel when you realize you are pregnant is shock and fear. Shock because you didn't think it could happen to you. Fear of what your parents and what your boyfriend might say.

When you're pregnant, you're looked down upon by many people, including your friends. You think someone will be there to help you. But you're wrong (well, in my case I was). When your parents find out you're pregnant, the way they look at you changes. You're not their sweet little girl anymore; you're the girl who was stupid and doesn't have a mind of her own. People stare at you when they notice the bulge in your shirt that has a baby inside, and look at you in contempt, in a way that makes you think that they think that you don't know what you're getting yourself into (I did, though).

When the baby is born, everything changes, especially the way your parents treat you. My parents treated me like I never knew what I was doing. Until the day I left.

You now have more responsibilities than you ever had before. After your child is born, you should know that your child is your number one priority. He comes ahead of everything, including when you go to school. If he's sick, you must stay home.

Those were all the negatives. Here are the positives. You're able to watch your child grow. You observe them learn new things. They do funny things that will make you laugh. You get to see the funny expressions they make. You feel proud when they do something new and when people say they are cute and big. I, myself, love the way my son smiles. It's so big and bright. He's a strong little boy who is always happy, except when he's sick.

One hard thing to handle is when they are sick. Sometimes you have to spend hours at the hospital trying to figure out what is wrong with your child. Not knowing, just worrying. They are constantly crying, while you feel helpless because there is nothing you can do to make them feel better except give them medicine and love. When they do get better, you forget they were sick, when they smile at you with the expression of love.

All that is written here is my life as a teen parent. If you think you can handle this with no regrets (only if you're pregnant already), then I think you should keep the baby. Even though things have been hard, I don't regret the day he was born and all that I have sacrificed for him.

MATERNAL AGE FACTORS

THE "OLDER" MOM

With more women deciding to delay childbearing until their careers are well established, this country is seeing an unprecedented number of births to women over 35. While there are risks associated with older maternal age, giving birth at an "advanced" age has its benefits. Mothers are generally more emotionally mature and prepared for the life changes that motherhood brings.

Down syndrome is the highest risk factor associated with older mothers. According to the March of Dimes Birth Defects Foundation, approximately 1 of every 1,250 25-year-olds have children with Down syndrome. Three in 1,000 35-year-olds have children with the syndrome, and the risk increases to 1 in 100 for 40-year-olds. While theories abound, it is generally agreed that the aging of the ovaries contributes to the increased possibility of genetic defects.

Women over 35 are more likely to miscarry than their younger counterparts, and twice as likely to develop diabetes during pregnancy. In the same age group, there is an increased risk of placental problems and bleeding, and these women are more likely to deliver by Cesarean section. On a happy note, the incidence of twins is highest for mothers ages 35-39.

How to best lower the risks? By following the generally prescribed rules of pregnancy: no smoking, drinking, or drugs; following a healthy diet, and taking 0.4 mg. of folic acid daily, preferably beginning before conception. Regular prenatal care is a must to have a healthy baby.

TEEN MOTHERS

According to Shelby Pasarell of Advocates for Youth (AFY) in Washington D.C., "Public perception holds that too-early childbearing leads to increased welfare costs, hopeless futures and a continuing cycle of poverty for adolescent mothers and their children. Many young teen mothers can, however, achieve academic success, have rewarding careers and lead productive and fulfilling lives." The key factors for the success of young mothers are educational and economic opportunities, along with social support services, and help from their families.

With more women deciding to delay childbearing, this country is seeing an unprecedented number of births to women over 35.

The Children's Defense Fund found that, regardless of ethnicity or race, teenage girls with poor basic skills were more than three times as likely to become mothers as those with average skills. Teen mothers have only a 60% chance of graduating from high school by age 25, 30% lower than their childless peers, according to AFY.

Many school districts offer programs for pregnant teens which allow them to continue their schooling, often including parenting courses and an on-site day care center. Education can make the difference between good and poor employment opportunities.

Teenagers are more likely to delay prenatal care, yet are more at risk than older moms for giving birth prematurely. They are also at higher risk for developing preeclampsia. Inadequate nutrition is often a factor. Finding a caring practitioner the pregnant teen can trust is of utmost importance.

Although more teens are keeping their babies than ever before, adoption is always an option. Over half the babies adopted today are placed through independent adoptions, usually through a private adoption attorney. Whether through independent or agency adoption, the adoptive parents pay for the birth mother's medical care through pregnancy, labor and delivery. Birth parents can review photos and letters from prospective adoptive families in order to make a placement choice. Adoption laws vary widely from state to state. Many areas have adoption counseling services that can make a referral.

❧ RESOURCES ❧

■ ADVOCACY FOR YOUTH
(202) 347-5700
1025 Vermont Ave., N.W., Ste. 200
Washington, DC 20005
Advocacy For Youth is a national advocacy program concerned mostly with the impact of teen sexuality. They can provide fact sheets and resources for teenagers and their families.

■ MARCH OF DIMES
888-MODIMES
1275 Mamaroneck Ave.
White Plains, NY 10605
E-mail: Resourcecenter@modimes.org
March of Dimes' Resource Center offers free publications, brochures, and public health information sheets on general pregnancy issues and specific birth defects, including "Pregnancy After Age 30," a public health education information sheet.

CHILD ABUSE

Child abuse is not something we like to think about, but it does happen—in all types of homes, with families from all ethnic groups and all income levels. Physical abuse and neglect hurt defenseless trusting children, and are most often caused by someone the child is familiar with: a relative, a child care provider or baby-sitter, a parent. If you see a child in imminent danger, contact law enforcement and your local child protective services agency, and explain the nature of the situation. Take action to make sure the child is in a safe environment.

PHYSICAL ABUSE

Physical abuse is any act which results in a non-accidental physical injury. This includes severe corporal punishment, including occasions where a person is frustrated or angry and strikes, shakes or throws a child. Other intentional forms of abuse may include burning, cutting, poking, twisting limbs, or otherwise torturing a child.

A disturbing form of physical abuse is shaken baby syndrome, which occurs mainly in children under 1 year of age, and seldom after age 2. A baby's brain and blood vessels are very fragile and vulnerable to whiplash motions, such as shaking, jerking and jolting. The neck muscles of an infant or small child are weak, so the child's head is relatively heavy and the neck cannot support the stress of shaking.

That means that vigorously shaking a very young child can cause irreversible brain damage, blindness, cerebral palsy, hearing loss, spinal cord injury, learning disabilities and even death. Shaking a baby can cause the brain to actually recoil against the skull, and since infants' brains are not well protected, shaking causes the brain to bleed and swell.

This is a partial list of neurological symptoms that might alert to a possible shaken baby:
- Unable to lift or turn head
- Pinpointed or dilated pupils
- Blood pooling in eyes
- Pupils unresponsive to light
- Semi-consciousness or lethargy
- Difficulty in breathing
- Seizures or spasms
- Swollen head (which may appear later)

No matter how impatient or angry you feel, never shake a baby—ever.

Approximately 75% to 90% of cases of shaken baby syndrome include retinal hemorrhages, a symptom almost never seen with accidental head injuries.

Be sure to tell others who are in contact with your child about the dangers of shaking a baby—baby-sitters, child care workers, siblings and other relatives. You can also protect your baby from head injury by making sure you don't shake your child when you play. Keep a baby's head well supported when holding, playing with or transporting.

It is not your responsibility to diagnose shaken baby syndrome or other physical abuse. If you suspect abuse, check with your pediatrician or a mental health professional.

NEGLECT

Babies' needs are few, but a small fraction of parents seem unaware of the necessity of adequate changing, bathing, feeding and loving. Neglect of a baby's nutritional intake is cruel, and the symptoms are quickly obvious: a baby who doesn't gain weight because of lower-than-necessary nutritional intake and who is at risk for dehydration. Diapers need changing whenever wet or soiled to avoid diaper rash and possible urinary tract infections. Just as important is simply spending time with your baby, talking to her, holding her gently and making her feel cherished.

Without a loving parent, a baby can learn to withdraw; crying will diminish as the baby learns not to expect attention from caretakers. This can lead to long-term attachment problems and difficulty in school. Babies do take a lot of time, but neglecting a baby's needs, even for a short while, can lead to disastrous consequences.

WHEN A BABY CRIES

Babies cry for a variety of reasons—when they're hungry or need to be changed—but sometimes babies cry because they are having a hard time adjusting to life. This is not unusual. If there is no medical reason for the crying, the best thing to do is let your baby cry and keep your frustration under control.

- No matter how impatient or angry you feel, never shake a baby—ever.
- Be patient. The baby is not crying to irritate you, but rather is just responding to an internal need to cry.
- If you've had all you can take, lay the baby on his or her back or side, making sure he or she is safe from harm, and take a break. Let the baby cry it out.
- Call a friend or relative to let them know how you're feeling. If a friend can spend an hour with the baby while you take a walk or spend some quiet time alone, you'll be better able to deal with a fussy infant.

Parenting classes and support groups are all excellent outlets to receive advice and input on your specific problem areas.

Have reasonable expectations for your child and yourself. Realize that not everything runs smoothly all the time, and that even the most difficult stages in your child's life will pass.

If you are facing a crisis situation, call your local Parents Anonymous office or the National Child Abuse Hotline (800-422-4453). Don't be afraid to reach out for help when needed.

Information provided by Anthony Urquiza, Ph.D., the California Department of Social Services and Children's Hospital in Seattle, Washington.

TAKING CARE OF YOURSELF AND YOUR FAMILY

KEEPING YOUR RELATIONSHIP ALIVE

By Kari E. Hazen

THE BALANCING ACT

Friday night arrives again. A week full of demands, deadlines and stress is coming to a close. I think I saw the father of my children about five hours this week if I was lucky. Now, another round of demands and duties arrive for the weekend...laundry, bills and picking up this house. My husband and I will take our daughters to the park, read stories and give them the love and encouragement they need. Balancing the day-to-day responsibilities of work, home and children, we search to find time for one another.

Having a good relationship, and children at the same time, may be difficult. Couples must come to terms with the conflicting feelings that say: "I want to be a good parent" and at the same time "I want our relationship to stay strong and intimate...and even a little spontaneous."

Some may laugh at the idea that there is even the slightest possibility the two roles are compatible. Others will cheer, pop the champagne bottle and say yes! I, too, believe this is possible—not only possible, but also extremely important. I think we all want a life filled with love from our significant other and love from our children. The real question lies in how to make it work for us.

PRIORITIZE YOUR RELATIONSHIP

Whether you are a working mom or a stay-at-home mom, it is clear you are giving a lot to your children. It is something instinctive that moms do well. Because we give so much to our families, it is much more challenging to give to the relationship that started the family. So, how do we make our relationship a priority again? By simply doing that...making it a priority. Pick it up from the bottom of your to-do list and move it to the top. Focus on the time, or lack of time, you're spending together and decide to make it better. To many, it may not sound too simple; yet there are some small steps that can be

Having a good relationship, and children at the same time, may be difficult for today's parents.

taken to get the relationship rekindled again. Here are some practical ideas that many parents suggest to help keep your relationship strong.

- Try to get a baby-sitter at least once a month. It doesn't matter what you do, just that you leave the house and spend time with one another.

- Take a walk. This may keep your children occupied and gives you a chance to talk with little interruption. Walking also releases stress and provides good exercise.

- Try a vacation alone. This one is difficult for most moms, especially the first trip. Yet once you enjoy a trip away and alone, you will find how good it is for your relationship. Nothing brings intimacy back better than complete and utter silence to enjoy with your partner.

- Celebrate! Celebrate your anniversary, your birthdays and even your small triumphs. It's the little things that keep a relationship growing strong.

- Surprise one another. Put a small note in a lunch bag, car or coat pocket, telling one another how important you are...and really mean it. It will make you smile all day.

- Take a nap or just be lazy together. Many times when you have the opportunity to be lazy together, it seems like the perfect time to do what really needs to be done. That usually means chores and household duties. Every once in a while ...don't do it. Just relax, watch a movie together, take a nap, snuggle, eat a bag of chips or candy, and forget the rest of the world.

- Take an individual time-out. Even if it is just an hour or two, do something you really want to do with a friend, or alone, and enjoy it. The happier you are, the better partner and parent you'll be. Leave the guilt behind.

- Talk to one another. Having children is stressful. When things build up or problems occur, talk about them. Don't hold your anger or thoughts inside. Chances are that before your children were born, it was easier to communicate (no crying to compete with). Make time to share your feelings.

- Before reacting in a stressful situation, try seeing it from your partner's viewpoint. Chances are he or she is trying just as hard, is just as tired as you are, and loves your kids just as much. You are both in this together with the same goals—a happy, fulfilling family life.

- Give yourself credit. Know you can't do it all without support from your family. The whole family structure doesn't have to revolve around one person. Remember, it took more than one of you to make a family, and it takes more than one of you to care for a family.

- Know that having a good relationship with children isn't easy. At times, your relationship may seem incredibly wonderful and other moments may seem bleak. It's just life. By committing to work on your relationship, you are one step ahead of many couples. In the long run, when your children are grown and gone, you'll have a relationship and the silence won't frighten you.

"Camaraderie Makes the Difference"

A Life Experience by Julie Hanson-Lynn, M.A.

"If only I had known it would be like this . . . ." "Why didn't anyone tell me, really tell me, it could be this way?" These thoughts crossed my mind several times a day after I brought my first child home from the hospital. "Am I the only one who feels this way?"

Although people said life with a newborn is hard, I was still unprepared for the realities of their demanding care, the disappointment in my postpartum body; the experience of months of sleep deprivation, and the isolation and loneliness of suddenly staying home.

Reading parenting magazines did little to reassure me. Their pictures showed moms happily exercising with their babies, serenely breastfeeding, and intently (enthusiastically, even!) stimulating their one-month-olds with all the proper paraphernalia. What's more, these moms were showered, fully dressed in clothes other than sweats, and had make-up on. Where was a picture of an exhausted mom, still in her pajamas at one o'clock in the afternoon, with her hair a mess and a breast pad unintentionally abandoned on the arm of the couch? Why wasn't I like the moms in the pictures?

I finally realized that I needed to be around other new moms. One day I was at a park and met a woman whose son was a week older than my daughter and we immediately connected. We laughed so hard when she told me she had been nursing just before the doorbell rang, opened the door to a delivery person and only after she shut the door did she realized her shirt was still unbuttoned! She invited me to join a play group she was a part of and it saved my sanity. None of us looked like the moms in the magazine pictures and I learned how to laugh about it. There was nothing wrong with me and I was doing a great job!

The friends I made in that group have been my closest friends for four years now, and my daughter thinks of their children as her own siblings. We get together as often as we can (with and without our kids); we share baby-sitting, and we are only a phone call away from each other when we need help or a supportive ear.

New parent support should be a part of every expectant parent's postpartum recovery plan. So completely do I believe this that I started my own private practice running support groups and educating health care professionals. If you don't find anything, start one yourself. Different groups do different things and attract different people so shop around to get ideas. At least then you'll know what is available to you after you have your baby. The key is to get out and get connected to others in a similar situation.

It is important to have a place where you can express all the emotions and thoughts you are having as a new mom and be reassured that you are not the only one. Most importantly, you too will learn how to laugh even though you have only had a few hours of sleep, your baby just spit up all over the shoulder of the third clean shirt you put on today, and you are late to an appointment. ❧

SUPPORT GROUPS

The arrival of a baby can unleash many new emotions and demands. Sometimes just being with other new parents helps to remind you that you aren't alone in your new role.

Participating in a support group is a great idea, especially for first-time parents, who often have many questions and concerns. The arrival of a baby can unleash many new emotions and demands. Sometimes just being with other new parents helps to remind you that you aren't alone in your new role. It is also fun to share your child's accomplishments and gain other parents' insights and clues to success.

This section includes national parenting support groups. Do some research to find out which group is right for your family. The hospital where you deliver may also offer support groups to serve your family's needs.

■ F.E.M.A.L.E. (FORMERLY EMPLOYED MOTHERS AT THE LEADING EDGE)
(630) 941-3553
P.O. Box 31
Elmhurst, IL 60126
Web site: http:\\members.aol.com\femaleofc\home.htm

F.E.M.A.L.E. is a national nonprofit support and advocacy group for women who have left full-time employment to care for their children. If you send a self-addressed stamped envelope to the address listed above, they will provide you with the nearest chapter. Most chapters hold two evening meetings per month as well as play groups and other activities to share with children. The $24 annual membership fee includes a monthly newsletter from the national organization.

■ MOMS CLUB (MOMS OFFERING MOMS SUPPORT)
(805) 526-2725
25371 Rye Canyon
Valencia, CA 91355

There are 4,000 chapters of this national nonprofit organization for women who are staying at home with their children (and for those who work part-time). Goals of the group include mental and social stimulation for parents, involvement in outreach projects which focus on the family, and social interaction for the kids. The groups typically meet monthly during the day with varying activities and child care options. In addition to the monthly meetings, some groups also plan field trips, playgroups, educational speakers and moms' nights out. Send $2 to the address above for an informational brochure.

■ MOPS INTERNATIONAL (MOTHERS OF PRESCHOOLERS)
(303) 733-5353
1311 S. Clarkson St.
Denver, CO 80210

This is a 25-year-old national support group which has nearly 1,500 groups nationwide. Groups typically meet twice a month during the day, and are geared to mothers of young children. The emphasis is outreach to moms who feel they may need support. Crafts, food and fun are all part of this group.

■ NATIONAL ASSOCIATION OF MOTHERS' CENTERS
800-645-3828
64 Division Ave.
Levittown, NY 11756

Mothers' Centers create an environment where women become part of a national network for support and exploration of issues that concern mothers and families. Over 50 centers are presently operating nationwide. The activities of different centers vary, but usually include workshops, seminars and discussion groups. A Mothers' Center representative will assist you in finding a local center, or send information on how to start and organize a center.

■ SELF-HELP CLEARINGHOUSE, NORTHWEST COVENANT MEDICAL CENTER
(201) 625-7101
25 Pocono Rd.
Denville, NJ 07834
Web site: www.cmhc.com/selfhelp/
E-mail: ashc@bc.cybernex.net

This organization provides information and a directory of more than 800 self-help and support groups, including parenting groups and those for a wide variety of medical conditions. The organization can also give you information about self-help clearinghouses that may serve your area. They also will mail a free handout on ideas for starting your own self-help group.

■ **STEPFAMILY ASSOCIATION OF AMERICA**
800-735-0329
650 J St., Ste. 205
Lincoln, NE 68508
For parents dealing with stepfamily issues, the Stepfamily Association offers support groups and education by trained facilitators at 50 chapters throughout the country. They also offer stepfamily education, information, referrals, books and a newsletter for stepfamilies and blended families.

■ **THE STEPFAMILY FOUNDATION**
(212) 877-3244
333 West End Ave.
New York, NY 10023
Web site: www.stepfamily.org
Membership in the nonprofit Stepfamily Foundation nets you a videotape, two audiotapes, publications, and a quarterly newsletter—eight pounds of information in all. The initial membership fee is $70, and $20 each subsequent year. Individual and family counseling sessions are available over the telephone. Although the organization sends no free information by mail, the web site contains more than 250 pages of interest to stepfamilies.

PUBLICATIONS OFFERING SUPPORT

■ **AT-HOME DAD NEWSLETTER**
(508) 685-7931, Peter Baylies
61 Brightwood Ave.
North Andover, MA 01845
This quarterly newsletter promoting the home-based father publishes a list of local coordinators who help fathers meet, get parenting advice, and plan activities. A subscription costs $12 per year. There are listings for books, online services, and magazines such as *Modern Dad* and an America Online chat group called "Stay-At-Home/Primary Care Dads Chat."

■ **THE COMPLEAT MOTHER**
(701) 852-2822
Box 209
Minot, ND 58702
Always provocative and sometimes outrageous, *Compleat Mother* is a quarterly magazine ($12/year or $20/two years) which celebrates breastfeeding and the family bed, and comes out strongly against disposable diapers and circumcision. While not for everyone, many will appreciate the pro-mothering viewpoint of this magazine.

■ **THE MOTHER IS ME**
800-693-6852
3919 Woodlawn Ave.
Falls Church, VA 22042
E-mail: zoey455@aol.com
Web site: ww.members.aol.com/zoey455/index.html
In 1997 the highly acclaimed quarterly *The Doula* merged with *The Mother Is Me*, a quarterly magazine edited by Amy

Condra-Peters. The magazine "offers all mothers, particularly feminist mothers, a collection of thought-provoking essays, fiction, commentary and book reviews" (of both adult and children's books). A sample issue costs $3.95, and a one-year subscription is $15.95.

■ MOTHERING
800-984-8116
P.O. Box 1690
Santa Fe, NM 87504
E-mail: mother@ni.net

"We are the publication for natural family living," proclaims *Mothering* magazine. In 1998 the magazine will be produced bimonthly. Supscriptions are $18 annually, $32 for two years, and $45 for three years. Beautiful photography illustrates articles on topics such as breastfeeding, home birth, educational methods—in all, a wide variety of articles and essays of interest to parents interested in natural family living. *Mothering* also publishes books on vaccinations, circumcision, fathering, homeschooling, and other topics.

■ THE NURTURING PARENT JOURNAL
800-810-8401
303 E. Gurley, Ste. 260
Prescott, AZ 86301
Web site: www.thenurturingparent.com
E-mail: letters@the nurturingparent.com

Attachment parenting is the theme of the quarterly *Nurturing Parent*. Articles encourage birth bonding, the family bed, unrestricted breastfeeding, father involvement, spousal commitment, and gentle discipline. The 40-plus page magazine ($18.50/year) includes in-depth articles enhanced with lots of photos, letters, essays, and parenting news briefs.

■ WELCOME HOME
800-783-4666
8310-A Old Courthouse Rd.
Vienna, VA 22182

Welcome Home is the product of the nonprofit Mothers at Home. Subscriptions to the 32-page advertising-free journal are $18. Each issue includes stories about joys and challenges of raising children, mother-to-mother problem solving, humor, and inspiring accounts of struggles and successes of at-home moms.

MASS CIRCULATION PARENTING MAGAZINES

■ **CHILD**
800-777-0987

■ **PARENTS**
800-727-3682

■ **PARENTING**
800-234-0847

■ **WORKING MOTHER**
800-627-0690

These widely circulated magazines are extremely helpful to new parents. All contain articles geared to parents of children from birth to teenage years, with doses of humor, advice, recipes, and ideas for family fun. You'll need to thumb through copies of each to see which is best suited to your needs.

Working Mother (10 issues/year) adds information of interest to moms heading back into the work force.

ONLINE SUPPORT

With just a computer, modem and phone line, parents can access a world of support and information. From checking an online version of a parenting book to chatting with other parents, the virtual community can be a wonderful resource. Here are some ways to get online. Note that the online world is rapidly growing; the resources were current when this book was published.

■ ONLINE SERVICES
America Online: 800-827-6364
CompuServe: 800-848-8990
Microsoft Network: 800-386-5550
Prodigy: 800-776-3449

The major online services, as well as a multitude of local providers, connect people throughout the country and beyond. You'll need to install their software and sign up as a member. It's easy to get free software and a free trial period, after which the monthly cost varies by the usage plan you prefer.

The major services offer bulletin boards for exchanging messages and "chat rooms" for real-time communication. They also offer e-mail, software files you can download and resource information on many subjects.

Each provides one or more areas specifically for parents. America Online has "Parent Soup" with message boards, experts, chat areas, reviews, and much more. Prodigy has message boards on parenting and a parenting page on their Internet site. Microsoft Network offers both "Home and Family" and "People and Communities" areas, with message boards, chat rooms, and resources. CompuServe, well-known for its business-related features, now offers a parenting forum.

All of these services also provide a way for users to access the Internet, which offers a multitude of places where parents can share and receive information. Here we've highlighted some of these sites.

■ INTERNET/WWW

Parents can access the Internet and its graphically-rich World Wide Web (WWW) through online services or through a direct Internet provider. With a direct provider, you'll also need Web browser software such as Netscape Navigator, which many companies include for free. Here's a small sampling:

Baby Online:
www.babyonline.com
This interactive site hosts expert panels to answer baby-rearing questions, and includes a parents' chat group.

Baby Web: www.netaxs.com/~iris/ infoweb/baby.html
Contains baby-related resources.

Birth Stories:
www.childbirth.org/articles/stories/ birth.html
For parents who love to read about birth stories, or would like to share their own, this is a great site.

Family.com: www.family.com
Family.com is part of Disney Online, and includes information from parenting newspapers throughout the U.S., feature articles and resources for parents.

Family Planet:
www.family.starwave.com
Family Planet offers daily news on family-related topics, experts discussing family issues, reviews, the *Parent's Resource Almanac* book online, and calendars of family events from around the country.

Father Net:
www.fsci.umn.edu/cyfc/ FatherNet.htp
Especially for fathers, Father Net includes excerpts of "Modern Dad" newsletter and chat groups.

Moms-at-Home:
www.iquest.com/~jsm/moms/
An online support area for moms who have chosen to stay at home.

National Parenting Center:
www.tnpc.com
Offers a variety of parenting resources, including thrice-yearly evaluations of toys, games and books.

Pampers Parenting Institute:
www.pampers.com
Organized by ages, this web site is a great general-purpose information site for parents. T. Berry Brazelton, M.D., is featured in an advice area.

Parent Soup:
www.parentsoup.com
This web site is the Internet version of AOL's parenting area, with much of the same information. There are bulletin boards and chat areas here, too.

Parents Place: www.parentsplace.com
Includes online news, resources, and areas to communicate with other parents. Parents Place's Web Doctor section answers parents' child health questions.

Parenttime:
www.ParentTime.com
Information geared to your child's age, expert advice, and the chance to chat with other parents are the main focus of ParentTime.

Dr. Toy: www.drtoy.com
At this site you'll find the Institute for Childhood Resources' list of the 100 best children's products and toys.

WorldVillage:
www.worldvillage.com
This "family-safe" web site includes articles, cartoons, reviews and contests.

"Real Life With Baby"

A Life Experience by Allison Blackham

I waddled through nine months of pregnancy and watched my belly expand to massive size. I visited the doctor and listened to a heartbeat, felt internal kicks and wiggles at all hours of the day and night. I furnished the nursery and bought tiny, cute baby clothes. I sat through childbirth classes and learned comical breathing techniques with ten other serious moms-to-be and their bemused partners. After months of anticipation, contractions began and I panted and grouched my way through labor. At labor's culmination, a wonderful nurse handed my newborn daughter to me and I was . . . surprised! There really was a baby in there!

That early surprise was a foreshadowing of things to come. No matter how well prepared I thought I was, the reality was still enough to knock me for a loop. The baby did difficult things, like cry. There were days when I seemed to cry a lot, too, especially when I'd had less than two hours of sleep the night before. My husband spent a lot of time cuddling two damp, sniffling females, both large and small, and wondered whether the end result of sex was all it's cracked up to be. Five babies later, I still remember postpartum as a wild and crazy ride. We grow into the calm, competent parents we want to be, but it takes time.

For most parents, sleep deprivation is the single biggest crisis of the postpartum period. Babies need a lot of sleep, but never when you do. Feedings every two hours around the clock, with fussing and crying in between, can make even the most compassionate and emotionally stable parent start to twitch. Let the housework go. Eat soup and sandwiches on paper plates, accept help from family and friends if it's offered, and ask for it if it's not. Get a support group going. This can be as informal as whining to your mom on the phone, but it's often good to talk to other new moms, sharing a weep and a laugh with women who are right there in the trenches with you.

With all the new and exciting things that come with a baby, it seems odd to talk about losses, but that's a reality of having a baby, too. Parts of your life are changed forever. You can no longer just up and do something you want to do, and romantic evenings alone are a thing of the past. Selfish pleasures (like an uninterrupted meal) go by the wayside. For the rest of your life, you will always have a child to consider. The advantages of having a child far outweigh the things you've lost, but you're not going to see all of that right away. Give yourself a break and feel a little sad or angry occasionally. Feelings never hurt anybody.

Poor Dad often gets lost in this postpartum time. Last week you were a couple, you had a life, things were good. Now you're Mom and Dad. The time you used to spend alone together is taken up in feeding, diapering, burping or, if you're lucky, sleeping. Sex? Who has the time or energy? Setting aside a few minutes each day to talk, smile at each other, hug and remember why you decided to be together in the first place is enough to keep you going. As soon as you feel comfortable leaving the baby with a friend or relative, it's great to establish a regular date night. Our children will someday grow up and leave us. We hope our partners will not. And after all, one of the best gifts parents can give their children is to love each other.

I was unprepared when I first held my newborn daughter, and felt inadequate in the days that followed. I've done almost as much growing as my daughter has in those 17 years. My biggest growth spurts have come out of the most difficult situations. As I've paced the floor with a wailing baby, spent the night sitting by the side of a wretchedly unwell toddler, curbed my temper when I'd rather yell, comforted when I'd rather scold, I've learned about unselfishness, patience, compassion and unconditional love. Those are big lessons to learn from such tiny people. It's too bad that we can't be magically transformed into wonderful, wise parents as soon as our children are born, but the process happens anyway. It's through the difficult, stressful, sometimes awful experiences of postpartum that we begin to grow into the good parents we are meant to be.

QUESTIONS AND ANSWERS
Postpartum Depression

Information on postpartum depression was provided by a host of experts: Marcia Kahn, M.D., and Ann Howard, M.D., of the Women's Psychiatric Resource Center in Beaverton, Oregon; Abby Myers, ARNP, and Dawn Gruen, ACSW, of Seattle, Washington; Kathe Pratt of Sacramento and Kerry Breeler of Antelope, California.

Q: What are postpartum mood disorders (PPMD)?

A: Pregnancy is a time of many changes. Reactions to these changes cannot be fully anticipated, and it is not uncommon for women to experience anxiety and/or depression during their pregnancies. The symptoms described below may also occur during pregnancy, or after a miscarriage or weaning.

Once your baby is born, many expect that the postpartum period will be the best time of your life. But instead of joy, you may feel sad, depressed, anxious, even angry. You are not alone. Many women experience significant postpartum symptoms. It is important to realize that these disorders are not self-induced. A woman cannot "pull herself together" any more than she could if she had the flu, diabetes, or any other physical illness.

The postpartum phase (up to one year) is one of the most vulnerable times for women and their partners. Giving birth is a physical, psychological, and emotional challenge, during which everything is in upheaval. Because of this it is difficult to know when normal transitional issues become problematic. In this culture, the turmoil surrounding childbirth is minimized so that many people ignore or deny any negative distress associated with it. The difficult emotions that many experience are often attributed to feelings of exhaustion, with the hope that they will just disappear. But if a woman or couple is experiencing problems, it is important to acknowledge even the mildest forms of distress. Awareness of these adjustment problems can alert the family to seek information and possible evaluation for a postpartum disorder. If the distress continues to be unrecognized, postpartum disorders may progress to more severe dysfunction.

Q. What causes postpartum illness?

A. Mechanisms involved in postpartum illness are not completely understood. Research indicates that these disorders are biochemical and hormonal. The brain's neurotransmitters are directly responsible for the way we feel. They are affected by heredity, hormonal changes and environmental stress. Unfortunately, psychological disorders are stigmatized. These illnesses are difficult to explain. Those closest to a distressed mother need to understand that while psychological and environmental stress may play a role, postpartum disorders are also physical and biochemical.

Q. What are symptoms of the various postpartum disorders?

A. *Baby blues.* Between 50% and 80% of women experience "baby blues." Feelings of depression, anxiety and irritability usually begin two to three days after birth and subside within a week or two.

Depression. Of women who give birth, 10%-20% develop postpartum depression. Postpartum depression can strike any time in the year postpartum or at the time of weaning from breastfeeding. Many women experience postpartum depression between the third and ninth month postpartum, whether or not they experienced the "baby blues." They experience intense feelings of sadness, anxiety and despair that do not go away within two weeks after onset. Instead, the feelings increase with each week and may last for a year or more.

Other symptoms include:
- Feelings of doubt, guilt, helplessness, hopelessness or worthlessness
- Trouble handling your usual responsibilities, feeling overwhelmed and unable to cope
- Insomnia or sleeping too much
- Marked changes in appetite
- Loss of interest in things that used to bring pleasure, including sex.

PPD: TIPS FOR COPING

- Learn and identify the symptoms of postpartum distress as early as possible.
- Understanding and awareness help alleviate guilt and confusion. Don't try to deal with this by yourself. Isolation only makes things worse. Talk to others, join a support group to know that you are not alone and are experiencing something that many other parents go through.
- Consult a health professional who is experienced in postpartum disorders.
- Get your thyroid checked.
- Explore with a health professional the possibility of using medicines that can reverse chemical changes in your body which may have contributed to the depression.
- Counseling can help you learn how to cope and care for yourself.
- Obtain help with domestic chores and care for the baby. This will help relieve pressure and increase the likelihood of a quicker recovery.
- Allow yourself to grieve about your feelings of loss.

- Trouble attaching to baby emotionally (or later loss of attachment)
- Extreme concern for your baby
- Fear of harming the baby
- Thoughts of harming yourself

Panic attacks. Women may experience severe anxiety attacks which include the following symptoms: shortness of breath, dizziness or faintness, increased heart rate or chest pain, sweating, nausea or choking, numbness and tingling, or fear of dying or "going crazy."

Obsessive-compulsive symptoms. Examples include recurrent, intrusive thoughts, urges or images that cause a distress, such as excessive concerns about the infant's health or of harming the infant. Another component is the need to perform repetitive behaviors, such as compulsive house cleaning or checking to make sure things are in order.

Postpartum psychosis. One in 1,000 women develops this severe reaction. Symptoms are severe and may include insomnia, hallucinations, agitation and bizarre feelings or behavior. Postpartum psychosis requires immediate medical help. Remember that postpartum psychosis is treatable and the sooner intervention occurs, the greater the likelihood for earlier recovery.

Q. *How long do postpartum disorders last?*

A. Depending on the degree of severity and type of treatment, postpartum depression may last only a few months or up to a year (with proper treatment). Long-term studies indicate, however, that without treatment, it may take up to four years to recover. If left untreated, children and the couple relationship may experience irrevocable impact.

Q: *How do I get help?*

A: If you think you are having symptoms (even mild ones) that have continued for more than two weeks, discuss them with your health care provider. Unfortunately, some providers are not trained to recognize signs and symptoms of PPD. They may minimize the problem, telling you to just get some exercise or take a break from the baby. This is good advice, but may not be enough. If your provider minimizes your symptoms and you still feel distressed, find another provider who has experience with postpartum disorders.

You should request a medical evaluation (including a thyroid exam). Low thyroid levels are a strong indicator of postpartum depression and physical symptoms including headaches, appetite and sleep disturbance, hair loss and dizziness. Often women's thyroid levels test at the "low-normal" range, and a more sensitive test, such as a TSH test, can identify subclinical hypothyroidism. Once medical causes are ruled out, a referral to a qualified mental health professional should be made.

For women with mild symptoms, information and strong emotional support from family or from a support group may be enough. Others may need individual or group psychotherapy to help understand the contributing factors to their postpartum difficulties, to learn more effective stress reduction and coping skills, and to rebuild self-esteem. Many women benefit from medication in addition to psychotherapy. There are antidepressants which have been researched and approved for use while breastfeeding. Medication should always be monitored under the supervision of a physician or nurse practitioner.

It is important to involve your partner in your treatment as emotional support is one of the main factors in an earlier recovery. Postpartum disorders are quite treatable and with early intervention, recovery and stability for you and your family will be forthcoming.

❧ RESOURCES ❧

■ DEPRESSION AFTER DELIVERY (D.A.D.)
800-944-4PPD (4773)
P.O. Box 278
Belle Mead, NJ 08502
Web site: www.behavenet.com/dadinc
This nonprofit group provides information on postpartum blues, depression and psychosis, including diagnostic information, available treatment methods, a local professional referral list, and a list of local support groups and volunteer telepone contacts. Annual membership is $30, and includes a quarterly newsletter. Enclosed in the basic mailing are items such as national meeting transcripts available for ordering.

■ POSTPARTUM SUPPORT, INTERNATIONAL
(805) 967-7636
927 N. Kellogg Ave.
Santa Barbara, CA 93111
This organization sends brochures on postpartum disorders, including symptoms, checklists and available services to women experiencing PPD. Sent free of charge, the self-assessment questionnaire can help you discover if it is truly PPD you are experiencing. Annual conferences have been held at locations across the country and in Toronto and London. Individual memberships in PSI are $30, and include a quarterly newsletter.

■ WOMEN'S HEALTH CONNECTION
800-366-6632
5708 Monona Dr.
Madison, WI 53716
For women with postpartum blues and depression, PMS and other hormone-related disorders, the Women's Health Connection staff pharmacists are available to answer your questions by phone. An educational division of Women's International Pharmacy, this group's information is unbiased and would be helpful for anyone suffering from PPD. They will send a packet with brochures and a free copy of the informative newsletter "Connection" on request.

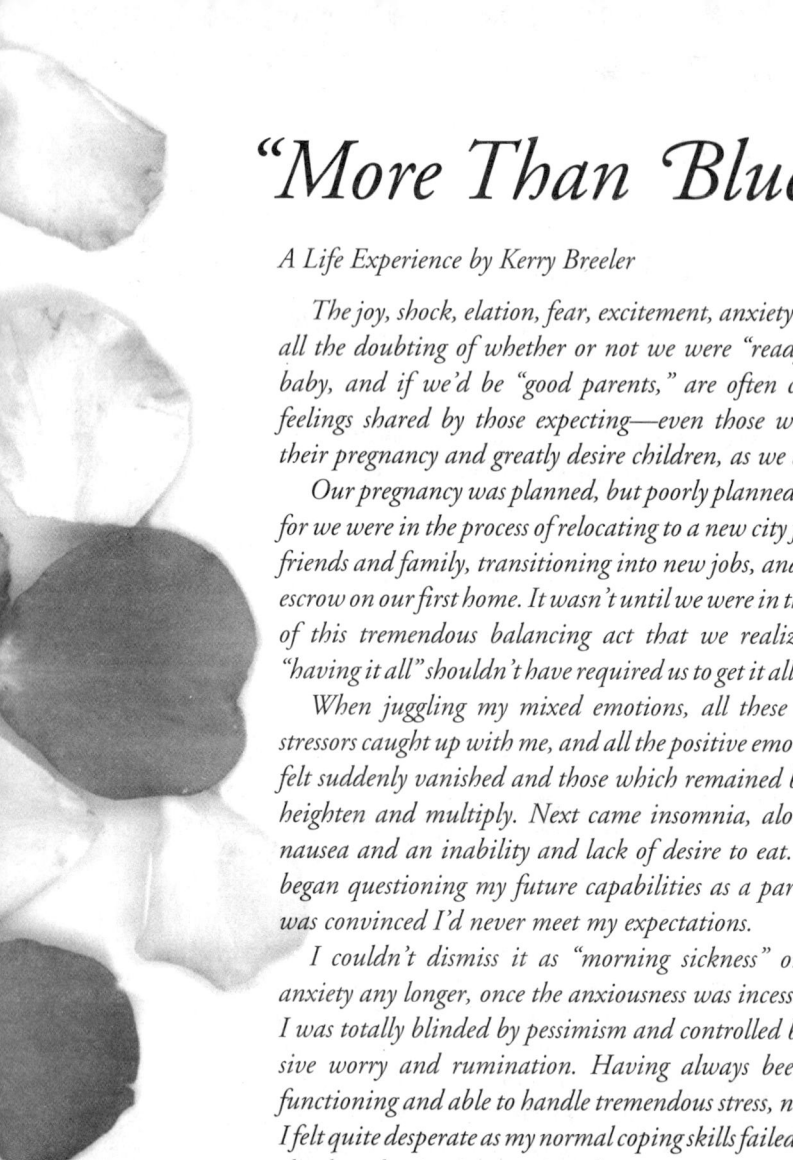

"More Than Blues"

A Life Experience by Kerry Breeler

The joy, shock, elation, fear, excitement, anxiety... and all the doubting of whether or not we were "ready" for a baby, and if we'd be "good parents," are often common feelings shared by those expecting—even those who plan their pregnancy and greatly desire children, as we did.

Our pregnancy was planned, but poorly planned at that, for we were in the process of relocating to a new city far from friends and family, transitioning into new jobs, and closing escrow on our first home. It wasn't until we were in the midst of this tremendous balancing act that we realized that "having it all" shouldn't have required us to get it all at once.

When juggling my mixed emotions, all these positive stressors caught up with me, and all the positive emotions I'd felt suddenly vanished and those which remained began to heighten and multiply. Next came insomnia, along with nausea and an inability and lack of desire to eat. Then I began questioning my future capabilities as a parent and was convinced I'd never meet my expectations.

I couldn't dismiss it as "morning sickness" or major anxiety any longer, once the anxiousness was incessant and I was totally blinded by pessimism and controlled by excessive worry and rumination. Having always been high-functioning and able to handle tremendous stress, naturally I felt quite desperate as my normal coping skills failed me and the sleep deprivation continued.

Luckily, with the help of a mild sleeping aid and the couple weeks off work ordered by my obstetrician, the feelings of hopelessness and incompetence diminished and I regained my self-esteem. Learning to lessen expectations of myself and to quit trying to be such a perfectionist through some brief counseling also contributed to my recovery.

What both the counselor and obstetrician failed to do, however, was warn me about what might be to come. They didn't warn me that I was at risk, let alone a higher risk, for *postpartum depression, and that after the remainder of my uncomplicated pregnancy, another even darker episode of depression might follow.*

My prepared childbirth classes didn't touch on the subject either. But postpartum depression did begin, far beyond six weeks postpartum—a slow, insidious development that gradually eroded away the love and happiness I'd had with my child and husband. Simple tasks became overwhelming, lethargy and lack of motivation set in, and every symptom I endured during my prenatal episode came back, only tenfold. Then emerged distressing thoughts that harm might come to my daughter (first at others' hands, later at my own), along with obsessive-compulsive behaviors to distract me from my own thoughts.

Denial, guilt and shame, along with mistaking my symptoms of depression as the cause of it, kept me from seeking help sooner. By the time I did, I had lost my sense of self and was vulnerable to everyone's interpretations and diagnosis. Co-dependent, child of divorce, unhappy marriage...? These and other "issues" handed out by both friends and professionals only complicated matters.

What would have helped was a diagnosis of PPD rather than that of "chronic depression." Also, therapy designed around the idea that "the fire has to be put out before the house is rewired." And finally, a support group where my feelings could be validated and normalized by others who had "walked the walk," and recovered! No such luck.

But the "fire" was eventually put out by a phalanx of medications. Gradually I improved as I went through the motions of daily life, and after a few months realized I'd fully recovered when enjoyment, spontaneity and a reconnection to my family all reemerged. It was then that I happened upon some excellent materials on PPD, and learned that both my illness and its mistreatment were all too common.

Now an advocate for heightened professional and public awareness of PPD, I facilitate a peer group and am a telephone support volunteer. I share the universal message "You are not alone, you are not to blame, and you will get better." It's a message I wish I had received.

GETTING TO KNOW YOUR BABY

By Troy Maslow Smith

In the first trying days of parenthood, it may be all you can do to keep up with your baby's feeding, diapering and bathing. But soon enough you and your baby will have a chance to spend time together as daily companions. These early months are crucial to your baby's development, and the best way to help your little one is to just be a guide to the world. With your guidance, you will help pass on to your baby the gifts of living and learning and loving. Each day is a new adventure for your child, and through her, you will see the world anew as well.

TEMPERAMENT

As you get acquainted with your newborn, you will notice right away what type of temperament she has. Some newborns sleep 23 hours out of the day, while others may be awake for 12, and want to be entertained each of those hours. Some babies crave stimulation while others shrink away from lights, loud sounds and too much handling. Parents must adjust their methods based on their child's preferences. Sometimes this comes naturally, but be prepared to be frustrated at times when you and your child seem incompatible. With a little patience and some experimenting, you will adjust.

WIDE-AWAKE BABIES

Wide-awake babies are both a joy and a frustration to their parents. Bright and interested in the world around them, they are the babies who kick themselves out of infant seats and prefer being held nonstop. These babies may be happiest in a front pack or sling, where they can go where you go and do what you do. They like motion and stimulation.

Sleeping will often be difficult for the wakeful baby. What you should be able to do, of course, is to put the baby in her bassinet or crib when you sense she is getting sleepy, and let her fuss before she falls asleep. This may work. Or it may not. You may need to rock her through each hard-earned nap and expect wakefulness every night for months on end.

> *These early months are crucial to your baby's development, and the best way to help your little one is to just be a guide to the world.*

Getting To Know Your Baby

Wakeful babies are sometimes soothed by pacifiers, by nursing, or just by being jiggled and danced with. (They are the best help for losing extra pregnancy pounds!) If colic is suspected, try some of the suggestions mentioned in the box. The biggest problem is finding a balance between stimulating the baby and finding a way to help the baby calm down and get enough sleep. The wakeful baby considers each hour spent sleeping an hour lost in which she could be playing, learning, and having fun!

SLEEPY BABIES

With a sleepy baby, parents may worry that their infant is not getting enough stimulation. The typical "good baby" may nurse easily, fall asleep quickly and cry rarely. When awake, he may be quiet and move little, preferring to watch the action going on around him. There is no cause for alarm; you have a calm, cool and collected child who will best thrive in a quiet atmosphere without a lot of outside stimulation. You will need to watch that your baby is not lethargic,

---

COPING WITH COLIC

A colicky baby is one who cries excessively, often in the evenings; not just once, but daily for up to four months. If you have a baby who cries excessively, it is best to have the child seen by the doctor in order to rule out any physical cause. Unfortunately, the cause of colic is unknown. Parents may try to comfort the baby using a number of time-tested techniques, and beyond that, they must just be patient.

Some helpful techniques for a colicky baby:
- Go for a ride in the car.
- Take the baby for a walk in the stroller.
- Carry the baby in a front pack or sling.
- Sing to, and play music for, the baby.
- Use the "colic hold"—baby lying stomach-down across the parent's forearm, resting her head on the parent's hand.
- Turn on the vacuum, washing machine or dishwasher—anything with a rhythmic sound or vibration.

If you find that you need time away from a crying baby, ask for help. See if your spouse, partner, a friend or a relative whom you trust will watch your child so you can get away for a short period. Go for a walk around the block or to the grocery store. Take time to relax and reassure yourself that you are not doing anything to cause your baby's colic. You may find that even a few minutes of relaxation can make all the difference in the world.

If the colic persists for a long period of time, make sure you work with your doctor. Join a support network to surround yourself with others who understand what you're going through. Colic for even one day may make the most excited new mother or father weary.

which may be an indicator of dehydration, along with diapers being wet less than every six to eight hours, a sunken appearance in her soft spot and eyes, and lack of saliva in the mouth. If you feel anything is physically wrong with your baby, give your pediatrician a call.

Whatever their temperament, most babies do best with a parent who is attempting to be calm and consistent. Even if the thought of giving that first bath at home (and dealing with the umbilical cord stump) fills you with dread, relax! Speak soothingly to your baby, and explain as you go what you are doing. Consider hiring a postpartum doula, or have a friend or relative with children over to give you pointers on bathing, breastfeeding and appropriate dressing for the weather. Just be confident that many parents have been in the same situation you are in, and have survived and thrived.

TALK, TALK, TALK

One way to keep yourself calm is to talk to your baby. At first it will not matter what you are saying; just hearing Mom's or Dad's voice will soothe the baby. You can say, "Now I'm going to change your wet diaper," and tell baby the steps involved. You can explain to the baby how you put her into her car seat, what color her hat is, and what the weather is like that day. Babies learn to process verbal information faster if they are spoken to regularly. Make eye contact when you talk, and wait after speaking for the baby to respond. Your baby will "talk" to you, if only by movements or an intent gaze. Soon she will coo back, and your "conversations" will naturally grow from there. Baby talk has its place as "play" language, but don't speak regularly to your child this way! You want him to learn to speak using real words.

By hearing your voice used in a warm and loving way, your child will know that you love him. Your voice becomes associated with good feelings. It's up to you to try not to yell, no matter what age your child is or what he has done! As Jane Healy, Ph.D., author of Your Child's Growing Mind, writes, "Children who have learned to 'tune out' adult voices because they were loud, bossy, or hurtful may start school with poor listening habits." Keep this in mind when choosing child care for your little one, as well.

Talking to your baby has real benefits for long-term learning. Recent research at the University of Chicago showed that at 20 months, children whose mothers frequently spoke to them knew 131 more words than those with less talkative mothers. By 24 months, children of talkative mothers knew 295 more words than the other children. You can think of an infant's brain as "hard-wired" to understand language, and early exposure just gets the circuitry going faster. By two or three years of age, your child will be the one who talks all the time!

SINGING AND DANCING

Singing is a great way to introduce music into your baby's life. You can sing lullabies, show tunes or rock ballads and—no matter how off-key you are—your baby will not criticize your singing voice. If you are inhibited, put a lullaby cassette in your tape player and sing along.

Dancing is great for both you and the baby. You can do ballroom, country-western or modern dance to your favorite music. Just hold on tight to your baby (sounds like a country tune!) and dance.

Getting To Know Your Baby

MUSICAL SELECTIONS

In the car or at home, music is a perfect accompaniment to your day. It's never too early to introduce your baby to music—both children's music and music in your family's own favorite style.

Lullaby tapes are a great start. The soothing melodies may even do the job they were originally designed to do—help your baby fall asleep. Record stores, baby retailers and discount stores generally have a good selection.

Children's tapes are usually more upbeat, encouraging sing-alongs. When your child gets to the toddler stage, he will probably have a favorite tape which he'll want played again and again. It may drive you batty to hear "The Wheels on the Bus" ten times a day, but that is just how kids are. Relax and try to enjoy it! Some favorite children's musicians are Raffi, Tom Chapin, Red Grammar, and Sharon, Lois, and Bram (from the TV show). Disney also has many recordings sure to please both the children and adults.

For a change of pace, you might try playing classical music for your baby as well. The complex arrangements and stirring melodies seem to be a foundation for music learning. Works of Vivaldi and Bach may be a little easier on baby's ears than Beethoven's "1812 Overture." Try a classical music station and you may learn to appreciate classical as well.

Think of other things you can do to music; for example, clapping hands or exercises such as "bicycling" baby's legs to a bouncy beat. You might like to find out more about infant massage and give your baby a soothing massage with a calming new-age CD playing. Music gives your child an introduction to rhythm and beat, early keys to both music and mathematics.

BABY'S PLAYTIME

A basic necessity for babies is a clean blanket on the floor. If a child is constantly being held, or in an infant seat or automatic swing, he misses the opportunity to explore. A tiny infant won't do much beside kick his legs when placed on the floor, but eventually he will enjoy feeling the blanket's texture, explore toys you have placed around him, and learn to roll or crawl to get at enticing toys just out of reach. One caveat: don't lay your baby down right after feedings, as a sitting-up posture is easier for digestion. Luckily, almost all babies like to sit in infant seats or bouncy chairs where they can watch you.

Mobiles entertain many small babies. You may want to put them in places other than over a crib. Many parents report great success with a mobile over a changing table, especially those which are designed to entertain the baby, not adults! Look for bright colors, or black and white designs, to capture and hold your baby's interest.

Your baby's first "toy" will be his own hands. By about six weeks he will be able to find his hands by touch, and will mouth them. By around two months, your baby will be able to grasp toys and will begin to enjoy toys that make noise as they are shaken. Some good toy ideas are rattles that strap on the wrist (you don't have to worry about them being dropped), and chewable toys with easily grasped handles. Never give an infant anything smaller than golf ball size to play with in order to avoid choking.

In the following month or two, your child will begin to grasp objects on his own. This is the time that an activity gym becomes a worthwhile plaything for many babies. Designed like a miniature swing set, with colorful objects hanging from straps, activity gyms allow children to lie beneath them and swing at and grasp the dangling toys.

When handing a three-month-old a toy, show the object, describe it ("here is your soft blue rattle") and let your baby reach out for it. Don't rush him. Once he makes the attempt to grab for it, put it in his hand. This will reward the reaching impulse. Over the next month he will be refining this technique, and will soon be able to grab just about anything he sets his mind to—including hair, earrings, and coffee cups. The danger time has begun! If you have not yet child-proofed your house, you must do so now.

THE GREAT OUTDOORS

When the weather is nice, a favorite activity of most babies is a stroller ride. The gentle breeze on the face, new sights and sounds, and the pleasant vibration from the wheels on pavement will often soothe a child. You may be able to park the stroller under a tree and let the baby watch the movement of leaves above while you catch up on some reading. Stroller rides, or walking with the baby in a sling or pack, get you out in the "real world" when the four walls of your home may be closing in on you. It's not too early to check out neighborhood parks to get acquainted with other moms.

The joys of nature are there for you to introduce to your child—the caress of wind on the cheek, the tickle of grass on bare feet, the scent of flowers, and the feel of rain on a bare head. You can introduce these things to your baby as soon as she's ready. Sand is great, but not when her first impulse is to eat it. But a six-month-old will enjoy splashing in a sprinkler set very low, and a three-month-old will like feeling the texture of leaves or grass.

What other experiences should be part of a baby's daily life? Not many. A baby's needs are simple—a quiet place to sleep, regular feedings, diaper changes when necessary, and the firm guidance of a loving caregiver. All the rest will fall into place. Remember, your baby is part of an already-existing family. Although it may prove difficult, try not to let your life be turned upside-down.

The best advice is to read a lot about baby and child care. Take your pediatrician's advice. Ask friends who are experienced mothers and whose parenting style you admire for guidance. And trust your own feelings and intuitions. To be a good parent, you don't have to buy every gadget that is available, dress your baby to the nines every day, or fuss over your baby unnecessarily. Use common sense and you and your baby will grow more in tune with each other as the months (and years) go by.

INFANT MASSAGE

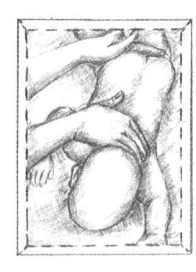

By Adrienne Disbrow, CIMI, Doula, CMT, ICCE

Touch . . . it is your baby's first sense and first means of communication. At six weeks gestation an embryo, less than an inch long, responds to touch. Many studies indicate that touch is an essential part of normal human development and that it is one of the basic necessities of life. With infant massage you will learn your baby's first language. You will also meet his basic needs and express your love and affection all at once.

In many cultures infant massage is an ancient skill passed down from generation to generation as a basic parenting tool. In our culture we are rediscovering the power of this ancient art. We can learn how to massage (touch) our infants and at the same time improve our confidence and competence in our ability to take care of our baby. With our complete attention during a massage, our baby learns about us as we discover him. Through massage, babies learn our smell, our voice, our touch, and how much we love them. We are learning our baby's nonverbal communication cues, likes and dislikes, and how he expresses himself. We are building a bond which will last a lifetime.

Touch is an essential part of normal human development and it is one of the basic necessities of life.

PHYSICAL AND EMOTIONAL BENEFITS

As modern science studies this ancient art, we are discovering infant massage induces many physiological benefits.

- Both the giver and receiver of the massage experience a wonderful, warm feeling of relaxation and closeness.
- Dad or Mom (the massage giver) releases the hormone prolactin. Called the "nurturing hormone," it creates that warm, fuzzy, "I love you forever" feeling in the parents.
- Massage improves circulation, digestion, and increases neurological organization in the infant.
- It reduces muscle tension and helps baby relieve stress in a way other than crying.
- Babies who are massaged get into a deeper sleep. Deep sleep is where children do a lot of growing and repair work their bodies need.
- By strengthening the development of the gastrointestinal and respiratory tracts, massage can help reduce the symptoms of gas and colic.

WHEN TO BEGIN

Massage can start at any age, including newborns and even preemies still in the hospital. With adaptations for each developmental stage, massage can be shared as a family tradition through the teen years and beyond. As an infant becomes more mobile, we urge parents to be flexible and adapt the massage to their child's needs. When a child learns to roll, just allow them to roll and massage whatever part appears available.

Crawling and walking are challenging because the child is often more interested in moving. Parents may find massages become quite a bit shorter. Inventing games, songs, and rhymes to go along with the massage may capture a newly mobile baby's interest.

Toddlers often go through a stage of independence vs. dependence and may decide that massage represents dependence and reject it for a while. Have no fear: as they work through this stage they will return to massage. From 3 years on it is fun to test your own creative abilities and invent massages and games that suit your child.

Older children might appreciate a massage after a soccer game or dance class. And, finally, when your children have children, they will pass the massage tradition and all its benefits down as they lovingly massage their own babies.

Anyone can learn infant massage: parents, grandparents, siblings or child care workers. Working parents especially find it a wonderful tool to reconnect and bond with baby after being away.

CHOOSING AN INSTRUCTOR

Courses are available ranging from group classes in one session to private classes, to several group sessions over a period of time. The International Association of Infant Massage's certified instructors have been through specialized training and receive updates in research and techniques quarterly. Some Certified Massage Therapists and other specialists who work with new parents and babies may also have special training in infant massage. Videos and books are also available for those who prefer to learn on their own.

❧ RESOURCES ❧

■ **INTERNATIONAL ASSOCIATION OF INFANT MASSAGE (IAIM)**
800-248-5432
1720 Willow Creek Cir., Ste. 516
Eugene, OR 97402
The purpose of IAIM is to promote nurturing touch and communication through training, education and research so that parents, caregivers, and children are loved, valued and respected through the world community. The association makes referrals to IAIM-certified infant massage instructors nationwide. IAIM also provides training and certification, a Gentle Touch warehouse for supplies and books, and a quarterly newsletter for association members.

"Zen and the Art of Mothering"

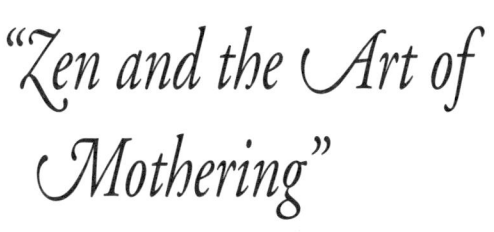

A Life Experience by Felice Lopez

Zoe Rosalie is our little wild one who we are teaching to be a gentle human being. She is a ball of energy—walking, running and talking, often all at the same time. She enjoys being read to; playing with blocks; rearranging our house; finding and greeting cats, dogs and squirrels; singing; dancing, and speaking her own language. As we have nurtured her, she has become a loving, observant, curious and eager child. In turn, Zoe has transformed us into more patient, thoughtful and resilient human beings. As we have grown to recognize how much our words, actions and moods shape her overall development, we begin to be aware of ourselves, so that she receives the best part of who we are and who we are becoming.

We have trained our ears and eyes to understand Zoe's questions and to recognize what, and how, she is learning from us and the world around her. When she was around nine months old, she began to sing along with her evening lullabies. She'd be nursing and when I'd get to "up above the world so high," she'd turn away from my breast and sing all three syllables: "up above." Her participation was subtle, yet unmistakable, and made me realize how closely she'd been listening to all my hours of singing.

By 14 months she had mastered all the little utterances we had taught her—hi, bye, yeah, yes, no, uh-oh, and some we hadn't taught her. Apparently we often ask "why?" around our house because Zoe started asking "why?" in response to our statements, and she'd wait for our answer, however incomprehensible to her.

Lately she's noticed that we begin to talk by saying "umm." One day she took great delight in playfully mocking me. As she was nursing I chatted with my husband, Scott, and when I spoke I began with "umm…" She stopped nursing, looked up at me, and said "umm…" and laughed. Scott and I continued our conversation, and Zoe proceeded to mimic me each time I said "umm," each time laughing harder, until all three of us were roaring with laughter.

Scott and I realized that just as we are her mirror to the world—reflecting our values back to her—she is a mirror to us, reflecting back who we are and what we do and say. I can observe her watching me, and catch fleeting parts of myself that can't be captured on film or tape. I can only see these parts of myself through Zoe's eyes.

We spend so much time planning what we want to impart to our children that we often don't pay attention to their teaching us. Although by nature we're able as mothers to nurse and as fathers to give tender care, we must learn how to do it. This learning is on a different curve than any other skill because, even though there are parenting books to read, the learning must be done by submitting to the child's timetable and personality. If we allow the mood, crying, or cooing of our babies to come forth and try to understand it without immediately quieting or recording it, then we can compassionately enter their reality. By listening to and learning about our babies as little people, we begin to go with their flow, start to teach them and in turn learn more about who we really are. Ultimately we realize that we are all children in the eyes of God.

As I've given and listened to Mother's Day greetings for the first time, I am reminded of the importance of savoring and reflecting upon each day's events—good and bad—that pass so quickly, yet add up to a child's lifetime of memories and experiences that mold their world view and personality. These are our experiences too, that can mold us if we let them. No matter how trying our tasks as parents may be, our job is made easier if we allow the days event's to wash over us— enveloping and becoming us—instead of resisting them, thinking they should be better, faster, less noisy. I submit myself fully to the role of parent, knowing I have much to offer and that I also have so much to learn that only Zoe can teach. ❧

THE VAST ADVANTAGES OF PARENTHOOD

By Joyce Armor

In trying to explain the deep and lasting significance of our wedding anniversary to our almost five-year-old son, I said, "If we hadn't gotten married, we never would have had you." He thought about this for a moment, then replied, "You mean Judie and Stephen (our very married but childless next door neighbors) aren't married?" I had obviously painted myself into a corner and tried to paint myself back out by explaining the differences between married couples with children and married couples without. He interrupted my riveting explanation to ask where lightning comes from, and I gave him my sage answer to such questions: "Go ask Daddy."

That was the end of the children vs. childless comparison for him, but not for me. My first thought was that Judie and Stephen have things that we don't. A new car, for one. Light (and clean) carpeting, for another. Time. But we have things they don't have, too. Toys, for instance. A refrigerator art gallery. Fruit by the Foot. Then again, they don't have to drag a bar stool outside, pry the screen off their bedroom window and somersault onto the bed, all in full view of passing traffic, because some little guttersnipe thinks it's funny to lock Mommy's bedroom door with the key inside at least once a week. They haven't changed enough diapers to cover the planet or broken up fistfights over a grain of sand. On a chilly, drizzling day, my son ran out of a friend's house into her front yard and sat on a huge pile of wet poop that had obviously been left by an elephant. I made the mistake of exclaiming, "Oh no! Look what you just sat in!" So he, naturally, scraped both hands across his backside and came up with handfuls of said elephant droppings. Horrified, he wiped the offending hands all over his brand new jacket.

Let's face it. Childless couples don't have to deal with the mounds of elephant and other droppings that parents do. They probably stay reasonably dry on rainy days. I am forever standing in a puddle in the rain fastening seat belts and trying to wrestle the car keys out of the fat little fist of someone who thinks it's funny to see Mommy's hair get plastered to her face.

My mother talks about the time my brother, age two, locked her out of the house in her nightgown in a snowstorm. For me it was the torrential rainstorm of 1986. I mean, haven't we all, at one time or another, had our front doors kicked in by the police? It's a tradition in our family. I'll bet Stephen and Judie don't have a locksmith listed in their personal phone directory. I see them come and go at odd hours, sometimes many times a day, and a hazy memory forms of a time when I could be spontaneous without hurrying to put on six shoes instead of two, or worse yet, trying to coax the kids into putting on their own shoes. Or standing over two little tooth brushers like a drill sergeant.

Okay, so Judie and Stephen can go where they want, when they want, and they're not at the mercy of baby-sitters or someone else's bowel movements. For their added enjoyment they have furniture without gouges, a clean house, a gorgeous boat and nice tans. Somewhere in our house are the missing pieces to 347 puzzles. We have a swing set with a lot of miles on it and an Aqua-Slide, slightly chewed by an Australian shepherd. But they don't have anybody to color with either, or play jacks or hopscotch or baseball with, or all the other joys of childhood that we're rediscovering.

There are no little arms reaching out over there, not only to get comfort, but to give it. And nobody lives at their house who believes they know everything. Maybe, just maybe, we have a small person living here who will one day make an important scientific or economic or ecological discovery or who will in some other way make this world a better place. As I tucked him into bed a few nights after our anniversary conversation, my son hugged me extra hard and said, "I'm happy you got married and had kids." Me too!

GREATER BOSTON RESOURCES

*Edited by
Allison Aley,
Felice Lopez
and Kelly O'Toole*

KELLY, FELICE, ALLISON AND CHILDREN

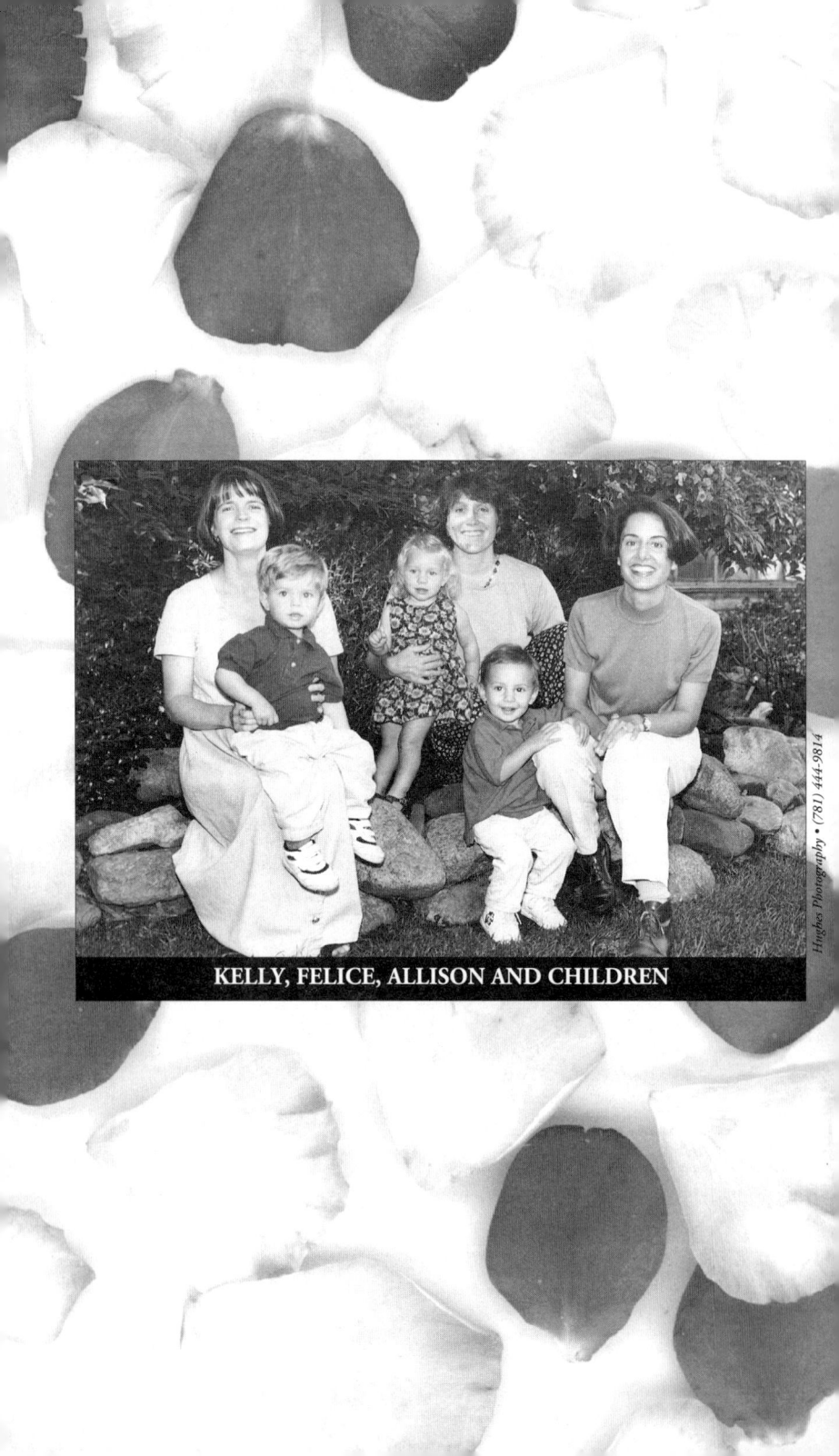

Hughes Photography • (781) 444-9814

"Birth of a Book"

By Kelly O'Toole

Nothing changes your life quite like having your first child. Gazing at your newborn's face changes how you look at the whole world. You suddenly have more love for this tiny person than you ever thought possible. Of course, your social life changes too. When my husband and I had our son Matthew, we started feeling isolated in a city that was very familiar. Neither of our families are from Boston and few of our friends had babies. We found ourselves wanting to connect with other new parents.

I established some new friendships through a new mothers' group but soon many of the women returned back to work. Then, one ordinary day at the park I met Felice and her daughter Zoe. Felice and I immediately felt like kindred spirits. We were both putting our teaching careers on hold to stay home with our children. She introduced me to Allison, a former lawyer who was staying home with her son Ben. We each felt the need to connect with other adults. We missed the stimulation of a professional life and the sense of community that comes with work.

When Felice suggested we start a neighborhood parents' group, I thought it was a wonderful idea. Many interesting moms and dads responded to the flyers we posted in Davis and Porter Squares. Soon we had a weekly play group and later organized a baby-sitting cooperative. We developed some great friendships and a wealth of community support to draw upon. It takes a village to raise a child, and we became that village for each other.

Soon Allison, Felice and I started to brainstorm about a project utilizing our professional backgrounds, yet still allowing us to stay home with our children. The idea of writing a book about having a baby in Boston seemed feasible. We felt there were many resources for parents but it was difficult and time consuming to locate them. A little research led us to The Seattle Baby Resource Guide. We thought, "Why not create the same thing for Boston parents?" It seemed like the natural extension of the local parenting support we had created.

We contacted the publisher. After lengthy discussions and soul searching about whether three stay-at-home moms with toddlers could actually find the time to write a baby resource guide, we decided to go ahead. We had a double stroller, lived within a few blocks of each other, and wanted to share the fun of a common professional venture. So we struck a co-publishing deal to create the Baby Resource Guide of Boston.

It was at this time that my husband and I found out we were expecting our second child at the end of September. We were overjoyed. I would be researching resources for expectant parents while I was myself pregnant, which gave us another factor to consider in our timeline.

Our goal was to write a book helpful for Boston parents and to balance our children's needs with our work. Our business phone number rang at Allison's house, the fax machine transmitted from Felice's house. When we needed a quiet get away, we often used Carberry's Coffee House as our meeting space. "Sneaker net," as Allison's husband refers to it, connected our Somerville homes for delivery of editorial material. At first, we gave each other six to nine hours per week of serious work time by caring for each others' children. It soon became clear we were going to need lots more time to complete the book.

Balancing the care of our toddlers with the completion of the Baby Resource Guide was challenging. Throughout the project and on Saturdays, our husbands took care of them while we worked. During the week, Fernanda Uliano, a wonderful high school student full of love for children, helped us take care of our children while we frantically tried to finish by summer's end. Our interns Lindy Forrester and Sandy Lima saved us many hours of research and fact checking. We dropped off mailings on our way to the park and we picked up resources with a child in a pack on our backs. One memorable business meeting was held at the playground. We climbed up the structure after our toddlers, helping them up ladders and catching them at the end of the *slide, all while having an in-depth conversation about what the article on a Boston obstetrician should look like.*

Throughout the project, we have been rallied and motivated by Allison's organizational energy and clarity of thought. Felice worked hard selling ads to fund the printing of our book. I plugged away, sharing the editorial responsibility with Allison. As the chapters grew, so did my belly. More than one store owner joked that I was really throwing myself into the book's research!

All of this is not to say it wasn't difficult at times. Our children, used to the luxury of a slower pace with their stay-at-home moms, did not always like to be rushed through their breakfasts so they could attend our cooperative child care. Dishes piled and dust accumulated as we worked diligently through every nap. Yet our children built a strong relationship with each other and their baby-sitter Fernanda. One night my husband and I took Matthew out to eat. Sitting in his high chair he started shouting a litany of names as people looked up from their meals: "Zoe, Ben, Felice, Allison, Nana (Fernanda)!" As I worked with Allison and Felice, these people had become a big part of his world.

I worked into September, only days before the birth of my second son Liam. I wouldn't have planned to work so long but the birth of a book is a little like the birth of a baby, it can be a long and excruciating process, but what joy at the end to be able to say, "I did it!" As we finish this resource guide, we feel an incredible sense of accomplishment. We have worked to build community among our three families and to provide a useful resource for Boston parents.

ACKNOWLEDGEMENTS

A project of this scope is a huge undertaking in any circumstances, but accomplishing it as full-time mothers required unbelievable commitment and support. We want to express our deepest gratitude to our husbands, without whose understanding and support this never would have been possible, and our children, who were obviously the impetus behind the idea and who exhibited patience and tolerance well beyond their years.

We also thank Linda Oshman, who introduced us to *The Seattle Baby Resource Guide* and its publisher, Kari Hazen. Our baby-sitter extraordinaire, Fernanda Uliano, gave us the time we needed to complete this book while providing excellent care for our children. The hundreds of people that we spoke to and corresponded with in the community were, almost without exception, informative and supportive. Several that went above and beyond the call were Deborah Kerr at South Shore Hospital; Rosalie Edes, Jeanne Mahoney, Sally Graham, and Beth Shearer at the Department of Public Health; Dr. Mari Kim Bunnell; many people at the Children's Trust Fund; Elise DeWinter at Connecting the Dots for Boston Tots, and numerous people at the area hospitals that gave us a wealth of information by responding to our survey. Many thanks to Bill Snow of Pro-Type Company for producing our cards, assisting with ads, and sharing general support and encouragement. Thanks to Diane Hughes Valente from Hughes Photography in Needham who did a remarkable job of our group photo.

We thank our local advertisers who saw the merit in this valuable guide and supported us with their ads and coupons.

Many sincere thanks to our precise editor Troy Smith and persistent layout artist Jude Lowell and patient publisher Kari Hazen.

HAVING A BABY, BOSTON STYLE

Congratulations—you or someone close to you is thinking about having or is already expecting a baby. You may have explored other books that discuss the details of pregnancy, and raise many other issues like choosing a care provider, keeping your baby healthy, deciding where and how you will give birth, and attending a childbirth class. But how do you find out about all the resources available to you and the local realities of meeting your new needs? This chapter will help you select a care provider, decide where to deliver, find out how to best ensure your baby is getting proper care, locate financial assistance to help cover your many new needs, find a pre/post partum exercise class, choose your childbirth education class, and help you decide what, if anything, to do with your baby's umbilical cord blood. It sounds like a lot to decide upon right now, but use this book to investigate the resources greater Boston has to offer in your journey through pregnancy and beyond.

CHOOSING YOUR PROVIDER

Your first step when you are considering pregnancy is to find a health care provider with whom you are comfortable. Those living in the greater Boston area are lucky to have a wide variety among which to choose. The medical schools at Harvard, Tufts, and Boston University, not to mention the reputable medical institutions with which they are affiliated, attract many of the most highly qualified care providers in the world. No matter what type of practitioner you are seeking (obstetrician, midwife, doula, neonatologist, family practitioner, naturopath, or perinatologist), you will find many qualified individuals practicing in and around Boston. If you are new to the area, do not have a health care provider, or are not satisfied with your current provider, consider the following information and resources to help you find a provider that meets your needs.

No matter what type of practitioner you are seeking, you will find many qualified individuals practicing in and around Boston.

QUESTIONS AND ANSWERS
An Interview With a Obstetrician

Almost every morning Dr. Mari Kim Bunnell wakes up to face a brand new life. As an obstetrician and gynecologist, she works long hours in a Brookline private practice with three other doctors. She also delivers at one of the country's most prestigious hospitals. Besides managing a full-time career, she is devoted to two young children and, like many other mothers, tries to prioritize her marriage with her pediatrician husband. To give you a glimpse of what an obstetrician's life is really like, we spent several hours interviewing her.

Q. *What is a typical day like as an obstetrician?*

A. There really is not a typical day. My days vary between seeing up to 30 to 40 patients in the office to being on call at the hospital. I'm always busy with patients. We see pregnant women in the office for prenatal care and non-pregnant women for annual appointments, surgeries or preventative care.

On the other hand, when I am on call or at the hospital, I handle births and surgeries. For instance, I was on call last week. I did 14 wonderful deliveries. I slept, but not at night, as I was with many women all night long. Fortunately, the deliveries were well spaced out, although a medical emergency took place with one mom while I was delivering another baby. Fortunately all went well. It was an incredible week bringing so many babies into the world.

Q. *Is it difficult to balance the medical needs of patients with the expected camaraderie?*

A. People seek out a health care provider who is good, yet good people tend to become busy. Unfortunately it's a hard balance between being busy and accommodating a patient's needs. Sometimes, you find yourself too busy and not being able to meet everybody's needs. So, like other fields, you do the best you can. I personally have a hard time saying no as I strive to give each patient the personal care they need. When someone asks, "Can I come in at 6:30 because I can't get out of work?" I try to meet their needs as much as possible. I spend a lot of my time reviewing my schedule and thinking about specifics about each patient. I'll think this patient needs more time and therefore I should cancel the next person and move her to another time. That's my way of managing time and my waiting room. I don't want to have a patient waiting for an hour for an appointment if I can help it.

Q. How many years did it take you to complete your education, and how well did it prepare you for your career?

A. I studied for more than 11 years. I have an undergraduate degree in biology, a four-year medical degree, and four years of specialty training which included residency and internship. During my residency, I was on call every third night. And other times I would literally spend three solid days at the hospital. Between the formal schooling and the hands-on training, I think it molded me into a competent and sensitive doctor. In order to keep my knowledge current and to renew my medical license, I attend at least 100 hours of continuing medical education every two years. I also attend other meetings in the hospital and work with the medical schools doing lectures.

The one thing I wasn't prepared for was the financial side of being a doctor. I was a biology major; I never took an economics class. I don't even balance my checkbook and all of a sudden I'm running a corporation. Most physicians aren't astute business people and, unfortunately, private practices will close unless someone understands the ins and outs of the business. So, on top of all the other demands, I'm taking a night class on managed care, to learn the business aspects of my job.

Q. What kind of financial hurdles do obstetricians face in order to practice?

A. The average beginning physician will start off usually with $70,000 worth of debt depending where they received their education. On top of the debt incurred, I pay about $30,000 per year in medical malpractice insurance. There was recently a $98.5 million dollar verdict written up in a malpractice prevention newsletter. My malpractice covers $5 million per occurrence, $10 million per year. And, if it's over that limit a suing patient could potentially put a lien on personal property. There is a huge personal risk and money commitment in becoming an obstetrician. I believe you can only do the best you can, make educated decisions and not focus on the risks involved.

Q. How do you balance your personal life and your career?

A. I don't think that there is a obstetrician with children in this world who feels that there are enough hours in the day. I take off between noon and 6:00 every Wednesday as my designated Mom time. That's when I schedule doctor's appointments, ballet classes, and teacher conferences.

I have wonderful child care; my nanny is my life. I have a cleaning service twice a month and I use a grocery service. My daughter goes to catechism every Sunday and I'm a lector. I play the piano every single night. That is one of my few releases. I don't play very well, but I play. I take six weeks of vacation a year. I've gotten very good at winding down. My husband always says that if my head hits the pillow I'm asleep.

This past Sunday, during an on-call weekend when I hadn't been home since Friday, my husband called me at noon and asked if I was going to the kids' soccer game and I said "no." Then he asked if I was going to make it to the walk around Jamaica Pond. When I said "no," he said, "Fine, I'll tell them you're not coming," and hung up. As understanding as he is, there is a point when he's been with the kids all weekend with no help that he lets me know it.

As I look back I do regret not staying home more. For both kids I stayed home for six weeks straight and then two weeks modified, so eight weeks. I wish that I had taken more time. Unfortunately in my career I was always on this track where I felt like I had to prove myself and I was going to get right in there and be as busy as the busiest person.

Q. *It sounds as if getting enough sleep is one of your greatest challenges.*

A. When I'm on call, my primary responsibility is to my patient. I live only two miles from the hospital. And, when I'm on call—even if anything else very important is happening at home—I must go to the hospital. It's not that I want to leave, it's that I have to leave and if it is in the middle of dinner, I have to give my family a kiss and run out the door. Last night when I was on call, I went to bed at 7:30 with the the kids because I didn't know if I would need to get up at 1:00 a.m. I was surprised because I was able to sleep all night. I was delighted and thought that was the greatest thing in the whole world! I'm on call one of every four nights and one of every four weekends. When you are on call, sleep is an unexpected bonus!

Q. *With all the demands you face, why and how do you do what you do?*

A. How many people get to bring life in the world? I always wanted to do something that can make an impact in someone's life. What can be better than guiding a patient through birth? I think people who choose obstetrics as their career genuinely love the field. You can walk into any OB ward and see how the staff shines. The job becomes a part of your life. Who else gets to start a morning delivering a baby? What could be more satisfying? I just could not imagine doing anything else.

THE MIDWIFE OPTION

By Laura Emmons, CNM, and Phyllis Gorman, CNM
Mount Auburn Midwifery Associates

Combining an ancient, nearly universal tradition with modern medical practices, certified nurse-midwives provide a safe and satisfying alternative to conventional obstetric care and childbirth. Women in Massachusetts are increasingly turning to nurse-midwives for a more holistic, family-centered approach that offers them quality medical care as well as a more personal experience. Midwives look at pregnancy and birth as normal events; the role of the midwife is to help you through this exciting (but sometimes stressful) life transition in a safe, supported, and educated way.

Certified nurse midwives (CNMs) are registered nurses with advanced training who have passed a national certification exam. CNMs are licensed to practice in all fifty states. Ninety-five percent of births attended by CNMs take place in a hospital setting, with the remainder delivering in a hospital or birth center.

CNMs assist women during labor, deliver babies, and provide prenatal and postpartum care. They also provide routine gynecologic care, including family planning services. CNMs in Massachusetts can order any test you might require (including bloodwork, ultrasound, or amniocentesis) and may also prescribe medications.

Nurse-midwives are experts in the normal birthing process, but are trained to recognize any complication that may arise. Obstetricians, on the other hand, are experts in complicated pregnancies and births. All CNMs have physician backup that is readily available should problems occur.

Many women worry that their medical histories make them "high risk," but this is often not the case. For instance, if you are over 35, or have a previous Cesarean section, a history of infertility, or a difficult delivery in the past, you may well be a candidate for midwifery care. If a complication such as high blood pressure or diabetes should develop, a midwife and obstetrician can work together as a team to provide you with the most complete care.

According to a recent study published in the *American Journal of Public Health*, mothers and babies are just as safely cared for by CNMs as obstetricians. However, women cared

---

Certified nurse-midwives provide a safe and satisfying alternative to conventional obstetric care and childbirth.

for by CNMs have lower rates of Cesareans, episiotomies, and induced labor. Medical and surgical interventions, which can be helpful in a complicated labor, can actually increase the risks to mom and baby in uncomplicated labors. Moreover, fewer interventions mean less chance of infection.

The physical and emotional support provided by a nurse-midwife often makes pain medication unnecessary. In the hospital setting, however, the same medical options for pain relief are available to women delivering with CNMs as for women delivering with physicians. Epidurals and, in the majority of cases, other pain medications are not available in birth centers or at home. It is always a good idea to ask your care provider about her or his philosophy regarding pain medication in order to avoid later misunderstandings.

A growing percentage of women in the greater Boston area are choosing to receive their care from CNMs and most insurance companies cover this care. However, nurse-midwives may not be included in the lists of providers published by your insurance company, so consult your local hospital or the resources in this book to find a nurse-midwifery practice near you.

PROVIDER REFERRALS

These services refer you to health care providers, including obstetricians, midwives, family practitioners and pediatricians. Generally the referral services are funded by specific hospitals or physician groups, and will therefore refer you to practitioners affiliated with those hospitals or groups. They can also answer questions about affiliations. Most referral lines operate during normal business hours; those with longer hours are noted.

■ ASK A NURSE
800-544-2424
(Beverly Hospital, Mount Auburn Hospital, Melrose-Wakefield Hospital, and South Shore Hospital)
Hours: M-F   24-hour service

■ BETH ISRAEL DEACONESS HEALTH INFORMATION LINE
800-667-5356

■ BRIGHAM AND WOMEN'S HOSPITAL PHYSICIAN REFERRAL LINE
800-294-9999

■ CAREFINDER
(617) 243-6566
(Newton-Wellesley Hospital)
Hours: M-F   8:00 a.m.-8:00 p.m.

■ DOCTOR REFERRAL LINE
617-782-6556
(Boston Medical Center, Boston University Medical Center, St. Elizabeth's Medical Center)
Hours: M-F   24-hour service

■ HEALTH CONNECTION
800-841-4325
(Boston Medical Center)

Boston: Provider Resources 245

■ **HEALTHY START HOTLINES** *Baby Pages*
800-531-MOMS (6667)
Massachusetts Dept. of Public Health

800-531-BABY (2229)
Boston Healthy Start Initiative
Telephone counselors assist women to locate a doctor or nurse-midwife and to access community support services. There are counselors who speak English, Spanish, French, Portuguese, Khmer, Haitian and Cape Verdean Creole.

■ **MASSACHUSETTS FRIENDS OF MIDWIVES (MFOM)**
800-948-4968, information and referral
This is a great place to call if you want to explore birthing alternatives or find providers who are willing to provide alternative care solutions. For example, they may be able to give you advice on how to seek out a provider who is experienced in performing external versions or who will deliver breech babies vaginally. They can also help you locate a midwife to attend your home birth. MFOM's has no formal relationship with any providers, but can provide you with many suggestions.

■ **MASSACHUSETTS GENERAL HOSPITAL PHYSICIAN REFERRAL SERVICE**
800-711-4644

■ **MOUNT AUBURN HOSPITAL PHYSICIAN REFERRAL**
800-322-6728

■ **NEW ENGLAND MEDICAL CENTER PHYSICIAN REFERRAL SERVICE**
(617) 636-9700
Hours: M-F   7:00 a.m.- 9:00 p.m.

■ **PHYSICIAN FINDER**
(978) 744-6000
(North Shore Medical Center/Salem Hospital)

■ **PHYSICIAN REFERRAL SERVICE AT ALANTICARE MEDICAL CENTER**
(781) 593-2000

PROVIDER RESOURCES

■ **BOARD OF REGISTRATION IN MEDICINE**
800-377-0550
(617) 727-0773
Web site: www.docboard.org
If you have questions or concerns about a physician licensed in Massachusetts, you can obtain a Physician Profile from the Board. The profile will include educational information, specialty board certifications, awards, recent publications, hospitals where the licensee has privileges, and whether the physician accepts Medicaid. It also includes disciplinary or malpractice information. This information is available on their web site as well as by phone.

■ **DIRECTORY OF BIRTHING RESOURCES**
P.O. Box 3188
Boston, MA 02130
The *Directory of Birthing Resources* is published by the Massachusetts Friends of Midwives (MFOM) to help women in Massachusetts find providers of women-centered birthing services. Here you will find midwives, labor support providers, childbirth educators, breast-

feeding counselors, and many other providers who serve pregnant and postpartum women. It can help you locate a yoga class for pregnant women, infertility services, an infant massage instructor, an acupuncturist, or a homeopath. There is also an index of bilingual and multilingual providers. The directory is available in its entirety on the Internet at www.bitwise.net/~midwife. You can obtain the booklet by sending $3.00 to MFOM at the above address.

■ **MASSACHUSETTS FRIENDS OF MIDWIVES (MFOM)**
(617) 497-0124
P.O. Box 3188
Boston, MA 02130
This nonprofit organization seeks to enable all families to have their children born safely in a manner consistent with each family's unique character and needs. MFOM also seeks to protect the right of birthing women to chose their provider and place of birth, be it home, birth center, or hospital. They have a resource library of videotapes, a telephone information and referral service, a speaker's bureau, and a schedule of lectures and conferences. You can become a member for $20 ($10 student), which includes a subscription to their newsletter.

■ **MASSACHUSETTS MIDWIVES ALLIANCE (MMA)**
(781) 444-6927
MMA is the professional trade organization of independent midwives attending most of the home births in Massachusetts. MMA provides apprentice training and education, as well as peer-review, protocols, and guidelines of practice. MMA midwives provide complete prenatal care, conduct normal deliveries at home, and provide postpartum care for the newborn and mother. For referrals to MMA midwives practicing in your area, call the organization's president, Linda Cozzolino at the number listed above.

COMMUNITY HEALTH CENTERS

These nonprofit, community-based organizations provide high quality, accessible health care to children and families, Medicaid/MassHealth recipients, high-risk populations, and uninsured or underinsured persons living in the Boston area.

These centers' services include pediatrics, family medicine, obstetrics and gynecology, social services and immunizations, dental care, nutrition/WIC programs, pharmacy and mental health services. Many offer child care services, teen programs, substance abuse prevention programs, and job training. Interpreters are often available for several languages. Fees are on a sliding scale basis, with many types of insurance accepted.

To locate the nearest center, call 800-475-8455 or (617) 426-2225, or stop by 100 Boylston Street, Suite 700, Boston, MA 02116.

"Birth, From A Doula's View"

By Donna Hudson-Bryant, C.D. (DONA)

"What was going through your mind during that last contraction?" I know by her stillness, with eyes closed, breathing deeply and silently, that Jean is still in an early part of her labor. She has rushed to the hospital, thinking her labor was far along because contractions felt different. Contractions are four to five minutes apart, lasting 45 seconds. The midwife checks her and finds that she is only two centimeters dilated, though fully effaced. I know she is disappointed. "I'm trying to imagine what the baby is doing now, how he is moving down and my cervix is opening." Jean isn't letting these numbers hold her back from the work she must do.

She looks tired to me; it is nearly midnight. Jean is having trouble relaxing; I see that happen when women make the car ride to the hospital. The adrenaline gets pumping in that "this is it" moment and inevitably slows the labor progress, while making the pain seem worse. I suggest a warm bath, and the midwife agrees this would be a nice idea. We all go down to the tub room and get the water running. Water can be so relaxing. The warmth, the buoyancy, and the sound of it running, washes the tension away.

Jean climbs into the tub. Bill, her partner, has been right with her throughout her labor. When she felt so different and wanted to come to the hospital, he felt as though he might be at his limit for helping her. But he is not afraid to be with her, to stay with her and accept her pain. Though he may doubt it, he is nowhere near his limit to help her.

Contractions come. "Let your body be heavy in the water. Let your shoulders drop, your bottom go loose, your legs be heavy. Yes, just like that; you're doing so well. Your baby is moving down; let that pressure be there. It's going away, so let it go…use your breath to blow the last of it away. Take a deep breath when it's gone and let everything go. Now, slow deep breaths, shut your eyes and rest. You're so beautiful; so strong." Within a half an hour, she is dozing between contractions, which are maintaining a nice pace, every five minutes, but now lasting a solid minute.

"What was going through your mind during that last contraction?" Jean is now only focused on the work of the labor. There is no outside conversation. "I'm so tired. I'm not sure I can keep doing this for as long as it will take." I know she's turned the corner, that her labor is progressing more quickly now. Women say these things as they near the end. It's only been two hours since we got to the hospital and one hour since Jean got in the tub, so I am pleased.

By now, Bill has found a ritual of words and pouring water over her belly, which helps Jean. "You guys are doing so well," I say. "That's it, just like that." His confidence has resurfaced. The nurse and the midwife check the well-being of mother and baby, and we take turns running errands, bringing Bill and Jean ice, juice, face cloths, music, etc., so that Bill doesn't need to leave. When he looks tired, I suggest that he change positions, and I massage his shoulders while Jean dozes. He's no good to her if he wears himself out. When Bill needs to leave, I am there to pick up the ritual. Jean is never alone.

Now Jean periodically belches and trembles. I can tell by the way she moans during these contractions that the pressure is very great; the baby is very low. "I'm trying to imagine where the baby is now, but it's hard…it hurts so much." The contractions are coming every three minutes now and are lasting well over a minute. "I want to get out of the tub." We wrap Jean in warm blankets. We walk towards her room but must stop every so often for the contractions. "The pressure doesn't go away," she says, looking at me with pleading eyes. With each contraction Jean sways her hips, hanging from Bill's neck. She moans and looks out at me with very wide eyes. The midwife suggests we check out how far along Jean has gotten; we both sense that it is time to push.

Sure enough, Jean's cervix is completely open and her baby's head is moving lower. Jean pushes with each contraction now, moving herself into positions which feel right for her. The baby's progress slows at a point. "I'm tired. What should I do?" I suggest she try kneeling, hanging from the back of the bed with the head of the bed up high. She tries this, and it works right away. I get the camera ready. Jean doesn't want birth shots, but wants pictures of the baby immediately. Her beautiful little boy is born moments later, and he is vigorous from the start. I snap away.

The time after the birth is a whirlwind which winds down after an hour or so. During this time, I help baby Peter nurse for the first time. I bring food and drink to mother and father, and take lots of pictures. I stay with Bill and the baby while Jean showers; he is nervous about being alone with his son. When things get quiet, and we have all talked ourselves out, I leave the family to savor this special time.

As I drive home, I relive the labor, and think about the other women whose births my doula friends and I have attended. These families have told us many wonderful things: "You spoke at length with us about our previous birth, validating our concerns and giving us hope that we would have a better experience this time." "You encouraged me when labor got slow and coached me through the very intense contractions when I had to hold still for the epidural." "When the baby's heart rate dropped, you supported me while the medical staff took care of the baby, making sure that I knew what was going on and reassuring me so that I wouldn't get too frightened." "Throughout the labor, you let my partner coach me as much as he wanted, and took over when he needed a break or when things got over his head." "I loved the written birth report you kept; now we know just how the labor went."

It's a privilege to serve women as they become mothers. As a doula, I can offer women many things, but we never know how birth will go. At the very last, I will stay with her until her baby is born, accepting her pain and sharing her joys, supporting her wishes to the end. ❧

ENSURING YOUR BABY'S HEALTH

■ **THE BOSTON HEALTHY START INITIATIVE** *[Baby Pages]*
(617) 534-7828
BHSI is a federally-funded urban health initiative whose primary goal is to reduce infant mortality. In partnership with the Boston Public Health Commission, BHSI seeks to improve the quality of life for all children in Boston's neighborhoods. It funds agencies to provide high quality case management, perinatal substance abuse, nutrition, transportation, and child care services.

■ **HEALTHY START** (DOTS PARTNER)
800-531-6667
Administered by the Massachusetts Department of Public Health, Healthy Start is a comprehensive prenatal care program for uninsured pregnant women designed to improve the health of their unborn babies. The program provides a variety of pregnancy-related services including prenatal visits, laboratory and pharmacy services, diagnostic services such as ultrasound and amniocentesis, home visits, delivery care for mom, routine hospital care for baby, psychiatric/psychological assessments, postpartum visits, and family planning. Eligibility is determined by income level and family size and these levels change every April 1st. In 1997, a single pregnant woman making up to $1769 monthly, or up to $21,228 annually, is eligible for Healthy Start. The application process is very easy and quick. Women can request an application by calling the 800 number listed above, or pick one up from a provider. The application must be returned with specific income verification. The program guarantees payment for the above services, but you should confirm that your provider accepts Healthy Start program reimbursement.

FINDING A DOULA

To locate a doula or labor assistant in the greater Boston area, ask for a recommendation or contact Doulas of North America (DONA) and the Association of Labor Assistants and Childbirth Educators (ALACE). If you have specific questions about doulas, contact Carolyn Ogren, DONA Massachusetts State Representative at (978) 664-4889 or reach her by e-mail at TheoCO@aol.com. Also, the *Directory of Birthing Resources*, discussed previously, lists women who provide labor support.

Fees usually range between $250-$500 depending on the person's experience and training, as well as the geographic area in which she is practicing. Most charge one all-inclusive fee rather than an hourly rate, and some offer sliding scale fees or bartering. This fee typically includes one prenatal visit and one postpartum visit, in addition to support during labor and birth.

Thanks to Carolyn Ogren, C.D. (DONA) for assisting with this information.

■ MASSACHUSETTS WOMEN, INFANTS AND CHILDREN NUTRITION PROGRAM (WIC)

800-942-1007

This state- and federally-funded health and nutrition program provides nutritious foods, nutrition and breastfeeding education to pregnant women, postpartum women, infants and children. WIC coordinates with community health services to ensure comprehensive health care and provides screening and referrals. It also provides checks that enable clients to purchase healthy and nutritious foods such as milk, cheese, eggs, juice, cereal, and peanut butter.

To be eligible an applicant must 1) live in Massachusetts; 2) be a pregnant, postpartum or breastfeeding woman, an infant, or a child under 5; 3) meet specific income guidelines (many WIC mothers work full or part-time, and two-income families are often eligible); and, 4) be at nutritional risk (this criteria is broadly construed and is easily met). In order to become "certified" to receive benefits, call or visit your local WIC office. You will be given a referral form to be completed by your provider prior to your appointment. Proof of the first three eligibility requirements must be brought as well. A nutritionist will assess your health and nutritional status. If eligible, WIC will give you food checks to be used at eligible stores.

■ MARCH OF DIMES

(781) 762-4747
1 Edgewater Dr.
Norwood, MA 02062
Web site: www.modimes.org

The Massachusetts chapter provides information through brochures and seminars to prevent birth defects and infant mortality. Their Campaign for Healthier Babies stresses a healthy lifestyle both before conception and during pregnancy. The March of Dimes makes referrals and can send you information on prenatal nutrition and care, genetic counseling, drug use, environmental hazards, and more. A video titled "Baby's First Months" is available for $20.

■ MATERNAL OUTREACH, INC.

(781) 340-9101
63 Winter St.
Weymouth, MA 02188

This unique home health agency specializes in perinatal home care. Their skilled nurses are trained in high-risk and normal obstetrics and provide services at your home. For pregnant women these services include: prenatal visits (available seven days a week and evenings) that encompass teaching, doctor-ordered management of complications, and planning for baby's arrival; and prepared childbirth education classes.

■ PROJECT PARENT TO PARENT

(617) 636-1626
New England Medical Center
750 Washington St., Box 116
Boston, MA 02111

Project Parent to Parent is a partnership between New England Medical Center and eight community health centers with a focus on serving at-risk pregnant and parenting women and their children. The program provides outreach, home visiting and advocacy, as well as linkage to prenatal and postnatal health care. Trained outreach staff at the participating health centers provide culturally sensitive health and socio-economic information to the families they serve.

■ SIDELINES OF NEW ENGLAND
(781) 294-4195
42 Fairview Ave.
Pembroke, MA 02359
This regional chapter of the national organization serves all of New England providing peer telephone support for women with high risk pregnancies, most of whom are on bedrest. They will try to match you up with a mom who had a similar experience. A newsletter is published quarterly and for $15 you can obtain a Parent's Packet which contains materials on how to survive bedrest.

AT-RISK RESOURCES

■ ADDICTION SERVICES
(617) 534-5554
Boston Public Health Commission
1010 Massachusetts Avenue
Boston, MA 02118
Addiction Services offers counseling and information and referrals for detoxification programs and outpatient services. They also provides a full range of outpatient counseling services for pregnant women as well as providing coordination with prenatal and medical services.

■ CHILDHOOD LEAD POISONING PREVENTION PROGRAM
(617) 753-8400
800-532-9571
Massachusetts D.P.H.
470 Atlantic Ave., 2nd Floor
Boston, MA 02210
Lead can harm a baby before birth by passing from the mother to her unborn child. High levels of lead can increase the risk of a miscarriage. It can also cause the baby to be born too early or too small. This program has information on all aspects of childhood lead poisoning prevention including a pamphlet on protecting your baby before birth.

■ COALITION ON ADDICTION, PREGNANCY, AND PARENTING (CAPP)
(617) 661-3991
349 Broadway St.
Cambridge, MA 02139
CAPP works to maintain and enhance services for women who are affected by the abuse of alcohol, tobacco, and other drugs. CAPP maintains a complete list of detoxification and rehabilitation programs for pregnant and postpartum women with infants and children. CAPP also facilitates access to substance abuse family treatment shelters.

■ FETAL ALCOHOL EDUCATION PROGRAM
(978) 369-7713
Boston University School of Medicine
1975 Main St.
Concord, MA 01742
The Fetal Alcohol Education Program provides consultation and training on the effects of alcohol use during pregnancy. Contact this program if you have questions about the risks of alcohol use during pregnancy or are concerned about Fetal Alcohol Syndrome and adoption.

■ HEALTHY BABY/HEALTHY CHILD PROGRAM (DOTS PARTNER)
(617) 534-5832
Boston Public Health Commission
26 Central Ave.
Hyde Park, MA 02136
The Healthy Baby/Healthy Child Program's mission is to increase the ability

Boston: At-Risk Resources

of infants and young children and their families to thrive, especially in neighborhoods and populations which are disproportionately impacted by infant mortality. They provide free home-based visits and group classes on parenting skills and health education, a food pantry for emergencies and advocacy and referral to community services.

■ MOM'S PROJECT
(617) 534-7411
Boston Public Health Commission
253 Roxbury St.
Roxbury, MA 02119
The Mom's project provides counseling and advocacy for pregnant substance abusers in the Boston metropolitan area. They make referrals to detoxification programs and prenatal care, run support and health education groups, offer family planning and reproductive health counseling and provide support services such as home visits, transportation and baby-sitting for clients. The Mom's Project offers services to women from pregnancy through 60 days postpartum.

■ PARENT LINE
(617) 624-8020
This computerized information line, sponsored by the United Way of Massachusetts Bay Success by Six Program, has prerecorded messages on a wide variety of topics. Each topic has a helpful four to five minute message. Topics on pregnancy include nutrition, drugs and your baby, and prenatal care. Messages are available in English and Spanish. You can also speak to a Parent Line specialist for additional support and information or to request a card with a complete list of topics.

■ PREGNANCY/ ENVIRONMENTAL HOTLINE
800-322-5014
Hours: M-F 9:00 a.m.-4:30 p.m.
This hotline is affiliated with the National Birth Defects Center. It provides the public and health care providers with information regarding the effects of exposure to environmental hazards and substances during pregnancy. The hotline staff provide information over the phone and a written follow up on topics such as x-rays, prescription and recreational drugs, exposure to chemicals, and more.

■ THE SMOKER'S QUITLINE
800-TRY TO STOP (879-8678)
800-8DEJA LO (833-5256) Spanish
If you are pregnant and are still smoking, this is the best time to quit. Smoking can cause real problems for you and your baby. It can make you more tired, cause worse morning sickness, contribute to miscarriage, or make breathing in labor more difficult. Smoking during pregnancy also increases the chances that your baby will be born smaller, will have breathing trouble, allergies, birth defects or lung infections. Even quitting late in pregnancy will help you and your baby. For free help, call the Smoker's Quitline between 9:00 a.m. and 9:00 p.m. Monday through Friday or 10:00 a.m. and 3:00 p.m. Saturday and Sunday. The Quitline experts can answer your questions about smoking, help you find programs in your community to help you quit, and provide counseling over the telephone.

- **STATEWIDE SUBSTANCE ABUSE INFORMATION AND EDUCATION HELPLINE**
800-327-5050
This Helpline is always open, and offers information, education, and referrals for both inpatient and outpatient alcoholism and substance abuse treatment. Specialized referral assistance is available for pregnant women and their families, both English and non-English speaking.

- **VNA CARE NETWORK, INC.**
800-728-1VNA (1862)
245 Winter St.
Waltham, MA 02154
This group offers home health and community care for 130 local communities. Their prenatal services include home visits to assess, care for and monitor pregnant women with conditions such as gestational diabetes, multiple pregnancies, hypertension and other high risk conditions. Many services are covered by insurance plans.

MATERNAL HEALTH COVERAGE

- **HEALTH CARE FOR ALL**
(DOTS PARTNER)
(617) 350-7279
800-272-4232 Health Helpline
30 Winter St., Suite 1007
Boston, MA 02108
Call this nonprofit health advocacy coalition if you need health care and have no health insurance, or some other problem prevents you from getting the health care you need. A Health Helpline staffperson or volunteer will provide you with information and referrals to programs that can help.

- **HEALTHY START PREGNANCY HOTLINE**
800-531-6667
Telephone counselors assist pregnant women applying for public insurance coverage and ensure that coverage is obtained and services accessed. They also advocate for clients who are denied coverage. Special assistance is available for teenagers, immigrants and refugees, and women at risk.

- **MASSHEALTH**
(617) 210-5000
800-841-2900
Formerly known as Medicaid, this program provides medical insurance for low income and disabled people. Eligibility is determined by financial and other criteria. Pregnant women are eligible for 45 days while their application is being processed. Call to locate your local Mass Health office for an application. You will need to show proof of income, residency, and citizenship (or documentation of alien status). If eligible, you will enroll in a managed care program and all prenatal and delivery costs will be covered. If your family continues to meet guidelines, your baby will also be covered.

- **MAYOR'S HEALTH LINE**
(617) 534-5050
800-847-0710
Hours: M-F 9:00 a.m.-5:00 p.m.
If you are without health insurance for yourself or your children, call the Mayor's Health Line. This information and referral line can direct you to free or low cost programs. They will also send you information and application forms.

WHERE TO DELIVER YOUR BABY

You can be confident in the knowledge that you are only a short distance away from some of the best medical care available.

Women who give birth in the greater Boston area can choose among a wide variety of birth settings. The vast majority of pregnant women are deemed low-risk and can therefore safely choose among all of the options—from the most technologically advanced hospitals with large numbers of medical specialists to a decidedly non-technical home birth with an independent midwife. Even those women who are considered high-risk, for whatever reason, still have many hospitals from which to choose. No matter what your decision, you can be confident in the knowledge that you are only a short distance away from some of the best medical care available anywhere in the world, should that become necessary. Keep in mind throughout your labor, birth and postpartum stay, that you are the consumer and your insurance is paying for the services provided. Exercise choice and voice your preferences.

Massachusetts law requires every hospital to provide certain maternity statistics to every maternity patient. As a result, most hospitals routinely compile a birth information fact sheet that you can usually obtain by calling either the public relations office or the labor and delivery floor. Be forewarned that some hospitals are more responsive than others, so you may have to be persistent. Even though they are legally required to provide it to women at preadmission, some are reluctant to release it prior to that time. However, we suggest that you get the information as early as possible so you may discuss it with your provider and address any concerns that it raises.

Chapter 111, Section 70E of the Massachusetts General Laws requires that hospitals provide maternity patients with the following information at the time of preadmission, all listed in annual percentage rates:

- primary, repeat, and total Cesarean sections
- vaginal births after Cesarean sections
- deliveries in birthing rooms, labor-delivery-recovery rooms, and labor-delivery-recovery-postpartum rooms
- deliveries by certified nurse midwives
- women monitored internally only and both externally and externally

- women receiving IVs, inductions, augmentations, forceps, episiotomies, spinals, epidurals and general anesthesia
- women breastfeeding upon discharge.

We surveyed the 21 hospitals in the greater Boston area, as well as the two operating birth centers (a third birth center, the Cambridge Birth Center, scheduled to open in December, 1997, answered our survey too). Most answered our surveys completely, but some left portions of the survey blank. If you have questions about where you will be delivering, discuss them with your provider.

COMPARISON CHART

On the following pages you will find our chart comparing the Boston area hospitals and birth centers. This information is intended to help people think about what is important to them in labor, birth, and postpartum and to make them aware that their experience can vary depending on where they choose to deliver. Be aware that percentages based on a smaller number of births tend to be skewed, because just a few births can greatly affect the numbers.

ANNUAL BIRTHS

The number of babies born each year in Boston area hospitals varies greatly, from less than 400 at Deaconess Waltham Hospital to more than 8500 at Brigham and Women's Hospital. The total number of 1996 births at the hospitals we surveyed was approximately 45,991 (Newton-Wellesley provided 1995 data). Add in the 320 births that occurred in the two birth centers and the 200 estimated home births, and you reach a total of 46,511 babies born in 1996 in the greater Boston area!

DELIVERY ROOMS

The majority of Boston area hospitals offer labor-delivery-recovery rooms (LDRs), which means you will be transferred to another room for your postpartum stay. A few offer LDRPs, which allow a woman to stay in the same room postpartum. Amenities vary—most hospitals have showers in labor rooms, and some, but not all, have whirlpool or regular tubs. Birthing beds are provided almost universally. A few hospital have birthing stools, and many provide squatting bars. Think about the amenities you want available throughout your labor and plan accordingly.

TEACHING HOSPITALS

Due to the large number of Boston area medical schools, 14 of the 21 hospitals are teaching hospitals. If you are to deliver at one of these hospitals, think about whether you mind being seen by residents and interns as well as fully licensed physicians or midwives. Hospitals should accommodate a woman's wish not to be seen by residents or interns if she makes those wishes known.

MIDWIFE DELIVERIES

The vast majority of the Boston area hospitals offer the opportunity for women to have their babies with a Certified Nurse Midwife (CNM). As can be seen from the chart, many birthing women (31.6% at Brigham and Women's Hospital in 1996) are taking advantage of this option.

CESAREAN RATES AND VBAC RATES

The 1996 primary Cesarean rate for each of the hospitals is shown in the chart. In 1996, 1.5% of North Shore Birth Center clients and 3.7% of clients at the Birthplace at Wellesley were transferred and had Casarean births. Secondary Cesarean rates in hospitals ranged from 5.2% to 10.6%, with most hospitals hovering around 7%. Total Cesarean rates, the combination of primary and secondary rates, ranged from 11.5% to 27%.

Most women—depending on the circumstances of their previous Cesarean—are now encouraged to attempt a vaginal birth after cesarean (VBAC). The 1996 VBAC rates for area hospitals and birth centers are shown on the chart.

VISITING HOURS

The visiting hours vary from hospital to hospital, but all of them allow certain people, particularly fathers/partners, grandparents, and siblings, to visit outside set hours.

HAVING OTHERS ACCOMPANY YOU

Policy varies, with many hospitals saying that the number of guests is up to the provider, while others limit it to a specific number. Discuss this with your provider.

With respect to Cesarean deliveries, most hospitals allow one support person into the operating room if it is a scheduled procedure. Whether a support person will be allowed into the operating room for an emergency procedure depends on the situation and the type of anesthesia being used. None of the hospitals allow a support person into the operating room if the woman is under general anesthesia.

POSTPARTUM ROOMS

Some of the area hospitals have all private postpartum rooms with private showers, but most hospitals have at least a few semiprivate rooms, which means you could be sharing your postpartum stay with another new mother. At some hospitals the private rooms cost more (generally $20-$35 per day) and the additional cost may or may not be picked up by your insurance.

ROOMING IN

Every hospital tries to give mom and baby some private time, generally one or two hours, directly after delivery. Admittedly, this time will be interrupted so that the nurses can make sure both are doing fine. You may decide to keep your baby with you at all times instead of leaving him or her in the nursery—this is called "rooming in." Most of the area hospitals indicate that they actively encourage rooming in, and all said they would allow it if the mom requested it.

BREASTFEEDING SUPPORT

Every hospital has lactation specialists to help moms get off to a good start in breastfeeding. Whether there is a charge for these services varies from hospital to hospital. In most places a mother need only request a consultation, but a few places require a referral from a nurse or a provider. A few of the hospitals have a lactation specialist contact the mother after she has been discharged to offer support or answer questions. You should investigate the specifics at your hospital prior to your delivery and take advantage of their services.

HOSPITAL COMPARISONS (1996 data unless otherwise indicated)	Annual Births	# of LDRs	Nursery Level
Beth Israel Deaconess Medical Center (617-667-8000)	5400*	11	II
Beverly Hospital* (978-922-3000)	2631	8	II
Boston Medical Center* (DOTS PARTNER) (617-534-5000)	1587	8	III
Boston Regional Medical Center* (781-979-7000)	1206	7	I
Brigham and Women's Hospital (DOTS PARTNER) (617-732-5500)	8600	24	III
Cambridge Hospital (617-498-1000)	600	5 LDRPs	I
Columbia Metrowest Medical Center (508-383-1000)	2808	8	II
Deaconess Waltham Hospital* (781-647-6000)	321	6	I
Emerson Hospital (978-369-1400)	1526*	8	II
The Malden Hospital (781-322-7560)	503	3LDRs, 4 LDRPs	I
Massachusetts General Hospital# (DOTS PARTNER) (617-726-2000)	1642	11	III
Melrose-Wakefield Hospital* (781-979-3000)	1337	7	I

* Fiscal year 10/1/95-9/30/96
# Fiscal year 9/1/96-8/31/97

Teaching Hospital	% CNM Delivery	% Prim. C-Section	% VBACs	% Epidurals	% Nursing at Discharge
Yes	5	14.8	57	69	75
Yes	13	13	49	40	71
Yes	24	12	65[#]	38	n/a
No	17.8	15.3	62.3	34.3	60
Yes	31.6	14.3	56.4	59	62.6
Yes	60	12.6	30.7	33	85
Yes	0.5	10.4	38	63	73
No	26	6	50	29	63
No	0	12.7	29.7	26.9	80.6
Yes	3	13	30	36	33
Yes	29.2	17.3	52.1	65.6	76.7
No	0	9.5	43.2	48.6	52.9

[+] Annual births based on calendar year; all other numbers based on fiscal year

HOSPITAL COMPARISONS (1996 data unless otherwise indicated)	Annual Births	# of LDRs	Nursery Level
Mount Auburn Hospital* (617-492-3500)	1163	6	II
New England Medical Center* (617-636-5000)	1600	7	III
Newton-Wellesley Hospital** (617-243-6000)	4295	6 LDRs, 27 LDRPs	II
The North Shore Medical Center/Salem Hospital (DOTS PARTNER) (978-741-1215)	1710	20 LDRPs	II
Norwood Hospital (781-769-4000)	1107	6	I
Quincy Hospital (617-773-6100)	806	4 LDRs, 8 LDRPs	I
St. Elizabeth's Medical Center (617-789-3000)	1800	11	III
South Shore Hospital (781-340-8000)	3129	11	II
Winchester Hospital* (781-729-9000)	2220	8	II
BIRTH CENTERS			
The Birthplace at Wellesley (800-431-4510)	55 (new program)	3 birthing rooms	n/a
North Shore Birth Center (978-927-7880)	265	2 birthing rooms	n/a

* Fiscal year 10/1/95-9/30/96
** Fiscal year 10/1/94-9/30/95

Teaching Hospital	% CNM Delivery	% Prim. C-Section	% VBACs	% Epidurals	% Nursing at Discharge
Yes	10	11.4	78[++]	48	79
Yes	6 (new program)	16	60	58	55
Yes	15	12	78[++]	35	82
Yes	5 (new program)	12.6	80.8[++]	35	60
No	0	13.7	62[++]	62	64
No	30.6	17	26.5	48.8	52.7
Yes	17	12.9	28	54	65
No	26	13	38	47	66
Yes	0	14.5	33	45.2	95
No	100	n/a	100	n/a	99
No	100	n/a	93	n/a	97

[++] Denominator is number of women who attempted a VBAC (rather than number of all women who have had a previous Cesarean)

BIRTH CENTERS

Women who are low risk may give birth at one of the freestanding birth centers in the area: The North Shore Birth Center (NSBC), the Birth Place at Wellesley or the Cambridge Birth Center. Their rooms, with private bathrooms, are like those found in a nice bed and breakfast, with medical equipment discreetly stored. Families may create their own setting with music, food, lighting, and guests.

Laboring women are attended by Certified Nurse-Midwives and, when a birth is imminent, birthing assistants (generally labor and delivery nurses). If complications arise women are transferred to a hospital (Beverly Hospital in the case of NSBC, Newton-Wellesley Hospital in the case of the Birthplace, and Cambridge Hospital for the Cambridge Birth Center). Transfer rates are generally around 15%. The Birthplace at Wellesley offers some pain medication, but the others do not. None offer epidurals. No security systems or nurseries are necessary because the baby never leaves the family once he or she is born. The length of stay ranges from four to 24 hours. If you deliver at the Birthplace and go home within 16 hours, they will offer you eight hours of MotherCare postpartum services.

■ **THE BIRTHPLACE AT WELLESLEY**
800-431-4510
173 Worcester St.
Wellesley Hills, MA 02181
Web site: www.birthplace.com

■ **CAMBRIDGE BIRTH CENTER**
(617) 498-1660
10 Camelia Ave.
Cambridge, MA 02139

■ **NORTH SHORE BIRTH CENTER**
(978) 927-7880
85 Herrick St.
Beverly, MA 01915
Web site: www.nhs-healthlink.org

HOME BIRTH IN MASSACHUSETTS

Massachusetts home births are attended by Certified Midwives. To be a candidate, you must be in good health, a nonsmoker, and eat well. You will be asked about risk factors that might prevent you from having a home birth. If your pregnancy situation changes, your midwife will help you transfer into the care of nurse-midwives or doctors who can attend you in a hospital.

Approximately one of every 100 Massachusetts babies is born at home. If you would like to explore this option contact the Massachusetts Midwives Alliance, listed in the first section of this chapter, to locate a home-birth midwife in your area. Fees vary among midwives, and many insurance companies pay for home birth, except for HMOs and Blue Cross/Blue Shield.

Thanks to Linda Cozzolino, M.Ed., C.P.M., President of Massachusetts Midwives Alliance, for confirming the accuracy of this information.

YOUR HOSPITAL STAY

By Christa Kelleher

Massachusetts was the fourth state in the nation to enact a law requiring a minimum standard of in-hospital coverage for mothers and newborns. This law applies to all women who are residents of Massachusetts and/or deliver in a Massachusetts hospital, except for individuals covered by self-insured health plans, discussed separately below.

THE 48-HOUR LAW

Under the new Massachusetts law, a woman and her baby are assured at least 48 hours in the hospital following a vaginal delivery and 96 hours following a Cesarean birth. These time periods begin at the time of delivery, unless you deliver between 8:00 p.m. and 8:00 a.m., in which case the clock does not start running until 8:00 a.m. that morning. Therefore, no hospital discharge may take place between 8:00 p.m. and 8:00 a.m. without the mother's agreement.

The law does not mandate that you stay for the minimum periods, and you and your care provider may decide that it would be appropriate for you and your baby to leave before the minimum time period expires. The Massachusetts law was adopted to ensure that mothers and newborns are not whisked out of the hospital inappropriately early. The law specifically gives the mother the ability to participate in the discharge decision.

FOLLOW-UP HOME VISITS

If you do leave early, then, upon your agreement, you will receive at least one home visit by a registered nurse, physician or certified nurse midwife trained in maternal and infant care. The first home visit will be covered by your insurer or HMO and must take place within 48 hours following discharge from the hospital. The initial home visit will include an examination of you and your infant, newborn screening tests, teaching of maternal self care, infant care, and breast/bottle feeding. Subsequent home visits determined to be medically necessary may be paid for by your insurance company or HMO, yet this will vary from plan to plan.

A woman and her baby are assured at least 48 hours in the hospital following a vaginal delivery and 96 hours following a Cesarean birth.

If, while you are in the hospital, you and your provider are having a problem determining your time of discharge, particularly if you are not in agreement about how long you should stay, you may contact the Massachusetts Department of Public Health at 800-436-7757 24 hours a day for assistance or clarification. If your provider or hospital attempts to discharge you without your consent prior to the expiration of the minimum time period, you may file an appeal through the Department of Public Health by calling this toll-free number. Filing an appeal will prevent you from being discharged (until the expiration of the minimum time periods) while the appeal is being considered.

You may also contact the Massachusetts Division of Insurance Consumer line at (617) 521-7465 with questions about coverage or the Massachusetts Department of Public Health's Bureau of Family and Community Health at (617) 624-6095 with inquiries related to hospital procedures or other non-insurance related questions. Both state agencies are involved in the implementation of the law and will assist you in any way they can.

SELF-INSURED PLANS

If your benefits are administered by your employer (or the employer of the person under whose insurance you are covered) rather than an HMO or separate insurance company, which is often the case with large companies, it is likely that your health plan falls into the "self-insured" category. You may contact your insurer or employer to find out if this is the case. Since self-insured plans (often known as ERISA plans) are regulated by the federal government, your coverage and your length of stay would then be determined by federal law and not state law. Please refer to the section on the federal maternity stay law in Chapter 2 for further clarification. It is important to note that the provisions of the Massachusetts regulations preventing discharge between 8:00 p.m. and 8:00 a.m. and guaranteeing a home visit if you leave before the minimum time periods expire are NOT included in the federal law (similar provisions may eventually be adopted in federal regulations, but had not been at the time this was written).

Christa Kelleher is a graduate student at Brandeis University who, as a Legislative Aide for Massachusetts State Senator Lois Pines (D-Newton), worked on the state law requiring a minimum standard of care for mothers and newborns.

STAYING IN SHAPE

Staying in shape is an important part of a healthy pregnancy and will better prepare you for a positive birth experience. Many of the hospitals offer prenatal exercise classes, as can be seen in the next section of this chapter. You can also find wonderful classes offered by individual instructors by asking your friends, reading the fliers in your provider's office, or looking in the *Directory of Birthing Resources* discussed in the first section of this chapter. Another option is to seek out a personal trainer at your local gym who is experienced in designing exercise programs for pregnant or postpartum women. Many gyms and health clubs offer classes and may even provide child care. The following places have ongoing programs designed for pregnant and postpartum women.

■ BEACON LIGHT YOGA CENTER
(617) 739-0717
1689 Beacon St.
Brookline, MA 02146
Beacon Light Yoga Center offers prenatal yoga, focusing on beneficial breathing techniques and postures.. The center also offers personalized Yoga To Go classes, for which the instructors will come to your home or office. Four classes costs $55 and eight classes cost $100. A drop-in class costs $16.

■ PORTIA BROCKWAY
(617) 492-6873
85 Prescott St.
Cambridge, MA 02138
Instructor Portia Brockway holds her classes at the Christ Church in Harvard Square. She offers prenatal yoga classes that focus on yoga-based breathing, postures, relaxation and visualization, and special exercises for the birth canal. Cost is $15 per class or six weeks for $90.

■ MOTHER CHILD CENTER FOR FITNESS & WELL BEING
(617) 864-4225
121 Reed St.
Cambridge, MA 02138
This center offers a prenatal class that focuses on exercising specific muscles that are used during pregnancy and birth. The class also addresses posture and alignment and how to ease the aches associated with pregnancy. Their postpartum class focuses on strengthening those muscles that were most affected during pregnancy and birth. Dance aerobics and massage are also offered. All classes are held in Arlington. Five classes cost $60, while ten cost $100. Drop-in classes are $15.

■ MOUNT AUBURN HEALTHCARE PHYSICAL AND OCCUPATIONAL THERAPY
(781) 643-6489
22 Mill St.
Arlington, MA 02174
This group, affiliated with Mount Auburn Hospital, offers a postpartum class "The A,B,C's of Health and Fitness—Exercises for New Moms," a low-impact, exercise class for mother and baby. It contains toning and strength training exercises for the back, pelvic and abdominal muscles, in addition to information on posture, infant massage, breastfeeding, and infant development. This six-week class is $50.

- **MYSTIC RIVER YOGA**
(781) 396-0808
196 Boston Ave., Suite 3900
Medford, MA 02155
Ongoing classes include Prenatal Yoga, Prenatal Exercise, and Mom and Baby Yoga. Workshops such as "Positions for Facilitating Labor" and "Pregnancy Massage for Couples" are also offered for generally less than $40, and sometimes free. Class prices range from $80-$175. Drop-in classes are $16.

- **NEW DIRECTIONS**
(617) 497-1675
5 Harvard Avenue
Brookline, MA 02146
Ulli Kesper-Grossman teaches Yoga for Pregnant Women (Fridays 9:30 a.m.-11:00 a.m.) and Postnatal Yoga (Fridays 11:15 a.m.-12:45 p.m.). Prenatal classes focus on stretching, breath awareness, and approaches to coping with labor. Postnatal classes help new moms relax, regain strength, and develop the necessary calm and inner balance to meet the demands of a newborn. Drop-in classes are $15 each, and ten classes are $130.

- **NEWTON-WELLESLEY HOSPITAL COMMUNITY EDUCATION**
(617) 243-6383
2014 Washington St.
Newton, MA 02162
Newton Wellesley Hospital offers a variety of prenatal and postpartum exercise classes, including Yoga For Pregnant Women (breathing and meditation), Prenatal Exercise (general low impact exercise), and Postpartum Shape-Up. There is also a highly recommended Exercise for Baby and Mom class, as well as a Baby Massage Class. Different pricing options are available for the Prenatal Exercise Class ($100 for once a week throughout your pregnancy, $150 for twice a week, or you may purchase blocks of classes). Prenatal Yoga is $85 for ten sessions and both postpartum classes are $40 for six sessions and $70 for 12.

- **POSITIVE PREGNANCY AND PARENTING FITNESS**
(978) 371-1371
308 Old Bedford Rd.
Concord, MA 01742
Esther Hausman, a certified childbirth and fitness instructor, leads prenatal and postpartum exercise classes. The pregnancy class includes prenatal strength training, stress management techniques, and relaxation/visualization training. She also discusses health information and support for pregnant women. Her postpartum class is designed for women and their babies from newborn to pre-crawling age. Esther also teaches in Spanish.

- **WEST SUBURBAN YMCA**
(617) 244-6050
276 Church St.
Newton, MA 02160
This YMCA offers both a prenatal and a postpartum exercise class, each meeting twice a week for seven weeks. The prenatal class is for pregnant women who want to maintain their fitness level and strengthen areas of the body that are stressed by pregnancy. The postpartum class is for moms and babies up to six months old, and helps new moms regain their fitness level. The cost for a seven week class is $42-$56, depending on whether you are a member or have particular insurance.

■ **WELLSTREET STATION**
(617) 923-1440
62 Mt. Auburn St.
Watertown, MA 02172
Close to Watertown Square, this prenatal yoga class focuses on breathing techniques, relaxation, stretching exercises and lower body strength. The instructor uses a holistic approach to discover ways to feel good about yourself and your baby. Cost is $15 per class or $95 for eight consecutive classes.

■ **YOGA CENTER OF JAMAICA PLAIN**
(617) 522-6822
57 Boylston St. #1
Jamaica Plain, MA 02130
The Center's Gentle Yoga for Beginners classes are suitable for pregnant women. Seven weeks of classes are $63 and meet once a week in the evening. The studio is convenient to bus and Green line.

CHILDBIRTH EDUCATION & CLASSES

Most people will take some sort of childbirth education class to help them prepare for labor and birth. There are many types of classes to choose from. Most hospitals offer a wide variety of classes taught by different types of professionals, often in both weekly series and weekend formats. There are also many independent childbirth educators who are free to teach their own philosophies without being constrained by hospital guidelines. Any childbirth educator is likely to be familiar with the procedures of the area hospitals. While the basic information should be similar in most classes, the emphasis and interpretation will be different. Similarly, each instructor will be different. Try to find one who shares some of your philosophies about giving birth.

In this section we have listed classes offered by area hospitals and other organizations. We have not listed the many classes taught by individual educators, but we encourage you to explore that option. Ask your provider or friends for a referral or look in the *Directory of Birthing Resources* discussed previously. There is so much choice in this area that you should be able to find a class or instructor that meets your needs.

■ **ASPO/LAMAZE OF NEW ENGLAND**
(978) 256-8148
This professional group of nationally certified ASPO/Lamaze childbirth educators offers quality Lamaze childbirth classes throughout New England. ASPO/Lamaze of New England was named national chapter of the year for 1997. It is affiliated with the ASPO/Lamaze teacher certification program at Salem State College. Dora Jean Brown is the expert on class information in the area.

■ **ASSOCIATION OF LABOR ASSISTANTS AND CHILDBIRTH EDUCATORS (ALACE)**
(617) 441-6244
ALACE can refer you to independent childbirth educators and labor assistants in your area, most of whom have been certified by ALACE. ALACE also has a mail order business carrying books and videos on pregnancy, birth and postpartum.

THE BOSTON ASSOCIATION FOR CHILDBIRTH EDUCATION, INC. (BACE)
(617) 244-5102
This nonprofit organization began offering the first childbirth classes in the area in 1953 and later became one of the founding organizations of the International Childbirth Education Association. The Nursing Mothers' Council (NMC), the first breastfeeding support group in New England, was established by BACE in 1962. Today, BACE provides referrals to BACE-certified educators. BACE also provides breastfeeding support, education, referrals, and training, and serves the community as a pregnancy/childbirth resource and referral organization.

CLASSES

PREGNANCY & BEYOND
(617) 232-1101
192 Washington St.
- Brookline, MA 02146
- Prepared Childbirth Classes
- Refresher Classes
- Breastfeeding Workshops
- Infant CPR Classes

BABY MATTERS
(978) 535-4503
888-83BABY1 (832-2211)
(classes at Beth Israel Deaconess Medical Center, as well as locations in Sharon, Needham, and Chelsea)
P.O. Box 229
Woodville, MA 01784-0229
- Prepared Childbirth
- Refresher
- Cesarean Birth
- VBAC Refresher
- Breastfeeding
- Sibling Preparation
- Infant/Child CPR
- New Parent "Survival Training"
- Parenting Multiples
- After Delivery Follow-Up
- Hospital Tour

BEVERLY HOSPITAL
(978) 927-9103
85 Herrick St.
Beverly, MA 01915
- Childbirth Preparation
- Mom/Baby Drop In Parenting
- Teen Childbirth Preparation
- Sibling Preparation
- Infant/Child Safety
- Prenatal Breastfeeding
- VBAC Preparation
- Hospital Tour

BOSTON REGIONAL MEDICAL CENTER
(781) 979-7060
5 Woodland Rd.
Stoneham, MA 02180
- Childbirth Preparation
- Refresher
- Cesarean Birth
- VBAC
- Sibling Preparation
- Infant/Child CPR
- Breastfeeding
- Caring For You and Your Newborn

BRIGHAM AND WOMEN'S HOSPITAL
(617) 732- 4082
75 Francis St.
Boston, MA 02115-6095
- Prepared Childbirth
- Refresher Prepared Childbirth
- Sibling Preparation
- Maternity/Hospital Tours
- Cesarean Childbirth
- Breastfeeding
- Baby's Breath/CPR
- Newborn Intensive Care Preparation
- Infant Care/Postpartum

Boston: Hospital Classes **269**

■ CAMBRIDGE HOSPITAL
(617) 498-1309
1493 Cambridge St.
Cambridge, MA 02139
- Childbirth Preparation

■ EMERSON HOSPITAL
(978) 287-3268
Old Road to Nine Acres (Route 2)
Concord, MA 01742
- Prenatal
- Refresher
- Breastfeeding
- Infant Care
- Sibling Preparation
- Trial of Labor After Cesarean

■ FAMILY HEALTH PROGRAMS
(781) 575-1089 or (508) 520-0651
(Newton/Wellesley Hospital-affiliated)
4 Estey Way
Canton, MA 02021
- Pregnancy and Childbirth
- Refresher
- Breastfeeding Success
- Infant Safety and CPR
- Sibling Preparation
- Infant Care

■ GREAT BEGINNINGS
(781) 322-7560, ext. 5218
Malden Hospital
Hospital Rd.
Malden, MA 02148
- Prepared Childbirth or Refresher
- Cesarean Birth
- VBAC
- Breastfeeding
- Sibling Preparation for Childbirth

■ HARVARD PILGRIM HEALTH CARE (HPHC)
(617) 731-7311
Most classes are open to the community and are offered at a variety of HPHC sites. Cost is $5-$10 per hour plus materials. Members receive a discount. Call or contact the Ob/Gyn department at individual HPHC health centers.
- Planning a Healthy Beginning
- Early Pregnancy Instruction Class
- Pregnancy Over 30
- Infant and Baby Massage
- Breastfeeding Class
- Newborn Baby Care
- Infant and Child CPR
- When Your Baby is Ill
- Infant Care and Feeding
- Infant/Child Safety
- Infant/Toddler Nutrition
- Mommy and Me
- New Mother & Parent Support Group
- Parent Effectiveness Training
- Prepared Childbirth Class
- Teen Childbirth Class
- What to Expect (Twins or More)
- Sibling Class
- Mother and Infant Postpartum Care
- Pre and Postnatal Exercise
- Postpartum Exercise
- Yoga for Pregnancy and Postpartum
- Massage for Pregnant Couples

■ MASSACHUSETTS GENERAL HOSPITAL
(617) 726-4312
55 Fruit St., Blake 1590
Boston, MA 02114-2696
- Prepared Childbirth
- Childbirth Refresher
- Cesarean Birth
- Grandparenting
- Sibling Preparation
- Breastfeeding and Infant Care
- VBAC
- Infant CPR

■ MELROSE WAKEFIELD HOSPITAL
(781) 979-3408
585 Lebanon St.
Melrose, MA 02176
- New Beginnings (Early Pregnancy)
- What to Expect (Mid-Pregnancy)
- Prepared Childbirth
- One More Time (Refresher)
- VBAC Awareness
- Anesthesia
- Early Infant Care I & II
- Breastfeeding: Basics and Beyond
- Working and Breastfeeding
- On Being A Sibling
- Meet the Experts
- Prenatal/Postpartum Exercise
- New Moms Network
- Toddler Developmental Play Program
- CPR (781) 979-3878
- First Aid (781) 979-3878

■ MOUNT AUBURN HOSPITAL
(617) 499-5121
330 Mount Auburn St.
Cambridge, MA 02238
- Prepared Childbirth
- Birth Refresher
- Breastfeeding
- Sibling Preparation
- Infant-Child CPR Certification
- Birthplace Hospital Tours
- Postpartum Exercise
- Infant Massage

■ NEW ENGLAND MEDICAL CENTER
(617) 636-4214
750 Washington St.
Boston, MA 02111
- Prepared Childbirth
- Refresher
- VBAC
- Sibling Preparation

■ NORTH SHORE MEDICAL CENTER/ SALEM HOSPITAL
(978) 777-1070, ext. 223
81 Highland Ave.
Salem, MA 01970
- Prepared Childbirth
- Childbirth Refresher
- Prepared Childbirth for Teens
- Prenatal Breastfeeding
- Breastfeeding and Back to Work
- Sibling Preparation
- Infant/Child Saver CPR
- VBAC
- Birthplace Hospital Tours
- Prenatal and Postpartum Exercise

■ NORWOOD HOSPITAL
(781) 769-2950, ext. 2343
800 Washington St.
Norwood, MA 02062
- Prepared Childbirth
- Refresher Course
- Sibling/Class Tour
- Breastfeeding
- Teen/Young Pregnant Moms-To-Be
- Me and My Baby
- Multiple Miracles
- Infant CPR

■ QUINCY HOSPITAL
(617) 376-4018
114 Whitwell St.
Quincy, MA 02169
- Prepared Childbirth
- Early Pregnancy
- Sibling Preparation
- VBAC
- Breastfeeding
- Young Adult Pregnancy

- **RESOURCE CENTER AT THE WOMEN'S PAVILION**
(508) 383-1580
Columbia Metrowest Medical Center
115 Lincoln St.
Framingham, MA 01702
- Prepared Childbirth & Refresher
- Pre-Pregnancy
- Prenatal
- Sibling Classes
- Teen Childbirth Preparation
- VBAC
- Breastfeeding
- Booty Camp (Basic Newborn Care)
- Home Bedrest
- Marvelous Multiples
- Prenatal Low Impact Aerobics

- **SOUTH SHORE HOSPITAL**
(781) 340-8332
55 Fogg Rd.
South Weymouth, MA 02190-2455
- Preparation for Labor and Birth
- Refresher
- Understanding Preterm Labor
- Preparing for Twins and More
- Newborn Care
- Infant Safety
- Breastfeeding
- Sibling Preparation
- VBAC
- Bootcamp for Dads
- Babes in Arms (Infant Massage)
- Prenatal Yoga
- Healthy Expectations (bedrest)

- **ST. ELIZABETH'S MEDICAL CENTER**
(617) 562-7095
736 Cambridge St.
Brighton, MA 02135
- Preparation for Childbirth
- Refresher
- Breastfeeding
- Sibling Preparation
- VBAC

- **WINCHESTER HOSPITAL COMMUNITY HEALTH INSTITUTE**
(781) 756-4700 or 756-2232 (tours)
41 Highland Ave.
Winchester, MA 01890
- Prepared Childbirth Series
- Refresher Class
- Care of Newborn
- Breastfeeding
- Sibling Preparation
- VBAC
- Prenatal Exercise
- Postpartum Exercise

CESAREAN SUPPORT AND PREVENTION

Educate yourself about Cesareans, even if you are having a textbook pregnancy and are considered low risk. If you've had a Cesarean, there are classes that will prepare you for a VBAC (vaginal birth after cesarean). Ask your provider for a recommendation. For support, awareness, and prevention information, contact the Central Massachusetts Chapter of ICAN.

- **INTERNATIONAL CESAREAN AWARENESS NETWORK (ICAN)**
Central Massachusetts Chapter
(508) 799-6340
ICAN offers pregnancy, postpartum and VBAC support. They can provide referrals regarding cesarean awareness and prevention. This central Massachusetts chapter holds support meetings in Worcester.

CORD BLOOD OPTIONS

Medical evidence indicates that umbilical cord blood is a rich source of stem cells—the building blocks of a new blood and immune system. Cord blood is increasingly being used as an alternative to bone marrow to treat a number of life-threatening diseases including leukemia, certain anemias and blood and genetic disorders. Cord blood collection is simple, painless, risk-free and cost effective when compared to a bone marrow harvest. Parents can now either store their newborn's cord blood privately for potential future use within their family or donate it to a public bank.

For families who want to store their baby's cord blood, there are two private cord blood banking companies in Boston—Viacord and New England Cord Blood Bank, and there are others across the country. Costs vary at each bank, but include up-front fees as well as an annual storage fee. Privately storing a newborn's cord blood ensures an exact match for that child and greatly increases the chance of a match for siblings and other immediate relatives. Transplants using allogenic (sibling) cord blood have been successful in treating the diseases mentioned above. Autologous (using one's own) cord blood has been successfully used in gene therapy.

Donating cord blood is a free and simple procedure in this area due to the presence of the American Cord Blood Program at the University of Massachusetts Medical Center (UMMC). Cord blood units are processed and stored at UMMC and made available to transplant centers around the world. Many of the area hospitals are collection sites for this program and should have the necessary materials and procedures in place for you to make a donation. If your hospital is not a collection site, arrangements can be made with the American Cord Blood program. As in normal donations of blood, the more cord blood donations that are made, the more likely it will be that the correct match will be found when a child needs it.

■ **AMERICAN CORD BLOOD PROGRAM**
(508) 756-3076
University of Massachusetts Medical Center (UMMC)
55 Lake Ave. North, Worcester, MA 01655

■ **NEW ENGLAND CORD BLOOD BANK** *Baby Pages*
888-700-CORD (2673)
665 Beacon St., Suite 302, Boston, MA 02215-3202

■ **VIACORD** *Baby Pages*
800-998-4226
551 Boylston St., Suite 40, Boston, MA 02116

MATERNITY LEAVE

There are both federal and state laws addressing the issue of maternity/paternity leave. Federal laws must always be followed, and, if state laws are more generous, those must be adhered to as well. The Massachusetts laws governing maternity leave are less generous than the federal Family and Medical Leave Act (FMLA), which is discussed in Chapter 2. So, if your situation is covered by the FMLA (if your employer has 50 or more employees and you have worked there for more than one year or for at least 1,250 hours in the last 12 months), you should refer to the FMLA in planning your leave. If you have questions, you should seek clarification from the resources listed at the end of that chapter, those following this section, and your human resources department.

Even if you are not covered by the FMLA, you may still be eligible for maternity leave under Massachusetts law. In Massachusetts, you are eligible for maternity leave if you are a full-time employee and work for a company with six or more employees. You also must have completed any probationary period, not to exceed six months. If there is no probationary period, you must have worked at least three months. Massachusetts law allows up to eight weeks of leave for the birth of a child, the adoption of a child under 18, or the adoption of a person under 23 who is mentally or physically disabled. Upon your return, your employer must offer the same position or a job with the same pay and benefits.

Whether you will be compensated during maternity leave will be determined by your employer's disability policy. Unlike some other states, Massachusetts does not have state-funded disability benefits. Disability is a compensation benefit that an employer may or may not offer. Depending on your employer's policies, you may also be able to use vacation, sick, or personal time during your maternity leave.

If, during your pregnancy, your provider determines that you need to stop work due to a medical condition, you will be considered a qualified handicapped individual, which may entitle you to disability benefits. This period of disability, before your child is born, will be subject to the disability/medical leave of absence policies of your employer and will not be considered maternity leave. Consult your employer's benefits office for specific information on its maternity leave and disability policies.

In Massachusetts, you are eligible for maternity leave if you are a full-time employee and work for a company with six or more employees.

RESOURCES

■ THE COMMONWEALTH OF MASSACHUSETTS COMMISSION AGAINST DISCRIMINATION
(617) 727-3990, ext. 577
1 Ashburton Place
6th Floor, Rm. 601
Boston, MA 02108
Hours: M-F   8:45 a.m.-5:00 p.m.
Contact the Commission if you feel you are being discriminated against for any reason, including pregnancy. File a report within six months and they will conduct an investigation of the situation. If you have questions about the differences between federal and state laws, they can answer your questions. You may get a recorded message when you call. Leave a detailed message and they will return your call.

■ U.S. DEPARTMENT OF LABOR EMPLOYMENT STANDARDS ADMINISTRATION, WAGE-HOUR DIVISION
(617) 424-4925
1 Bowdoin Square, 8th Floor
P.O. Box 8668
Boston, MA 02114
Hours: M-F   8:30 a.m.-5:00 p.m.
This local office of the Department of Labor can answer questions about the Family and Medical Leave Act (FMLA). Upon request, they will also send you a copy of the legislation. Contact them if you feel you are not receiving the benefits due to you under the FMLA.

CHILD CARE OPTIONS

Babies need someone to care for them 24 hours a day and not every family is lucky enough to have a member who is able to do that. Fortunately, the greater Boston area has a huge variety of child care options from which to choose. We have also included ideas on how to find an occasional sitter.

There are many questions to consider: what are your financial constraints, how many hours will you need, are those hours flexible, do you want your child to have social interaction with other children or the complete attention of an adult? The following individuals have adopted different approaches to child care. Their stories may inspire you as you explore and decide upon a child care arrangement that suits your needs.

- **Andrew:** I am a freelance writer who works at home. Though my income can be erratic, the hours are flexible. When I was a boy, my mother taught me how crucial the first years are in a child's development, and I had always looked forward to helping guide my own children. When my wife became pregnant, she finished her last year of psychiatric training, then took a half-time position. By each working half-time we have been able to raise our son Benjamin without child care. It hasn't always been easy, but with the help of friends and family, a good parenting group and baby-sitting coop, we are making our way.

- **Gina:** I work 20 hours a week and my husband works full-time. Our 2-year-old daughter attends a Cambridge coop preschool three days a week, and spends two half days with her grandparents. We are fortunate to live near my parents and they are able to watch our daughter. We choose a cooperative preschool because it is less expensive and offers scholarships. More importantly, we like being a part of a community of parents who actively participate in the school. My husband spends one day a month as a helping in the classroom, and we feel at ease knowing there is always a parent present.

- **Jill:** When our son Benjamin was born, my husband and I were both partners at large law firms. While we considered various options, a live-in provider was most attractive given our professions and schedules. We wanted someone

There are many questions to consider when thinking about your child care needs.

who was affectionate, responsible, honest and energetic. In addition, we needed someone who could be flexible. Fortunately we found Sarah, and she has lived with us for a little over a year. Despite initial reservations about having a new person living in our home, it has worked out fantastically, in large part because of the layout of our house. While Sarah is always welcome anywhere in the house, she has the downstairs to herself with her own bathroom, television and phone line. We have been enormously pleased with Sarah and the arrangement and are thrilled that she will be taking care of Ben for another year.

- **Lee:** I trained, during my pregnancy and after Rosita was born, to become a certified infant and toddler teacher. After requisite legwork, aided by my daughter's turning 15 months, I found a place where I could teach and she could attend. I'm very happy with my choice, although it is a long and hard day for a single parent, because I'm seeing my daughter blossom and I'm learning a lot about toddlers. This option will only work if you truly want to work with children, if you can let go of your child to let her bond with her teachers, and if you have some other financial help, because the pay is woefully small.

- **Rebecca:** I needed to return to work four months after my son Jacob was born, so my husband and I looked at many different options for child care. My primary goal was to have him near enough to my office so that I could easily visit and nurse him at lunchtime. Stability and dependability were also very important—we didn't want to have to worry about finding an alternative at the last minute if a caretaker got sick. For all of these reasons and the fact that we felt comfortable with the checks and balances and support systems in place for caretakers, we choose a child care center very close to where I work.

- **Helene:** My husband and I decided I would return to work part-time after our daughter Olivia was born, but my mother kept telling me: "Helene, you can't have it all." As my maternity leave drew to the end, our daughter still would not take a bottle. She wouldn't even take it from the nanny as everyone told us she would. She stood her ground, refused that bottle, and cried a lot. After a month of the nanny squeezing a nurser bag of breast milk into her mouth, I realized that our daughter needed me and this was her unmistakable way of telling us. We could never capture these early impressionable years with her again, and I could always get a job. Having it all wasn't worth it (you're right Mom), and my paycheck would just barely cover the cost of child care and my work clothes. We decided that my job would be to raise that little rascal to be full of wonder and love, and to be an asset to the planet.

CHILD CARE CENTERS

Massachusetts child care centers are licensed facilities that generally care for a minimum of 10 children. Centers that care for infants must have one teacher for the first three infants and an additional teacher or assistant for the next four infants. The group size should not exceed seven infants. Toddlers, ages 15 months to 2 years 9 months, should be in a group of nine or less. One teacher for the first four toddlers and an additional teacher or assistant for the next five toddlers is required. For ages 2 years 9 months and older, the ratio is 1:10 (one adult for every 10 preschoolers) for a full day or 1:12 for a half day.

LICENSED FAMILY CHILD CARE

Licensed family child care refers to child care in the private home of a licensed individual. There are two types: single provider and large family child care. A single provider may watch a maximum of six children, of which no more than three may be age two or under (and one of the three must be at least 15 months and able to walk). Licensed large family child care allows up to 10 children under the care of a licensed provider and an approved assistant.

REFERRAL AGENCIES

A number of public and private agencies will provide names, phone numbers and information on care providers. We do not list specific child care facilities since providers change frequently. Instead, this guide refers you to local child care agencies that will help you find the right caregiver for your specific needs.

The following are public agencies that are part of the statewide Child Care Resource and Referral Network. Each agency covers a specific geographical area and refers parents to licensed family child care and child care centers. Referrals are made on a sliding-scale fee. They also offer referrals if your child has a disability. Each agency distributes vouchers or subsidies to qualifying families. All offer parent and child care provider workshops. To identify the public child care referral agency that serves your area, call 800-345-0131. The hours for each agency are 9:00 a.m.-5:00 p.m., Monday to Friday, unless otherwise stated.

PUBLIC CHILD CARE REFERRAL AGENCIES

■ **CHILD CARE CHOICES OF BOSTON (CCCB)**
(617) 542-5437, ext. 641
105 Chauncy St., 2nd Floor
Boston, MA 02111
Hours: M-F 9:00 a.m.-2:00 p.m.
CCCB assists parents in selecting the child care arrangements best suited to their needs. The agency maintains an extensive database of all licensed providers in Boston. Information and Referral Specialists will consult with parents regarding hours of operation, fees, and program content. For children with disabilities, a customized search to locate programs able to support and meet individual needs is available. The Specialist continues to work with the parents and provider once care is selected in order to assure a quality experience. They also make referrals for sick child care.

■ **CHILD CARE CIRCUIT**
(978) 686-4288
190 Hampshire St.
Lawrence, MA 01840

(978) 921-1631
196R Cabot St.
Beverly, MA 01915
This agency's database, updated every four to six weeks, covers 45 cities and towns north and northeast of Boston. Payment of the sliding-scale fee gives you membership for one year. Members are entitled to child care referrals, a parent newsletter published twice a year, publications on choosing child care, questions to ask providers, and more. In addition, they can provide referral for sick child, back up and temporary care.

ABOUT LICENSING

Child care centers and family child care homes in Massachusetts must be licensed by the Office of Child Care Services (OCCS). A child care license limits the number and ages of children in care. A license requires that all child care providers are checked for criminal records and tuberculosis clearance. Before a license is issued, all child care centers and homes are checked for health and safety hazards. To evaluate each licensed provider, the OCCS visits each child care site before the initial licensing, at the time the license is renewed (every two to three years), and upon a complaint.

If you have questions about the care your child is receiving at a center or home, talk to the teacher, director or home provider about your concerns or impressions. If you think the children in care are at risk of health and safety hazards and you have talked to the provider without any results, you can call the OCCS regional office near you and request an investigation of the care situation. These offices can also inform you of the complaint history of a provider or center and send you more detailed information on licensing. The web site includes a list of every licensed child care provider in the state.

■ **MASSACHUSETTS OFFICE OF CHILD CARE SERVICES**
(617) 626-2000
Main Office
1 Ashburton Place
Boston, MA 02108
Web site: www.machildcare.com

Greater Boston:
(617) 727-8898
24 Farnsworth St.
Boston, MA 02210

Worcester and the Metrowest region:
(508) 792-7341
75A Grove St.
Worcester, MA 01605

The North Shore:
(978) 524-0014 or (617) 727-6853
66 Cherry Hill Dr., Suite 100
Beverly, MA 01915

The South Shore:
(508) 947-1133 or (617) 727-1444
109 Rhode Island Rd.
Lakeville, MA 02347

■ **CHILD CARE RESOURCE CENTER**
(617) 547-9861, ext. 72
130 Bishop Allen Dr.
Cambridge, MA 02139
Hours: M-F 9:00 a.m.-3:00 p.m.
Counselors answering the Parent InfoLine will assist you in finding child care in communities surrounding Boston. Ask about their numerous publications covering topics such as choosing child care, in-home care, balancing family and work and more. Many are available in other languages.

■ **CHILD CARE SEARCH**
(978) 263-7744
800-455-8326
43 Nagog Park
Acton, MA 01720
Child Care Search provides referrals in 37 towns in the Greater Lowell, Central Middlesex and Metrowest areas. Their database, updated monthly, includes information on vacancy, fees, how long a provider has been licensed, and more. They have publications on how to choose child care and an evaluation checklist.

■ **COMMUNITY CARE FOR KIDS**
(617) 471-6473 or 800-637-2011
1509 Hancock St.
Quincy, MA 02169
Hours: M-F 8:30 a.m.-4:30 p.m.
Serving the South Shore, Community Care for Kids offers unlimited referrals for six months by an Information and Referral Counselor, a packet of information on choosing quality child care, enhanced referrals for special needs, and technical assistance for parenting questions and concerns. Payment based on a sliding scale.

OTHER CHILD CARE REFERRAL AGENCIES

■ **CHILD CARE PROJECT**
(617) 825-6554
1485 Dorchester Ave., Room 203
P.O. Box 503
Dorchester, MA 02122
The Child Care Project serves the neighborhoods of Boston and has various subsidy programs for working families. If you qualify for a voucher or are income eligible, this agency will assist you in locating licensed family child care. They also conduct parent and child care provider workshops.

■ **CHILD DEVELOPMENT FAMILY SYSTEM**
(617) 494-1644
1 Kendall Square
Building 200, 4th Floor
Cambridge, MA 02139
Free referrals for licensed family child care in the greater Boston area are available through this agency. The majority of their clients are families who qualify for vouchers. Qualification criteria include meeting income eligibility, receiving AFDC and attending school for at least 20 hours per week, or participating in the Massachusetts Department of Transitional Assistance education and training programs. If you qualify, counselors will help you set up appointments, drive you to visit various family child care sites, and assist you with proper voucher authorization.

■ **GROVE HALL DEVELOPMENT CHILD CARE COLLABORATIVE**
(617) 298-5907
438 River St.
Mattapan, MA 02126
Hours: M-F   7:30 a.m.-5:30 p.m.
For 24 years this agency has been serving the Boston communities of Mattapan, Dorchester, Roxbury, Hyde Park, and Roslindale. They provide free referrals for child care centers and licensed family child care in those areas.

■ **NEWTON CHILD CARE COMMISSION AND FUND**
(617) 332-6723
100 Walnut St., Rm. 100
Newton, MA 02160
Hours: M-F   9:00 a.m.-3:00 p.m.
Newton Child Care Commission and Fund will provide free lists of licensed Newton family child care and center based child care providers. Low and middle-income residents who meet income qualifications can enter their child in a child care scholarship lottery in the spring. They also sponsor single parent support groups.

■ **WARMLINES PARENT RESOURCES**   [Baby Pages]
(617) 244-INFO (4636)
206 Waltham St.
W. Newton, MA 02165
Web site: www.warmlines.org
Since 1978, WarmLines has been providing much needed support and information to area parents. Many businesses in the greater Boston area offer WarmLines services to their employees free of charge. Even if your company does not offer this service (Corporate Alliance Program), you can become an individual member for $75 and take advantage of their many services for no additional cost or at a discount. Several programs are also available to non-members on a fee for service basis.

WarmLines can provide you with computerized referrals to a variety of child care options in Allston, Belmont, Brighton, Brookline, Needham, Newton, Waltham, Watertown, Wellesley, and Weston. A knowledgeable staff person will work with you to tailor the search to your individual requirements. A search is $40 for members and $65 for non-members. WarmLines publishes "Sitter Solutions," a booklet listing area babysitting resources and helpful hints for obtaining a sitter.

■ **WORKPLACE CONNECTIONS**
(781) 890-8781
300 Bear Hill Rd.
Waltham, MA 02154
Workplace Connections offers referrals to licensed family child care, child care centers, and in-home care placement agencies as a benefit to their client companies. The general public can pay a flat fee to receive a list of resources that meet age and hour requirements. As of fall 1997, this fee is $30 for child care center and family child care information and $30 for in-home care placement agency information. They will search as many towns as you like. Additional requests require fee repayment. Their database lists child care providers for all of Massachusetts. If your search encompasses several regions due to home, work or commuting locations, it may be beneficial to use this service. You will also receive a summary of licensing regulations, guidelines for choosing child care and a checklist to use when visiting programs.

IN-HOME AGENCIES

The rates for in-home child care providers, unless otherwise noted under a particular agency, are negotiated directly with the caregiver and generally fall within the following ranges: live-out nannies generally get paid $7-$12 per hour; live-in nannies providing full-time child care typically get room and board and $250-$350 per week (although, depending on their credentials, some are paid as little as $200 per week or as much as $500 per week). These amounts are in addition to the placement or referral fees charged by the agency. All organizations referenced in these sections have well-established screening procedures ranging from background criminal checks to written references and personal interviews. You should become familiar and comfortable with any agency's screening procedures prior to using their services.

■ AMERICAN NANNY CO.
(617) 244-5154
P.O. Box 97
New Town Branch
Boston, MA 02258

The American Nanny Co. specializes in full-time (which they consider to be 30-55 hours per week), live-in and live-out child care, primarily in the greater Boston area. They also occasionally place temporary, part-time, or summer nannies. All of their nannies are American women who range in age from 19 to mid 50's. Their fee is $1950. They place a high priority on developing good relationships with nannies and families and on making good matches between the two.

■ BEACON HILL NANNIES
(617) 630-1577
825 Beacon St.
Newton, MA 02157

This agency places live-in caregivers nationally and both live-in and live-out caregivers for the greater Boston area. Both placements are full-time with a minimum commitment of one year. Their fees vary depending on whether you hire an au pair or a nanny. Au pairs are 18 or older; nannies must be 21 or older and have more child care experience. The application fee is $125 for an au pair and $375 for a nanny. Placement fees are $1700 for an au pair or $3350 for a nanny. Use their payroll service and receive a reduced placement fee. This service will take care of all initial state and federal tax forms as well as make quarterly tax filings for you.

■ BOSTON NANNY CENTRE, INC.
(617) 527-0114
135 Selwyn Rd.
Newton, MA. 02161

Boston Nanny Centre serves all of greater Boston, placing full-time live-in or live-out nannies for a referral agency minimum of one year. They received the "1997 Agency of the Year Award for Outstanding Ethical Business Practices" from the Alliance of Professional Nanny Agencies. They recruit both locally and nationally and provide a strong support network and training program for their nannies. Their fee is $1950, $350 of which is paid when the nanny is hired and the balance due one month after the nanny begins, building a trial period which benefits everyone.

■ CONTEMPORARY NANNY, INC.
800-358-0702
53 Langley Rd.
Newton, MA 02159

This local organization places live-in American nannies anywhere in the United States, including the greater Boston area. They have an extensive screening process which includes both psychological and employment reliability testing. Their nannies range in age from early 20's to retirement and all of them have prior experience as a nanny or a degree in education. They also offer a "lease a nanny" program for short-term needs ranging from one week to several months, as well as some after school nannies.

■ DESIGNATED SITTERS, INC.
(978) 774-8580
P.O. Box 409
Danvers, MA 01923

Serving the North Shore, this full service nanny placement agency specializes in placing full-time live-out nannies, but can often fulfill other needs as well. Fees range from $575-$1800, depending on the number of months and the number of hours per week for which you are seeking child care. All of their nannies are local. They can also provide a replacement nanny from their substitute care service should your nanny become sick or need some time off.

■ DOMESTIC SPECIALTIES
(617) 570-9009
151 Merrimac St., 6th Floor
Boston, MA 02114

Domestic Specialties places live-in and live-out nannies for full and part-time positions. All of their nannies have a minimum of two years experience working with children and hold a valid driver's license. The fee for a live-out nanny is generally four times her weekly salary. The fee for live-in nannies is $2000 or four times her weekly salary, whichever is greater. This agency will soon implement an intensive nanny training program lasting one to two weeks. Domestic Specialties also places housekeepers and house managers.

■ INDEPENDENT NANNY SEARCH
(617) 725-4009
1 Longfellow Place, Suite 1515
Boston, MA 02114

An alternative to hiring a nanny agency, this organization provides you with a kit that includes everything you will need to find your own nanny. The kit includes information on how to do a search, screen candidates over the phone, conduct an interview and check references. The kit includes specific questions to ask, an initial application and hiring forms. Once you decide on a candidate, Independent Nanny Search will do a seven year criminal check for you. The price of the kit is $250.

■ IN SEARCH OF NANNY, INC.
(978) 777-9891
5 Cherry Hill Dr., Suite L100
Danvers, MA 01923

For 10 years this full service nanny agency has been focusing primarily on the North Shore, but also serves clients in Boston and the Metrowest area. It places full-time, part-time, short-term, long-term, and summer nannies, almost all local. Their fees for a permanent, part-time nanny range from $400 to $1200 and from $1450 to $2350 for a permanent full-time nanny. They also offer several options for temporary nanny care.

■ MINUTE WOMEN, INC.
(781) 862-3300 Lexington
(617) 964-1188 Newton
(978) 369-3171 Concord
49 Waltham St.
Lexington, MA 02173
In business for 28 years, this privately owned and licensed employment agency specializes in placing full-time, live-out nannies in the greater Boston area. They can also fill requests for live-in nannies. There is a $90 registration fee to use their services and a $1950 referral fee for a full-time nanny. Most of their nannies are local. They also provide cleaning services and elder care.

■ NANNIES NOOK
(781) 749-8097
3 Wanders Dr.
Hingham, MA 02043
Nannies Nook does national recruitment to find American nannies for families in the greater Boston area. They place both live-in and live-out nannies for full and part-time positions. All of their nannies are carefully screened and have current first aid and CPR certification or are willing to receive training. The fee is $1700 for both live-in and full-time live-out nannies. The fee for a part-time live-out nanny is $1300. All contracts are for a minimum of one year. They also provide caregiver support by sponsoring social meetings for nannies.

■ NANNY POPPINS, INC.
(617) 227-KIDS (5437)
(978) 927-1811
100 Cummings Center, Suite 311h
Beverly, MA 01915
The owners of this full service nanny referral agency are mothers and/or have past experience working as nannies. Serving greater Boston, as well as the North Shore, South Shore, and Martha's Vineyard, Nanny Poppins places live-in and live-out nannies in full and part-time situations. They also place summer nannies and after school nannies. They have an extensive standard screening procedure. They guarantee their service for a period of up to one year. Their fees vary depending on the number of hours per week and the number of months, ranging from $15 for one day to $1500 for a full-time nanny for a year. Clients with nannies also receive discounted rates on their occasional baby-sitting service.

■ PARENTS IN A PINCH
(617) 739-5437
45 Bartlett Crescent
Brookline, MA 02146
This full service agency places live-out nannies on both a full and part-time basis. Parents in a Pinch is very picky in their screening process, accepting only about 20% of all that apply to work for them. All of their nannies have previous experience. There is a one-time referral fee ranging from $500-$1700, depending on the number of months and the number of hours per week. The services of Parents in a Pinch are available as a corporate benefit to over 20 companies in the Boston area. This organization also arranges back-up child care and postpartum (including overnight) care, as well as group care.

- **QANNA: QUALITY ASSURANCE NETWORK OF PROFESSIONAL NANNY AGENCIES**
(781) 237-0212
1 Grove St.
P.O. Box 812209
Wellesley Square, MA 02181

(508) 650-8889
Clarks Block
2 Summer St., Suite 14
Natick, MA 01760

This agency places live-in and live-out full-time nannies for a one to two year commitment. They require an application fee of $150 and a placement fee of $2500. The fee for a mother's helper is $1700. All of their in-home providers are carefully screened. Qanna provides extensive support and training for their nannies. They run a comprehensive nanny certification program that all nannies must attend while employed. They also offer a Nanny Stress Hotline, weekly nanny gatherings and a program that pairs new and established nannies together. Qanna serves clients in the greater Boston area and throughout New England.

TAX INFORMATION

It is your responsibility to follow federal and state tax laws when hiring an in-home provider. In Massachusetts, if you withhold federal income tax, you must also withhold state income tax. The federal identification number you receive from the IRS will also be your state identification number. You will need to register with the Department of Revenue by submitting Form TA-1, and you must submit quarterly wage reports.

The frequency of state tax payments will depend on the amount withheld from your employee's salary. If you are withholding $101-$1200 in taxes per year, you will be required to make quarterly tax payments using Form M-942. You will also need to pay state unemployment tax if you pay your in-home help more than $1000 per calendar quarter. Contact the Division of Employment and Training and ask for their Employer Status Report.

Check with your accountant, the IRS, the Department of Revenue and the Division of Employment and Training for further instructions and forms.

AU PAIR AGENCIES

There are many organizations that specialize in bringing au pairs from all over the world and placing them with families in the United States. These groups are all regulated by the federal government and tend to be fairly similar in their programs. Generally there is a fee of about $4000 which covers selection, placement, screening, local counseling and an orientation. Families provide room, board, pocket money (approximately $130 per week) and up to $500 for education. The candidates are required to speak at least conversational English, but some agencies require fluency. Details regarding au pair agencies can be found in Chapter 2.

The laws in this area often change, so it is important to stay informed or consult with a professional. There are businesses listed at the end of this section that can help you.

■ **THE INTERNAL REVENUE SERVICE**
800-829-1040
JFK Building, Rm. E100
Boston, MA 02201

■ **COMMONWEALTH OF MASSACHUSETTS DEPARTMENT OF REVENUE**
800-392-6089
(617) 887-6367
P.O. Box 7010
Boston, MA 02204

■ **COMMONWEALTH OF MASSACHUSETTS DIVISION OF EMPLOYMENT AND TRAINING**
(617) 626-5050
19 Staniford St.
Boston, MA 02114

PRIVATE CHILD CARE TAX/INSURANCE FIRMS

The following organizations can assist you in complying with federal and state tax laws or help you provide insurance for your care provider. Many offer payroll services that will take care of everything from filing initial tax forms to electronically depositing your employee's check into her bank account. This is only a partial list of payroll, tax filing and insurance companies.

■ **GTM ASSOCIATES**
800-929-9213
16 Computer Dr. West
Albany, NY 12205
Web site: www.gtmassoc.com
GTM is a payroll and tax filing service that will assist you in complying with state and federal tax laws. For $28 per month they will prepare signature-ready tax forms that you need only to sign and send. For $30 per month they will submit quarterly tax forms for you. GTM will handle your employee's payroll, including a direct deposit feature, as well as submit tax forms for $35 per month. Each option includes the completion of initial forms to ensure compliance with all state and federal tax laws.

■ **BREEDLOVE & ASSOCIATES INC.**
800-723-9961
25958 Genesee Trail Rd. #503
Golden, CO 80401
This company offers a payroll and tax service for your household employees. Their full service includes initial set up of federal and state tax forms, management of payroll, filing of tax returns and handling all correspondence with the IRS and state tax agencies. They also sell a software package that will lead you step-by-step through the tax and payroll process for household employees.

■ **HOME/WORK SOLUTIONS NANITAX** [Baby Pages]
800-626-4829
2 Pidgeon Hill Dr., Suite 210
Sterling, VA 20165
Web site: www.4nannytaxes.com
A one-time fee of $175 for their Quick-Start program includes completion of initial state and federal tax forms, a breakdown of employee withholdings and employer contributions and a how-to booklet. For $275 per year plus a one-time $75 registration fee, Nanitax will complete the initial tax forms and prepare quarterly and annual tax filings for one employee. They also offer a payroll service including electronic payroll reporting and funds transfer. Visit their web site for more information about hiring in-home help and use the tax calculator to determine employee deductions and employer estimated contributions.

■ **RICHARD A. EISENBERG ASSOCIATES** [Baby Pages]
800-777-5765
1340 Centre St., Suite 203
Newton, MA 02159
The official Insurance representative of the International Nanny Association, Eisenberg Associates has been in business since 1970, and can help you understand the laws pertaining to insurance for nannies, which are complicated and constantly changing. They offer disability and retirement plans for your nanny as well as portable health insurance that your nanny can keep even if she leaves your employment.

TEMPORARY AND SICK CHILD CARE AGENCIES

Even if you are home with your child full-time or have the most dependable child care provider in the area, there may be a time when you need child care on a temporary basis. This may occur when a provider takes a vacation (most centers and family day care homes take one or two weeks off a year and nannies can get sick or have personal emergencies like the rest of us), when your current situation becomes unsatisfactory for any reason and you need time to find another, or when your child is ill. Most centers and many family day care providers will provide you with guidelines about when you should keep your child home due to illness. Generally, if your child experiences any of the following in the 24 hours prior to being delivered to the care provider, you should probably keep him or her home:

- A temperature of 100 orally or 101 rectally
- Diarrhea—two or more instances close together could indicate a contagious virus
- Vomiting
- Pronounced or persistent coughing
- A contagious condition of any kind (strep throat, flu, respiratory infection, conjunctivitis, chicken pox, infectious rash)
- Head lice
- Red or runny eyes or a runny nose that you suspect is a cold

The current rate for temporary sitters in the greater Boston area is $7-$12 per hour, depending on the qualifications of the sitter. This is in addition to membership, replacement and referral fees

Boston: Temporary and Sick Child Care Agencies

charged by the agency. All organizations referenced in these sections have well-established screening procedures ranging from background criminal checks to written references and personal interviews. You should become familiar and comfortable with any agency's screening procedures prior to using their services. Most of these organizations will provide sitters for mildly ill children.

■ BROCKWELL AGENCY, INC.
(781) 235-5823
P.O. Box 812246
Wellesley, MA 02181
In business since 1964, this agency specializes in temporary, hourly or overnight child care for business trips or vacations as well as long-term care with a one-year commitment. They will accommodate requests to interview a temporary caregiver if time allows. Their fees vary depending on factors such as number of children and length of the temporary placement. They also offer new baby care and postpartum support.

■ CHILD CARE RESOURCES DIVISION OF NANNIES NOOK
(781) 749-9889
3 Wanders Dr.
Hingham, MA 02043
In business for 12 years, this agency places temporary nannies by the day, month or for overnight child care. Their nannies are carefully screened and include students, retired women and mothers. They charge $20 per day in addition to the nanny's fee. Reduced rates are available for placements longer than a month.

■ DESIGNATED SITTERS, INC.
(978) 774-8580
P.O. Box 409
Danvers, MA 01923
This full service nanny placement agency also provides short-term or substitute care. There is a registration fee of $50 that entitles you to call and get referrals for baby-sitting needs. There is a minimum of four hours. Unregistered families can use the service as well, but must pay an additional $2 per hour fee, over and above the hourly rate for the sitter. Overnight care is also available at an all-inclusive price of $108 per 24-hour period (plus $10 for each additional child).

■ IN SEARCH OF NANNY, INC.
(978) 777-9891
5 Cherry Hill Dr., Suite L100
Danvers, MA 01923
This full service nanny placement agency offers at least two options for temporary care. For $160 you can subscribe to their list, updated three times a year, of over 60 screened providers available for evening and weekend child care. For $100 you can also register for their temporary nanny service which entitles you to call them when you have a specific need. The agency charge associated with this service is $22 per day.

■ MINUTE WOMEN, INC.
(781) 862-3300 Lexington
(617) 964-1188 Newton
(978) 369-3171 Concord
49 Waltham St.
Lexington, MA 02173
This employment agency, in addition to placing full-time nannies, can fill temporary and sporadic requests for sitters with at least three to four business days'

notice. There is a $90 registration fee to use their services and an additional $3 per hour charge (in addition to the sitter's hourly rate). Most of their sitters are local and have been carefully screened and interviewed. They also provide cleaning services and elder care.

■ **NANNY POPPINS, INC.** *Baby Pages*
(617) 227-KIDS (5437)
(978) 927-1811
100 Cummings Center, Suite 311h
Beverly, MA 01915
In addition to being a full service nanny referral agency, this organization offers an occasional baby-sitting service. You can become a member for $150 and receive referrals for up to 6 hours of sitting per week at no additional cost and discounted rates on referrals over 6 hours. Referral fees for non-members range from $10 for a half day to $75 for seven days/overnights. Clients with nannies receive discounted rates. Gift certificates are available.

■ **NEWBORN AND FAMILY CARE**
(781) 444-2198
75 Bird St.
Needham, MA 02192
This service, started 14 years ago, provides newborn, day, overnight or 24 hour live-in family care. Their carefully screened, experienced caregivers also provide general postpartum support including household chores, meal preparation, laundry and food shopping.

■ **PARENTS IN A PINCH**
(617) 739-5437
45 Bartlett Crescent
Brookline, MA 02146
In addition to full and part-time nanny care, group care, and postpartum care, Parents in a Pinch, as suggested by their name, provides temporary back-up child care in your home with very short notice, although they prefer 24 hours' notice. They can help in almost any situation, including unexpected illness and school vacations. They are also affiliated with a number of family child care settings and can set up a play date rather than a baby-sitting situation for healthy kids, if that is preferable. There is a daily agency referral fee of $50 for a full day ($30 for a half day), unless your employer has contracted to offer these services as a corporate benefit.

■ **TOWN & COUNTRY SITTERS**
(781) 422-1010
P.O. Box 812296
Wesley, MA 02181
This 24-hour baby-sitting service provides caregivers on a short-term, sporadic or temporary basis in the greater Boston area and as far west as Framingham. They fill requests for overnight sitters, and, while they never make guarantees, have gotten very good at finding caregivers on very short notice. You can become a lifetime member of the service for $40 which entitles you to a $10 discount on the placement fees—$25 for a half day and $35 for a full day for non-members. Town & Country Sitters has a variety of sitters ranging from college students to professionals and active retirees.

ONSITE GROUP CARE

Because more people are traveling with their children for business and holidays, a demand for group care is growing in the Boston area. Both Parents in A Pinch and Town & Country Sitters, listed in the previous section, are addressing this need. They will come in and set up temporary on-site child care for company picnics, holiday parties, weddings, meetings, conventions, and commencements.

OTHER CHILD CARE RESOURCES

■ COMMONWEALTH OF MASSACHUSETTS CRIMINAL HISTORY SYSTEMS BOARD
(617) 660-4600
200 Arlington St., Suite 2200
Chelsea, MA 02150
Contact this office for public access to Criminal Offender Record Information (CORI). By submitting $25 and filing a Public Record Request Form, you can receive conviction information on certain persons currently or recently convicted, in custody, or supervised within the Massachusetts criminal justice system. You may also request, at no charge, a Sex Offender report on an individual, and receive information as to whether a person has convictions for sex offenses pursuant to the Massachusetts Sex Offender Registration and Notification Law.

■ PARENTS UNITED FOR CHILD CARE (PUCC)
(DOTS PARTNER)
800-264-7001
(617) 426-8288
30 Winter St., 7th Floor
Boston, MA 02108
This multiracial organization of low and moderate income parents works to increase the supply of quality, affordable child care in Massachusetts and to advocate on issues related to family, children and the work place.

Parents participate in PUCC's many projects, including the Public Action Committee, which looks at ways to work with the legislature to improve child care in Massachusetts. There are also neighborhood organizing groups and parent leadership trainings, as well as the Boston School Age Child Care Project. Finally, PUCC publishes a quarterly newsletter with information on the organization's activities, and an annual guide to before and after school programs.

BABY-SITTING: THE SEARCH FOR A SITTER

By Carolyn Curtis, WarmLines Staff

Finding an occasional sitter takes creativity, time, energy, and a positive attitude, according to child care experts at WarmLines Parent Resources in Newton. They suggest that parents break the process down into manageable steps.

- **Make a wish list.** Consider the age of your child, and the tasks your sitter will be responsible for: meals, bedtime, driving, etc. For example, do you want an adult with extensive newborn experience or a teenager who will play with your 7-year-old while you work at home?

- **Put it in writing.** State the type of care sought, the age and sex of your child, any special requirements, and your general location ("Kenmore Square area"). Never include your full name or address.

- **Spread the word.** The two most common approaches are placing classified ads and distributing flyers. Think of ways to get your flyer noticed: enlarge it to poster size, reduce it to index card size, print it on brightly colored paper, add children's drawings, use tabs with tear off phone numbers.

HELPFUL SUGGESTIONS

- **Think creatively.** For instance, can you offer room and board in exchange for sitting? If so, you might contact student housing at local colleges and universities.
- **Think cooperatively.** Swap free care with other parents by joining or starting a baby-sitting cooperative.
- **Think about an agency.** Many in-home placement agencies recognize families' needs for occasional or last minute baby-sitters, and offer these specialized services.

FROM DIAPERS TO DORMITORIES

With all of the wonderful information in this book about baby products you'll need and where to get them (not to mention all of the coupons in the back of this book to help you pay for them), it seemed appropriate to provide some concrete information about those other expenses that are looming in the not-so-distant future.

Here in the greater Boston area we are surrounded by many of the most sought-after and esteemed colleges in the country. Every day, as Boston area parents watch the news or read the paper, they are reminded of these four-year institutions and the opportunities that are available to those who attend them. We're sure most new parents hope that one day their little bundle will be one of those mature and self-confident students

The point is not to wait— start saving something, anything, now.

ANNUAL COLLEGE COSTS

College	1996-97	2015-16
UMass Boston	$4,405	$14,889
UMass Amherst	$9,702	$32,792
Suffolk University	$11,440	$38,666
Wentworth Institute	$17,350	$58,642
Northeastern University	$20,226	$68,363
Emmanuel College	$20,525	$69,373
Wheelock College	$20,700	$69,965
Bentley College	$21,015	$71,029
Babson College	$23,284	$78,698
Emerson College	$24,169	$81,690
Boston College	$25,626	$86,614
Harvard University	$27,575	$93,202
MIT	$27,762	$93,834
Brandeis University	$27,884	$94,246
Boston University	$27,964	$94,516

walking across some campus with a load of books under their arm. The reality is, unless you can reasonably expect to come into a lot of money before that first tuition bill comes, you should start saving as soon as you can toward that day.

The table on the previous page is a look at what it costs to attend area colleges and what it is likely to cost in the 2015-2016 academic year, the year that a baby born in 1997 is likely to start.

All of this may seem a little overwhelming, especially because with the birth of a new baby and the decrease in disposable income that generally comes with that event, the prospect of putting a significant monthly sum in the bank may seem impossible. The point is not to wait—start saving something, anything, now. You may want to seek out a financial planner to come up with both short and long term goals and a workable plan to achieve them.

Thanks to Paul Derbyshire of American Express Financial Advisors for contributing to this article.

WHERE TO SHOP

From Boston proper, up to Beverly on the North Shore, out west to Concord and Framingham, and down to Hingham on the South Shore, parents and parents-to-be will find an amazing shopping selection, which ranges from the basic to the truly unique, to the outstanding bargain, and even the wildly overwhelming. As one of the largest and most densely populated metropolitan areas in the country, products are abundant and the stores are plentiful, but getting around the area is always an adventure. In Massachusetts we don't believe in street signs, love to go around and around rotaries, and rave when we can't turn around on one-way, no U-turn roads like Rte. 9. We've tried to make this easier by providing relevant landmarks in our store reviews, but your trusty street map will still come in handy. In some cases you may want to skip the driving and opt for public transportation, babies love it!

Given our famously changing seasons here in New England one must be prepared for any weather, and given our vastly varied terrain, any circumstance! You know what they say "If you don't like the weather in New England, wait a minute." So being prepared to meet the day will put you at ease...so you and your baby can enjoy the mountains, the beach and the city streets. Here are some ideas for clothing you'll need:

Parents and parents-to-be will find an amazing shopping selection, which ranges from the basic to the truly unique.

AUTUMN/WINTER
- Polar fleece, hat and mittens, bunting, and baby blanket
- Socks and booties
- Boots for yourself (for those long walks to soothe baby)
- Lots of onesies (gotta layer!)
- Cozy one-piece suits with snaps
- Wool sweaters

SPRING/SUMMER
- Hat with brim
- Swim diaper
- Tanks
- Lots of onesies (gotta layer!)
- Sweat shirt/pants (for when that wind whips up)
- Aqua socks or sandals for toddlers (for those rocky beaches and water playgrounds)
- Cotton sweaters

Here are some can't-miss products for the different seasons:

AUTUMN/WINTER
- Baby carrier for infant
  Once baby is very sturdy and sitting up, the following are great options:
- Back pack with sun/rain shield
- Pull sled with seat belt

SPRING/SUMMER
- Sand toys (complete with castle molds, babies love to crush our careful creations)
- Beach umbrella (once that nap hits, you can do some reading)
- Insulated lunch sack with refreezable ice (for baby's bottle/cup and all those snacks)
- Stroller with large storage basket
- Lip balm and sun screen (once baby turns 6 months old)

MALLS

There are many malls in the greater Boston area and their locations are listed below with the mall hours. We have not repeated this information for each of the stores that are located in these malls.

■ THE ATRIUM MALL
300 Boylston St. (Rte. 9, Eastbound)
Newton, MA 02158
Hours: M-Sat. 10:00 a.m.-9:30 p.m.
       Sun. 11:00 a.m.-6:00 p.m.

■ ARSENAL MALL
485 Arsenal St.
Watertown, MA 02172
Hours: M-Sat. 10:00 a.m.-9:30 p.m.
       Sun. 11:00 a.m.-6:00 p.m.

■ BRAINTREE MALL
South Shore Plaza
Braintree, MA 02184
Hours: M-Sat. 10:00 a.m.-10:00 p.m.
       Sun. 11:00 a.m.-6:00 p.m.

■ BURLINGTON MALL
1100 Middlesex Turnpike
Burlington, MA 01083
Hours: M-Sat. 10:00 a.m.-10:00 p.m.
       Sun. 11:00 a.m.-6:00 p.m.

■ CAMBRIDGESIDE GALLERIA
100 CambridgeSide Place.
Cambridge, MA 02141
Hours: M-Sat. 9:30 a.m.-9:30 p.m.
       Sun. 11:00 a.m.-7:00 p.m.

■ COPLEY PLACE
100 Huntington Ave.
Boston, MA 02112
Hours: M-Sat. 10:00 a.m.-8:00 p.m.
       Sun. 12:00 p.m.-6:00 p.m.

■ LIBERTY TREE MALL
Danvers, MA 01923
Hours: M-Sat. 9:30 a.m.-9:30 p.m.
       Sun. 11:00 a.m.-6:00 p.m.

■ THE MALL AT CHESTNUT HILL
225 Boylston St. (Rte. 9, Westbound)
Boston, MA 02112
Hours: M-Sat. 10:00 a.m.-9:30 p.m.
       Sun. 11:00 a.m.-6:00 p.m.

■ MEADOW GLEN MALL
Rte. 16 (Locust St.)
Medford, MA 02155
Hours: M-Sat. 10:00 a.m.-9:30 p.m.
       Sun. 11:00 a.m.-6:00 p.m.

■ NATICK MALL
1245 Worcester Rd.
(Rte. 9, Westbound)
Natick, MA 01760
Hours: M-Sat. 10:00 a.m.-10:00 p.m.
        Sun.   11:00 a.m.-6:00 p.m.

■ NORTHGATE SHOPPING PLAZA
66 Squire Rd.
Revere, MA 02151
Hours: M-Sat. 9:30 a.m.-9:30 p.m.
        Sun.   10:00 a.m.-6:00 p.m.

■ NORTH SHORE MALL
210 Andover St.
(Routes 114 and 128)
Peabody, MA 01960
Hours: M-Sat. 10:00 a.m.-10:00 p.m.
        Sun.   11:00 a.m.-6:00 p.m.

■ PRUDENTIAL PLAZA
800 Boylston St.
Boston, MA 02112
Hours: M-Sat. 10:00 a.m.-8:00 p.m.
        Sun.   11:00 a.m.-6:00 p.m.

■ SQUARE ONE MALL
Rte. 1 South
Saugus, MA 01906
Hours: M-Sat. 10:00 a.m.-10:00 p.m.
        Sun.   11:00 a.m.-6:00 p.m.

FURNISHINGS AND EQUIPMENT

■ BABY CLUB
(781) 396-4422
129A Corporation Way
Medford, MA 02155
Hours: Th, F   10:00 a.m.-6:00 p.m.
        Sat.   10:00 a.m.-5:00 p.m.
        Sun.   12:00 p.m.-5:00 p.m.

Baby Club is located near Wellington station in one of many warehouses facing the railroad tracks. They offer first quality cribs at affordable prices. Crib prices range from $150 for a crib that converts to a toddler bed to European cribs for $349. They carry Child Craft and Bassett as well as some European designs you will find for more elsewhere. You will also find changing tables, dressers, crib mattresses, Dutailier gliders, wooden high chairs, nursery decorations and more. They have 100% cotton sheets and blankets, and all crib bedding sets are under $250. They have a shower registry and offer a flexible layaway plan. Another big plus for this store is that at the time of print all the sales associates were moms!

BABY FURNITURE WAREHOUSE STORE, INC.

(781) 942-7978
128 North Industrial Park
One General Ave.
Reading, MA 01867
Hours: M   10:00 a.m.-3:00 p.m.
        Th   10:00 a.m.-8:00 p.m.
        F, Sat.   10:00 a.m.-5:30 p.m.
        Sun.   12:00 p.m.-4:00 p.m.

(781) 843-5353
20 Mill Lane
Braintree, MA 02184
Hours: Same for both locations

The Baby Furniture Warehouse has everything you will need for your baby. They carry Ragazzi cribs as well as Bassett, C & T International and more. Most crib prices fall in the $250-$300 range. Matching changing tables and dressers are also available. The Baby Furniture Warehouse has one of the largest selections of Dutailier glider rockers in New England and at excellent prices. They have a large selection of crib bedding sets, several under $200. You will also find infant toys, nursery decorations, car seats, high chairs and other accessories useful for baby's first year. In addition, they have strollers by Graco, Aprica, and Kolcraft, among others. For your older child, they sell beautiful beds, bunks, desks, and dressers by Ragazzi. I found the sales staff friendly and helpful.

THE BABY PLACE

(508) 655-5305
50 Worcester Rd. (Rte. 9, Eastbound)
Natick, MA 01760
Hours: M, T, F, Sat. 10:00 a.m.-5:30 p.m.
       W, Th   10:00 a.m.-8:30 p.m.
       Sun.   12:00 p.m.-5:00 p.m.

Located on the Wellesley-Natick Line, this 15-year-old family-owned business is designed to be one-stop shopping for all of your baby purchases. This service-oriented store has friendly and extremely knowledgeable staff and a huge assortment of attractively displayed merchandise. They encourage browsing in their extensive stock which includes everything from cribs (ranging from $199-$699 including a mattress), strollers and car seats, to specialty items like hand painted rocking horses, christening gifts, safety products, and clothing. They carry many brands such as Child Craft, Peg Perego, Combi, MacLaren, Aprica and Baby Jogger, including three Italian brands of cribs—Pali, Bonavita, C & T, and Lexington Furniture (often sought after for its old world distressed look). They have the largest selection of crib bedding in New England, including custom designs. You'll find almost everything for the breastfeeding mom, including Medela pumps, and the premature baby and they are happy to work with you to find items they don't have. The staff works hard to educate the customer on making purchases that will satisfy their taste and fit in with their lifestyle. They will help moms on bedrest by phoning, faxing pictures and sending literature. They also assist out-of-towners in choosing the right gift from their baby registry. Gift certificates, gift wrapping, discounts for multiples, set up and delivery, and layaway are also available. Don't forget to check out their web site, www.thebabyplace.com, for inquiries, orders and rotating pictures of their customers' babies.

■ BABY SPECIALTIES
Baby Pages

(508) 653-2229
1276 Worcester Rd.
(Rte. 9, Eastbound)
Natick, MA 01760
Hours: M, T, F, Sat. 10:00 a.m.-6:00 p.m.
   W, Th   10:00 a.m. 9:00 p.m.
   Sun.   12:00 p.m.-5:00 p.m.

Located behind Pizza Hut, this family-owned business offers a large assortment of baby furniture, products and accessories. This store specializes in customer service, room planning, and extended product knowledge. Baby Specialties carries lines such as Ragazzi, Child Craft, Simmons and Pali, which are attractively displayed with coordinated bedding. Crib prices range from $199-$499. They have a wide selection of strollers including Peg Perego, Combi, Maclaren, and Emmaljunga, as well as Graco and Century, ranging in price from $79-$499. They carry breastfeeding supplies, specializing in Medela and Avent, and most sought after items including glider rockers and car seats. There is a comprehensive baby registry, free layaway and discounts for multiples. Their larger second store and warehouse is located in Worcester, and the clerks can quickly check to see whether items are in stock.

■ BELLINI
(781) 449-9909
944 Highland Ave.
Needham, MA 02194
Hours: M-Sat.   9:30 a.m.-5:30 p.m.
   Th   9:30 a.m.-8:00 p.m.

Bellini presents a beautiful display of cribs, bedroom sets, and accessories. The products are high quality with a definite designer feel. You can think of Bellini as the kind of store that sells only the best. The store also carries Perego strollers as well as beautiful quilts and linens, both affordable and heirloom quality. Bellini is best known for their cribs. Every Bellini crib converts to a youth bed, saving parents the extra expense of purchasing a toddler bed later. The furniture you purchase at Bellini will last for years and retain its quality. Prices are more affordable than you may think, with cribs in the $400 range.

■ BOSTON BABY SUPERSTORE
Baby Pages

(617) 332-1400
30 Tower Rd.
Newton, MA 02164
Hours: M, T, F   9:30 a.m.-6:00 p.m.
   W, Th   9:30 a.m.-9:00 p.m.
   Sat.   9:30 a.m.-5:30 p.m.

(781) 749-5770
Hingham Plaza
100 Derby St.
Hingham, MA 02043
Hours: same as above

(978) 771-1414
10 Newbury St. (Rte. 1 South)
Danvers, MA 01923
Hours: same as above, plus:
   Sun.   12:00 p.m.-5:00 p.m.

I visited the Newton store located off of

Highland Ave. on Tower Road behind the Filene's Basement parking garage. In all of their stores, they carry everything for baby from bottles and breast pumps to cribs and high chairs. Boston Baby features one of the best selections of cribs in Boston including models by Simmons, Legacy, Morigeau and Pali. Cribs start at $230. You can choose from six different crib mattresses and a huge selection of crib bedding sets, as well as other bedding. They also carry a wide variety of changing tables and dressers. If you are looking for medium to high-end strollers, Boston Baby's selection is hard to beat. You will find Graco, Emmaljunga and Peg Perego among others. They carry some wonderful 100% cotton infant layette pieces from preemie sizes to 12 months. Their sales associates are well trained and do not work on commission. They are happy to give you information about products without any pressure to buy on the spot. There is a good layaway program and shower registry. Ask about their baby date contest. You can receive up to $500 back from your previous purchases if your baby is born on their lucky dates.

■ BURLINGTON COAT FACTORY
(617) 848-3200
705 Granite St.
Braintree, MA 02184
Hours:　M-Sat.　10:00 a.m.-9:00 p.m.
　　　　　Sun.　　11:00 a.m.-6:00 p.m.

(508) 651-2526
Speen St. and Rte. 9
Natick, MA 01760
Hours:　Same as above
While Burlington does sell coats (lots and lots of them), they also have a complete baby department, selling everything from clothing to furniture. Many cribs and toddler beds are on display, all with coordinated bedding and accessories and attractive themes. There are plenty of strollers, car seats, playpens, swings, rocking chairs, lamps, mobiles and other furniture items. The Baby Depot at Burlington Coat Factory carries names like Child Craft, Graco, Century, Simmons, Aprica and Perego at prices discounted about 20%-30% below other retail outlets.

Besides furniture, a well-stocked accessories section includes nursing supplies, safety items, baby bottles, bibs, toys, books, car seat covers, diaper bags and more. The store has a large baby clothing section with popular brands in both casual and dressy styles, again at discounted prices. They have preemie sizes as well as christening gowns. There is also a small maternity section with casual and career wear, nursing lingerie, and maternity hose.

Be aware of the store's return policy which states that items must be returned within 30 days for store credit only. Just make sure if you are doing some early, pre-baby shopping that you are sure you won't need to return it.

■ KIDS CONVERTIBLES FURNITURE
(508) 626-0011
680 Worcester Rd. (Rte. 9, Eastbound)
Framingham, MA 01702
Hours:　M-Sat.　10:00 a.m.-6:00 p.m.
　　　　　Sun.　　12:00 p.m.-5:00 p.m.
Located a couple of miles west of Shopper's World, this store is the place to go for beautifully constructed solid wood convertible furniture. It specializes in Babies Dream furniture, carrying

six complete lines. All of the cribs convert to toddler beds and then to very attractive double beds. The changing tables convert to dressers. There are matching armoires, nightstands, mirrors, toy chests and bookcases. You can choose among oak, birch, beech and pine and from three different stains. The cribs range from $299-$599 and the changers/dressers range from $299-$589. Conet Ball glider rockers ranging from $299-$499 are available, as well as bedding and coordinated accessories from Lambs & Ivy, Brandee Danielle, and Cotton Tale.

■ THE RIGHT START
(508) 647-0907
Natick Mall

(781) 272-3353
Burlington Mall

If a specialty baby gadget exists, it's probably available at the Right Start. This is one of the few stores where you'll find such items as baby wipe warmers, a device that rocks your baby's crib for you, the Sleep Guardian Air Delivery System to prevent SIDS, pest-repellent nightlights, crib tents, and tapes simulating the sounds of rain or a parent's heartbeat. In addition to gadgets, you'll find cribs, including the Dura Crib-Go-Round, crib bedding, a huge selection of safety products, infant development toys, and books. The Right Start carries a few strollers including Peg Perego and Combi. The stores are bright and spacious, and the staff is really up to date on the latest in baby products. They can often suggest a product to help you that you never knew existed.

Call ahead to confirm hours and locations.

■ TOYS "R" US
(781) 289-1181
Northgate Shopping Plaza

(781) 396-6885
630 Fellsway West
Medford, MA 02155

(781) 935-7654
366 Cambridge St.
Woburn, MA 01801

(617) 445-5159
South Bay
14 Allstate Rd.
Dorchester, MA 02125

(617) 576-8697
Fresh Pond Mall
200 Alewife Brook Pkwy.
Cambridge, MA 02138

(508) 370-4445
One Worcester Rd.
Framingham, MA 01701

(781) 329-4924
100 Providence Hwy.
Dedham, MA 02026
Hours: M-Sat. 9:30 a.m.-9:30 p.m.
Sun. 10:00 a.m.-6:00 p.m.

(978) 532-0978
North Shore Mall

Besides toys, Toys R Us carries all of the baby basics including diapers and formula, car seats and strollers, baby bottles and diaper bags. Check out the Baby Registry, where you can register for all your baby needs. Baby product brands include Fisher Price, Graco, Kolcraft, Gerry, Century, Evenflo, and Cosco. About half of the products are over head and difficult to reach. To remedy that, you'll have to ask for help. You'll find high chairs, exercisers, baby carriers, strollers, portable cribs and much more.

Toys R Us also carries some baby clothing sleepers and play outfits, T-shirts, bibs and socks. Sleepers are reasonably priced starting at about $7, and play outfits begin at about $10. With prices and selection like this, Toys R Us is a mainstay for all parents.

MATERNITY STORES

■ A PEA IN THE POD
(617) 969-1132
The Atrium Mall

(508) 532-3010
North Shore Mall

A Pea In The Pod is well known for their stylish maternity wear. Believing that women shouldn't have to compromise fashion during pregnancy, A Pea In The Pod offers tailored business suits, career and casual wear in beautiful styles. The store even carries special occasion dresses and a variety of maternity lingerie.

■ DAN HOWARD MATERNITY
(781) 233-5254
Augustine's Plaza
120-134 Broadway (Rte. 1)
Saugus, MA 01906

(508) 653-4722
Sherwood Plaza
1298 Worcester (Rte. 9, Eastbound)
Natick, MA 01760

(617) 848-9397
Granite Plaza
717 Granite St.
Braintree, MA 02184

(781) 272-4003
Crossroads Shopping Center
34 Cambridge St.
Burlington, MA 01803
Hours: Hours vary by store

Dan Howard's is one of the oldest self-manufactured maternity clothing stores. Nationwide the chain has more than 100 stores. It sells a wide variety of clothing, ranging from career attire to casual, comfortable clothes. Pricing is competitive, with casual clothing beginning at $19 and career apparel at $39.

GIFTS TO CONSIDER GIVING AND RECEIVING
- Front baby carrier, baby sling or backpack
- Diaper bag/backpack with fold up changing pad and compartments
- Polar fleece bunting, hat and mittens and booties
- Customized playsuits and onesies with handpainting or stitching
- Child's play tent (to shade an infant in the sun or chill, and give a toddler her own space)
- Kid's music tapes (for those long car rides to the mountains, beach, or sitting in city traffic jams)
- Nursery cassette tape player that attaches to crib
- Membership to the Museum of Science, The Children's Museum, Drumlin Farm, or one of the indoor playspaces
- Three months of a diaper service.

Dan Howard's has bathing suits, pantyhose, undergarments and nursing shirts. They also have career coordinates to mix and match, including a three-piece suit with a top, pants, and skirt for $59. They also stock semiformal cocktail dresses starting at $39. Most of the dresses are extremely fashionable and fun, and many have ties in the back to not only accommodate growth during a pregnancy, but allow the garment to be used afterwards. You can also purchase maternity clothes through the company's catalog, available through the above number.

■ MATERNITE
(508) 651-8811
Natick Mall

■ MIMI MATERNITY
(617) 262-8012
10 Newbury St.
Boston, MA 02112

(617) 266-1275
Copley Place

(781) 273-4994
Burlington Mall

(617) 964-5833
The Mall at Chestnut Hill
Hours: Hours vary by store

■ MOTHERHOOD
(781) 233-8271
Square One Mall

■ MOTHER'S WORK
(617) 356-1812
Braintree Mall

(781) 273-4447
Burlington Mall

(617) 577-0211
CambridgeSide Galleria
Mimi Maternity, Motherhood, Mother's Work and Maternite are all owned by the same company. Mimi offers very contemporary casual and dressy clothes, Motherhood and Maternite carry some quality basics and dresses, and Mother's Work caters to the working mother. Quality, fun, and fashionable is the best way to describe these stores. The clothing is designed in the latest styles, and is very professional. All of the stores carry nursing bras, underwear, and lingerie. Nice dresses start at $118, and they offer the popular "4 Essentials" package for $118 as well. Casual shorts and tops cost between $20 and $40, while work dresses range from $50-$100. They often have great sales of 20%-50% off when the new season of clothing comes in, which is convenient since it's difficult to shop ahead when you're pregnant. The staff is helpful, and can help direct you to versatile pieces which will give you a lot of use.

■ MATERNITY WORKS OUTLET
(617) 542-6344
10 Milk St.
Boston, MA 02108
Hours: M, T, F 10:00 a.m.-6:00 p.m.
W, Th 10:00 a.m.-7:00 p.m.
Sat. 9:00 a.m.- 5:00 p.m.
Located in the heart of downtown Boston, less than two blocks from Downtown Crossing, this outlet store is tucked away on the mezzanine just down the hill from the Old South Meeting House. It is a must for anyone working in the area and worth a special trip into the city for those who do not. Its racks and shelves are packed with top quality brand name maternity wear (Mother's Work,

Steena, Maternity Works, Mimi Maternity, Maternite and A Pea In The Pod) at prices 30% to 75% less than retail (and often it is the same merchandise available elsewhere!). They carry jeans, sweaters, jumpsuits, tops, T-shirts, swimwear, shorts, special occasion wear, sleepwear, lingerie, hose, tights, bras and more. Check out the "As Is" room where items are marked down 25% to 90% off the already discounted prices. For example, I saw a Motherhood pink cotton tank top for $4 and A Pea In The Pod special occasion pantsuit for $45.

■ **MOTHERTIME**
(617) 923-1201
The Arsenal Mall
This maternity and children's clothing store, owned by the same company that owns Dan Howard and Mother's Work, has a good selection of stylish career wear and sporty casual wear for pregnant women, as well as a smaller selection of clothing for babies 3-24 months. Popular brands include Meg Lauren, Jessica Lauren, Dan Howard, and Oh! Mamma. For the working pregnant women there are attractive dresses and coordinated tops and slacks, as well as tights, bras and hose. I admired a maroon and white houndstooth print top with solid maroon slacks for $69. They often carry coordinated boxed sets (top, skirt, slacks). The more casual, but still very attractive and well-made, clothes included jeans in several colors for $36, print mock turtlenecks for $24, and fleece tops for cooler weather at $39. There were two sale racks where the clothing was marked down 50%. There was also a good selection of nursing tops and nightshirts in different styles, as well as nursing pads and bras. One corner of the store was dedicated to baby clothes, including one and two piece outfits ranging from $15-$30, sweaters, layette items, and snowsuits. I saw several adorable Halloween costumes, which made me smile as I contemplated my 15-month-old toddling around dressed as a pumpkin, rabbit or dinosaur. Don't forget to ask about their frequent buyer club or their gift baskets, which can be custom made for $39.99 and up.

■ **SARAH JULIAN MATERNITY** *Baby Pages*
(617) 558-1280
1381 Washington St. (Rte. 16)
W. Newton, MA 02165
Hours: T-Th 6:00 p.m.-9:00 p.m.
And by appointment
Instead of buying maternity clothes for the office, why not rent them? This rental maternity shop has an excellent selection of high-end independent labels. I found lots of well made, tasteful outfits appropriate for office wear. You pay a deposit and $45-$50 per outfit for 30 days. At the end of the month, they take care of the dry cleaning and you can choose a whole new wardrobe if you wish. This flexibility is perfect when your pregnancy spans more than one season, you need corporate clothes for a short amount of time, or you simply welcome some variety in your maternity wardrobe. Sarah Julian also rents special occasion dresses and outfits for a three-day period starting at $40 per outfit and sells stockings, underwear, and tights. There is a convenient drop-off box for returns made outside business hours.

ɜ˞ *Call ahead to confirm hours and locations.*

■ THE STORK EXCHANGE
(617) 325-5689
81 Dwinell St.
W. Roxbury, MA 02132
Trish Gill took advantage of corporate downsizing to start her own secondhand maternity wear business. Her high-end, gently used executive, business and casual wear go for about 40% of retail price. Trish offers a personalized service where she talks with you to find out your size, style and tastes and selects six to ten items, packs them up and brings them to your house. If you are buying several outfits, she is flexible with the price.

■ STORK TIME
Baby Pages
(617) 969-5930
1015 Boylston St. (Rte. 9, Westbound)
Newton, MA 02161
Hours: M-Sat. 10:00 a.m.-5:00 p.m.
           Th   10:00 a.m.-7:00 p.m.
           Sun.   1:00 p.m.-4:00 p.m.

Stork Time is a small store with a good selection. They carry Take Nine, Mama Mia, Hayley Michaels, and others at 20%-50% less than retail. Jeans start around $30 and most shorts are $24. I especially liked the khaki pants and shorts by Rebel, with a discreet expansion panel, at 20% off retail price. You will also find leggings, nursing tops, dresses, and great bathing suits by Mama Pavlova. The only items not discounted are clothes by Japanese Weekend and fun block-print items by Newton-based Kiwi. If you are looking for a specific item, you might want to call ahead to check for availability and size. Hose and nursing bras by Leading Lady, while not discounted, are well-stocked in sizes and styles.

DEPARTMENT AND DISCOUNT STORES

■ AMES DEPARTMENT STORE
(978) 927-1010
81 Dodge St.
Beverly, MA 01915

(781) 329-8098
737 Providence Highway (Rte. 1)
Dedham, MA 02026

(781) 395-6850
760 Fellsway
Medford, MA

(781) 289-5111
Northgate Shopping Plaza

(781) 233-5650
333 Broadway
Saugus, MA 01906

(781) 935-2350
2 Elm St.
Woburn, MA
Hours: M-Sat. 9:00 a.m.-9:30 p.m.
           Sun.   9:00 a.m.-7:00 p.m.

These large discount department stores really do offer great prices, although their selection is limited. Their infant and toddler section is relatively small (compared to other department store discounters), but has a nice selection across the board. The day I visited the Medford store they had a 25% off all newborn, infant, and toddler Playskool fleece sets and coveralls. I saw Basic Editions overalls for $6, Looney Tunes Lovables outfits for $8, and the most adorable three-piece 100% cotton little girls' outfit for $13. Their layette was filled with cozy cotton clothing by Gerber. Some safety devices, baby toys and general baby paraphernalia were stocked. Ames carries high chairs, playpens, strollers, and car seats in the price range of $27-$40 by such makers as Graco, Cosco, J. Mason, and Kolcraft. They have a huge toy section filled with Little Tykes, Fisher Price and Playskool, among other brands, all at very reasonable prices. Ames has frequent sales on their already great prices (check your Sunday circular), but call ahead to verify stock as availability varies widely.

■ ANN & HOPE
(617) 924-3400
615 Arsenal St.
Watertown, MA 02172

(978) 777-1300
159 Endicott St.
Danvers, MA 01923
Hours: M-Sat. 9:30 a.m.-9:30 p.m.
Sun. 11:00 a.m.-6:00 p.m.

The Ann & Hope adjacent to the Arsenal Mall is a huge store, with a large selection of layette, infant and toddlers clothes, equipment and toys. If their selection isn't enough to bring you in, then their rock-bottom prices, which are often discounted even further (check your Sunday circular), will certainly entice you. The largest of the three sections devoted to babies was a maze of clothing racks filled with a wide selection of clothes by such names as Tiny Tots, Playskool, Carter's, and French Toast ranging in price from $10-$42. I saw a Baby Beluga overall set and shirt for $13, Bugle Boy overalls for $14, and a gorgeous 100% green cotton velvet dress was $22. They have a small but nice christening selection, as well as a densely packed complete layette, diaper bag and bedding section. One entire wall contained the largest selection I've ever seen of any kind of baby needs, bottle, pacifier, teether, and safety device imaginable by brands such as Safety 1st, Gerber, The First Years, Playtex and others. This discount department store stocks cribs, car seats, strollers, playpens and vaporizers by companies such as Graco, Cosco, Evenflo, Gerry, and Fisher Price. They also carry a large selection of formula and diapers. A very helpful sales person answered my questions.

■ BLOOMINGDALE'S
(617) 630-6000
The Mall at Chestnut Hill

Go up to the second floor, walk between the escalators, bear all the way to the right and you'll find the layette, infant and toddler clothing section. Their layette section was filled with brands such as Little Me, Carter's, and Baby Dior among others, ranging in price from $10 for a onesie to $36 for a quilted union suit. Bloomies has their own plush store brand clothing, called b Kids, which is well made and priced—a polar fleece jacket with lined pants, and a handknit 100% cotton sweater both went for $32, each. They carry Ralph Lauren casual and weekend wear for babies. There was an extensive bunting selection: Beatrix Potter $40-$60, a teddy bear shaped bunting by Little Me for $36 and a faux leopard skin by Causal Time for $57. Bloomingdale's carries a nice selection of Carter's and Bambino bedding and layette. The toddler section was filled with b Kids and Flap doodles. Staff are knowledgeable and attentive.

Call ahead to confirm hours and locations.

Boston: Department and Discount Stores

■ BRADLEE'S
(781) 272-7120
150 Lexington
Burlington, MA 01803

(617) 889-0234
1100 Revere Beach Pkwy.
Chelsea, MA 02150

(617) 327-9283
950 American Legion Hwy.
Roslindale, MA 02131

(617) 628-3426
180 Somerville Ave.
Somerville, MA 02143

(617) 926-4410
Watertown Mall
550 Arsenal St.
Watertown, MA 02172

(617) 282-0222
725 Morrissey Blvd.
Dorchester, MA 02125

(508) 620-1810
1 Worcester Rd.
Framingham, MA 01701

(781) 749-5031
100 Derby St.
Hingham, MA 02043

(781) 391-1050
Meadow Glen Mall

(617) 472-8881
Presidents Plaza
215 Quincy Ave.
Quincy, MA 02171

(781) 329-4425
300 VFW Pkwy.
Dedham, MA 02026

(617) 436-6540
500 Geneva Ave.
Dorchester, MA 02125
Hours: Hours vary by store

This discount department store has a fairly good selection of infant and toddler clothing and equipment at very reasonable prices. Their frequent sales (check the Sunday circular) make the bargain potential even better. At the time I visited the Watertown store, they offered 30% off Gerber layette, Tiny Toes coveralls and all coordinated bedding. There were many 100% cotton union suits for between $10-$17 by such names as Little Red Hen, Lovespun and Weeplay. They had beautiful Beatrix Potter buntings for $45, regularly $75! Bradlee's had a nice selection of baby paraphernalia such as diaper bags, bottles, pacifiers, and safety devices. They carry a basic selection of car seats, high chairs, playpens and strollers, by brands such as Graco and Century. Call to verify stock and sales prices as they vary widely from store to store.

■ COSTCO
(978) 777-3936
11 Newbury St.
Danvers, MA 01923

(781) 890-9600
520 Winter St.
Waltham, MA 02154
Hours: M-F   11:00 a.m.-8:30 p.m.
         Sat.   9:30 a.m.-6:00 p.m.
         Sun.   10:00 a.m.-5:00 p.m.

This membership-only store is an excellent place to find bargains. Unfortunately, however, it does not always carry the same brands and so you never know what you'll find from one visit to the next. You also cannot depend on any sales help in making your baby product purchases. Costco usually does carry Huggies diapers in large packages of 160 in size medium and 120 in the large size. Also, Baby Fresh diaper wipes are often in stock. Products such as strollers and car seats usually can be found but the selection is limited to one or two brands, including Century and Fisher Price. Books are always a great bargain at the Costco. This section includes tape cassettes and, at times, crayons, paints and markers. The toys are sometimes plentiful, especially during the summer and winter holiday seasons, but again, it is hit and miss. The prices usually beat any items you may find on sale at other stores.

■ **DECELLE FAMILY FASHIONS**
(617) 325-1400
1870 Centre St.
W. Roxbury, MA 02132

(781) 431-2234
50 Central St.
Wellesley, MA 02181

(781) 861-8554
1690 Massachusetts Ave.
Lexington, MA 02173

(617) 354-7214
37 White St. (Porter Square)
Cambridge, MA 02142
Hours: Hours vary by store
Visit this bargain department store for their excellent prices and varied selection. The Porter Square location has a large infants/toddlers section filled with good quality name brands such as Carter's and Weebok at very reasonable prices. Decelle's merchandise is in season and first quality, the same as seen in larger department stores, but their prices are discounted at least 20%, and often by as much as 30%-50%. I was impressed by the large selection of layette items and 100% cotton clothing by brands including Absorba (really soft thick cotton), Baby Rageous, Little Me, and Baby B'Gosh. Of particular note is their little boys' section. Decelle carries a range of boys' clothes in brand names such as Bobby Stix, Danny Stones and Cotton Club, which go beyond the usual truck and sport motifs. They also stock a small selection of christening gowns, gifts, and crib bedding. Visit the store often, as they get new stock in almost daily. Call in advance if you are looking for something in particular, but if you're seeking basics such as layette items, footed suits, darling outfits, and sleepers, you'll certainly find something to please your eye and your wallet.

■ **FILENE'S**
(617) 357-2100
426 Washington St.
Boston, MA 02111

(617) 484-3800
75 Leonard St.
Belmont, MA 02178

(617) 848-3800
Braintree Mall

(781) 272-3800
Burlington Mall

(617) 621-3800
CambridgeSide Galleria

(508) 653-3800
Natick Mall

(617) 965-3800
The Mall at Chestnut Hill

(781) 231-8400
Square One Mall
Hours: Hours vary by store

I visited the Boston store, located at Downtown Crossing at the intersection of Washington and Summer streets. Their children's department, located on the fifth floor, had an impressive section dedicated to babies and toddlers. It was well-stocked with everything from the basics (face cloths, towels, blankets, sleepwear, toys and gift sets) to more specialized items like christening wear by Madonna, outerwear, and special occasion outfits. Many brands like Baby B'gosh, Vitamins, Welcome Home, Disney, and Little Me were creatively displayed and styles included the cute and cuddly, the sporty, and the formal. There was a large layette section containing a wide range of brands, including Carter's, Little Me, Baby Dior, Ralph Lauren. Terry cloth footed pajamas were $9.99 and embroidered layette gowns were $14.99. There were many sale racks where clothes were 25%-75% off. Their baby gift registry was not computerized, so one would have to call or visit that particular store to use it. Filene's no longer sells maternity clothes. Attractive gift wrapping is available for $3.50-$8.50, depending on the size of the box.

■ **FILENE'S BASEMENT**
(617) 542-2001
426 Washington St.
Boston, MA 02111

(617) 849-0031
Braintree Mall

(781) 229-2130
Burlington Mall

(508) 620-1680
Framingham Mall
Rte. 30
Framingham, MA 01701

(617) 332-1295
215 Needham St.
Newton, MA 02165

(978) 532-2400
North Shore Mall

(781) 231-8153
Square One Mall

(617) 926-4474
Arsenal Mall

This famous Boston store is no longer part of Filene's, even though some of the locations are still the same. Filene's Basement carries both maternity clothing and clothing for babies at huge discounts. You need to visit often and check items over thoroughly, but astute bargain hunters will often be very pleased with their finds. Many brands are the same as you'd expect to find in department stores, but the prices are substantially less. In the infants' section, I saw a Baby Beluga plush two-piece outfit with an appliqued bear for $14.99 and a Little Me tan one-piece outfit with dinosaurs for $17.99. The maternity section had everything from casual wear to career and formal wear, with a range of brands and styles represented. Don't forget to check the date on the price tag; if it's more than two weeks old, you'll get even more savings with the Automatic Markdown Plan.

Call ahead to confirm hours and locations.

■ JC PENNEY
(978) 977-3050
North Shore Mall

Penney's has a nice selection of maternity and children's wear. Mid-priced maternity clothes are available with casual jumpers starting at $30 and career dresses starting at $50. They also have name-brand jeans and other casual attire that start at $20. For summer, they carry several cute floral outfits and Cherokee brand relaxing wear. In the fall, the store offers corduroy jumpers and paisley patterns. The maternity section has the basics and then some.

The infants' and toddlers' area features clothing, baby products, and a gift section. The clothing includes name brands such as Arizona, Baby B'Gosh and Little Mc. A few preemie and christening outfits are also offered. A small selection of baby products are available. Books, toys, and stuffed animals are also in this department.

Penney's catalog offers a wide selection of merchandise. Delivery is now available to your home. They also offer a gift registry which is a plus for any new parent.

■ K-MART
(978) 777-2354
139 Endicott St.
Danvers, MA 01923
Hours: M-Sun. 8:00 a.m.-7:00 p.m.

(781) 231-0404
180 Main St.
Saugus, MA 01906
Hours: M-Sun. 8:00 a.m.-10:00 p.m.

(617) 541-4959
7 Allstate Rd.
Boston, MA 02112
Hours: M-Sun. 8:00 a.m.-10:00 p.m.

(617) 843-5400
350 Grossman Dr.
Braintree, MA 02184
Hours: M-Sun. 8:00 a.m.-10:00 p.m.

(617) 628-9500
Assembly Square Mall
77 Middlesex Ave.
Somerville, MA 02144
Hours: M-Sat. 8:00 a.m.-10:00 p.m.
       Sun. 8:00 a.m.-6:00 p.m.

K-Mart is among the lowest priced local stores for maternity and infant wear. The maternity section has some fashionable outfits including the New Edition line and Jaclyn Smith's clothes in larger sizes that would easily work for maternity use. Casual tops begin about $10, and casual dresses start at $25. Nursing bras and maternity underwear, located in this section, are around $6.

Infant attire ranges in price from $5 to $20. Sesame Street, Disney Babies, Dundee and Route 66 are the available brands, with a sleeper or summer outfit starting at about $10. K-Mart also offers a large section containing bottles, feeding accessories, rattles, bibs, cotton diapers, safety products, crib bedding and room decorations.

The baby product selection equals that of other discount stores and is very well-priced. Evenflo, Graco, Kolcraft and Century brands are usually stocked. You'll find a few cribs, and a moderate selection of car seats, high chairs, playpens and swings. The prices are among the lowest we've found, even for dependable name brands. Their diaper sales can be a great deal as well.

■ LORD & TAYLOR
(617) 262-6000
760 Boylston St.
Boston, MA 02111

(978) 273-1461
Burlington Mall

(978) 977-7400
North Shore Mall

(508) 651-0744
Natick Mall

(781) 848-1970
Braintree Mall

Hours: Hours vary by store

The children's department of the Boston store had a nice selection of infant clothing, but I was told that the Burlington Store has an even bigger one. In addition to the many familiar brands like Baby B'Gosh, Little Me, Vitamins, and Carter's, Lord & Taylor also carries its own attractive brand, Small Creations. There is a well-stocked layette section, including the familiar Carter's items, as well as things from Ralph Lauren. I was particularly impressed with their large selection of soft soled shoes by Baby Deer in sizes 1-3. You will find a lot to choose from in both sleepwear and outerwear. They have christening outfits by Alexis and Madonna starting at around $25. There is no gift registry or gift wrapping, but the attractive gift boxes with the Lord & Taylor rose are free. Lord & Taylor does not carry maternity clothing.

■ MACY'S
(617) 357-3000
450 Washington St.
Boston, MA 02111

(617) 848-1500
Braintree Mall

(781) 272-6000
Burlington Mall

(508) 650-6400
Natick Mall

(508) 531-9000
North Shore Mall

Hours: Hours vary by store

Macy's has a great selection of infants' and children's clothing. The department is large and nicely separated into sections, making it easy to find your child's age group. Surprisingly, Macy's offers many children's items at a very affordable price. Dresses, T-shirts, shoes, and play wear are all available at Macy's. A summer play dress starts as low as $15. Dresses begin in the low $20's. Macy's clothing is fairly upscale, offering brands like Guess, Charter Club, and Baby B'Gosh. Prices can be expensive, but sales are good and occur fairly often. Macy's clothing really stands the test of time, too. After two years of owning Macy's infant sleepwear and toddler clothing, I have found it withstands numerous wearing and frequent laundering. Yet, the clothing still looks like it is in tip top shape. In addition to clothing, Macy's has a small toy department primarily for gift items. The stores also have children's shoe departments that carry some very fine brand names at, again, affordable prices.

Call ahead to confirm hours and locations.

■ MARSHALL'S
(617) 442-5050
8 Allstate St.
Dorchester, MA 02122

(617) 923-1044
Arsenal Mall

(617) 262-6066
500 Boylston St.
Boston, MA 02112

(781) 272-6362
34 Cambridge St.
Burlington, MA 01803

(781) 749-6162
Rte. 3A
Hingham, MA 02043

(781) 944-6150
1343 Main St.
Reading, MA 01867

(617) 391-1331
Meadow Glen Mall

(617) 964-4987
275 Needham St.
Newton Upper Falls, MA 02164

(781) 337-5816
Pleasant Plaza
50 Pleasant St. (Rte. 18)
South Weymouth, MA 02188

(781) 438-1520
Stoneham, MA 02180

(617) 338-6205
350 Washington St.
Boston, MA 02112
Hours: Hours vary by store

Marshall's infant/toddler section is well-marked with signs which are easily noticeable. You can find excellent name brands here, including Baby B'Gosh and Little Me, that elsewhere may cost at least 20% more. They also have a small toy and book selection. We found Dr. Seuss books at half price, and videos $4 off the regular price. Marshall's also has a small maternity clothing selection. You can count on a bargain at Marshall's.

■ PRICELESS...KIDS
(781) 740-4252
Hingham Shopping Center
100 Derby St.
Hingham, MA 02043

(617) 623-8033
Twin City Plaza
22 McGrath Hwy.
Somerville, MA 02143

(781) 233-5029
635 Broadway (Rte. 1)
Saugus, MA 01906
Hours: M-F   10:00 a.m.-9:00 p.m.
            Sat.   10:00 a.m.-6:00 p.m.
            Sun.   11:00 a.m.-5:00 p.m.

About one quarter of this discount store's large inventory is devoted to infant and toddler clothing. The day I visited I was met by enticing racks of darling Baby b'Gosh spring play suits for $10 and soft, faded Old Navy overalls and dresses for $10, all in sizes 3-24 months. Priceless offers such good prices because they buy overstock and a few irregulars. Throughout the tightly arranged infant/toddler section you will find racks of clothing organized by price and type: for example, Tiny Tots playsuits (many 100% cotton) are two for $10. There is an abundance of little boy wear in sport, traffic and outdoor motifs. Brand names include Health Tex, Carter's, Little Me, Baby Paris, Winnie-the-Pooh Wear, and

Nanette. They feature girls' shoes only, up to little girls' size 3. Priceless also carries crib bedding and accessories, infant toys, baby blankets, bibs, photo albums, for all under $10! This bargain store has great prices and selection to recommend it, and it also has a Kids' Video Corner with a television and benches to amuse your older children.

■ SAKS FIFTH AVENUE
(617) 262-8500
Prudential Plaza
Boston, MA 02112
Hours: M-Sat. 10:00 a.m.-8:00 p.m.
Sun. 12:00 p.m.-6:00 p.m.

This upscale department store has a small but beautiful children's department carrying private label clothing, as well as other brands like New Potatoes, Little Me, Jean Bourget, Marimekko, and Babymini. There were adorable layette items by Petite Bateau, Ralph Lauren, and Miniclasix. The prices are what you'd expect to pay for these brands. A simple cotton onesie with side snaps was $18 and a one-piece quilted outfit by Jean Bourget was $74. There were some blankets, toys and other accessories. If you are looking for a special gift or heirloom item, peruse the glass cases on either side of the register. One had sterling silver rattles, brush and comb sets, spoons, and frames, and the other featured dolls by Madame Alexander.

■ SEARS
(781) 231-4529
1325 Broadway
Saugus, MA 01906

(617) 252-9001
CambridgeSide Galleria

(781) 231-4500
Square One Mall

(781) 320-5177
300 Providence Hwy.
Dedham, MA 02026

(781) 221-4929
Burlington Mall

(617) 356-6029
250 Granite St.
Braintree, MA 02184

(781) 977-7529
North Shore Mall
Hours: Hours vary by store

Sears is a great place to shop for all the necessary baby basics. Sears carries baby furniture, including cribs, play yards, high chairs, car seats, and crib accessories. You'll find Graco, Evenflo, Century, Cosco and Gerry here, all competitively priced. They also have a nice toy section including Fisher Price, Sesame Street and others. Sears clothing is reasonably priced and plentiful. They primarily offer Carter's brand, which is known for quality and durability, but you'll also find Disney and Pooh clothes and toys. Sears is a good place to shop for the "staples" such as underwear, T-shirts, socks, etc. The children's section is large and the service friendly and helpful. Ask about the KidVantage plan: if the clothes wear out before they're outgrown, Sears will replace them.

❧ Call ahead to confirm hours and locations.

Sears also has a nice maternity clothing selection, offering primarily the Take 9 brand. Tops average about $25, pants $30, and dresses start at $39. The store also carries nursing bras, maternity panty hose and undergarments.

■ TJ MAXX
(781) 329-8162
300 VFW Pkwy.
Dedham, MA 02026
Hours:　M-Sat.　9:30 a.m.-9:30 p.m.
　　　　Sun.　　12:00 p.m.-6:00 p.m.

(617) 356-3564
250 Grove St.
Braintree, MA 02184
Hours:　M-Sat.　9:30 a.m.-9:30 p.m.
　　　　Sun.　　10:00 a.m.-6:00 p.m.

(781) 393-0027
750 Fellsway
Medford, MA 02155
Hours:　M-Sat.　9:30 a.m.-9:30 p.m.
　　　　Sun.　　10:00 a.m.-6:00 p.m.

(617) 492-8500
Fresh Pond Mall
200 Alewife Brook Pkwy.
Cambridge, MA 02138
Hours:　M-Sat.　9:30 a.m.-9:30 p.m.
　　　　Sun.　　10:00 a.m.-6:00 p.m.

T.J. Maxx is a brand name discount store with a small infants' and children's department. Prices here are very good, although the selection is somewhat limited. This is a good place to shop if you have the time to go through the racks. It is also the kind of store you'll want to visit frequently, since the merchandise is always changing. When we visited, there was a nice selection of children's underwear, and several Little Me and Winnie the Pooh outfits for only $20.

■ WAL-MART
(781) 592-4300
780 Lynn Way.
Lynn, MA 01905
Hours:　M-Sat.　7:00 a.m.-10:00 p.m.
　　　　Sun.　　8:00 a.m.-9:00 p.m.

Wal-Mart is a huge discount store where you can find a variety of baby products and equipment from Evenflo, Fisher Price, Gerry, Graco, Cosco and Kolcraft. Many of the strollers, portable cribs and swings were displayed on high shelves, so bring a friend to help if you want to try out an item. The store is also well-stocked with other necessities such as nursery items, baby bathtubs, diaper bags, bottles, diapers, formula and crib bedding. They offer a large safety selection including the Safety 1st line. Prices are competitive with other large discount stores.

Wal-Mart also has a wide variety and excellent prices on infant and toddler clothing. You can pick up a two-piece newborn outfit for as little as $5-$9. All the basic clothing items are available.

For maternity shopping, the expectant mom may be a little disappointed, as it may be difficult to find a wide selection of clothing. It was hit-or-miss depending what store we visited. Some stores carry large T-shirts and stretch leggings at reasonable prices.

Call ahead to confirm hours and locations.

CHILDREN'S CLOTHING STORES

■ ABIGAIL'S CHILDREN'S BOUTIQUE
(781) 235-3333
93 Central St.
Wellesley, MA 02181
Hours: M-Sat. 9:30 a.m.-5:30 p.m.
This lovely store in Wellesley Center has wonderful clothes for infants and toddlers as well as older children. You will find an excellent selection of outfits by Little Me, Sweet Potatoes, Flapdoodles and more, many from $20-$30. They have sales in January and June. When I visited, summer merchandise was marked down 50%. I found an adorable romper by Flaphappy for $9. They carry christening gowns, dress clothes, hats, tights, socks, Padders and outerwear. Abigail's also has beautiful infant gifts such as teddy bear lamps, Ambi toys and frames. Customer service is their specialty. They offer shopping by phone, free gift-wrapping, monogramming items such as blankets and sweaters, and will special order hard to find items for you. Their sales staff is friendly and very helpful.

■ BABY BOOM
(781) 848-1600
1000 Washington St.
Braintree, MA 02184
Hours:
M 12:00 p.m.-5:00 p.m.
T, Sat. 10:00 a.m.-5:00 p.m.
W, Th 10:00 a.m.-6:00 p.m.
F 10:00 a.m.-7:00 p.m.

Baby Boom sells children's clothing at excellent prices. The owner personally visits New York to purchase quality clothes at affordable prices. I found items by Little Me, Tiny Tots, Health Tex and more. A cute two-piece short set by LA Kid was $17. T-shirts by French Toast at $4 each were stocked in a huge selection of colors. When I visited in mid-summer, they had a special: buy two sets of shorts, get one free. Baby Boom also has a good selection of christening gowns. They sell shoes including Osh Kosh, Weebok, and Step & Stride, among others, and their friendly and helpful staff will professionally fit them for you.

■ BAY VIEW CLOTHING & LITTLE BRITCHES
(617) 269-3272
473 W. Broadway
South Boston, MA 02127
Hours:
M-W 9:00 a.m.-5:30 p.m.
Th, F 9:00 a.m.-6:00 p.m.
Sat. 9:00 a.m.-5:00 p.m.

Little Britches sells children's clothes as well as hats and other accessories. I found many newborn outfits by Little Me for under $20 and they have a good selection of clothing by Osh Kosh at reasonable prices. You will also find clothes by Beyond Basics Kids and Little Red Hen among others. Little Britches carries a selection of christening gowns as well. When I visited they were having a special sale: buy one item at the original price and get a second item for a penny!

■ CALLIOPE
(617) 876-4149
33 Brattle Street
Cambridge, MA 02138
Hours: M-W 10:00 a.m.-6:30 p.m.
Th, F 10:00 a.m.-8:00 p.m.
Sat. 10:00 a.m.-6:00 p.m.
Sun. 12:00 p.m.-6:00 p.m.

Located in Harvard Square for 25 years, this shop carries gorgeous 100% cotton infant and toddler clothing. Prices range from $8 for a Baby Basics onesie to $40 for a Midori dress with hat, to $80 for a girl's dress. Baby clothes from such brands as Toot Petite, Baby's Own, Absorba, Le Top, and Rebble Pebble range from $25-$35 for a two piece cotton suit. They have an especially good selection of infant toys from Chicco, Ambi, Kouvalias and Primitive Playthings and a plush and cozy collection of stuffed animals. Handmade items that caught my eye were adorable buntings by Tinis To Go in several shapes like sunflowers, bumblebees, and peapods for $52. There were similar jackets and bibs. They also sell Stride Rite seconds, which are structurally fine but may have a smudge here and there, for $19.99. Calliope offers free gift-wrapping, shower registry and very attentive sales clerks.

■ CAROLANN'S CHILDREN'S SHOP
(781) 749-8060
31-35 Main St.
Hingham, MA 02043
Hours: M-Sat. 9:30 a.m.-5:30 p.m.

This old-fashioned children's clothing store, located in Hingham Center, reminds me of stores that, as a child, I looked longingly into the windows. You are enticed through the doors by a unique selection of toys, such as Montgomery School House Vermont wooden toys, and swept through a whirl of beautiful colors, fabrics and textures. Carolann's offers full customer service and is still able to offer 20%-50% off regular retail prices. The owner, Carol Baron, proudly showed off their complete layette, infant, and toddler wear, all in 100% cotton. Carolann's prides themselves on carrying better brand clothing: Flapdoodles, Kitestrings, Le Top, Sweet Potatoes, Marimekko and Wes & Willy. Carol was especially excited to show me their unique boys' clothing in yummy garment-dyed cottons. Carolann's specializes in Cherry Tree, Ali Mac and other polar fleece brands. Given the discounted prices for better brand, distinctive children's clothing and personal service, a special trip to Hingham may be worth the while.

■ CENTRE BOUTIQUE— CHILDREN'S CLOTHING
(617) 524-4839
314 Centre St.
Jamaica Plain, MA 02130
Hours: M-Sat. 10:00 a.m.-7:00 p.m.

Located near the intersection of Perkins Avenue, this children's boutique has been serving Jamaica Plain for the past 15 years. An entire wall was devoted to cute little two-piece rompers for $14.99-$17.99 by Top-Top and Bon Cha Cha Sports. A complete winter-welcoming knitted outfit of blanket, booties, hat and jacket is $24.99. An embroidered pillow case and summer weight blanket is $17. A complete line of christening wear is priced at $35-$70. Owner and community development organizer Tony Barros has plans to greatly expand the baby line over the next year. They offer layaway and gift-wrapping. Se habla espanol.

■ THE CHILDREN'S BOUTIQUE
(781) 259-3432
2 Lewis St.
Lincoln, MA 01773
Hours: Vary with the season; call ahead.
This small store is tucked away along the railroad tracks, kitty corner from the Mall at Lincoln Station. You will find high quality domestic and imported brands including Carriage Boutique, Cacharel and Petite Bateau. You will also find imported shoes from size 3 on up and many beautiful handmade items. Prices range from $10 for a summer outfit by Little Me to $450 for a christening gown by Cacharel. I saw a gorgeous gingham one-piece coverall with embroidered animals and matching booties for $70. The owner enjoys catering to her customers and expects them to be choosy. She will order anything in any line that she carries and has a very flexible return policy.

■ CHILDREN'S CAROUSEL
(781) 455-8705
1500 Highland Ave.
Needham, MA 02192
Hours: M-F 9:30 a.m.-5:30 p.m.
       Sat. 9:30 a.m.-5:00 p.m.
Located in Needham Center, Children's Carousel offers quality clothes at good prices. You will find outfits by Carriage Boutiques, New Potatoes, Marimekko, Flapdoodles and more, many in the $20-$30 range. Children's Carousel also has some unique gifts such as interesting motion clocks and stuffed animals by Eco Toys. I saw a delightful mouse, unlike any plush animal I'd seen before for $18.50. He was handmade from natural fibers and smartly dressed in earth tones. Children's Carousel sells christening gowns and offers gift-wrapping.

■ THE CHILDREN'S PLACE
(617) 924-6605
Arsenal Mall

(781) 229-6678
Burlington Mall

(617) 494-6085
CambridgeSide Galleria

(508) 655-9605
Natick Mall

(978) 532-5494
North Shore Mall

(781) 231-9515
Square One Mall

(617) 356-7799
Braintree Mall

This East Coast chain is a good place to go for reasonably priced casual, sporty clothes, all of which are private label. For babies, the sizes range from 3-24 months. The boys' selection is as wide and varied as the girls' and most of the clothes for infants are 100% cotton. You'll find cute rugby shirts in bright colors, coveralls, lots of coordinated outfits, and a large selection of Extra Tiny Sweats. I found comfy quilted overalls in an assortment of fall colors for $14, pink wide-wale corduroy overalls for $18, and flowered turtlenecks for $10. I saw a whole wall of layette items, including all cotton stretchies at two for $20. Definitely check out their sale rack where you can usually find great deals.

■ DEL VALLE'S CHILDREN'S GIFT SHOP
(617) 522-0885
360 Centre St.
Jamaica Plain, MA 02130
Hours: M-Sat. 10:00 a.m.-6:00 p.m.
A half-block past Centre Boutique is a children's shop that carries some unique items. Most of their clothing is imported from Puerto Rico and Columbia and is very reasonably priced. I saw a two-piece silky 100% cotton beautifully machine-crocheted suit by Vamy for $20 and Galsin has a three-piece plush 100% cotton ensemble for $29. Del Valle's has a complete line of christening outfits from a very simple crocheted 100% cotton gown for $29 to a more elaborate sequined suit for $60. They carry fancy bassinette ensembles including skirt, net and pole for $179. There is a nice selection of shoes by Carola, Hedy, and Bebitos. Most are all leather and leather lined for $20-$40. When a few sizes remain, those shoes are marked down to 50% off. They always have a sale rack with great bargains for 30%-50% off, for example, boys' three-piece suits for $20.00. Dell Valle's is a neighborhood store that offers senior citizens and regular customers a discount. They gift wrap and offer layaway. Se habla espanol.

■ THE DISNEY STORE
(617) 248-3900
Faneuil Hall Marketplace
200 State St.
Boston, MA 02109

(617) 926-2129
Arsenal Mall

(617) 266-5200
Copley Place

(617) 577-8833
CambridgeSide Galleria

(617) 380-7700
Braintree Mall

(781) 941-8001
Square One Mall

(781) 229-7766
Burlington Mall

(508) 653-1883
Natick Mall
Hours: Hours vary by store
What a fun place to shop, like a little taste of Disneyland right in your own backyard. The window displays are bright and attractive and movie screens play favorite Disney shows. Children love to go here, which is both good and bad! The store sells clothing items, all depicting some Disney character or scene, and a large selection of gift items and Disney memorabilia. The store has beautiful sleepwear starting at $20, and cute outfits from $24 on up. They also have a huge selection of stuffed animals and figurines, including many of the lesser characters in Disney movies. Of course, they have the latest and greatest Disney videos for sale, usually along with a special discount on store products.

Call ahead to confirm hours and locations.

■ FISH KIDS
(617) 738-1006
1378A Beacon St.
Brookline, MA 02146
Hours: M-Sat. 10:00 a.m.-5:00 p.m.*
　　　　Th. 10:00 a.m.-6:00 p.m.*
*Call regarding extended hours in the fall

This fun children's clothing store is located just a couple of blocks up from Harvard Street on the outbound side of Beacon. Quality clothing is attractively displayed among the brightly painted fittings and unique hanging fish. There is a mix of American and European brands including Sweet Potatoes, Mullberribush, Clayeux, Baby Lulu, Pingo, and Petit Bateau. Prices for baby outfits range from $20 up to $100. I saw a cute blue and white long sleeve one-piece by New Potatoes for $21 and a leggings and top outfit by Flapdoodles for $36. There are many attractive gender-neutral clothes, and a wide selection of outerwear including Cherry Tree and Corky & Co. There are also accessories, baby bags, hats and swim diapers.

■ FROG POND KIDS
(978) 922-3585
50 Dodge St.
Beverly, MA 01915
Hours: M-Sat. 9:30 a.m.-5:30 p.m.
　　　　Th. 9:30 a.m.-8:00 p.m.
　　　　Sun. 12:30 p.m.-4:30 p.m.

Located on Rte. 1A, just off Rte. 128 towards Hamilton, Frog Pond Kids sells it own unique brand of appliqued children's clothing. They have a range of colors and styles for babies 3-24 months. All prices in this store are 40% off retail. Coordinated outfits are the specialty so you can easily find clothes for twins or siblings that have the same patterns in different colors or the same colors in different patterns. For instance, there was a one-piece coverall with dots and stripes and a large appliqued rabbit for $18 available in both pink and blue. The fabrics are mostly 100% cotton and the appliques for infants are fun—animals, fruit, rockets, and balls. They also sell coordinating hats, socks, bibs, and headbands.

■ GAP KIDS
(617) 424-8778
201 Newbury St.
Boston, MA 02116

(617) 262-2370
Copley Place

(617) 923-1966
550 Arsenal St.
Watertown, MA 02172

(617) 864-0719
15 Brattle St. (Harvard Square)
Cambridge, MA 02138

(781) 270-3503
Burlington Mall

(617) 439-7844
Faneuil Hall Marketplace
200 State St.
Boston, MA 02109

(617) 494-9181
CambridgeSide Galleria

(781) 233-9200
Square One Mall

(781) 237-6766
74 Central St.
Wellesley, MA 02181

■ GAP KIDS ...
(978) 531-4894
North Shore Mall
Hours: Hours vary by store
Gap Kids and Baby Gap are known for quality 100% cotton clothing that lasts and lasts. Not unlike the regular Gap, Gap Kids carries a preppie look including jeans, jean jackets, button-down shirts, and T-shirts. The style is comfortable and looks great on kids. Another plus is that Gap clothes are sized realistically, so your six-month old will really wear a size 6 months. Baby Gap clothes are similar in color to the other Gap clothes, but they are generally of softer material, and they still have that famous coordinated style. Belts, socks and hair accessories are available to finish off the outfit. In the back of the store are sale items where you can really find a good bargain. You can expect to spend $12 for onesies and $26 for an outfit.

■ THE GOLDEN GOOSE
(617) 893-5111
405 Boston Post Rd.
Weston, MA 02193
Hours: M-Sat. 10:00 a.m.-5:00 p.m.
The Golden Goose, in the heart of the beautiful town of Weston, has a good selection of clothing for babies. They carry a mix of American and European brands, including Flapdoodles, Sophie, Katie & Co., and Clayeux, and a range of styles including layette, casual, and dressy. Christening gowns and special occasion dresses are sold as well. I saw a two-piece navy print outfit by Galipette on sale for $29, a cozy Petit Bateau velour sleeper for $42, and a Wes & Willy long sleeve thick cotton overall for $42. The Golden Goose carries a small selection of underclothes, socks, tights and booties. There are many Winnie-the-Pooh items, as well as stuffed animals, frames and handpainted furniture. Gift-wrapping is free on non-sale items.

■ GYMBOREE
(781) 272-0967
Burlington Mall

(617) 437-1191
Copley Place

(617) 969-9936
The Mall at Chestnut Hill

(781) 848-6113
Braintree Mall

(508) 651-1123
Natick Mall

(978) 532-6644
North Shore Mall

Gymboree is a franchise that carries its own label. The styles are simple and comfortable. Most of the clothing is 100% cotton. Gymboree has its own style of mix-and-match clothing that is vibrantly colored. Sale items are in the back of the store and you'll find bargains here: 25% to 50% off. Some toy items and Gymboree videotapes are also sold here. The sales staff is friendly. You can expect to spend about $35 and up for a whole outfit. Gymboree outfits grow with your child, using special cuffs that roll up or down. You can get an extra year of wear out of the outfit in some cases.

Call ahead to confirm hours and locations.

■ ICINGS GIFT BOUTIQUE
(781) 593-7670
254 Eastern Ave.
Lynn, MA 01902
Hours: T-Sat. 10:00 a.m.-5:30 p.m.
Icings is a beautiful store decorated with a Victorian theme. Clothing, displayed separately by gender, including a neutral section, is attractively arranged among gifts, toys, and jewelry. They sell high-end children's clothes in preemie sizes up to 4T. You will find items by Little Me priced around $20 as well as more expensive labels such as Petit Bateau and Kite Strings. Icings has a wonderful selection of baby gifts including baby books and blankets and pillows available for monogramming. They carry beautiful christening gowns and offer gift-wrap and new baby gift baskets. I found the staff extremely enthusiastic and helpful.

■ IMAGINATIONS
(781) 639-4626
9 Bessom St.
Marblehead, MA 01945
Hours: M-Sat. 10:00 a.m.-5:00 p.m.
Imaginations, run by two sisters, carries a beautiful line of clothes including Petit Bateau, Cow and Lizard, Flapdoodles and New Potatoes. Prices start at around $20. A one-piece cotton outfit by Creme de la Creme adorned with teddy bears and a small stuffed bear tucked into the pocket was $31. Gorgeous handmade sweaters were $76. Imaginations has some darling baby gifts. I found a wonderful selection of frames, baby books, and a cute marbleized newborn cotton hat for $10. They also carry christening gowns.

■ KATIE'S INFANTS & TODDLERS
(617) 846-6010
32 Woodside Ave.
Winthrop, MA 02152
Hours: T-Sat. 10:00 a.m.-5:00 p.m.
Named for a granddaughter, Katie's Infant & Toddlers is run by a mother-daughter duo who loves and specializes in fine baby clothing, preemie through size 4-6. This understated boutique is located in Winthrop Center: look for the street number or the little clothes in the window, as there is no sign! Katie's carries a wide array of unique clothing in 100% cotton, wonderfully different prints and delightful coordinates. Their prices range from the under $10 gift to a complete christening outfit for anywhere from $50-$300. Although off the beaten path, it is worth the trip to find really special items such as a great baby wrap by Teddy Toes or a darling onesie camisole with a frilly bottom. Katie's also carries some sweet and unusual toys and gifts. They have fun toddler boys' clothes that shouldn't be missed. Katie's offers gift-wrapping, complete layette and preemie wear and specializes in personalized service for christening wear.

■ KENZIE KIDS
(617) 965-5566
The Mall at Chestnut Hill
This family-owned store has been around for more than ten years and was recently named one of the top children's specialty stores in the country by both *Child* magazine and *Kid's Fashions*. You'll find a wide range of quality clothing, from T-shirt and short sets by Flapdoodles for $27 and layette stretchies by Jean Bourget for $34, to mix and match cotton infant

sets by Zutano. Other brands include Little Me, Wes & Willy, and Le Chat. Kenzie Kids carries a wide selection of more unique items like hand-smocked dresses, silk buntings, distinctive diaper bags, fun hooded bath towels, and handknit chenille cardigans with matching caps. They have beautiful christening gowns ranging from around $70 to well over $300, and a large selection of outerwear, including fleece jackets, buntings and very fancy snow suits. You can also find different accessories and gift ideas. The friendly staff is knowledgeable and helpful.

■ KIDS "R" US

See address listings under Toys "R" Us. Owned by Toys R Us, this is a good place to shop for clothing that is both reasonably priced and fashionable. Kids R Us stores are well designed, making it an easy place to shop. They have a wide variety of seasonal clothing, including swim suits and related gear, and all sorts of accessories, including children's jewelry. The shoe department is not large but has some good buys. The store is great for layette items as well as back to school clothes. Like Toys R Us, it also has a price guarantee. You can find excellent bargains on the clearance rack: dresses for less than $15 and T-shirts for less than $8.

■ KUSSIN'S, INC.
THE CHILDREN'S SHOP

(978) 369-3253
79 Main St.
Concord, MA 01742
Hours: M-Sat. 9:00 a.m.-5:30 p.m.
Sun. 12:30 p.m.-4:30 p.m.
This wonderful store opened 60 years ago and is run by the same family today.

You can find almost any type of clothing you might need for your new baby including Carter's sleepwear and underwear; Cherry Tree fleece outerwear; clothing in brands like Agabang, Flapdoodles, and Sweet Baby Jess; and gorgeous christening gowns and special occasion dresses. I saw an adorable yellow one-piece outfit by Le Top with an embroidered collar for $28. You will find all kinds of accessories, bedding, child carriers, frames, stuffed animals, and piggy banks. Antiques that pertain to babies are attractively displayed throughout the store and may be purchased. The upstairs "Attic" has clothing sold at discount prices with no frills attached (stricter return policy and no gift-wrapping). Older kids will enjoy the playground in the back of the building.

■ LITTLE DREAMS—A STORE
FOR NEW PEOPLE

(781) 740-0211
77 Water St.
Hingham, MA 02043
Hours: Hours vary; call to confirm
Right off Hingham Harbor on Rte. 3A, this store, like its name, has a fun and whimsical feel. Little Dreams specializes in unique clothing made of natural fibers, carefully chosen for superior quality, intended to survive several children's tough and tumble wear. You'll find colorful and charming dresses with matching leggings, handmade sweaters for all seasons and special birthday hats with fantastic adornments. Little Dreams has plenty of polar fleece with matching hats and mittens. Visit the store for special options such as out of the ordinary seasonal wear and irresistible infant gifts.

❧ Call ahead to confirm hours and locations.

■ MARSHA FACTORY OUTLET
(781) 631-5511
32 Tioga Way
Marblehead, MA 01945
Hours: M-Sat. 10:00 a.m.-4:00 p.m.*
*Often closes early on Sat.; call ahead.

A true factory outlet, Marsha's prices everything at least 40% below retail. Sizes start at 6 months and nearly all items are cotton with some sort of decoration, ribbon or applique. Boys shortalls adorned with large baseballs and footballs were $12 and a pink dress with rosebuds and lace was $7. Plain cotton T-shirts and shorts were $3-$5 each. Seasonal clothes are sold later in the year than retail stores. Fall items are not put out until October, for example. Call for dates for special sales and summer Saturday hours.

■ NEXT
(617) 236-6398
206 Newbury St.
Boston, MA 02116
Hours: M-Sat. 10:00 a.m.-8:00 p.m.
Sun. 12:00 p.m.-6:00 p.m.

(508) 655-6398
Natick Mall

(978) 977-6398
North Shore Mall

The U.S. flagship location for NEXT, a chic British clothing and home accessory store, rests in our very own Back Bay. The only four-storied NEXT in the U.S., this cutting-edge fashion store also carries children's clothing for newborn-24 months nestled in its own nook on the third floor. Thick 100% cotton onesies were $18 and cozy union suits were $24, although they don't carry much more in the way of layette. They do have a handsome selection of overalls, pants, shirts and sweaters for boys and adorable leggings and shirts, overalls, jumpers, dresses and sweaters for girls. Prices ranged from $12 for a shirt to plush corduroy overalls or a two-piece cushy velour outfit for $28-$42 to 100% cotton sweaters for $34. They had some great reversible coats for $48 with matching hats for $8. NEXT has taken classic clothing and updated the style using contemporary cuts and fashionable color combos (for instance, lime green, electric yellow, and orange on a dark blue background) in thick cottons, velours, corduroys, and polar fleece. Most items are coordinated, from shoes and socks to onesies, overall sets, sweaters, coats and hats. NEXT has a preferred customer program where 10% of all purchases is rebated back to customer as an in-store credit.

■ OILILY
(617) 247-9299
31 Newbury St.
Boston, MA 02116
Hours: M-Sat. 10:00 a.m.-6:00 p.m.
Th 10:00 a.m.-7:00 p.m.
Sun. 12:00 p.m.-5:00 p.m.

(617) 630-0605
The Mall at Chestnut Hill

In Boston, Oilily is located on the first block of Newbury St., near the Public Garden. Oilily is an upscale children's shop with a distinctively fresh look on children's clothes. If you are looking for something different than the usual brands and color combinations, a visit to Oilily is a must. While smaller sizes are often in softer colors, I saw adorable toddler clothes for the fall/winter for boys in brown and gold shades. Soft blue corduroys for girls were $58 and an adorable white shirt with an embroidered Peter Pan collar was $45. Oilily also carries shoes, hats, baby gifts and bedding and they have a mail order catalog. The Boston sales staff was extremely helpful and friendly.

■ OLD NAVY
(781) 740-1022
Anchor Plaza
Hingham, MA 02043

(781) 393-0697
Meadow Glen Mall

(617) 926-0098
Arsenal Mall

(978) 762-8557
Liberty Tree Mall
Hours: Hours vary by store

Old Navy is one of our favorite stores for shopping for the whole family as they carry sizes from infants to adults. Their selection of children's clothing is large and the prices are unbeatable. Old Navy's clothing styles are very similar to Gap but much lower in price. You'll find lots of onesies and leggings along with casual outfits and a great variety of socks, hats, and bibs. If you are looking for your own child or for a great gift at a reasonable price, you can't beat Old Navy.

■ PEANUT BUTTER 'N JELLY KIDS
(978) 777-1122
110 Newbury St. (Rte. 1 South)
Danvers, MA 01923
Hours: T-Sat.   10:00 a.m.-5:00 p.m.

If price is not your primary concern, you will always be able to find new and different clothing and accessories of the highest quality at this upscale children's clothing store. The owner is always searching for unique clothing "on the cutting edge of fashion and quality." The brands change, but in among the unfamiliar imports you'll also find brands like Galipette, Bebe Mode, and Flapdoodles. The store specializes in christening gowns and carries many novelty items like teddy bears, party hats and handknit matching child/adult sweaters. It is also the place to go for cruisewear for your children starting in December. Customers often come by on their way to a christening or party to find a wonderful gift, and extremely elegant gift-wrapping is included in the price of all non-sale items.

■ PEEK A BOO
(617) 569-0933
76 Bennington St.
E. Boston, MA 02128
Hours: M, W, Th,
         Sat.   10:00 a.m.-5:00 p.m.
         F   10:00 a.m.-6:00 p.m.

No search for unique children's clothing would be complete without a visit to Peek A Boo. Tucked in a row of stores and townhouses, this tiny treasure trove is located just outside of Central Square in East Boston. They have a complete layette line, gorgeous custom made christening gowns from $50-$200 and up, and ornate first birthday princess outfits complete with hats trimmed in ribbons, fur and beads. This wild little boutique carries other custom items such as a pink leather snowsuit with shearling hat to match and appliqued bomber jackets by Identity for $135. Peek A Boo also carries traditional camel hair coats and linen/cotton sailor suits for boys. A preview of their autumn polar fleece collection featured Ali Mac items from $75-$100. You can custom order a handmade sweater for $60 or pillow, $65, that are only available at Rodeo Drive, Aspen, and in E. Boston!

■ PETIT PATAPON
(781) 235-8909
27 Central St.
Wellesley, MA 02181
Hours: M-Sat. 9:30 a.m.-5:30 p.m.
Sun. 12:00 p.m.-5:00 p.m.

Petit Patapon is a French label made in Portugal. All of their clothes are cotton and have an adorable European look. When I visited, their summer merchandise in fun, bright colors was attractively displayed. You might expect to pay more for well-made European clothes but most items were $20-$30. I also found several items, both summer and winter, priced up to 50% off. A T-shirt adorned with a very cute dog was $8 from $12 and a few of last year's snowsuits were priced at $38 from $76.

■ PINK DOMINO
(617) 964-7465
1280 Centre St.
Newton Centre, MA 02159
Hours: T-Sat. 10:00 a.m.-5:30p.m.
Th. 10:30 a.m.-7:00 p.m.
Sun. 12:00 p.m.-5:00 p.m.

Located on the second floor in Picadilly Square, this unique store offers "fine fashions for young ladies," but also has a fun and colorful selection of infant and toddler girls' clothing. It would be a wonderful place to find a well-made and unique gift for a special baby girl. When I was there I saw an adorable Mardigras red and blue checked sleeveless romper for $42, a cotton bathing suit with a huge sunflower for $39, and a gorgeous knitted chenille hat and cardigan for $100. They also have formal dresses. Brands include Baby Lulu, San Francisco Blues, Lilly Pulitzer, and Confetti.

■ THE QUILTED GIRAFFE
(617) 332-7633
50 Winchester St.
Newton, MA 02161
Hours: M-F 9:30 a.m.-5:00 p.m.
Sat. 10:00 a.m.-5:00 p.m.

Located on the left-hand side of Winchester Street, which passes under Rte. 9 as you come from the Highlands, this children's boutique is a good place to find imported clothing for infants and both imported and domestic clothing for older children. You'll find a good selection of clothes ranging in price from $20 for a onesie to $110 for a nicely made two-piece pants/jacket outfit. There is a large selection of sleepers and some accessories including bibs, blankets, and hooded towels. Sizes for babies range from one month to 24 months. Brands include Jean Bourget, Petit Bateau, Galipette, and Flapdoodles.

■ THE RUGGED BEAR
(617) 739-3320
49 Boylston St. (Rte. 9, Westbound)
Chestnut Hill, MA 02167

(978) 927-9212
2-4 Enon St. (Rte. 1A)
N. Beverly, MA 01915

(781) 431-1715
34 Central St.
Wellesley, MA 02181
Hours: Hours vary by store

This specialty chain for children's clothing and camping equipment carries a good selection of sporty clothing for babies 0-24 months. The Chestnut Hill store near Legal Seafood had many reasonably priced private label clothes, all 100% cotton, in a wide variety of prints and colors. Polo shirts were $11, body suits were $13, and cotton cardigans were $20. They also carry other brands including Agabang, Kitestrings, and Stamp. An adorable 100% cotton sailor print top with striped pants by Zutano Baby was $30. Accessories included Flaphappy hats, swim diapers bibs, Padders, baby bags, towels, blankets, and layette items by Le Top. Rugged Bear carries the complete line of Kelty Kids child carrier backpacks and accessories.

■ SATURDAY'S CHILD
(617) 661-6402
1762 Mass. Ave.
Cambridge, MA 02140
Hours: M-Sat. 10:00 a.m.-6:00 p.m.
Sun. 12:00 p.m.-5:00 p.m.
(seasonal)

Located on Mass. Ave. about halfway between Harvard and Porter Squares, this store captures the idyllic quality of babyhood and childhood with its gorgeous high quality clothing, shoes, and accessories. They carry some preemie clothing, and will special order any item, especially Baby Bjorn. You'll find the most delicious baby clothes from such makers as Marimekko, Minibasix, New Potatoes, and Flapdoodles. There were onesies from $12-$50, outfits from $34-$100 and dresses from $24-$120. Most of their clothing is European, as are nearly all of their shoes. Shoe prices range from a simple (yet mode) pair of sneakers at $17, to glistening red patent leather Mary Janes at $60. They have a beautiful selection of crib accessories, a variety of baby carriers, potties, step stools, music tapes, baby books and some delightful infant toys. They offer cheery free gift-wrap and will arrange a shower registry if you ask. Get on their mailing list to receive advance notice of their clearance sales, which offer substantial savings.

■ VILLAGE KIDS
(617) 332-7654
35A Lincoln St.
Newton Highlands, MA 02161
Hours: M-Sat. 10:00 a.m.-5:30 p.m.
Sun. 12:00 p.m.-5:00 p.m.
(except some holidays and the summer months)

The couple that owns this attractive children's clothing store has three sons, so they make sure that those who are shopping for boys will be pleased with the selection, as will those searching for girls' outfits. The store is deceptively large, with meandering rooms of competitively priced quality clothes with brands like San Francisco Blues, Three Wishes, Flapdoodles, Pluto's, and Cow & Lizard. There is a large selection of Sara's Prints natural fiber clothing and a wall full of accessories. You can find outfits from $20 on up to over $100. I saw a Flapdoodle denim coverall with vest for $47.50, a fun girl's fleece jacket for $29.99 and an adorable T-shirt/leggings/hat set by BabySacks for $39. There is also a huge selection of toddler clothes.

■ THE WARNER BROTHERS STUDIO STORE
(617) 859-3770
Prudential Plaza
800 Boylston St.
Boston, MA 02112
Hours: Hours vary by store

(617) 227-1101
Faneuil Hall Marketplace
200 State St.
Boston, MA 02109

(978) 977-0482
North Shore Mall

(617) 356-5681
Braintree Mall

The Warner Brothers Studio Store is filled with (you guessed it) Warner Brothers character clothing and items. Tweety Bird, Batman and Robin, Bugs Bunny and more await you at this lively store! Rocket ships and large movie screens keep your child occupied. Prices are what you would expect from a specialty store, with clothing starting at around $22 on up. You'll find play clothes, jeans, shorts, sweats, and onesies, all with a variety of choices in color and Warner Brothers character. They also have some really cute crib toys, hats and coordinated outfits, as well as unique memorabilia and items that you could not buy elsewhere. Like the other character stores, this is a fun place to shop for kids and adults.

ૐ

Call ahead to confirm hours and locations.

RESALE AND CONSIGNMENT STORES

■ APPLE TREE
(617) 469-6887
1785 Centre St.
West Roxbury, MA 02132
Hours: T, Th, Sat. 10:00 a.m.-5:00 p.m.
W, Fri. 10:00 a.m.-3:00 p.m.

Located in the heart of West Roxbury, this consignment store carries baby clothes, shoes, toys, equipment and books. Creepers were $6-$7 and two-piece stretchie sleepers were $5-$8. I saw brands such as Little Me, Baby Beluga, Baby Gap, Gymboree, Osh Kosh, and Laura Ashley. They have a nice maternity selection (some pricing examples: $17-$20 for a two-piece dress, $25 for a dress, $14 for a blouse). After 30 days merchandise is reduced to half-off the marked price. Apple Tree always has a $1 sale rack and seasonal and holiday wear sales. They produce a quarterly informative newsletter discussing upcoming sales, changing equipment laws and local preschool recommendations.

■ CECE'S MATERNITY RESALE
(508) 370-9828
419 Worcester Rd. (Rte. 9, Westbound)
Framingham, MA 01701
Hours: T, Th. F,
Sat. 10:00 a.m.-5:00 p.m.
W 11:00 a.m.-5:00 p.m.

Owned and operated by a former manger of Dan Howard's, this store offers high quality, hardly worn clothes at about 75% less than at retail shops. Almost all of the top brands were well represented in all sizes and styles. She has casual, career, lingerie, swimwear, and black tie items at extremely attractive prices. I saw

Mother's Work jeans for $14, a Maternite stirrup jumpsuit for $39, a Dan Howard suit for $28, and a Meg Lauren dress for $39. All of the clothes were cleaned, pressed and attractively displayed.

■ CHIC REPEATS
(617) 536-8580
117 Newbury St.
Boston, MA 02116
Hours: M-Sat. 10:00 a.m.-6:00 p.m.
Sun. 12:00 p.m.-5:00 p.m.

Chic Repeats is an upscale resale store sponsored by the Junior League of Boston. The upper level sells women's fashions and the lower level sells maternity and children's clothes. I saw a Laura Ashley girl's dress for $25 and a Baby Dior infant outfit for $9 as well as clothes by Osh Kosh and Gymboree. The maternity racks feature labels such as Dan Howard, Take Nine, and Pea In The Pod. Chic Repeats also sells toys, car seats and baby equipment.

■ CHILDREN'S ATTIC AND MY SISTER'S CLOSET
(617) 471-8602
142 Willard St.
Quincy, MA 02169
Hours: M- Sat. 10:00 a.m. - 5:00 p.m.

You might be surprised as you ride through this residential area when you come upon a house that has become Children's Attic and My Sister's Closet. As you enter the first floor, you'll see a nice variety of cribs, high chairs, strollers and other baby equipment. To the right you'll find toys and books, to the left a room devoted to baby clothes, all well-priced. I saw onesies for $1, strechie sleepers for $3, overalls at $6, and jumpers for $4. In August they had already begun stocking their winter coats. I saw a Baby B'Gosh snow suit for $22, and a nice purple Rothschild coat and hat for $50. The toy selection moves in just as fast as it moves out, so ask to put your name on a waiting list if you're looking for something specific. I saw a ride-on Little Tykes tractor and wagon set for around $30. Its buyer was waiting on a list or I would've snapped it up.

Upstairs you'll find My Sister's Closet, a bedroom packed on three walls with maternity clothes, all in excellent condition. I saw a very nice work dress for $16, a two-piece 100% cotton jersey casual outfit for $22, a two-piece dress suit for $30, and a formal black velvet dress with sequins for $40. My Sister's Closet stocks maternity clothes in a variety of styles, sizes and for any occasion and plans to expand to an additional bedroom.

■ CHILDREN'S EXCHANGE
(781) 665-4522
12 Essex St.
Melrose, MA 02176
Hours: T-Sat. 10:00 a.m.-4:00 p.m.

This small store in Melrose Center is packed with good used children's clothes at excellent prices. A cute Cow and Lizard outfit was $10 and a two-piece Osh Kosh set was $7. They also had lots of dress and holiday clothes marked down 20%. An adorable Christmas dress was $16. I also found a Peg Perego high chair in excellent condition. I recommend a visit to this store as they had one of the largest inventories of the resale shops I visited.

Call ahead to confirm hours and locations.

■ CHILDREN'S CORNER CONSIGNMENT
(781) 740-8135
24 North St.
Hingham, MA 02043
Hours: T, W, Sat. 10:00 a.m.-5:30 p.m.
        Th   10:00 a.m.-3:30 p.m.
        F   1:00 p.m.-8:00 p.m.

Located just up from the Hingham Harbor, this quaint consignment shop is packed with goodies. Clothing and shoes range from newborn to teenage sizes. Name brands include the Gap, Limited, Talbots, and Children's Place. Their automatic markdown, 25% off marked price after 30 days and 50% off after 60 days, ensures really good deals. Children's Corner offers strollers, car seats, cribs and other baby equipment, toys, children's videos at half retail prices. New equipment is offered at wholesale club prices or below. Their maternity section is very limited, but features brand names and less-than-a-year-old-fashions.

■ CHILDREN'S EXPRESS
(978) 657-5718
281 Main St.
Wilmington, MA 01887
Hours: T-Sat. 10:00 a.m.-5:00 p.m.
        F   10:00 a.m.-7:00 p.m.

This resale shop has a good selection of children's and maternity clothes. Clothes are conveniently separated into boy's and girl's sections. I found girl's dress shoes for $2 and a newborn Baby Beluga outfit for $6 as well as other quality brands. Children's Express also sells toys and equipment. When I visited they had a beautiful Child Craft crib for $100 and a like-new Graco umbrella stroller for $9. In their maternity department I found a special occasion dress by Mimi Maternity for $50.

■ CHILDREN'S ORCHARD   *Baby Pages*
(617) 277-3006
807 Boylston St. (Rte. 9, Westbound)
Chestnut Hill, MA 02167

(978) 777-3355
139 Endicott St. (Endicott Plaza)
Danvers, MA 01923

(508) 788-0072
861 Edgell Rd.
Framingham, MA 01701

(508) 651-9386
132 E. Central St.
Natick, MA 01760

(617) 244-0030
2088 Commonwealth Ave.
Newton, MA 02166

(617) 770-4979
Pilgrim Plaza
15 Scammell St.
Quincy, MA 02169
Hours: Hours vary by store

Each of these individually-owned franchises buys and sells merchandise that meets strict standards. This is a great place to find good quality used baby and maternity clothes, toys, equipment, and furniture at great prices. Half of their inventory is under $8. The Chestnut Hill store had a whole wall of clothes just for babies, with brands such as Baby Gap, Healthtex, Mini K, and Patagonia. There was a NEXT two-piece cotton outfit for $7.99 and an Esprit cotton/linen romper for $6.44. They also sell new hats, belts, sunglasses, tights, socks, soft-soled shoes, and hair accessories at competitive prices. You may also be able to find jogger strollers, gates, nursing pillows, child carriers and toys.

■ **CHILDREN'S TREASURES**
(617) 289-5437
90 Squire Rd. (Rte 60, Westbound)
Northgate Shopping Center
Revere, MA 02151
Hours: M-Sat. 10:00 a.m.-9:00 p.m.
Sun. 12:00 p.m.-5:00 p.m.
Children's Treasures is a spacious, well-stocked secondhand store. They carry clothing and shoes for newborns to teenagers, as well as baby equipment, furniture, toys and books. Prices are one-third of retail, for example: $2 for a simple onesie, $8 for Osh Kosh overalls, and $13 for a London Fog fleece bunting in excellent condition. They have a markdown rack with prices from $1-$6 filled with items that haven't moved in the past year. Expect to pay half of retail prices for baby equipment in the best condition. They carry a nice selection of toys from $3-$6 depending on the condition. Children's Treasures also offers new strollers, car seats, crib mattress and changing tables at approximately 10% off retail price. They offer a foster parent discount of 10% on new and 20% for secondhand items. Staff are friendly and knowledgeable about their merchandise.

■ **CHILDREN'S WEARABOUTS AND MATERNITY**
(781) 335 -5533
21 Park Ave.
Weymouth, MA 02190
Hours: M-Sat. 9:30 a.m.-5:00 p.m.
Sun. 12:00 p.m.-5:00 p.m.
This bright and tidy resale shop is off Rte. 18. It sells gently used children's clothing, toys, books, and baby equipment at half of retail cost. It had fun, distinctive and reasonably priced new polar fleece hats. Suits and overalls were $6, onesies $3, 2 piece sets were $5.75-$8.50. They had a very good maternity selection. For example, a two-piece set was $18-$20 and dresses sold for $16-$25. They offer documented foster parents a 20% discount on all items. Customers have the option to return items after 15 days for cash and after 30 days for store credit.

■ **KIDDY LITTER**
(617) 527-7997
851 Washington St.
Newtonville, MA 02160
Hours: M-Sat. 10:00 a.m.-5:00 p.m.
True bargain hunters should enjoy searching through the vast array of used merchandise packed into this little shop. You can find many brands like Gymboree and Baby Gap, as well as more upscale brands like Sweet Potatoes and Baby Sasson. I saw some Osh Kosh corduroy overalls with feet for $7.50 and a Fusen Usagi cotton romper for just $5.50. The infants' clothes are organized by size along two of the walls. There is a good selection of outerwear and shoes, along with some toys, books, car seats and strollers.

■ **THE LOLLIPOP TREE**
(978) 535-3441
3 Bourbon St.
W. Peabody, MA 01960
Hours: M, T, W
Sat. 9:30 a.m.-5:00 p.m.
Th., F 9:30 a.m.-7:00 p.m.
Sun. 12:00 p.m.-5:00 p.m.
This resale store is spacious, clean and very well organized. There is a huge assortment of well-priced clothing in many brands including Weebok, Bugle Boy, and Gymboree. I saw a Baby Gap print dress for $10, a Healthtex shorts

outfit for $4, and Osh Kosh overalls for $8. There were 21 car seats neatly displayed along the wall, including an Evenflo Ultra for $40. I saw several strollers, gates, furniture, and games. The whole back wall was filled with used toys, all well priced and in great condition. This store is just off Lowell Street, heading toward Peabody from Rte. 95.

■ **SAMANTHA'S KIDS**
(978) 745-5767
181 Essex St.
Salem, MA 01970
Hours: M-Sat. 11:00 a.m.-5:00 p.m.
This resale store is located in the heart of historic Salem, just a few doors down from the Peabody Essex Museum Cafe on the Pedestrian Mall. The clothing is conveniently displayed separately by gender and organized by age. They have a good selection in all sizes and many different brands. I saw a London Fog windbreaker for a nine-month-old for $10, Carter's sleepers for $2, and a two-piece outfit from Gymboree for $6. They also frequently sell baby equipment, but tend to have people waiting for items, so the strollers, cribs and car seats go almost as fast as they come in.

■ **SMALL CHANGES**
(781) 647-KIDS (5437)
85 River St.
Waltham, MA 02154
Hours: T, Th, F 9:30 a.m.-5:30 p.m.
       W   9:30 a.m.-4:00 p.m.
       Sat.   9:30 a.m.-5:00 p.m.
Located in the Colonial Shopping Plaza, Small Changes sells used clothing at excellent prices. I found quality brands such as Gymboree, Gap and Absorba. An all-cotton dress by Osh Kosh was $4 and a snowsuit by London Fog was $19. Everything is in excellent condition without stains, tears or missing buttons. The exception is their bargain table. You will find good clothes for play or even for dolls at $3 and under. Small Changes also carries used toys.

■ **WEAR IT AGAIN KIDS**
(617) 244-7060
32 Lincoln St.
Newton Highlands, MA 02161
Hours: M-Sat. 10:00 a.m.-4:00 p.m.
Shopping in this family-run consignment shop is a pleasant experience. You'll be helped by friendly, knowledgeable staff as you look through a wide selection of inexpensive used clothing. They specialize in high-end clothes (Jean Borget, Petit Bateau, Clayeux, Ralph Lauren) but carry everything (Gap, Flapdoodle). Almost everything in the store is made of natural fibers. I saw a Disney romper for $6, a Good Fellas short suit for $10, Osh Kosh overalls for $10 and newborn onesies for $1-$6. They have a huge selection of hair accessories at great prices. You'll also find barely worn shoes, bathing suits, coats, snowsuits, and a sale rack in the back.

ે&

ે& *Call ahead to confirm hours and locations.*

TOY AND BOOK STORES

Shopping for infant toys and books is fun. Many stores go out of the way to make the experience enjoyable for the whole family. Buy items that are appropriate for your baby's development, always taking safety into account. Even tiny infants enjoy books and noisy, colorful toys. Here are some toy stores with irresistible selections of toys and books:

■ **ANIMAL VEGETABLE MINERAL** *Baby Pages*
(617) 547-2404
2400 Massachusetts Ave.
Cambridge, MA 02140

■ **BELMONT TOYS**
(617) 484-1101
71 Leonard St.
Belmont, MA 02178

■ **BUTTONWOOD FOR KIDS**
(781) 749-2665
28 South St.
Hingham, MA 02043

■ **THE CHILDREN'S MUSEUM SHOP**
(617) 426-6500, ext. 236
300 Congress St., Museum Wharf
Boston, MA 02210-1034

■ **CONCORD TOY SHOP**
(978) 369-2553
4 Walden St.
Concord, MA 01742

■ **CURIOUS GEORGE GOES TO WORDSWORTH** *Baby Pages*
(617) 498-0062
1 JFK St. (Harvard Square)
Cambridge, MA 02138

■ **HENRY BEAR'S PARK**
(617) 547-8424
361 Huron Ave.
Cambridge, MA 02138

(617) 969-8616
81 Union St. (Picadilly Square)
Newton Center, MA 02159

■ **NO KIDDING**
(617) 739-2477
19 Harvard St.
Brookline, MA 02146

■ **NOODLEKIDOODLE**
(781) 272-8530
Burlington Gateway
51 Middlesex Turnpike
Burlington, MA 01803

(508) 650-6244
Sherwood Plaza
1324 Worcester Rd.
Natick, MA 01760

(781) 848-9835
South Shore Plaza
250 Granite St.
Braintree, MA 02184

■ **SANDY & SON TOY STORE**
(617) 491-6290
Inman Square
1360 Cambridge St.
Cambridge, MA 02139

■ **TOY STOP**
(781) 235-1250
324 Weston Rd.
Wellesley, MA 02181

Call ahead to confirm hours and locations.

SPECIALTY STORES

■ ASSOCIATION OF LABOR ASSISTANTS AND CHILDBIRTH EDUCATORS
(617) 441-2500
552 Mass. Ave.
(Central Square)
Cambridge, MA 02139
Hours: M-F 10:00 a.m.-5:00 p.m.*
*Call ahead if you plan to go at lunchtime

In addition to books and videos on pregnancy, birth, breastfeeding, midwifery, teen parenting, labor assistants, Cesarean prevention, and postpartum (also available through their catalog, but you'll have to pay shipping charges), ALACE also sells massage tools, birth balls, and note cards by Harriet Hartigan out of its offices. ALACE is tucked away on the second floor of the Cambridge Business Center. You'll need to ring their buzzer in the foyer to gain access to the building, but you'll be greeted by the voice of a friendly staffperson.

■ CHINOOK OUTDOOR ADVENTURE [Baby Pages]
(617) 776-8616
93 Holland St.
Davis Square
Somerville, MA 02144
Hours:* M-F 11:00 a.m.-7:00 p.m.
Sat. 10:00 a.m.-6:00 p.m.
Sun. 12:00 p.m.-5:00 p.m.
*Extended during holidays

Although it is located on Holland Street leaving Davis Square, when you walk into Chinook you get the feeling you've just walked into a wild west frontier country store. The clothing is sturdy, no-nonsense yet beautiful, and meant to prepare you and your baby for any outdoor adventure. The most popular items are the polar fleece baby bunting and baby blankets. At $38 the baby bunting is sized for newborns through 18 months and comes in a wide variety of gorgeous colors and patterns. The fleece baby blanket is 3' x 2' and is $16 for a solid and $18 for a print. They also carry polar fleece mittens for $8-$10, and Peruvian style hats at $12 for babies, toddlers and small children. They'll create special order items for an additional charge. From their scraps they've created very special bears ($38-$58), the profits of which they have donated to the Malden Mills (where the polar fleece is manufactured) Fire Victims Fund. You should also check out Chinook's seasonal handmade or painted clothing. For example, their summertime offering was Quiggles Kidwear, who makes delightful 100% cotton clothes. Be sure to see their new fall lines. They've recently stocked 100% cotton Flaphappy clothing and hats.

■ MATERNAL OUTREACH [Baby Pages]
(781) 340-9101
63 Winter St.
Weymouth, MA 02188
Hours: M-F 9:00 a.m.-5:00 p.m.
Sat. 9:00 a.m.-1:00 p.m.
Also by appointment

Located within the office of a perinatal home health agency of the same name, this little store is stocked with any supplies the pregnant and/or nursing mother may need. The staff are knowledgeable about all material and are certified bra fitters. You'll enjoy their extensive selection of maternity underwear and girdles and nursing bras from Medela, Olga, White

River and some Italian imports. Maternal Outreach rents the Medela Lactina breast pump and sells other Medela and Little Hearts pumps. Just when you thought those romantic sexy numbers were a thing of the past, Maternal Outreach carries or can order gorgeous 100% cotton nursing nightgowns. For baby, the store carries bottles, pacifiers, White River Easy Feeder Medicine Dispensers, and a variety of milk storage supplies. There are also general books on pregnancy and birth, parenting, and nursing, as well as resources for bereaved mothers.

■ **MOTHERWEAR'S FACTORY OUTLET STORE** *Baby Pages*
(413) 586-2175
320 Riverside Dr.
Northampton, MA 01060
Hours: Th 12:00 p.m.-8:00 p.m.
F, Sat. 10:00 a.m.-4:00 p.m.

The hour and a half that it takes to get from Boston to this store will seem well worth it to any breastfeeding mom who is looking for dresses, shirts, bras or separates specifically designed for nursing easily and discreetly. Take a look at a Motherwear catalog (call 800-950-2500 for your copy) to get an idea of the kind of clothing you will find here. This outlet store carries previous season inventory, irregular garments and returned items at substantially discounted prices, sometimes as much 75%. All nursing bras are $5.

ꙮ *Call ahead to confirm hours and locations.*

■ **NEW WORDS: A WOMEN'S BOOKSTORE**
(617) 876-5310
186 Hampshire St.
Cambridge, MA 02139
Hours: M-F 10:00 a.m.-8:00 p.m.
Sat. 10:00 a.m.-6:00 p.m.
Sun. 12:00 p.m.-6:00 p.m.

New Words is a wonderful bookstore for women located in Inman Square. In addition to books on politics, fiction, spirituality, and lesbian and multicultural titles, they also have lots of books on pregnancy and parenting. You can find everything from the standard books found in mall bookstores to more alternative titles. New Words has an excellent selection of titles on fertility, motherhood, natural childbirth, and single parenting. They also have lots of quality children's books, many of them multicultural titles. Don't forget to check out their bulletin board, organized into sections such as book groups and volunteer opportunities. It would be a great place to connect with other moms, find (or start!) a babysitting cooperative or support group.

■ **PERIWINKLES**
(781) 237-8844
386 Washington St.*
Wellesley Hills, MA 02181
Hours: M-Sat. 8:00 a.m.-6:00 p.m.
(call for extended fall hours)

Periwinkles began ten years ago as makers of custom handpainted furniture—stunning heirlooms of the future. Today they continue to handpaint a variety of gorgeous quality furniture of their own design (cribs go from $695-$890, rockers from $425-$700, depending on style and detail) that will take baby into

adulthood. They offer outstanding accouterments including custom linens, toys, accessories, clothes (newborn to 6x for girls and to 24 months for boys), and a wide array of personalized gifts that extend the furniture's gentle ambiance into life and home's dimensions. Visit the store to work with helpful staff who will help you plan, decorate and furnish your baby's very first room.
*Periwinkles plans to relocate to a new space at 67 Central Street in Wellesley Centre on February 15, 1998.

■ **PREGNANCY & BEYOND**
(617) 232-1101
192 Washington St.
Brookline, MA 02146
Hours: M- Sat. 10:00 a.m.-5:00 p.m.
Take the Greenline to Brookline Village or park on Washington Street or Rte. 9 to visit Pregnancy & Beyond. This little shop contains a surprising amount of useful and hard-to-find items for pregnant women and breastfeeding moms. The owner tries hard to carry the things her customers need. She has Biobands to help with morning sickness and the Prenatal Cradle for belly and back support. She'll also rent you a beeper for short-term use or a breast pump for as long as you'd like. You'll find Medela products (including bras and unique accessories such as cigarette lighter adapters for electric pumps), Avent nursing products (including the conversion kit, which enables you to pump directly into them), shells that prevent leaking, and nursing stools and pillows. There are nursing clothes and bras, baby slings, books and rental videos on a variety of topics.

■ **SCRIBBLE IT**
(617) 964-9897
50 Winchester St.
Newton, MA 02161
Hours: M-F 9:30 a.m.-5:00 p.m.
Sat. 10:00 a.m.-5:00 p.m.
Located on the left-hand side of Winchester Street, which passes under Rte. 9 as you come from the Highlands, this unique store is a great place to go for a creative gift. Everything in the store can be personalized with a child's name (free of charge). Their designers will work with you on colors and designs and, for an extra charge, can even duplicate special fabric or wallpaper designs. You will find a wide selection of toys, furniture and accessories, including lamps, stepstools, tables and chairs, frames, rugs, beds, piggy banks, and wall hangings. Gorgeous handpainted solid wood toy boxes sold for $450. There is free gift-wrapping and a shower registry. The sales people are friendly, fun and creative. They ship UPS everywhere and will work with you on the telephone to send that perfect gift.

■ **SUSI'S: A GALLERY FOR CHILDREN**
(617) 876-7874
888-278-4111
348 Huron Ave.
Cambridge, MA 02138
Hours: T-F 11:00 a.m.-6:00 p.m.
Sat. 10:00 a.m.-5:00 p.m.
The bright colors, different textures, and sheer quantity of handpainted, one-of-a-kind, whimsical art objects make being in this store a visually exciting experience. It is a good place to find unusual and creative gifts to add a touch of fun and color to your baby's room. You'll

find many different kinds of mobiles and hanging items—my favorites were a gold and red old-fashioned airplane covered with blue spotted dinosaurs and a huge stuffed smiling sun made out of felt. Susi's has a lot of handpainted furniture and unique mirrors. There are clocks, mirrors, music boxes, stools, toy boxes, and bookcases in many different colors and themes. Fun and funky monsters and animals show up on all kinds of items. You can also find handpainted clothing—onesies, T-shirts, sweatshirts, booties and blankets—made of different materials. There are creative items in all price ranges, from bibs and booties for $10-$15 to the larger handpainted furniture pieces that can go for several hundred dollars.

LOCAL PRODUCTS AND ARTISTS

■ ART BY DESIGN
(781) 891-5997

Susan Shepard can add a touch of color and whimsy to your child's room or provide you with a one-of-a-kind gift. She handpaints furniture with original designs, from celestial stars, suns and moons to favorite toys and pets (including The Attitude Bears). Any piece of furniture can be designed, custom made, and coordinated to any environment. Her most popular pieces are growth charts, footstools, toy chests, rockers, and coat racks. Prices and pictures are available upon request.

PHOTOGRAPHERS

The presence of a new baby—the tiny little toes, silly smiles, and shining eyes—somehow makes us want to memorialize every irretrievable moment. You'll likely start taking more photos, and you may want to go further and have more formal portraits taken. The least expensive way to do this is at places like Sears where you can choose from different backgrounds and packages. If, however, you want to have a sitting with one of the many professional photographers in this area, many of whom offer baby portrait clubs, special photos, or black and white hand-tinted photography, here are several:

- **Bobbie Bush**, Salem (978) 744-6918
- **Hughes Photography**, Needham (781) 444-9814 *Baby Pages*
- **Marorie Nichols**, Somerville (617) 776-6320
- **Portraits By Andree**, Boston (617) 738-9553
- **Quasi Photo**, Roslindale (617) 323-2765
- **Loren Sklar**, Newton (617) 969-9448
- **Studio Eleven**, Newton (617) 244-2766
- **Lee Weaver**, Acton (978) 259-0749

■ BABY BLESSINGS
(781) 449-9518
22 Pershing Rd.
Needham, MA 02194

Tina Chisolm began sewing special occasion and christening gowns when she wanted handcrafted, old-fashioned designs in natural fibers for her children. Now she works from home designing and sewing special occasion clothing for babies and young children. She will restore antique gowns, make a new pattern from an old gown, or make something new inspired by vintage designs. When I visited she hung her angelic offerings on Shaker pegs across the wall, each one a unique and lovely vision. This special clothing costs from $69-$200 depending on your choice of fabric, trim, and intricacy of detail. She will work with you to keep within your price range.

■ CASTLEMAKERS
(978) 658-2370

Deborah Fedele has ten years' experience bringing babies' rooms to life with her murals and handpainted furniture. She can create anything from a spark of detailing around a window to a full-charactered wall scene. Pricing examples include $25-$50 for a stool to $400 for a generally detailed 6' X 6' wall space. Call to receive a complimentary color brochure or a free estimate.

■ EXPRESSIONS ENTERPRISES
(617) 825-7006

Jackie Cooper creates darling children's clothing and accessories (newborn to toddler) with her own basic designs cut from lush, gorgeous 100% cotton fabric from Senegal, Ghana and the Ivory Coast. Jumpers, overalls, dresses and other outfits start at $25. Her clothing is often available at Caribbean and African Creations at 54 JFK Street in Harvard Square Cambridge. Call ahead to see what is in stock: (617) 491-3192. You can also contact Jackie directly and she'll make your children custom clothing, or you may choose from her inventory.

■ LOUISA MARSHAL DESIGNS
(508) 376-0856

Louisa Marshall will work with you to design and transform the walls of your baby's room. One may choose from a simple nursery character, a border of your choice, or a full mural. Prices vary depending on what you want done, but can range from $100 for a few characters to around $700 for a mural on an average-sized wall. She has a large portfolio full of varied styles and concepts and provides free consultations and estimates. You can see an amazing example of her work by going to Birthday Wonderland in Dedham where she designed and painted the fantasy world that covers the walls.

■ MATERIAL THINGS
(508) 829-4637

Nancy Goodhile has designed and copyrighted a unique window treatment called Kangaroo Pouches. She created a valance to be used in your child's room from infancy through adolescence that will hold special stuffed animal friends in a decorative, organized fashion. These quality valances can be purchased ready-made, in a variety of solid chintz colors, or can be custom made with your choice of material. Call Nancy to find out where you can purchase them in the Boston area, or to work with her directly.

■ S.T.A.R. ENTERPRISES, INC.

Baby Pages

(617) 332-8382

Stacey Lee Crowell designed, manufactured and now sells the Beach 'n' Sport Caddie by mail order. This caddie helps parents lug their children's growing myriad of stuff more efficiently. It is designed to roll over sand, but will also tote your picnic, toys, equipment and umbrella over most terrain. Constructed of recycled plastic, it is sturdy and converts into a handy tabletop uniquely designed with six recessed drink holders. You may see her at the beach in the summer traversing the sand and selling her caddie. It sells for $99 plus $12.95 (eastern USA) for shipping.

⁂

DIAPERING OPTIONS

Until December of 1996, Dydee Diaper Service of Dorchester had been the major supplier of cloth diapers in eastern Massachusetts. In recent years Dydee had continued to expand as it acquired many smaller diaper services. When it closed its doors at the end of 1996, it was the only game in town, so parents (other than people on the North Shore due to the presence of Baby's Laundry and Diaper Service in Salem) were left choosing between laundering their own cloth diapers and using disposables. Luckily, Kimberly's Diaper Service of West Yarmouth (formerly Dydee of Cape Cod) has greatly expanded to the serve the greater Boston area. It now delivers cloth diapers to communities as far north as Stoneham and as far west as Concord and Framingham and has plans for further expansion..

■ BOSTON DIAPER CO-OP

(978) 463-7615

This direct-to-public wholesale diaper service is a cooperative in the sense that the more people who buy disposable diapers through them, the better the price for everyone. Boston Diaper Co-op provides a complete range of disposable diapers, similar in quality to those you could buy in the stores, at prices that are generally 15%-20% less. They have four sizes of diapers in standard, premium, and supreme grades. Diapers are shipped to your home or office through the U.S. mail and typically arrive within three days of placing your order. Next day delivery is available for an additional charge. Reorder reminders and automatic reorder programs can be set up. If there is a Neighborhood Distribution Center in your area, your diapers can be sent there to save you the cost of shipping. They plan to offer a complete line of baby care products and nursery supplies at wholesale prices soon.

■ BABY'S LAUNDRY AND DIAPER SERVICE

(978) 744-4162

Serving Essex County, this family business is also a professional laundry and dry cleaning service offering weekly pickups. For $17.50 a week, it will deliver 80 freshly laundered diapers in two different sizes. Diaper liners and deodorizers are free and diaper pails can be purchased for $8. You get back the number of diapers you use each week and they will work with you if you need to change that number.

■ KIMBERLY'S DIAPER SERVICE
800-479-6161

Kimberly's is a family owned and operated business that has been faithfully delivering freshly cleaned cloth diapers to doorsteps of Cape Cod for many years. It now serves families of the greater Boston area as well. For $13.95 per week they will deliver 80 diapers in diaper pail liners. Parents with twins get a substantial discount: 160 diapers for $17.95 per week. Diaper pails can be purchased for $16.99, and deodorizer discs are complimentary. They offer a start up special which includes ten weeks of service, a diaper pail, and four diaper wraps for $150. Also, the ninth week of diaper service is free after paying for eight weeks in advance. A subscription to *Baby Magazine* comes free with the service and will be dropped off by your delivery person every other month. In many areas, Kimberly's also delivers Tushies, which are gel-free cotton disposable diapers. Kimberly's service is available as a shower gift.

BIRTH ANNOUNCEMENTS

There are many different ways to announce to the world the birth of your child. Stationery and Hallmark stores carry prepackaged announcements that you simply write out yourself. Printing companies and many stationery stores carry catalogs from which you can choose a customized announcement. Finally there are more artistic, customized announcements available. You can find everything from hand calligraphy to hand colored, or individually designed announcements that will be as unique as your new baby. Here are a few places to find birth announcements.

- **BY INVITATION ONLY**, Needham, (781) 444-1119
- **CALLIGRAPHERS**, Newton, (617) 244-6660
- **CR PRINTING**, Waltham (781) 893-8787
- **FOREVER YOURS**, Lexington, (781) 862-3777
- **INVITATIONS AND CO.**, Boston, (617) 227-2127
- **J. OLIVER'S**, Boston, (617) 723-3388
- **ONE OF A KIND**, Brookline (617) 566-3500
- **PAPER CAPER**, Boston (617) 367-6254
- **THE PAPER TREE**, Newton, (617) 964-9282
- **STATIONERS INC.**, Concord (978) 369-1692
- **UNIQUE SIMCHAS**, Newton, (617) 734-3114

CARING FOR YOUR BABY

Even before your baby was born you began taking care of him. You ate healthfully, got enough sleep and exercise, attended your prenatal care visits and endured numerous tests—all to assure your baby's health. Once that baby leaves the security of your womb his care will involve more immediate decisions and considerations based upon your health coverage, finances, location and personal preferences.

We've gathered resources on a range of issues that you may want to consider before your baby's birth: choosing a pediatrician, deciding whether and how to circumcise, immunize and breastfeed. There are many factors to weigh here and many groups that can help you do it. The earlier you settle on your choices the more comfortable you'll feel when you see that wrinkled darling come into the world. Which isn't to say you won't change your mind when you thought it was made up!

Once you've mastered the first months of parenthood, you recognize a new range of questions: What and how do we feed the love bug? What about those safety considerations that change with every new achievement? How do we go about childproofing? Relax, prepare what you can ahead and refer to the many resources below if you have questions. Trust your common sense and follow your heart as you make a safe place in the world for your fresh and tender baby blossom.

CHOOSING A PEDIATRICIAN

Remember to trust your common sense and follow your heart.

Due in part to the large number of medical schools and highly acclaimed medical institutions in and around Boston, there are literally hundreds of skilled pediatricians and family practitioners in this area. The advantage of such a large number is that you can most likely find a practitioner who shares and can be supportive of your health care philosophies. Unfortunately, word travels fast and the most popular and established practitioners in certain communities often are not taking new patients, so it is important for you to start looking at practices and interviewing doctors early. Any effort you expend in the search for the right doctor will seem well worth it the first time your baby's temperature goes above 101 in the middle of the night. Ask your friends and your provider for a recommendation. Referral services offered by area hospitals can provide you with names of pediatricians in your area.

CIRCUMCISION

■ **CIRCUMCISION RESOURCE CENTER (CRC)**
(617) 523-0088
P.O. Box 232
Boston, MA 02133
This nonprofit organization was founded to educate the public about circumcision. It collects and disseminates the latest information and research about both the American cultural practice and the Jewish religious practice of circumcision. CRC is a valuable source of information for expectant parents, childbirth educators, medical professionals, counselors and others. Contact them for a free brochure, as well as more detailed information in the form of books and video tapes. The founder, Ronald Goldman, is a psychologist who has written two books on the topic of circumcision. He counsels expectant parents and others who need support around the issue of circumcision.

■ **SYNAGOGUE COUNCIL OF MASSACHUSETTS**
(617) 244-6506
1320 Centre St.
Newton Centre, MA 02159
In addition to publishing a directory of all Jewish organizations and congregations in Massachusetts, this group attempts to maintain an accurate list of practicing mohels. A referral to a mohel practicing in your area is available upon request.

NEWBORN SCREENING PROGRAM

This Program fulfills the mandate of Massachusetts law that all newborns be tested for early indicators of certain serious, but treatable, disorders. Babies born in a hospital will have blood drawn from their heel prior to discharge. Arrangements should be made for babies born outside of a hospital to be tested as well.

The blood will be screened for the following disorders: congenital hypothyroidism; phenylketonuria (PKU); hemoglobin disorders, including sickle cell disease; congenital toxoplasmosis; biotinidase deficiency; galactosemia; "maple syrup" urine disease (MSUD); homocystinuria; and congenital adrenal hyperplasia. Normal test results will be reported to the hospital of your baby's birth. If a retest is indicated, the doctor listed on the collection form will be notified. You may object to these tests being performed on your baby based on religious grounds, but you may be asked to sign a waiver relieving your doctor of any liability.

For information, the Newborn Screening Program may be contacted at the State Laboratory Institute, 305 South Street, Jamaica Plain, MA 02130, or by phone at (617) 983-6300.

"Our Circumcision Decision"

A Life Experience by Allison Aley

When we first confirmed that I was pregnant, for some reason we both assumed it would be a girl. But as my husband and I adjusted to the idea of having a baby, we started to realize that, while we had always envisioned having a girl first, there was just as much chance that we'd have a boy. We both agreed that we wanted to find out, if that was possible.

We went in for an ultrasound on the day after Christmas and told the technician that we'd like to know the sex if she thought she could tell. Because it was a slow day at the hospital and the images of the baby were particularly clear, she took quite a long time showing us every wonderful detail—fingers, toes, feet, eyes, beating heart, bladder, umbilical cord. We were overwhelmed with the miracle of it all and blissfully happy as we heard words like "normal," "perfect," and "beautiful." We had completely forgotten about the gender question. We were being told that I was carrying what looked like a perfectly healthy baby and that was all that mattered.

As we continued to watch images float across the screen, she said, "So you want to know the sex?" We looked at each other, smiled and then nodded. "Well...it's a boy." "Are you sure?" "Yes, that's his penis." Wow, just like that? No hedging at all when all of my friends had heard things like "It's most likely a girl" or "I can't really tell, the baby is not cooperating." I was still high from the news that he looked normal and this new piece of information was interesting and exciting, but then the thought crossed my mind: "Now we have to address the circumcision issue."

I didn't bring it up right away and when I did I got the reaction that I fully expected. Tom hadn't even considered that there was a decision to be made. He was circumcised, all of his friends were circumcised, so of course our son would be circumcised. Wasn't it a routine procedure anyway? So began the process of making our first difficult decision as parents. It was such a different experience for us both. We were overwhelmed with the responsibility for the new little life that was growing inside me. And, while we both ended up on the same side of the issue and very comfortable and pleased with our decision, we started on opposite sides.

I had done a lot of reading about natural childbirth, breastfeeding and care of the newborn. I knew that circumcision was no longer routine and that the American Academy of Pediatricians no longer recommended that it be done. I was putting so much energy into preparing for a peaceful, natural, welcoming birth, that the idea of cutting off my baby's foreskin seemed contradictory, especially since we had no religious reason to do it. Tom looked at it completely differently. He was less concerned about the pain of the procedure (after all, he didn't remember it), than he was about our son looking different from him and possibly different from his friends as he was growing up.

We discussed it for hours and at times we both got very emotional. We read articles and learned that there is support for every argument on both sides. We quickly realized that it was a decision that had to be made from the heart and gut. We managed to be respectful of each other's feelings, knowing that we each wanted only to do the right thing. I finally said that, although I would choose not to have him circumcised, I thought it should be Tom's decision because he would most likely be the one to explain that decision to our son down the road. I asked only that he really think about it.

After that I didn't bring it up and tried to remain objective when Tom wanted to talk about it. He took the decision very seriously and talked about it with everyone—friends, family, co-workers, and our midwives. We were continually amazed at how misinformed some people were about the procedure and the reasons for having it done. Others were thoughtful and tried to be helpful. My mother assured us that whatever we decided to do would be fine. My stepmother said he'd look just like all of the Greek statues if he wasn't circumcised. Tom's little brother had a friend who had chosen to be circumcised at 15 because he was the only one of his friends who was not. A lawyer friend had worked on an insurance defense case involving a botched circumcision where the little boy had to undergo reconstructive surgery. All of this was food for thought.

During this time I had the opportunity to watch two circumcisions being performed side by side as part of a clinical rotation. It was hard to watch and I found myself putting my hands protectively over my pregnant belly. The babies were strapped on special boards so that they could not move, and they screamed in what must have been fear and frustration. The obstetricians came in and performed the procedure, each using a different method. Both babies were obviously in pain. The doctors left them strapped to the boards and then the nurses came and swaddled them back up. The parents were not there to comfort them. I felt sick.

When we discussed it at one of our prenatal visits, we learned that, if we chose to have it done (which the midwives did not recommend), the birth center's policy was to have us bring him back to the center when he was eight days old because a baby's blood clots more effectively at that time. We would be there to comfort and nurse the baby immediately. I felt better when I learned this.

Interestingly, my Jewish friends tell me that a ritual bris is done at day eight when the baby is surrounded by family and friends and often given a cloth dipped in wine to suck on to ease the pain. This seems so much more humane. Indeed, many people recommended that we have a mohel perform the circumcision.

One day Tom came home and out of the blue said, "I've decided that we won't have our son circumcised." I was relieved and happy that he had come to the decision that I had hoped for. Looking back now, I am amazed at how much energy and emotion went into that decision, but the process was good for us and helped us to begin to be a cohesive parenting team. And, we both still feel that we made the right decision for us, and for our son, Ben. ☙

IMMUNIZATIONS

Massachusetts has one of the highest immunization rates, and one of the lowest rates for outbreaks of vaccine-preventable diseases, in the country. As a universal distribution state, Massachusetts' Department of Public Health (DPH) makes vaccines available to providers at no cost. Providers may not charge patients for these vaccines (they may charge for vaccines obtained from other sources). Providers may charge a minimal administrative fee, however, but must waive it if the parents cannot afford to pay. In any event, no Massachusetts child should go without immunizations due to financial constraints.

Your newborn may be given his or her first immunization (Hepatitis B) at the newborn exam, if born in a hospital, or at the first visit to the pediatrician, if born in a birth center or at home. Thereafter, if you follow the schedule recommended by DPH (which is almost identical to the schedule shown in Chapter 4), your baby will receive immunizations at two months, four months, six months, 12 months and 15 months. In other words, you should expect them at almost every well-baby check-up until your baby is a year and a half old. A few additional vaccinations are recommended as your child approaches school age, again before becoming a teenager, and at college entrance.

DPH has developed minimal immunization requirements, as required by state regulation, which must be satisfied before a child can attend child care, kindergarten, school, summer camp or college. By state law, no child will be admitted to school unless proper documentation of immunization, or a medical or religious exemption from immunization, is provided. A medical exemption must be obtained from a doctor and is usually only valid for a specific vaccine due to allergies or a previous serious adverse effect in the child or a close relative. A religious exemption in Massachusetts requires that you write an affidavit stating that vaccinating your child is against your "sincerely held religious beliefs." When your baby receives his or her first immunization, you will be given a Massachusetts Lifetime Health and Vaccination Record, a small booklet where all immunizations will be recorded. You should keep this record in a safe place and bring it to every health care visit. You will need to present this record often during your baby's childhood to demonstrate immunization status.

No Massachusetts child should go without immunizations due to financial constraints.

While DPH strongly recommends that all children be immunized, it is not unusual for parents to be concerned about the safety and efficacy of vaccines. There is a great deal of information to address these concerns aside from the pamphlet you may get at your doctor's office. There are books, research studies in medical journals, web sites, and the manufacturer's own product inserts. It is always possible to delay vaccinations until you feel you have the information you need to make your decision. You should thoroughly discuss any concerns, fears or objections with your provider. Similarly, you should make your provider aware of any health concerns, including illnesses and allergies, specifically related to your child before any vaccines are given.

Your pediatrician or family practitioner should discuss immunizations with you at some length, as they will be a big part of your initial contacts with him or her. If you do not have a doctor for your baby, you should find one that you are comfortable with as soon as possible. But the lack of a doctor should not prevent you from having your child immunized. Most of the Community Health Centers and many visiting nurses associations will immunize your baby and can help you find a provider as well.

For a list of places in your area where you can have your child vaccinated, call 800-232-2522 (English), 800-232-0233 (Spanish), or the Massachusetts Immunization Program at (617) 983-6800.

RESOURCES

■ MASSACHUSETTS CITIZENS FOR VACCINATION CHOICE (MCVC)
(781) 646-4797
P.O. Box 1033
East Arlington, MA 02174
E-mail: MCVCHQ@Juno.com

The mission of MCVC is to provide encouragement, information, and resources that will help individuals make informed vaccination decisions. MCVC is composed of parents, professionals and others from across the state. Some have vaccinated their children completely, others have chosen to decline all vaccinations, and still others have chosen to accept certain vaccines but not all. The group members are united in the belief that unbiased information should be readily accessible and choice should rest with the individual.

■ VACCINATION AND CHILDHOOD DISEASE DISCUSSION GROUP
(781) 643-7043

This group meets monthly to discuss vaccines (their components, efficacy, and side effects), childhood illnesses, alternative health treatments for childhood illnesses, and ways to build a healthy immune system. The group's premise is that every person has the right to make an informed decision about the best course for their child's health.

HEALTH COVERAGE

■ THE CHILDREN'S MEDICAL SECURITY PLAN
800-909-2677
Sponsored by the Department of Public Health and administered by John Hancock Mutual Life Insurance Company, this health insurance program provides affordable access to preventive and primary care services for children under 18 who are not eligible for Medicaid/MassHealth. You can enroll immediately over the telephone or you may request their one-page application by calling the number listed above. Providers may also obtain limited authorization for eligible children in emergency situations, in which event the child will be covered for 45 days and a letter will be sent to the parents to see if they want to become a permanent part of the Plan. Contributions toward premiums are based on family size and income. In 1997 for a family of four earning $32,100 or below there is no premium and a $1 co-pay. For a family of four earning between $32,101 and $64,200 the premium is $10.50 per child per month with a $3 co-pay, and a four-person family earning more than $64,201 would have a premium of $52.50 per child per month with a $5 co-pay. This plan covers children for well-child check-ups, vaccinations, diagnostic tests, emergency care up to $1000, prescription drugs up to $100, and other services.

■ HEALTH CARE FOR ALL
(DOTS PARTNER)
(617) 350-7279
30 Winter St., Suite 1007
Boston, MA 02108
HCFA is a nonprofit health advocacy coalition that is a good place to call when you or your baby need health care and have no health insurance, or some other problem prevents you from getting the

---

ABOUT *FIRST*LINK

*FIRST*Link is a special service for families with newborns, sponsored by the Department of Public Health (DPH). It connects new parents with resources and programs for children and families in their own community. Before a new baby goes home from the hospital, parents are asked if they want to receive this service. The local *FIRST*Link program contacts the new family and will visit them in their home to answer questions or discuss concerns that having a new baby may raise. The *FIRST*Link home visitor also helps connect the family to services or other resources according to their own needs and interests, such as health care, food and nutrition programs, parenting groups, child care, and education and job training. The *FIRST*Link home visit is entirely voluntary, and is provided at no cost to families.

*FIRST*Link is a new program and is not yet available in all areas of the state. For more information, call (617) 624-6060. To request a home visitor, call 800-531-MOMS (6667). Bilingual staff are available at the "800" number to answer questions about *FIRST*Link services.

care you need. The staff or volunteer who answers the Health Helpline (800-272-4232) can provide you with information about different programs and referrals to programs that can help. Advocacy and legal assistance are also available. HCFA analyzes health care policies and proposals and makes them understandable for the public and the media. They also lobby on behalf of consumers and teach consumers how to lobby on their own behalf.

■ HEALTHY START HOTLINE
800-531-6667
Telephone counselors are available to assist women in obtaining medical coverage for their infants. There are counselors who speak English, Spanish, Portuguese, Haitian Creole, French, Khmer and Cape Verdean Creole.

■ MASSHEALTH
(617) 210-5000 or 800-841-2900
This federally and state-funded program, formally known as Medicaid, is administered by the Massachusetts Division of Medical Assistance and provides medical insurance for low income, elderly and disabled people. Eligibility is determined by financial and other criteria. All recipients of Transitional Aid to Families with Dependent Children (TAFDC) and/or Supplemental Security Income (SSI) are automatically eligible. Applications can be obtained from your local MassHealth office, which can be located by calling the 800 number listed above. You will need to show proof of income, residency, and U.S. citizenship (or documentation of alien status). They will also want to know about your family situation. If you and your family are found eligible, you will be enrolled in a managed care program.

■ MAYOR'S HEALTH LINE
(617) 534-5050 or 800-847-0710
Hours: M-F 9:00 a.m.-5:00 p.m.
If you are without health insurance for you or your children, call the Mayor's Health Line. This information and referral line can direct you to free or low cost programs. They will also send you information and application forms.

CHILD SUPPORT SERVICES

Child Support Services will work to locate an absent parent, to establish paternity for a child born to unmarried parents, and obtain a court order for child support. Women receiving public assistance automatically receive these services. Once the father is located, either parent has the right to request a genetic test. The test costs $200 and the man will be asked to pay if it is determined that he is the father. The test, a swab brushed against the inside of the cheeks of the man, the mother and the baby, is non-invasive and painless. The results are very accurate and are accepted by courts to determine paternity. If a woman is receiving public assistance and the man is determined to be the father, a child support order will be issued. If she is not receiving assistance, a child support order will be issued only if she requests it. For more information regarding paternity, child support, and genetic tests, call 800-332-2733.

BREASTFEEDING

More and more women in the greater Boston area are choosing to nurse their babies. Based on 1996 data provided by area hospitals anywhere between 30% and 80% of women were breastfeeding their babies when they were discharged. This is an encouraging trend as the benefits of breastfeeding for mom and baby are enormous.

Even though women have the physical ability to breastfeed, it is still very much a learned skill. Like any learned skill, it will be easier if you take the time to prepare yourself mentally prior to attempting it, and then have patience with yourself and your baby once you begin. You should also take advantage of those who are trained to help breastfeeding moms. Seeking out other people and groups supportive of breastfeeding will give you the comfort and security you need in your new endeavor. This section provides you with local resources that will help you take these steps toward a positive breastfeeding experience.

CLASSES

One of the best things you can do to prepare yourself for nursing your baby is to attend a breastfeeding class prior to birth. Most of the hospital-affiliated classes are one or two evenings in length and fairly inexpensive. Many midwifery practices and obstetrical practices also have listings of classes in the area. The *Directory of Birthing Resources* is a wonderful source for breastfeeding counselors and lactation consultants who teach private classes. Some practitioners will even come to your home for a private consultation. You could also contact the Massachusetts Lactation Consultant Association (see the resources at the end of this section) for a referral. If at all possible you should attend a class with your partner, as research has shown that one of the biggest factors in breastfeeding success is the support of the women's partner.

LACTATION CONSULTANTS

Lactation consultants are especially trained in breastfeeding education, management and support. Their goal is to help you breastfeed successfully, and to help you through any challenging breastfeeding situation. Lactation consultants who are International Board Certified Lactation Consultants (IBCLC)

More and more women in the greater Boston area are choosing to nurse their babies.

have met the necessary qualifications set by the International Board of Lactation Consultant Examiners and meet continuing education requirements. Lactation consultants may also sell and rent electric pumps and related supplies. Since there are so many lactation consultants in the area, we have chosen not to list all those in individual private practice. Your pediatrician or the Massachusetts Lactation Consultant Association, listed below, can be happy to refer you to a trained lactation consultant.

BREAST PUMPS

Whether returning to work or planning for an occasional night out, most breastfeeding mothers need to express their milk at some time. Milk can be expressed manually (the technique is shown in most breastfeeding books) or by using a breast pump. Many kinds of breast pumps are available, and choosing the right one for you may be confusing.

Look for someone who is trained to help breastfeeding moms and consult them regarding the type of pump that is best for you and how to use it most efficiently. Make sure you spend your money wisely by buying or renting a good quality pump with a brand associated with breastfeeding. Medela and Ameda Egnell are two of the most well-known breast pump companies and offer a wide range of quality breast pumps and breastfeeding accessories. Both have referral numbers to help you locate the breast pump rental station nearest you. Call the Breastfeeding National Network regarding Medela products at 800-TELL-YOU (835-5968). You can locate the nearest Ameda-Egnell distributor by calling 800-323-8750. In addition, if you call the Boston Association for Childbirth Education at (617) 244-5102, they can refer you to a member of the Nursing Mothers' Council in your area who also rents breast pumps.

RESOURCES

■ **BOSTON ASSOCIATION FOR CHILDBIRTH EDUCATION INC./ NURSING MOTHERS' COUNCIL (NMC)**
(617) 244-5102
P.O. Box 29
Newtonville, MA 02160
NMC is the oldest volunteer breastfeeding support group in New England and has been actively supporting breastfeeding mothers since 1962, when it was founded by the Boston Association for Childbirth Education (BACE). Its mission is to provide women with the information and support necessary to help them make informed decisions about infant feeding. Through BACE, NMC provides breastfeeding support and education by trained lay counselors, as well as referrals to lactation consultants. NMC also makes breast pumps and hard-to-find breastfeeding aids available to families at a reasonable cost.

When you call the number listed above, you will get the names and phone numbers of the NMC counselors who are handling phone calls for that month. They will be able to help you with your breastfeeding questions or concerns or refer you to someone who can. If you do not reach them on the first try, leave your name, phone number and a message and they will call you back soon. NMC counselors are women who have breastfed at least one child and have been trained in breastfeeding management, support and counseling. They are also required to participate in continuing education to keep their breastfeeding management knowledge as current as possible in a rapidly advancing field of research and information.

■ **LACTATION CARE, INC.** *Baby Pages*
(617) 244-5593
25 Fisher Ave.
Newton, MA 02161
This practice of three Board Certified Lactation Consultants (IBCLC) offers many breastfeeding support services. Classes include "Getting Started with Breastfeeding," and "Transitioning Back to Work and Continuing to Breastfeed." Lactation Care is available for private breastfeeding consultations, and Medela breast pump rentals and sales with telephone support. Lactation Care is the largest breast pump depot in New England.

■ **LACTATION SUPPORT SERVICES**
(617) 732-8045
Brigham and Women's Hospital
75 Francis St.
Boston, MA 02115
Certified lactation consultants provide emotional and educational support, as well as diagnosis and treatment of breastfeeding problems, both prenatally and for new mothers in the hospital after birth. The Center also offers prenatal breastfeeding classes, telephone support, and outpatient visits with lactation consultants by appointment. A weekly drop-in support group for breastfeeding mothers meets on Thursdays from 10:00 a.m.-12:00 noon at the Women's Resource Center, 850 Boylston St. in Boston. To RSVP for the group, call (617) 732-5763.

■ **LA LECHE LEAGUE OF MA/RI/VT**
(781) 245-3270
To locate an accredited La Leche League Leader in your area call (617) 469-9423. The recording will give you the numbers of Leaders who are handling phone referrals in the greater Boston area for that month. Due to the high volume of calls, the area Leaders share responsibility for inquiries, referrals and questions. You should call one of the numbers given on the recording (even if none are in your geographic area) and the Leader who answers will refer you to the Leader in your area. La Leche League Leaders are volunteer mothers who have breastfed at least one child. They provide breastfeeding information, help, and support over the telephone free of charge. They also host monthly meetings which cover a wide variety of topics relating to breastfeeding. These meetings are great places to meet other nursing mothers and to ask questions or share concerns in a supportive environment. The Area Coordinator of Leaders for La Leche League of MA/RI/VT is Victoria Doran, who can be reached at the above number.

■ THE LACTATION CENTER AT WINCHESTER HOSPITAL
(781) 756-4788
41 Highland Ave.
Winchester, MA 01890
Lactation Consultants are available to support and encourage you and your family in your decision to breastfeed. A basic breastfeeding class is offered, as well as a more specialized class for women who must be separated from their babies due to illness or returning to work outside the home. Medela breast pumps are available for sale or rent and maternity nursing bras are sold. The Center is open 7 days a week by appointment.

■ MASSACHUSETTS LACTATION CONSULTANT ASSOCIATION (MLCA)
(508) 520-6863
57 Fruit St.
Norfolk, MA 02056
If you are looking for a Lactation Consultant, contact MLCA. For $1 they will send you their publication, *Lactation Consultants Practicing in Massachusetts*. MLCA will also give you a referral over the phone. Their comprehensive list includes Lactation Consultants working in private practice, hospitals and clinics and those providing breast pump rentals and sales.

■ MASSACHUSETTS WOMEN, INFANTS AND CHILDREN NUTRITION PROGRAM (WIC)
800-942-1007
WIC offers support, information and counseling to eligible breastfeeding women for six months after the birth of the baby and possibly longer if still breastfeeding. WIC actively encourages its mothers to breastfeed and provides printed material about why it is better for both mom and baby. Many local WIC programs offer a peer counseling program for breastfeeding mothers. Staff at the number listed above will help you locate the nearest local WIC program.

GROWING UP HEALTHY
"Growing Up Healthy," published by the Bureau of Family and Community Health at the Department of Public Health, is a portable health record for children from birth to 6 years of age with record keeping pages for immunizations, allergies, and more. The diary also includes information on parenting, child development, health and safety, and a list of agencies and organizations useful for parents. *Creciendo Sano*, a Spanish edition, is also available. *Growing Up Healthy* will be available statewide to parents of children from birth to age 6 beginning in January 1998.

■ **MATERNAL OUTREACH, INC.** *Baby Pages*
(781) 340-9101
63 Winter St.
Weymouth, MA 02188
This unique home health agency provides lactation consultation visits in homes throughout the greater Boston area seven days a week and evenings. Through its store of the same name (see the store review in Boston Chapter 3) you can also find Medela breast pumps and other breastfeeding supplies. Therese Sentas, an experienced labor and delivery nurse, is the owner of this business.

■ **MILK BANK AND BREASTFEEDING CENTER**
(508) 793-6005
Memorial Hospital
119 Belmont St.
Worcester, MA 01605
The Milk Bank and Breastfeeding Center is one of seven donor milk banks in North America. It follows the guidelines of the Human Milk Bank Association of North America (HMBANA) in collecting, storing, and distributing donated breastmilk. Milk is used for sick infants who may not survive without human milk. Donors are screened through a blood test and a questionnaire. If you think you would like to donate, arrangements will be made to have your blood drawn and tested free of charge.

■ **PREGNANCY & BEYOND**
(617) 232-1101
192 Washington St.
Brookline, MA 02146
Hours: M-Sat. 10:00 a.m.-5:00 p.m.
A call or visit to this little store can probably fulfill any need a nursing mother might have. In addition to Medela breast pumps and other useful breastfeeding equipment and accessories (more specifically detailed in the store review section), you'll find books and videos on breastfeeding. The owner, Rina Jacobson, is an experienced labor and delivery nurse and very knowledgeable about all aspects of breastfeeding and cares deeply about her customers. She also teaches breastfeeding workshops.

FINANCIAL ASSISTANCE

The prospect of having a baby raises financial issues for everyone. If you need assistance or feel that you might be eligible for a public program, call 800-249-2007 and speak with the Department of Transitional Assistance, formerly known as the Department of Public Welfare. A staffperson will discuss your situation to determine whether you meet requirements necessary to qualify for cash payments through Transitional Aid to Families with Dependent Children (TAFDC) or Food Stamp benefits. Even if you are not eligible for either of these programs, you may still qualify for other public programs, including MassHealth, formerly known as Medicaid. Public program regulations are often difficult to interpret, so it's worth a visit to a local office to get more information—call the above number for the office nearest you.

FEEDING BABY

▪ EXPANDED FOOD AND NUTRITION EDUCATION PROGRAM (EFNEP)
(617) 522-8567
P.O. Box 1196
19 St. Rose St.
Jamaica Plain, MA 02130
EFNEP is a federally-funded program of the University of Massachusetts Extension at Amherst. Its nutrition and food-related education program is designed for low income families with young children. Persons participating in any other food assistance program (i.e. WIC, Food Stamps) or with incomes at or below 125% of the federal poverty level are eligible. A 10 hour program is offered to small agency groups, such as employment training programs, adult education, and pregnant and parenting teen programs. There is also a Learn at Home Course for individuals. Participants learn how to plan inexpensive and nutritious meals, prepare food safely and manage their resources. Parts of the curriculum deal with pregnancy and infant feeding.

▪ FOOD STAMP BENEFITS
Department of Transitional Assistance
800-249-2007
Food stamp benefits help eligible households buy the food they need. The monthly allotment of food stamp benefits received by a household is based on net monthly income and household size. As of July 1, 1997, the maximum allotment (which changes yearly) is $220 for a household of two and $400 for a household of four. Applications may be picked up and filed in person or by mail at the Department of Transitional Assistance office serving your area. Call the Application Information Unit at the 800 number listed above for more information or to locate the office nearest you. You may also call Project Bread at (617) 723-5000.

▪ MASSACHUSETTS WOMEN, INFANTS AND CHILDREN NUTRITION PROGRAM (WIC)
800-942-1007
This unique nutrition program can help you meet the important nutritional needs of your rapidly growing infant and your children under five. Infants are certified up to age one and children are certified for six-month periods. Every six months, children must be reevaluated to determine eligibility. If your child is eligible, you will receive food checks for milk, cheese, eggs, beans, fruit juice, cereals, peanut butter, and other foods necessary for kids to grow big and strong. WIC also continually monitors and evaluates nutritional health status and provides referrals for pediatric health care and immunizations.

▪ NORTHEAST ORGANIC FARMING ASSOCIATION OF MASSACHUSETTS
(978) 355-2270
411 Sheldon Rd.
Barre, MA 01005
Send your address and 55 cents in stamps to this organization to obtain a free copy of the Organic Food Guide, which lists organic foods that are available from the nearly 100 local organic farms, retail stores, and cooperatives statewide.

- **PROJECT BREAD'S FOODSOURCE HOTLINE**
800-645-8333
(617) 523-7010
This information and referral service is for anyone having difficulty getting the food they need. It can help people gain access to programs that will meet their basic nutritional needs. Over half of the people who call this Hotline are families with children. The following services are available: referrals to food pantries and meal programs; information, screening and applications for food stamp benefits; information on group meal sites; information regarding the nutritional program for WIC; referrals to programs that supply food at little or no cost.

- **SHARE-NEW ENGLAND**
888-742-7363
146 Will Drive
Canton, MA 02021
SHARE stands for Self-Help A Resource Exchange. This program promotes local level community building in conjunction with a nonprofit food distribution program that provides a supplemental package of nutritious food. The package, containing 6-10 pounds of frozen meat, fresh fruits and vegetables, and other staples, costs $14 in cash or food stamps plus 2 hours of community service a month. SHARE operates through host organizations such as churches, union halls, schools, and community centers. There are no eligibility requirements, but applicants must sign up in advance. Call the above number to find the closest host organization.

CHILDPROOFING COMPANIES

- **HANDY WORKS, INC. CHILDPROOFING SERVICES**
(617) 738-1977
4 Copley St.
Brookline, MA 02146
Run by a licensed contractor with 20 years experience, this company offers full service child proofing. They will come to your home for an initial evaluation and will also child proof your home charging an hourly fee and cost of materials. Handy Works will do custom work as well as install any necessary safety devices.

- **SAFE BEGINNINGS**
(978) 670-7189
800-598-8911
13 Alexander Rd., #5
Billerica, MA 01821
This local company is run by a husband and wife team who are also parents. They charge an hourly fee plus the cost of the items installed to childproof your home. You can also pay the hourly fee for a safety assessment. Call for their free catalog which has an extensive selection of childproofing items. They are very knowledgeable about the use and installation of the products in their catalog since they actively use them in their child proofing business.

LEAD POISONING PREVENTION

Lead poisoning is a disease caused by swallowing lead. It can permanently damage the brain, kidneys, nervous system, and red blood cells of young children. Low levels can slow growth and cause learning and behavioral problems. Very high levels can cause retardation, convulsions, and coma. Adults who were lead poisoned as children continue to be affected by the consequences such as having a greater vulnerability for high blood pressure.

Children are most often poisoned by lead dust and lead paint in older homes. Lead dust can come from repairing areas with lead paint, opening and closing windows, and through normal wear and tear of painted areas. Lead dust settles to the floor, on window sills, and other surfaces and gets on children's hands and toys. It enters their bodies when they put their hands or toys into their mouths. Children can also become poisoned by eating, chewing, or sucking on things with lead paint such as window sills, railings, or other painted surfaces. Repairs and renovations of older homes increase the risk of lead poisoning. Children and pregnant women should not be in the home when this work is being done.

Children are at higher risk if they live in homes built before 1978 that are in poor shape or are being renovated. Children will absorb more lead into their systems if their diets are low in calcium and iron, and high in fat. Also, if parents work with lead, they may bring lead dust home on their clothes or hair.

A blood test is the only way to tell if your child has lead poisoning. Every child in Massachusetts under the age of four must be tested for lead each year. Some children should be tested more often if they are at higher risk. Ask you doctor, local lead program, or health center to test your child for lead.

The Massachusetts Lead Law requires the removal or covering, or interim control, of lead hazards in homes built before 1978 in which a child under the age of six lives. Have your home tested for lead by a licensed lead paint inspector. A licensed deleader has to do all removal of leaded paint and all other high risk work. The owner, or someone who works for him or her who is not a licensed deleader, can do certain low

Children are most often poisoned by lead dust and lead paint in older homes

risk deleading and interim control work. Simple home repairs like scraping paint before repainting or removing woodwork can make lead dust. This may create a hazard for the whole family. If you are a tenant and are not sure if your home has lead paint, ask the owner. If the owner doesn't know, ask him or her about hiring a lead inspector to test the home. You can also call the board of health or your local lead program to do an inspection. Tenants with children may not be evicted or harassed because of lead paint.

This information is reprinted with permission from Lead Poisoning: Facts and Guidelines published by the Massachusetts Department of Public Health Childhood Lead Poisoning Prevention Program.

■ CHILDHOOD LEAD POISONING PREVENTION PROGRAM

(617) 753-8400
800-532-9571
Department of Public Health
470 Atlantic Ave., 2nd Floor
Boston, MA 02210

This program provides free information on the Massachusetts Lead Law, lead testing, preventing childhood lead poisoning, reducing lead hazards and more. They publish numerous pamphlets in several languages including protecting your baby before birth, safely renovating your home, and financing a deleading project. They assist home owners as well as tenants. For families with children who have lead poisoning or with elevated levels of lead, this agency offers assistance in inspection and enforcement of the Lead Law.

CAR SAFETY

In Massachusetts, the Child Passenger Safety Law requires that all children under age 13 be restrained in an age appropriate child car seat or safety belt. However, you need to do more than simply use a car seat to ensure your baby's safety. Incorrect use of car seats is a significant problem. The following agencies can help you locate a free or low cost car seat, instruct you in its proper use, and give you additional information.

■ BUCKLE UP HOTLINE
800-443-SAFE (7233)
Call this hotline for educational materials on car seats and the Massachusetts Child Passenger Safety Law. They also have information on low cost car seats. Report the registration number of a car in which you see a child riding unrestrained and they will send the owner a friendly reminder and the above publications.

■ GOVERNOR'S HIGHWAY SAFETY BUREAU
(617) 727-5073
100 Cambridge St., Room 2104
Boston, MA 02202
This agency has a video on the correct installation and use of car seats. It is available in both Spanish and English and is titled *Protecting Your Child's Life*. Like the 800-443-SAFE program, they can refer you to car seat loan and rental programs in Massachusetts.

■ INJURY PREVENTION AND CONTROL PROGRAM
800-CAR-SAFE (227-7233)
250 Washington St., 4th Floor
Boston, MA 02108
This agency provides general information on child passenger car safety. Call for information on laws, correct use of car seats and safety belts, air bags, car seat recalls, seats for children with special needs, and car seat loan and distribution programs. They can help answer your questions as well as send you printed materials.

OTHER SAFETY RESOURCES

■ CHILDHOOD INJURY PREVENTION PROGRAM
(617) 534-5197
Boston Public Health Commission
1010 Massachusetts Ave., 2nd Floor
Boston, MA 02118
This agency provides information and resources on the prevention of unintentional injuries. Call for educational materials on car safety, bike helmets, window fall prevention, water safety, poison prevention, fire safety and more. They hold trainings for Boston parent and provider groups on topics such as such as how to childproof your home. They collaborate with various hospitals, health centers, schools, public safety agencies and other groups on injury prevention projects for the Greater Boston SAFE-KIDS Coalition. They also provide a speaker's list and a calendar of safety observances. The SAFE KIDS Coalition sponsors a Safe Kids Week in the Spring.

■ INJURY PREVENTION AND CONTROL PROGRAM
250 Washington St., 4th Floor
Boston, MA 02108-4619
Write to this agency to receive a "Safe Home Checklist" and "Creating Safe Kids" brochure. The brochure, produced in conjunction with The Boston Globe Child Safety Campaign, addresses home, traffic, recreational safety and more.

■ MASSACHUSETTS PREVENTION CENTER
Boston:
(617) 423-4337
95 Berkeley St.
Boston, MA 02116

Metro Suburban:
(617) 441-0700
552 Massachusetts Ave., Suite 203
Cambridge, MA 02139
These Mass Prevention Centers are among ten in the state that work to promote education on public health issues. Their libraries are open to the public Monday through Friday from 9:00 a.m.-5:00 p.m., although you should call for an appointment. Some centers also have evening hours by appointment. The libraries have a selection of free resources, lending materials, and references to be used on site. You will find information on pregnancy, parenting, nutrition, alcohol, drug and tobacco use, immunizations, house, play and fire safety and more. The centers also offer workshops that parents can attend. Representatives at either office can tell you which office serves the community in which you live or work.

■ MASSACHUSETTS SAFETY COUNCIL
800-732-6729
This private, nonprofit organization provides safety and health information and training to area businesses and members of the community. They have brochures on car seats, childproofing, and storing and handling household chemicals. They can also provide you with a list of EMTs who give infant and child safety and CPR classes to area businesses.

■ OFFICE OF COMMUNITY FIRE SAFETY EDUCATION
Boston Fire Department
(617) 343-3397
115 S. Hampton St.
Boston, MA 02118
The mission of this office includes undertaking efforts to reduce loss of life, injury and property from preventable incidents. To do this they provide effective life safety educational programs to children and other members of the community. Call them with questions concerning children and fire safety or fire play or to set up a workshop. They also have literature on baby-sitting safety, household safety and teaching preschoolers.

■ POISON CONTROL HOTLINE
800-682-9211
(617) 232-2120
300 Longwood Ave.
Boston, MA 02115
Funded largely by the Department of Public Health and run by Children's Hospital, this 24 hour toll-free hotline provides information and assistance for poisoning emergencies. You can also call for poison information and prevention,

although they may put you on hold to handle emergencies. To have information mailed to you, send a self addressed stamped envelope.

CPR AND FIRST AID TRAINING

A crucial step to ensure your family's safety is to take a CPR and First Aid Training class. Classes are very affordable and are often given at night and on weekends. You can take an infant/child CPR class which teaches techniques to be used with babies and small children or one geared towards adults. In addition to those organizations listed below, most hospitals offer classes. Refer to the hospital-affiliated classes for a complete list of CPR classes.

■ AMERICAN HEART ASSOCIATION (MASS. AFFILIATE)
(508) 620-1700
20 Speen St.
Framingham, MA 01701
The American Heart Association has many trained instructors in Massachusetts who teach a Pediatric Basic Life Support course covering CPR and choking in the infant and child. The course is generally 4-6 hours long and the fees range from $5-$30 per person. Contact them to find the training center nearest you.

■ AMERICAN RED CROSS OF MASSACHUSETTS BAY
(617) 375-0700 ext. 221
285 Columbus Ave.
Boston, MA 02116-5114
The American Red Cross has many certified instructors in Massachusetts who teach two different courses: 1) Infant and Child CPR; and 2) Massachusetts Child Care Progression (first aid). The CPR course can be completed in two evenings or one Saturday and the first aid course takes one evening. The course fees are $47 for CPR, $35 for first aid, and $75 for both. They also offer a 10 hour baby-sitting course for $25. Some discounts are available. The current schedule is available upon request.

■ CHILD CARE PROJECT
(DOTS PARTNER)
(617) 825-6554
1485 Dorchester Ave., Room 203
P.O. Box 503
Dorchester, MA 02122
This child care referral and advocacy group offers first aid and CPR workshops in both Spanish and English. A combined class is $40 and up. A schedule is available upon request.

■ CHILD CARE RESOURCE CENTER
(617) 547-1063, ext. 231
130 Bishop Allen Drive
Cambridge, MA 02139
In addition to child care referral, this agency holds CPR and first aid training for child care providers and parents. A CPR class is $40 and a combined CPR and first aid is $50. Contact them for a current schedule.

■ COMMUNITY CARE FOR KIDS
(617) 471-6473
800-637-2011
1509 Hancock St.
Quincy, MA 02169

Call for their newsletter which lists times and locations of first aid and CPR training. The cost is $30 for an individual class in first aid, CPR or CPR renewal and $45 for a combined first aid and CPR class. They offer Saturday and evening classes but early registration is encouraged as many classes fill two months in advance.

■ CPR SERVICES, INC.
800-547-5107
(617) 330-1255
(508) 881-5107
22 Stoney Brook Dr.
Ashland, MA 01721

Started twelve years ago by a Registered Nurse who is also the Coordinator of Community Education at Newton-Wellesley Hospital, this innovative company travels around the greater Boston area teaching first aid, safety and CPR to individuals in their own homes, as well as to staff in doctors' and dentists' offices, child care centers, nursery schools, and public schools. The First Aid for Families course provides an overview of CPR and the Heimlich maneuver, and covers many topics including emergency drills, fire drills, home safety, bike safety, equipment safety and poisons. The classes involve a lot of hands-on participation and role playing and a manual is provided. The fee is generally $35-$45 per person depending on the number of people and the travel time involved. This would be a convenient idea for your neighborhood parent's group.

"SURVIVAL STRATEGIES"

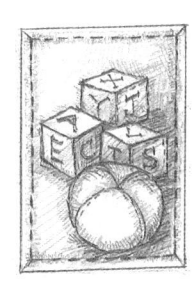

By Allison Blackham

I sat on my deck, nose pressed against the glass of the locked sliding door, watching my two-year-old, Laura, cavort around the room in her soggy diaper while eight-month-old Kirsten rocked happily back and forth on her bottom, gnawing away at my key ring. Unable to get in, unable to explain to my largely nonverbal toddler how to unlock the door she had so cleverly locked behind me, I sat fuming.

Alternating between a Mister Rogers-like gentle patience and insane shouting, I lured Laura back to the door again and again, coaxing her to open it. I could see both children and knew they were safe. Everything was okay, until the baby lost interest in my keys and crawled away into the unseen reaches of the hall. At that point I broke the bathroom window, struggled through, and rescued my wandering infant.

Later, as I painfully picked broken glass shards from the window frame, baby Kirsten watched, bouncing furiously in her jumper in the bathroom doorway, demanding to be held. Laura, free of mother's watchful eye, stripped all of the sheets from her sisters' beds and got stuck head first in a pillowcase. Quick to reach the scene of this latest household disaster, I watched the wildly screaming bundle of bedding on the floor for a moment. "This is funny," I thought. "This would make a great script for some dumb sitcom. Why am I not laughing?"

Catastrophe and crisis are a regular part of family life. There may be some robotic "wonder parents" out there with lukewarm children who never push the limits, but I have never met them. Every family I know has broken window days, trips to the emergency room, tantrums and general craziness from time to time. I, personally, am the mother of six children. In my early mom-work, I assumed that each crisis was a reflection of my own total inadequacy as a parent. After years of experience and a lot of commiseration with other frazzled moms and dads, I now know we all go through this stuff. Kids and chaos go together like bread and butter. From the non-sleeping newborn stage when we're all walking around like characters from "Night of the Living Dead" to the eerie episodes of hearing our mother's voice come out of our own mouths when we face off with a defiant teenager, these exciting times take their toll. I haven't uncovered any ways of avoiding the

Sibling arguments, broken windows and lost lunchboxes are really unimportant things in the whole scope of what life is about.

problems yet, because my husband insists that I live in the same house with the rest of the family, so I've had to deal with them. Here are some ideas that have helped at our house.

Save hysteria for life-and-death situations. Sibling arguments, broken windows and lost lunchboxes are really unimportant things in the whole scope of what life is about. When small things start to bug me, I stop and pull out my mental picture of myself at age 85 (still very peppy and active, by the way). At 85 will I care that my son lost four pairs of shoes in one year? Will it matter that my youngest child ate a worm? (I only found half.) Will my children blame me because we had cold cereal for dinner on Cub Scout night six years running? I hope not. I hope that what is important is that we said "I love you" and made cookies together and played pretend games. What doesn't matter in the long run is not worth getting tense about now.

Avoid out-of-body experiences. We tend to wish ourselves into another time or place when our current moment in life feels nasty. We think, "When the baby sleeps through the night/when the toddler is toilet trained/when my teenager gets through this awful phase, *then* everything will be better." Hey, by the time the kids are all perfect and out of our hair, we'll be dealing with Medicare and nursing home placement. There will always be challenges. No one is excused from the ups and downs of life. Even the Queen of England has to wear silly hats and put up with a lot of deranged relatives. Some day those shiny-eyed kids with their big mouths and sticky fingers will be grown and gone. We need to live with the awareness that what we have and take for granted now changes and becomes a poignant memory tomorrow.

Seek joy. Life is jammed full of beauty and magic. A warm shower, sun shining on the grass, the smell of chocolate, a baby's smile—all of these things are miracles. Why wait for a trip to Disneyland or a letter of commendation from the President to feel like life is great? One of the best feelings I've ever had is seeing my daughter's face light up when I offer to read her a story, and that happens every day.

Treat yourself. Raising kids takes much more energy than any eight-hour-a-day job. Don't you work hard? Don't you deserve a reward? When was the last time your child kissed your hand and said, "Thank you, dear Mother, for all of your effort on my behalf?" It's not going to happen. Well, maybe at your funeral. We need to take time to reward ourselves. Go for a leisurely walk, eat an unshared candy bar, have lunch with friends, go to the pool and soak up the sunshine. Give to yourself so that you will have something to give away.

Sometimes on a really crazy day, I ask myself why I had children. And, after I answer that question, I ask myself why I had six children. Mostly, it's because I love kids, especially mine. And though I spend most of my days fishing the baby out of the cat food dish, fishing the cat food out of the baby, and pulling small people out of heating ducts and sofa cushions, I know I am actually making an investment, because love lasts, and broken windows can always be replaced.

SPECIAL CONCERNS

The arrival of a sweet and helpless new baby, even a normal and healthy one, is an emotional time for parents as they struggle to gain a footing on unfamiliar terrain. When a baby is born with a problem, or things don't turn out as expected or worse, there is a death, it is even more difficult to cope. For those dealing with infertility, the struggle is compounded by complete uncertainty. If you are a teenager, you have many different challenges ahead. After the first few days and nights as a single parent or as a parent of multiples, you'll know you can't go it alone. There are many Boston area groups and organizations that can provide you with support and information to help you grasp your situation and deal with it more effectively. Those summarized below can offer understanding, support, and resources to help parents with special and unexpected concerns create networks of strength allowing them to deal with the day and face the future.

If your baby is born with special needs, you may want to begin by calling the Federation for Children with Special Needs. You'll be able to speak with other parents of children with special needs as well as obtain a wealth of information. The staff at the Public Benefits Information Line can help you determine whether you are eligible for public benefits to help pay for your child's care. The Family Resource Center at Children's Hospital or the FIRST program at UMass Medical Center can help you find additional information on your child's condition. Boston is home to both Children's Hospital and the Floating Hospital for Children at New England Medical Center—some of the best medical care for children anywhere in the world.

Babies who leave the safety of their mother's womb prematurely have their own set of problems. Fortunately, the most advanced therapies and some of the most highly trained specialists are here in Boston. A wonderful group, NICU: Parent Support, Inc., offers much to families during this difficult time.

Losing a baby is a hurt that only subsides over time. There are many support groups where you can share your grief with others who have experienced a similar loss. These groups offer a first place to seek refuge, understanding and recovery.

There are many Boston area groups and organizations that can provide you with support and information to help you.

Infertility is an increasing concern. We have gathered the many resources that are available in the greater Boston area for individuals and couples facing this problem. State-of-the-art treatment, as well as compassionate counseling and support, is readily available. Both the national and state chapters of Resolve, Inc. are located in this area.

While not as staggering as infertility, prematurity, loss, or having an imperfect baby, other situations can be cause for special concern. Parents of multiples can easily find each other and share tips for coping with the extra demands through the groups listed in this section. Single parents will be relieved to find that they are not necessarily alone. Teenage parents face very special circumstances and should know about the numerous resources available to them in the community.

Above all, recognize that humans are social animals and we need each other, especially in trying circumstances. Take the leap, reach out and these resources will guide you on your journey toward support, health and healing.

"The Perfect Baby"

By Sheryl Rosner

As most people expect, I truly felt that my pregnancy and the birth of my first child would be marked by joy and emotional bliss. I had a very uneventful pregnancy, in fact, I hardly ever felt sick. I went through all of the usual pregnancy screening tests without a hitch. I had three ultrasounds, all of which showed a perfectly healthy developing fetus. All signs indicated that I would have an unremarkable birth of an undoubtedly remarkable baby.

My labor began when my water broke as I sat watching "Get Shorty" at a movie theater, just two days before my expected due date. My husband and friends whisked me off and the doctor on call instructed me to come in to the hospital since I would need to deliver the baby within 24 hours. My doctor was not on call that night so I was introduced to a doctor who I had never met before. My labor progressed rapidly and the baby was born after just a few hours of pushing.

As the baby emerged I could see my husband David's face, as the head was flipped around. I said, "Is it a girl or a boy?" and I heard David ask the doctor, "Is that a cleft lip?" The doctor looked quickly at the baby and stated matter-of-factly, "Yes, I believe it is." At that moment, everything had changed. The blissful birth that was expected turned into one of the most stressful and traumatic moments of my life. I screamed, "Is the baby okay? Can I see it?" and David said, "It's a girl and she has a cleft lip." All I wanted to do was hold the baby and make sure I would be able to feed her.

Samantha was born with a bilateral, incomplete cleft lip. Her palate was intact, which allowed her to nurse right away. I had already been slightly familiar with clefts since a friend of mine from work had a baby with a cleft just six months prior to Samantha's birth. When her baby was born, I did some rough research since I was curious about the condition. I was relieved to learn that it is predominately a cosmetic condition that can been fixed through plastic surgery.

The next few days in the hospital involved frustration, fear, confusion and sadness. I felt very uninformed about Samantha's condition, although I did receive some assurance from Samantha's pediatrician that things were going to be all right. I tapped into every resource in the medical community that I knew to help us locate the best plastic surgeon to conduct Samantha's surgery. All avenues pointed us to Children's Hospital in Boston, with a team of highly skilled plastic surgeons and craniofacial experts led by Dr. John Mulliken. I was unable to get an appointment for Samantha for one week after she was born, but in the meantime, she was turning out to be the most delightful, adorable child I had ever seen. She nursed easily and we bonded instantaneously.

Dr. Mulliken and Dotty MacDonald, his assistant, helped reassure us that everything was, in fact, going to be fine. We scheduled Samantha's surgery for 12 weeks after she was born. I was told that she would not be able to nurse for two weeks after the surgery, so I would need to get her used to a special bottle. She would also need to wear cuffs around her elbows so that she would be unable to touch her lip after the surgery.

The surgery was long and heart-wrenching, but thanks to Dr. Mulliken's genius, Samantha looks gorgeous. People often stop me and tell me how beautiful she is. She will probably need a few more small procedures before she is 12 and she will ultimately need a lot of dental work—but all in all, we feel extremely lucky and thankful to have such a wonderful, perfect child. ❧

SPECIAL NEEDS — GENERAL RESOURCES

■ CASE MANAGEMENT PROGRAM
(617) 727-0747 or 727-0748
Greater Boston Regional Office
Lemuel Shattuck Hospital
180 Morton St., 3rd Floor
Jamaica Plain, MA 02130
Administered by the Division for Children with Special Health Care Needs at the Department of Public Health, this program provides support to families whose children have complex health care needs. Services are free, voluntary and confidential. Regional case managers provide information and referral, case-specific consultation, and trainings. They can help you identify the needs of your family and child, understand the range of public benefits, identify community resources, and access those services.

■ DISABILITY LAW CENTER, INC.
800-872-9992
11 Beacon St., Suite 925
Boston, MA 02108
The Disability Law Center (DLC) is a private, nonprofit public interest law firm providing free legal assistance, information, and referral to people with disabilities throughout Massachusetts. DLC works with policy makers to address issues that impact persons with disabilities. Through its Speakers Bureau, experts speak about their areas of expertise with groups, agencies and organizations. DLC also produces publications on a variety of disability law issues, some of which are available in several languages.

■ EARLY INTERVENTION SERVICES
(617) 624-5070
Department of Public Health (DPH)
250 Washington St., 4th Fl.
Boston, MA 02108
Early Intervention is a community-based program of developmental services run by DPH that serves all cities and towns statewide. It serves families of children 0-3 years of age for whom there are developmental concerns or whose development is at risk due to certain birth or environmental circumstances. Early Intervention provides developmental, therapeutic and supportive services to the child and the family, including home visits, toddler groups, support groups, and referral services. Transportation can also be arranged. Parent(s) will be involved in assessments and ongoing programming for the child. Referrals may be made by anyone concerned about a child's development. For the location of Early Intervention Programs in your area, contact DPH or the Family Ties program, listed below.

■ FAMILY RESOURCE CENTER
(617) 355-6279
Children's Hospital
300 Longwood Ave., Farley 111
Boston, MA 02115
Hours: M-F 8:30 a.m.-5:00 p.m.
E-mail: FAMRES@A1.tch.harvard.edu.
The staff of Children's Hospital's Family Resource Center answer families' questions about their children's diagnosis or hospital stays, and help families find the information they need to understand and take part in their child's care. Information and educational materials are available on a wide range of

topics, including pediatric illnesses and conditions, disease-specific support groups, health care financing, community programs, special education, nutrition and safety, and parenting. The center's staff will do literature searches on any topic. Their services are available free of charge to patients, families and members of the community. They have an extensive lending library available for families of Children's Hospital patients.

■ **FAMILY TIES**
800-905-TIES (8437)
Family TIES is a statewide information and support network for families of children with disabilities or chronic illness, supported by DPH Bureau of Family and Community Health, Division for Children with Special Health Care Needs. Regional parent coordinators inform families about community resources, lectures, workshops, conferences, and support groups. The coordinators are available to assist anyone caring for a child with disabilities or chronic illness. Family TIES has an Annual Statewide Parent Networking Conference.

■ **FEDERATION FOR CHILDREN WITH SPECIAL NEEDS**
(617) 482-2915
800-331-0688
95 Berkely St., Suite 104
Boston, MA 02116
On behalf of children with special needs and their families, this nonprofit child advocacy and information center helps parents and parent organizations work together. Most staff members and volunteers are themselves parents of children with special needs. Speak with one of their information specialists regarding early intervention, special education, disability rights, health care financing, and other related topics. The Federation offers a variety of services which include workshops in various Massachusetts communities throughout the year, conferences, program consultation, newsletters and fact sheets.

FINDING CHILD CARE FOR CHILDREN WITH SPECIAL NEEDS

There are several public agencies that make up the statewide Massachusetts Child Care Resource and Referral Network. These agencies assist parents in locating licensed child care in a specific geographical area. Each agency also offers enhanced referrals if your child has a disability. This means that you will receive special assistance in locating child care that is suitable for your child. Some agencies will even work with the child care provider to assist in creating a safe and appropriate environment for your child. Call 800-345-0131 to locate the public child care referral agency that serves your area. The Child Care section in Boston Chapter 2 has more information on these agencies.

■ FINDING INFORMATION AND SERVICES THROUGH TECHNOLOGY (FIRST)
(508) 856-6286
UMass Medical Center (UMMC)
55 Lake Ave. North
Worcester, MA 01655

This free parent-professional information service can help locate information concerning medical conditions in children and their medical care needs. FIRST is a collaborative effort between DPH and the UMMC Department of Pediatrics. It provides written information about specific diagnoses and procedures, bibliographies of selected readings, parent support networks and newsletters. It has access to medical journals, genetic and public library information databases, as well as regional contacts with other parent-professional libraries. The office is staffed part-time, so leave a message and a staff person will call you back. Be sure to include the age, sex, and condition of your child, as well as the general type of information you are seeking.

■ FIRSTSTEPS HOME VISITING SERVICES FOR FAMILIES IN PREGNANCY AND EARLY CHILDHOOD

The FIRSTSteps program, administered by DPH, provides comprehensive home visiting services for families with children from pregnancy through age 3, who have certain characteristics or conditions in their lives that may lead to poor health outcomes, developmental delays, and/or child abuse or neglect. A multidisciplinary team assigned to a family includes home visitors, who are members of the community and share the family's language and culture. Other team members include a maternal and child health nurse, an early childhood development specialist, and a mental health professional. This prevention-oriented, voluntary program is intended to reduce or avert problems. Services include parenting education and support, infant/toddler developmental screening and health assessment and monitoring.

Women and teens are eligible to enroll in FIRSTSteps during pregnancy and up to six months after giving birth. Referrals may be made by calling Dorchester CARES at (617) 474-1256 or Martha Eliot Health Center at (617) 971-2129. Self-referrals are acceptable. Once a referral is made and the woman gives her consent, a needs assessment will determine eligibility. All FIRSTSteps programs will participate in FIRSTLink, a statewide screening and referral program, as it becomes available.

■ MASSACHUSETTS EASTER SEALS SOCIETY
800-922-8290
484 Main St.
Worcester, MA 01608

This statewide organization responds to unmet needs of children and adults with disabilities through rehabilitation services, recreational activities, technological assistance, home health care, advocacy, and public education. It has a free equipment loan program. One of their Information Specialists can provide answers regarding programs, services, and equipment in communities throughout the state.

■ MASSACHUSETTS GENETICS PROGRAM (MGP)
(617) 624-5070
Department of Public Health
250 Washington St., 4th Floor
Boston, MA 02108
MGP is a statewide program that helps keep consumers and professionals informed about medical and scientific developments in human genetics, as well as the associated ethical, legal and social issues. It develops genetics education and training programs; provides information on genetic conditions, tests and treatments; provides technical assistance regarding availability of medical, genetic, and support services; and provides information and referral about genetic-related conditions.

■ MASSACHUSETTS NETWORK OF INFORMATION PROVIDERS FOR PEOPLE WITH DISABILITIES (MNIP)
800-642-0219
(617) 642-0122
c/o New England INDEX
200 Trapelo Rd.
Waltham, MA 02254
MNIP consists of disability-related agencies from across the state that provide information and referral to people with disabilities. A computer network allows information specialists to quickly provide resources, support and information. These agencies also have access to a library of disability specific fact sheets and other information. Anyone may contact MNIP and take advantage of this service free of charge.

■ NEW ENGLAND SERVE
(617) 574-9493
101 Tremont St., Suite 812
Boston, MA 02108
New England SERVE published "Paying the Bills: Tips for Families on Financing Health Care for Children with Special Needs" in 1992. This booklet, developed by parents who have children with special needs, contains information and strategies on getting payment for a child's health care. It costs $5 per copy, but quantities may be limited. Send a check or money order to receive a copy (call prior to ordering large quantities).

■ PUBLIC BENEFITS INFORMATION LINE
800 882-1435
The DPH Division for Children with Special Health Care Needs operates this help line. You will reach a trained staff person who can give you information about public benefits and case management for your child with special health care needs. You can also get information on the DPH Hearing Evaluation Program for Infants and Toddlers, a hearing aid program for children, and a program for children with PKU.

PUBLIC BENEFITS FOR CHILDREN

If your child has a chronic illness, blindness, or a disability, or has complex medical needs then investigate the following public benefits by calling the Public Benefits Information Line, 800-882-1435:

- **Supplemental Security Income (SSI).** A federal program that provides a monthly cash benefit and automatic eligibility for MassHealth.
- **CommonHealth**: A state program to purchase MassHealth coverage for children with disabilities through a sliding fee based on income and family size.
- **Kaileigh Mulligan Home Care for Disabled Children.** A state waiver program that does not count parent income for SSI MassHealth eligibility and allows a child to return or remain home with MassHealth coverage while receiving medical care.

SPECIAL NEEDS— DIAGNOSIS SPECIFIC RESOURCES

■ ARC MASSACHUSETTS
(781) 891-6270
217 South St.
Waltham, MA 02154
Web site: www.gis.net/~arcmass
E-mail: arcmass@gis.net
Formerly called the Massachusetts Association for Retarded Citizens, this organization can provide information regarding available resources and statewide referrals (including referrals to local Arc organizations) for persons with mental retardation and related disabilities. It also engages in legislative advocacy and the shaping of public policy on issues affecting this population.

■ AUTISM SOCIETY OF AMERICA: MASSACHUSETTS CHAPTER
(781) 329-4244
789 Clapboardtree St.
Westwood, MA 02090
This nonprofit, volunteer organization serves individuals across the state (along with the Central Massachusetts and Western Massachusetts Chapters) with Autism Spectrum Disorder (Autism, PDD-NOS, and related disorders) providing information and referrals, and encouraging research and education related to autism. The organization holds open informational meetings, publishes a newsletter, engages in legislative advocacy, and maintains a lending library. The office is staffed part time, so leave a message and someone will call you back.

- **BOSTON PEDIATRIC AND FAMILY AIDS PROJECT (BPFAP)**
(617) 442-8800, ext. 331
Dimock Community Health Center
55 Dimock St.
Roxbury, MA 02119
The goal of this family-centered community-based program is to improve and expand the system of care to address the needs of women, children, youth, and families at risk of or infected with HIV in the greater Boston area. BPFAP's 12-member collaboration includes community health centers, teaching hospitals, and human service and home health agencies. This collaboration provides prevention, early intervention, access, comprehensive case management for families living with HIV, HIV pregnancy care, and links to clinical trials. Educational materials are available. MassCARE is a similar program serving the rest of the state.

- **FETAL ALCOHOL EDUCATION PROGRAM**
(978) 369-7713
Boston University School of Medicine
975 Main St.
Concord, MA 01742
The Fetal Alcohol Education Program provides consultation and training on the effects of alcohol use during pregnancy. If your child has Fetal Alcohol Syndrome (FAS), this program can help make referrals to available resources. Their handbook, "FAS: Parent and Child," which discusses eating, sleeping, behavior and learning problems in children with FAS, costs $7.50.

OTHER AUTISM RESOURCES

The following organizations serve different parts of the greater Boston area providing information, referrals and technical assistance to families who have a child with Autism/PDD. Each conducts parent training workshops and conferences, and publishes a newsletter. Some offer support groups, study groups, speakers, legislative advocacy, and vacation programs for children.

- **Autism Support Center**
(978) 777-9135
800-728-8476 in Eastern MA
64 Holten St.
Danvers, MA 01923

- **Community Autism Resources**
800-588-9239
P.O. Box 1511
Fall River, MA 02722

- **The Family Autism Center**
(617) 762-4001
789 Clapboardtree St.
Westwood, MA 02090
Web site: www.snarc.org.

- **The Parent-Till Partnership for Autism**
(617) 329-6150 ext. PPD (773)
20 Eastbrook Road
Dedham, MA 02026

FOUNDATION FOR FACES OF CHILDREN
800-417-5500
40 Grove St., Suite 375
Wellesley, MA 02181
This nonprofit organization supports children with craniofacial differences and their families. It funds research activities at the Craniofacial Centre at Children's Hospital—a leading facility for treatment of cleft lip/palate, craniofacial and maxillofacial conditions—and provides financial support to families for services and treatment costs not covered by insurance. The parent support/resource group offers telephone and face to face support. Foundation parents helped the Centre publish "Cleft Lip and Cleft Palate: Questions and Answers for Parents." The Foundation publishes a newsletter, conducts outreach programs, and hosts social support outings. The Foundation is also the Boston chapter for AboutFace, a craniofacial support network that provides education and support to families.

GBARC
(617) 783-3900
1505 Commonwealth Ave.
Boston, MA 02135
Improving the quality of life for all persons with mental retardation and related disabilities is this nonprofit organization's mission. It serves Arlington, Belmont, Boston, Brookline, Cambridge, Chelsea, Everett, Malden, Medford, Newton, Revere, Somerville, Watertown and Winthrop. GBArc staff offer support groups, guidance, information and referral, as well as access to other resources. Its Parent to Parent program links parents together for support. The Respitality Program at GBArc works with local hotels to provide parents of children with disabilities an opportunity to get away. GBArc also has an Advocacy Program and a Guardianship Program available on sliding scale fees.

HELPING HANDS FOUNDATION, INC.
(781) 631-5895
46 Peach Highlands
Marblehead, MA 01945
A regional support group for families of children with hand or arm anomalies, this group meets twice a year for a weekend winter outing on Cape Cod and a afternoon summer outing in Canton. These gatherings allow the children to see other kids like themselves and provide opportunities for parents to share thoughts and experiences. In addition, Helping Hands publishes a biannual newsletter and family directory.

HEARING EVALUATION PROGRAM FOR INFANTS AND TODDLERS
800-882-1435
This Department of Public Health Program can tell you where to get your child's hearing tested locally, and, if your child is under 3 and you have no insurance, the program may pay for the test.

MASSACHUSETTS COMMISSION FOR THE BLIND (MCB)
800-392-6450
88 Kingston St.
Boston, MA 02111
Physicians and optometrists have a legal obligation to report all cases of legal blindness to MCB. Once legal blindness is established, a child will be registered with MCB and a Children's Service

Worker will contact the family in order to explain available services. MCB provides information, resources, and advocacy, and can assist with early education, daily living skills, and recreation. Support and counseling are available to assist with concerns related to vision loss.

■ **MASSACHUSETTS COMMISSION FOR THE DEAF AND HARD OF HEARING (MCDHH)**
(617) 695-7500
210 South St., 5th Floor
Boston, MA 02111
MCDHH serves as the principal agency in the state on behalf of deaf, late deafened and hard of hearing people. It maintains a statewide interpreter referral service and coordinates referrals for Computer Aided Realtime Translation (CART) Services. MCDHH also provides public education, materials, and general information related to deaf, late deafened and hard of hearing persons. The Department for Case Management and Social Services provides crisis intervention, needs assessment, cross-agency plan development, outreach, and personal counseling. Its contract with the Massachusetts Assistive Technology Partnership (MATP) provides disabled people of all ages increased access to assistive technology. It coordinates several Specialized Early Intervention Programs for deaf or hard of hearing children 0-3 years old.

■ **MASSACHUSETTS DOWN SYNDROME CONGRESS (MDSC)**
800-664-MDSC (6372)
P.O. Box 866
Melrose, MA 02176
This nonprofit organization is made up of parents, professionals, and others interested in Down syndrome. It provides new parents with information, resources, and support, and encourages research and education related to Down syndrome. Parents' First Call is a statewide volunteer network of informed parents who make themselves available to parents of children newly diagnosed. UPDATE is a quarterly newsletter about Down syndrome. MDSC sponsors social functions, conferences and workshops. You can become a member for as little as $20 annually.

■ **MASSACHUSETTS SPINA BIFIDA ASSOCIATION**
(617) 239-1919 (24 hours)
25 Devon St.
N. Andover, MA 01845
This volunteer organization is made up of parents of children and individuals born with spina bifida. Services include family support, financial assistance, a lending library of written materials (accessible through the mail) and an equipment loan library. They publish a bimonthly newsletter and provide scholarships for camps and schools. Their Parent Helping Parent program provides much-needed support. An annual membership is $35. You may leave a message with the answering service or call Cindy Ward, one of the volunteer parents, directly at (978) 682-9330.

■ MASSACHUSETTS WOMEN'S HIV CARE AND ADVOCACY PROJECT (MASSCAP)

(617) 624-5966
Department of Public Health
250 Washington St., 4th Floor
Boston, MA 02108

The goal of the MassCAP project is to enhance early and comprehensive testing, counseling, and care of HIV infected women and adolescents. It also supports providers in the implementation of standards of care for pregnant women and adolescents who are HIV positive or at-risk for HIV infection. Teams consisting of a Nurse Coordinator and a Peer Advocate provide training and technical assistance to providers, help link HIV infected women and adolescents to early care and support services, and offer one-on-one peer support and advocacy to women and adolescents. The Boston team is housed at Dimock Community Health Center in Roxbury.

■ UNITED CEREBRAL PALSY ASSOCIATION OF METROBOSTON, INC.

(617) 926-4180
71 Arsenal St.
Watertown, MA 02172

This nonprofit affiliate of United Cerebral Palsy Associations provides services and support to children and adults with cerebral palsy and their families in the greater Boston area. Services include residential support, assistive technology, information and referral, advocacy, financial assistance, and community education. UCP operates a Tech Tots Lending Library, which contains adaptive switches, toys with large knobs and other specialized modifications, books, computers, and other resources. The library enables families of disabled infants, toddlers and preschoolers to bring home adaptive toys for their children.

■ NEW ENGLAND CHAPTER OF THE ASSOCIATION OF PERSONS WITH SEVERE HANDICAPS (TASH)

(508) 468-1484
P.O. Box 491
Wenham, MA 01984

TASH actively promotes the full inclusion and participation of children and adults with disabilities in all aspects of life. TASH's mission is to eliminate physical and social obstacles that prevent equity, diversity, and quality of life. The New England chapter conducts annual workshops and conferences, disseminates information and resources regarding issues consistent with the values and vision of TASH.

INFERTILITY

■ BEHAVIORAL MEDICINE INFERTILITY PROGRAM
(617) 632-9529
Beth Israel Deaconess Medical Center
One Deaconess Rd.
Boston, MA 02215
Web site: www.med.harvard.edu/programs/mindbody

The Mind/Body Medical Clinic at Beth Israel Deaconess Medical Center offers both a ten-week program and a single session program for all women having difficulty conceiving. The treatment plans in the $920, ten-week program include elicitation of the relaxation response, cognitive-behavioral strategies to enhance coping skills, stretching exercises and nutrition. Participants report feeling less depressed, anxious, angry and fatigued and, for unconfirmed reasons, about one-third of participants conceive within six months of completing the program. To participate, you must have been trying to conceive for at least one year. The single session program teaches women to elicit the relaxation response and informs them about what to expect during infertility treatment cycles, and costs $88. Check with your insurance provider about whether these programs are covered. Financial assistance may be available.

■ FERTILITY AWARENESS SERVICES
(508) 660-1126
52 Cedar St.
Walpole, MA 02081

Fertility Awareness Services provides education and support around fertility issues. This organization, through its infertility self-help program, can help you better understand and take control of your fertility, develop a "holistic action plan" and become a more savvy consumer of infertility services. They charge a $30 resource fee that includes printed materials, use of the resource center and access to its referral network. Private consultations are $40. They also run community workshops and professional seminars.

■ RESOLVE OF THE BAY STATE, INC.
(781) 647-1614
P.O. Box 1553
Waltham, MA 02254

This is certainly the most important organization to know about for anyone who is experiencing or who has experienced an infertility crisis. Resolve of the Bay State, Inc. is the Massachusetts chapter of Resolve, Inc., located in Somerville, MA). Call the above number for a sympathetic ear or to get information on each of the infertility treatment programs in the area, drop-in discussions, workshops, adoption, insurance, advocacy efforts, and support groups. You can become a member by sending $45 and will receive their newsletter, a Directory of Services (an up-to-date resource book of infertility information and services and adoption resources), and access to their Member to Member Contact System. By joining you automatically become a member of the national and Massachusetts chapters and will receive valuable services and information from both.

INFERTILITY PROGRAMS

If you or someone you know is experiencing infertility and hope to find a medical treatment, the programs listed below offer a range of the most advanced diagnostic and assistive reproductive technologies. Some are free standing and some are affiliated with academic medical institutions. Many offer donor egg programs, donor semen programs, and cryopreservation services. Some have satellite locations throughout the state.

■ BOSTON IVF
(617) 735-9000
One Brookline Place
Brookline, MA 02146

■ BOSTON REGIONAL CENTER FOR REPRODUCTIVE MEDICINE
(781) 979-4700
3 Woodland Rd., Suite 321
Stoneham, MA 02180

■ BRIGHAM AND WOMEN'S HOSPITAL CENTER FOR REPRODUCTIVE MEDICINE
(617) 732-4222
75 Francis St.
Boston, MA 02115
Web site: www.bwh.harvard.edu
*Evening appointments available

■ CENTER FOR REPRODUCTIVE ENDOCRINOLOGY
(617) 421-2987
The Health Centers of Harvard Pilgrim Health Care
One Fenway Plaza
Boston, MA 02215

■ FAULKNER CENTRE FOR REPRODUCTIVE MEDICINE
(617) 983-7300
1153 Centre St.
Boston, MA 02130
E-mail: IVFinfo@AOL.com

■ FERTILITY CENTER OF NEW ENGLAND
(781) 942-7000
20 Pond Meadow Dr., Suite 101
Reading, MA 01867
Web site: www.fertilitycenter.com

■ MASSACHUSETTS GENERAL HOSPITAL VINCENT MEMORIAL IN VITRO FERTILIZATION UNIT
888-221-4IVF (4483)
Fruit St.
Boston, MA 02114

■ NEW ENGLAND MEDICAL CENTER/ TUFTS UNIVERSITY SCHOOL OF MEDICINE
(617) 636-6066
Division of Reproductive Endocrinology
750 Washington St., North Mezzanine
Boston, MA 02111

■ REPRODUCTIVE SCIENCE CENTER OF BOSTON
(781) 647-6263
Deaconess-Waltham Hospital
Hope Ave.
Waltham, MA 02254
E-mail: rscbostn@cris.com

BEREAVEMENT RESOURCES

■ THE COMPASSIONATE FRIENDS, INC. (TCF)
(508) 877-1363
21 Corrine Dr.
Framingham, MA 01701
TCF is an international organization for bereaved parents and siblings. Peer support in the form of friendship and understanding is offered to those suffering from the death of a child at any age, from any cause. Local chapters, comprised of parents who have suffered the death of a child, provide telephone support, newsletters, and resource libraries. Some chapters have sibling groups. There are several local chapters in the greater Boston area. A referral to current local chapter leaders can be obtained by contacting the regional coordinator, Rick Dugan, at the above address or number.

■ MASSACHUSETTS CENTER FOR SUDDEN INFANT DEATH SYNDROME
(617) 534-SIDS (7437)
800-641-7437 Crisis Hotline
Boston Medical Center
One Boston Medical Center Place
Boston, MA 02118
Families who have suffered any type of unexpected death in children ages 0-3 should contact this statewide bereavement counseling and information center. Center staff can refer you to a support group in your area and put you in touch with parents who have experienced a similar loss. They also make referrals for home visits by SIDS counselors. Trained counselors are available on their crisis hotline 24 hours a day.

■ NICU: PARENT SUPPORT, INC.
800-964-NICU (6428)
(617) 964-8778
18 Lovett Rd.
Newton Centre, MA 02159
This volunteer group offers peer support and practical advice to families experiencing a high-risk pregnancy or the birth of a critically ill baby. They also offer bereavement support services to families experiencing pregnancy or infant loss. Trained outreach parents offer telephone support and hospital visits. Other resources include breast pumps, referrals for professional support, education, and a quarterly newsletter.

PREGNANCY/PERINATAL LOSS SUPPORT GROUPS

There are many support groups in the area for individuals or parents who have suffered miscarriage, stillbirth, or the loss of a newborn. The focus of these groups generally encompasses mutual support, sharing of experiences, coping strategies, and reducing one's sense of isolation. Some groups meet monthly or weekly on an ongoing basis. Others meet for six to eight weekly sessions. Groups are facilitated by professionals who work closely with people who have had pregnancy losses. There is rarely a fee for attending these groups.

■ ENDED BEGINNINGS
(617) 322-9309 or 979-3515
Melrose-Wakefield Hospital
24 Porter St.
Melrose, MA 02176

■ HOPE
(781) 340-8423
South Shore Hospital
55 Fogg Rd.
S. Weymouth, MA 02190

■ HOPE (HELPING OTHER PARENTS ENDURE)
(617) 273-2624
(781) 729-9000 (Winchester Hospital Social Services)
Baldwin Park II, Alfred St., 3rd Floor
Woburn, MA 01801

■ L.O.S.S. (LIFTING OTHER SORROWFUL SPIRITS)
(978) 922-3000, ext. 2200
Beverly Hospital
Herrick St.
Beverly, MA 01915

■ PARENT'S SUPPORT GROUP: FOLLOWING THE LOSS OF AN INFANT
(617) 732-6462
The Care Coordination/Social Work Services Department
Brigham and Women's Hospital
75 Francis St.
Boston, MA 02115

■ PERINATAL DEATH SUPPORT GROUP
(978) 287-3270
Emerson Hospital Hospice Program
Rte. 2
Concord, MA 01742

■ PERINATAL LOSS PARENT SUPPORT GROUP
(617) 636-4662
New England Medical Center
750 Washington St.
Boston, MA 02111

■ PERINATAL LOSS SUPPORT GROUP
(978) 741-1215 ext. 2637
North Shore Medical Center
81 Highland Ave.
Salem, MA 01970

■ PREGNANCY LOSS GROUP
(508) 383-1377
Columbia Metrowest Medical Center
115 Lincoln St.
Framingham, MA 01702

■ PREGNANCY LOSS SUPPORT GROUP
(617) 667-3433
(617) 667-3421
Social Work Department
Beth Israel Deaconess Medical Center
330 Brookline Ave.
Boston, MA 02215

■ SHARE
(781) 769-2950 ext. 2343
Norwood Hospital
800 Washington St.
Norwood, MA 02062

■ SHARE OF THE SOUTH SHORE
(781) 331-1562
(781) 331-9677
(508) 747-8917
Old South Union Church
25 Columbian St.
S. Weymouth, MA 02190

OTHER PREGNANCY/ PERINATAL LOSS SUPPORT GROUPS

These support groups differ in focus and content from those listed previously.

■ AFTERWORDS
(781) 862-1171
Prenatal Diagnostic Center, Inc.
80 Hayden Ave., Suite 200
Lexington, MA 02173
This support group is for patients who have decided to terminate a pregnancy after the diagnosis of an abnormality in the fetus. A group of six to ten meets for a series of two-hour sessions co-facilitated by a genetic counselor and a professional therapist with experience in pregnancy loss and grief counseling.

■ KALEIDOSCOPES
(781) 794-7803
Hospice of the South Shore
100 Bay State Dr.
Braintree, MA 02185
Children ages 3-17 accompanied by an adult family member may attend this bereavement support group. Children are divided into age-appropriate groups, which are facilitated by experienced counselors. It meets eight consecutive Tuesdays, 6:30-8:00 p.m. An interview and registration is required and there are no fees within the first year after a loss.

■ NICU BEREAVEMENT GROUP
(617) 724-3177
Massachusetts General Hospital
32 Fruit St.
Boston, MA 02114
This support group is for parents and individuals who have suffered late pregnancy loss, stillbirth, or the death of a baby in his or her first year of life. It is facilitated by a nurse and a clinical social worker and meets for eight to ten weekly sessions.

■ PREGNANCY LOSS BEREAVEMENT SUPPORT GROUP
(617) 667-7110 or 667-3421
Beth Israel Deaconess Medical Center
330 Brookline Ave.
Boston, MA 02215
Individuals or couples who have made the difficult decision to interrupt a pregnancy after prenatal testing has revealed a fetal abnormality will find support at this group. It is co-led by the Department of Clinical Genetics and the Department of Social Work and meets for six sessions.

■ SUPPORT GROUPS FOR THOSE WHO HAVE SUFFERED MULTIPLE MISCARRIAGES
(617) 732-6079
The Care Coordination/Social Work Services Department
Brigham and Women's Hospital
75 Francis St.
Boston, MA 02115
Two support groups are offered for individuals and couples who have had more than one miscarriage. One group is for those who have had a previous successful pregnancy and the other is for those who have not. Both groups are led by a clinical social worker and meet twice a month.

PREMATURE INFANTS

If your baby is born eight to ten weeks prematurely and you delivered at a hospital with a Level II nursery, he or she may be able to remain at that hospital. Babies born more than ten weeks early, or when other medical conditions require, are transferred to the Level III nurseries (also called Neonatal Intensive Care Units or NICUs) at the hospitals discussed below. All of these hospitals are teaching hospitals located in Boston and have staff and equipment capable of caring for the special needs of very premature infants.

■ NICU: PARENT SUPPORT, INC.
800-964-NICU (6428)
(617) 964-8778
18 Lovett Rd.
Newton Centre, MA 02159
This parent to parent support group has much to offer the parents of a premature baby. Telephone support, hospital visits, and preemie clothing and diapers are offered to parents of a premature baby.

HOSPITAL FACILITIES

Beth Israel Deaconess Medical Center • (617) 667-4042   25 beds
Beth Israel Deaconess has a Level III nursery for the care of premature newborns. In addition, they offer an eight-bed Transitional Care Unit (Level II nursery), and a large normal newborn nursery. Beth Israel Deaconess has nine neonatologists on staff. They provide surfactant therapy. Premature newborns requiring surgery are transferred across the street to Children's Hospital.

Boston Medical Center • (617) 534-4359   15 beds
Boston Medical Center has a 15-bed Level III nursery, and also provides step-down (Level II) and normal newborn care. BMC specializes in the care of high-risk infants. There are four neonatologists on staff. Surfactant therapy is provided. Premature newborns requiring surgery are transferred to Children's or Mass General.

Brigham and Women's Hospital • (617) 732-5420   46 beds
The Newborn Intensive Care Unit Provides acute and stabilization care for intensely ill neonates as well as developmentally and family oriented care for growing premature infants and other high risk newborns. Unit-based services include medicine, nursing, respiratory therapy, and social work. The medical staff are available on the unit 24 hours a day. The unit provides state-of-the-art therapy, including surfactant therapy. Babies are transferred to their home community hospitals when they no longer require complex NICU care. In the event the NICU is full, babies may be transferred to other local level III nurseries.

Children's Hospital • (617) 355-6000   16 beds
Children's Hospital's NICU is a 16-bed unit designed to provide intensive care for newborn infants with critical medical or surgical problems. There are 27 neonatologists on staff. Infants are transported to the NICU from community hospitals and other tertiary NICUs. Children's provides a full range of therapies including surfactant replacement, high frequency ventilation, nitric oxide, and ECMO. In addition, patients have access to all specialty and subspecialty consulting services within the hospital.

Massachusetts General Hospital • (617) 724-4310   18 beds
Mass General's Level III nursery provides advanced care for premature or critically ill newborns. Mass General also provides neonatal step-down (Level II) care as well as normal newborn care. There are five neonatologists on staff who use state-of-the-art therapies, including ECMO, nitric oxide and surfactant therapies as required. Babies are transferred to Brigham and Women's Hospital when the NICU is full.

New England Medical Center • (617) 636-5008   40 beds
The Floating Hospital for Children at New England Medical Center has a state-of-the-art Level III nursery. Neonatal step-down (Level II) care is provided either at the Floating Hospital or in one of six community Level II nurseries. Normal newborn care is also provided. There are 30 neonatologists on staff. Surfactant therapy, high frequency ventilation, nitric oxide, and all pediatric subspecialty services, including cardiac and general surgery, are provided.

St. Elizabeth's Medical Center • (617) 789-3000   30 beds
St. Elizabeth's Level III nursery offers state-of-the-art care for premature newborns. Neonatal step-down (Level II) care, as well as normal newborn care, is also provided. There are five neonatologists on staff and surfactant therapy is provided. Any infant requiring surgery is transferred to the Floating Hospital at New England Medical Center, or, in special insurance situations, Children's Hospital.

RESOURCES FOR PARENTS OF MULTIPLES

■ TRIPLETS, MOMS AND MORE
(781) 986-2308
73 Acorn Dr.
Randolph, MA 02368
E-mail: TMANDMORE@aol.com
This statewide support network has seven regional groups in Massachusetts providing support and information to families with triplets, quadruplets or more. Triplets, Moms and More offers telephone support to expectant women, including those on bed rest, from others with similar experience. Other support activities include moms' and dads' nights out, playgroups, parties, and speakers. Some groups have outreach programs including meal deliveries and home and hospital visits. Their monthly newsletter includes parenting tips, personal stories, and activity updates.

■ TWINS, INC.
(781) 275-0256
12 Pickman Dr.
Bedford, MA 01730
Run by a psychotherapist and educator who is also an identical twin, Twins, Inc. works to build community and support for twins and the people in their lives. A Parents of Twins support group meets bimonthly in Arlington and Bedford and a day-long Parents of Twins Workshop is offered as well. Additional support and classes for parents of twins and other multiples are also available.

■ MOTHERS OF TWINS (OR MULTIPLES) CHAPTERS
800-243-2276
There are approximately ten local chapters of the National Organization of Mothers of Twins in the greater Boston area. Every chapter is slightly different, but each offers a place for moms to share the joy and frustration of raising twins or multiples. They typically have monthly meetings, as well as playgroups, support groups, speakers and other club functions. The chapters are loosely organized by geography. As with many volunteer organizations, contact phone numbers frequently change. You can get a current list of all of the local chapters in the area by calling the national organization at the 800 number listed above. The largest chapter in the area is the Massachusetts Mothers of Twins Founding Chapter, which can be reached by calling (617) 646-8946 and leaving a message. Another large chapter is the Dedham Regional Chapter of Mothers of Twins. Its president, Jean Panciocco, can be reached at (508) 660-1277.

TEEN PREGNANCY AND PARENTING

■ ALLIANCE FOR YOUNG FAMILIES
(617) 482-9122
800-645-3750 Teen Hotline
30 Winter St., 11th Floor
Boston, MA 02108

This nonprofit corporation provides leadership to prevent teenage pregnancy, promote adolescent health, and meet the needs of pregnant and parenting teens. In addition to research and advocacy, the Alliance operates a Benefits Access Project through its teen hotline. Trained counselors can advise teens regarding financial and other problems, including child custody, guardianship, and child support. The Alliance also houses the Boston Initiative for Teen Pregnancy Prevention.

■ BOSTON CHILDREN'S SERVICES
(617) 267-3700
271 Huntington Ave.
Boston, MA 02115

BCS is the oldest child welfare agency in the country. It offers a wide range of programs for children and families, including several specifically geared toward teen parents. These include: the Empowering Young Mothers Program, a teen living program though which teenage moms learn parenting, household management, and other necessary skills in supervised apartments in Dorchester; and Teen Parent Aides who make home visits to provide support, teach parenting skills, and help teens access needed services.

MASSACHUSETTS TEEN LIVING PROGRAMS

Recent reforms in the state welfare system have included provisions requiring that teen mothers, in order to receive cash benefits, must live with a parent, guardian, or family member over the age of 20. If this is not possible due to potential for abuse, neglect, addiction, or other extraordinary circumstances, they may still receive benefits if they live in one of 22 structured Teen Living Programs (TLPs).

TLPs were established by the Massachusetts Department of Social Services (DSS) and the Massachusetts Department of Transitional Assistance (DTA) to enable teen parents to develop parenting and life skills, to connect them with school and child care, and to provide a safe and supportive living environment. The goal is for teens to lead independent lives after completion of the program. A resident can remain in a TLP until her 20th birthday. To live in a TLP, a resident must contribute all of her food stamps and 30% of her monthly income. To be eligible for placement, teens must first be deemed eligible to receive Transitional Aid to Families with Dependent Children. For more information, contact your local DTA ("welfare") office or call DSS at (617) 727-3171, ext. 414.

■ CHILDREN'S TRUST FUND
(DOTS PARTNER)
800-252-8403
(617) 727-8957
294 Washington St., Suite 640
Boston, MA 02108
The Children's Trust Fund promotes and funds programs specifically geared toward teenage parents, including different types of support groups and parenting and life skills classes. Contact CTF to learn about these types of programs that are being offered in your area.

■ CRITTENTON HASTINGS HOUSE (DOTS PARTNER)
(617) 782-7600
10 Perthshire Rd.
Boston, MA 02135
Crittenton has a long and impressive history of assisting pregnant teenagers. Today it helps young families in the Boston area with programs including education and job training; housing (including an on-site transitional housing program for teens and their children); reproductive health care services; child care for children of teen parents finishing high school; preparation of meals for pregnant and parenting women; and counseling services. Crittenton also runs a highly acclaimed school-based Young Fathers program in Boston high schools.

■ EARLY INTERVENTION SERVICES
(617) 624-5070
Early Intervention offers many programs geared toward teenage parents including support groups, child care, classes and education.

■ THE FUTURES FOR YOUNG PARENTS PROGRAM
(617) 623-6667
432 Columbia St.
Cambridge, MA 02138
Futures is a free GED program for pregnant and parenting young people from Cambridge, Charlestown, Everett, Malden, Medford, Somerville, and greater Boston. To be eligible one must be 21 years of age or younger and must be receiving Transitional Assistance. The program offers classes, counseling, individualized instruction and tutoring, as well as career exploration and speakers. Futures also provides assistance in solving problems related to parenting, pregnancy, nutrition, housing, finances, domestic violence, and self-esteem. Eligible participants may receive financial assistance with child care and transportation.

■ LITTLE HOUSE HEALTH CENTER
(617) 282-3700
990 Dorchester Ave.
Dorchester, MA 02125
This health center offers an eight-week instructional program called "Building Healthy Families and Children" for teen parents and young parents. A variety of practical topics are covered emphasizing child health and behavior including taking a temperature, medicines for children, nutrition, temper tantrums, and first aid. There is also a less structured peer support group for young parents. Assistance with transportation and child care is provided. Advocacy and outreach services are also available.

- **NEWTON COMMUNITY SERVICE CENTERS, INC. (NCSC)**
(617) 969-5906
492 Waltham St.
West Newton, MA 02165
NCSC's Young Parents Program offers a comprehensive network of support services during pregnancy and throughout the years of parenting. Services include individual counseling, child care placement, support groups, job training and internship placement, and advocacy and referral. NCSC uses a tri-generational approach, seeking to involve parents, children and grandparents. Transitional housing is available for young parents who are homeless or at risk of homelessness. NCSC also has Parent Aides who make home visits and provide support. You need not be a resident of Newton to use the services offered by NCSC.

- **THE PARENTING PROJECT AND YOUNG PARENTS PROGRAM**
(617) 355-7718
Children's Hospital
300 Longwood Ave.
Boston, MA 02115
This project is open to all mothers (whether currently pregnant, currently parenting, or both) who are 18 or younger, and to all expectant or current fathers or partners of eligible mothers. Services include medical care for infants and toddlers, postpartum medical care for teen mothers (including birth control and gynecological care), referrals for

---

HEALTHY FAMILIES

This newborn home visiting program is a free, confidential, universally accessible and completely voluntary family support service available to every first time parent under 20 years of age living in Massachusetts. A joint initiative between Children's Trust Fund (CTF) and the Department of Public Health, this program addresses the concerns, added responsibilities, and need for reliable information that a baby's arrival brings. A trained Family Partner visits the young family to discuss questions and concerns about taking care of a new baby. He or she can also provide referrals to resources and services within the community, provide information about what to expect as a baby grows, help baby proof homes, and help parents stay up to date with a child's immunizations and other health matters. These services are available prenatally and continue through to the child's third birthday with visits as often as once a week.

All first-time parents under the age of 20 are eligible for this program. After obtaining the mother's consent, referrals to Healthy Families programs can be made either during pregnancy or upon the birth of the child by health care professional, service providers, or birthing hospitals. Self-referrals are also encouraged. Programs can be located by contacting CTF at 800-252-8403.

medical care for young fathers, a teen mother's parenting group, advocacy for young fathers, a young fathers club, help with school and job plans, support, education, and referrals to community resources. Transportation is provided. Many staff speak Spanish.

■ A WOMEN'S CONCERN
(617) 825-0838
1876A Dorchester Ave.
Boston, MA 02124

(781) 433-0466
1211 Highland Ave.
Needham, MA 02192

(781) 284-8747
103 Broadway (Route 107)
Revere, MA 02151

These private nonprofit centers serve thousands of young women who have faced unplanned pregnancies. Each center provides free pregnancy tests, information and resources about all pregnancy concerns including abortion procedures and alternatives, referrals for medical care, social services, adoption, housing, and counseling. Diapers, clothing, and other baby items are available in some situations. The trained volunteers help each woman explore her situation and make well-informed decisions using goal-setting skills and child development information. Evening and weekend appointments are available.

■ DAYBREAK CRISIS PREGNANCY CENTER
(617) 576-1981
(617) 576-1982 (24 hour helpline)
1384 Massachusetts Ave.
Cambridge, MA 02138

Daybreak serves men and women facing crisis pregnancies, many of whom are teens. Their goal is to give realistic alternatives to abortion. Daybreak provides free pregnancy testing, a 24-hour helpline, peer counseling, some private housing, maternity and baby clothing, referrals for adoption, and post-abortion counseling and support groups. The center is affiliated with Care Net (formerly the Christian Action Council) and does not perform or refer for abortions.

■ EXPANDED FOOD AND NUTRITION EDUCATION PROGRAM (EFNEP)
(617) 522-8567
P.O. Box 1196
19 St. Rose St.
Jamaica Plain, MA 02130

This education program serves pregnant and parenting teens, in addition to low-income families with children. Its nutrition educators are trained in the "Great Expectations" course, which has been developed specifically for young pregnant women. Participants learn the importance of nutrition during pregnancy, as well as how to prepare food safely, manage their resources, encourage healthy eating habits in children, and effectively use food assistance programs.

"A Single Mother's Story"

By Lee F. Doyle

To raise a child is the most important and the most difficult job on the planet, bar none. That has long been my belief, but never in my tender dreams of motherhood did I imagine I would be a single parent. I'm not very representative of the single mothers I know, though, because my situation arose not out of divorce but as an unexpected pregnancy in the context of an off-again-on-again, long-term involvement with a guy (I can't bring myself to call him a man). I covered my denial about his problems with my addiction to the exhilarating, oceanic intensity of our sexual connection. When I told him the results of my pregnancy test, I learned that if I chose to have the baby, I would be an emphatically single mother.

The crossroads I stood at was the most profound of my life. At the age of 38, I had largely accepted the idea that children just weren't in the cards for me, and I had been accepted into a masters program to become an ESL teacher. I did not have the income of a Murphy Brown, in fact, I had no income at all at the time.

I firmly believe that children need, want and deserve to have both a mama and a daddy. The discussions I had with myself were searing, and they tangled with my deepest spiritual beliefs. The short version of my decision is that I couldn't not have the baby.

How bizarre it sounds to me now to say "the baby." She's not a generic baby, she's herself, the incredibly sweet, blindingly beautiful, fantastic human critter who shares my life and occupies pretty much every conscious moment and probably many of the subconscious moments as well. I've slowly been working through my defensiveness about her genesis, yet my dream of a warm-and-fuzzy, complete family and my *sorrow at its lack persists: what will I tell my daughter when she asks, inevitably, for her father? How can he not be here to share these wonderful times when she first laughed, ate pizza, crawled, and yes, even farted in the bathtub? She will only be this age once. I pray constantly for a nice, grown-up man to appear and be a genuine partner to me and a genuine daddy to my daughter.*

Fatigue, chores, fatigue, loneliness, fatigue, money worries, fatigue, illness, fatigue....mothers of young children experience these grimmer sides of childrearing. My supposition is that married mothers experience them to a more moderate degree. There is, after all, the hope that once Daddy comes home, a trip to the gym or even a decent supper may be possible. More times that I care to count, this single mama lies down after her child is bathed and tucked in, exhausted on the couch, without eating much dinner and without cleaning up the kitchen. When I wake up at 6:00 the next morning the same undone chores greet me. Where were the elves when I needed them?

What a sense of victory I feel upon getting us both fed a balanced supper that includes all four food groups! Or upon actually getting a set of sit-ups and push-ups done! The day is spent wresting one task after another out of the overwhelmingly constant pile of tasks. All mothers face these concerns. It's just that for single mothers, the fresh horses do not arrive and are not even on the way.

I have heard married mothers say "I don't know if I could do it alone"—yes, they could, if they had to. I have heard single mothers express ideas such that married mothers have no problems and have it all taken care of. Well, sorry, there's no free lunch for mothers. Through being part of both a new moms group in which I am the only single mother and a single mothers group where I am the only one not single by divorce and through knowing at least one single father with full-time custody of his children, I am able to see across the circumstantial differences between us mother-types (of whatever gender) and to arrive where I began when I fantasized the perfect family so many years ago: to raise a child is the most important and difficult job on the planet, bar none. ❧

SINGLE PARENTING

■ MASSACHUSETTS PATERNITY ACKNOWLEDGMENT PROGRAM
800-332-2733
(617) 577-7200
141 Portland St.
Cambridge, MA 02139

When a baby is born to parents who are not married to each other the baby automatically has one legal parent—the mother. In order to establish legal paternity for their child, parents of children born in Massachusetts now have the option of participating in the Paternity Acknowledgment Program, a voluntary program which allows unmarried parents to establish legal paternity without going to court.

This can be done in one of two ways. The easiest way to do it is at the time of birth in a hospital or birth center. The father must give the same information as the mother to the birth registrar and both must sign a Voluntary Acknowledgment of Parentage form. If the father is not present at the time of birth for whatever reason, a Post-Birth Acknowledgment can be completed and signed at the clerk's office in the city or town where the baby was born. A fee is charged (usually $20-$40) to cover the costs of amending the birth certificate to include the father's name. Call (617) 753-8601 for questions regarding birth certificates or to locate the city or town clerk's office where your child was born.

If both parties sign the Voluntary Acknowledgment of Parentage form at the time of birth, or if they file the Post-Birth Acknowledgment while the baby is still under six months of age, either parent has the right to request genetic marker testing within 60 days to confirm paternity. This testing can be done privately or through Child Support Services. A court can use the results of the tests to decide whether or not the man is the father.

The benefits of establishing legal paternity are many. It provides the child with two legal parents and the networks that come with them. The child will also have access to the father's medical history, health insurance, and other benefits. Although an unmarried mother is presumed to have custody, a father who has established legal paternity has the right to petition the court with regard to custody and visitation, and to have a say in any adoption plans. Having legal paternity established also helps to ensure that the child will receive financial support from both parents.

■ NEW BEGINNINGS
(781) 235-8612
207 Washington St.
Wellesley Hills, MA 02181

This free support group focuses on emotional, physical, intellectual, and spiritual issues that single adults face in their lives. It helps single people to experience growth and healing from the loss of a relationship. New Beginnings meets every Thursday evening at 7:00 p.m. on a drop-in basis. Several subgroups have formed from this larger group, one of which focuses specifically on single parenting issues.

■ BOSTON SINGLE MOTHERS BY CHOICE
800-721-7007 or (617) 964-9949
P.O. Box 600027
Newtonville, MA 02160

BSMC is an independent organization affiliated with the national Single Mothers by Choice. It offers support and resource information to all women who are either considering single motherhood or are already single mothers. Annual membership is $30, prorated from September. Meetings are generally held the second Sunday of the month and child care is provided. First meetings are free for nonmembers, and there is a $5 fee for nonmembers for each meeting thereafter. There is a monthly newsletter, as well as speakers, discussion groups and social events.

■ NEWTON CHILD CARE COMMISSION AND FUND
(617) 332-6723
100 Walnut St., Rm. 100
Newton, MA 02160

Newton Child Care Commission facilitates single parent support groups with baby-sitting and transportation provided. It sponsors a baby-sitting reimbursement program for occasional baby-sitting needs. Both programs are funded through a grant from the Rebecca Pomroy Foundation, and are available to single parents residing in Newton.

■ PARENTS WITHOUT PARTNERS
(508) 832-2445
P.O. Box 510
Auburn, MA 01501

Parents Without Partners is an international organization whose local chapters provide family activities, support, adult social activities, newsletters, and a friendly forum in which to discuss issues related to single parenting. It is open to all single parents. Membership fees vary chapter to chapter. There are seven local chapters in the greater Boston area. A referral to current local chapter leaders can be obtained by contacting Sally Tracy at the above number.

■ SINGLE ISSUES
(617) 558-7034
49 Pearl St. #2
Newton, MA 02158

This nine-session workshop/discussion group is open to all single women, regardless of sexual orientation, considering pregnancy, adoption or childfree living. It provides support, information, and empowerment for women as they make this important life decision. The group is facilitated by an experienced psychotherapist who is a single mother by choice. There is a fee and enrollment is limited to ten participants.

■ YOUNG WIDOWS AND WIDOWERS, LTD. (YWW)
888-YWW-LTD8 (999-5838)
(978) 475-5556
P.O. Box 4091 BV
Andover, MA 01810

This nonprofit group was formed in 1983 to address the needs of younger widowed persons. Widows and widowers in the group range in age from 20s to 50s, many of whom are parents of young children. Different programs address the changing needs of widowed people with an underlying goal of turning grief into growth. There are several YWW chapters in eastern Massachusetts.

CHILD ABUSE PREVENTION

Parenting can be a very difficult task. At times it may be helpful to have someone to talk to when you are feeling angry or overwhelmed by the demands of raising children. The following agencies work to prevent child abuse by supporting parents. They can make referrals and provide a listening ear.

■ CHILD-AT-RISK HOTLINE
800-792-5200
This hotline is the Department of Social Services (DSS) after-hours reporting line for incidents of child abuse/neglect. Open 24 hours a day, they will make referrals to DSS, as well as referrals to mental health, parenting, self-help groups, and others.

■ MASSACHUSETTS COMMITTEE FOR CHILDREN AND YOUTH (MCCY)
800-CHILDREN
14 Beacon St., Suite 706
Boston, MA 02108
MCCY's mission is to prevent child abuse through education and advocacy work. The Don't Shake the Baby Campaign is designed to prevent Shaken Baby Syndrome (SBS). Call for a helpful brochure describing SBS and tips on what to do for your baby and yourself when your baby cries.

■ PARENTAL STRESS LINE
800-632-8188
The Parental Stress Line is available 24 hours a day, seven days a week. If you are a parent or child care provider, you can call this line if you need help with feelings of stress or anger, or if you just need someone to talk to. The hotline provides a listening ear and can help you problem-solve and brainstorm solutions. Hotline operators also make referrals.

■ PARENTS ANONYMOUS
800-882-1250
140 Clarendon St.
Boston, MA 02116
Hours: M-F   9:00 a.m.-5:00 p.m.
Parents who feel isolated, stressed, or angry towards their children can call for support and a listening ear. They can send you information and refer you to one of 70 local support groups across the state. Groups hold weekly evening meetings, free of charge, for parents of children of all ages.

■ UNITED WAY'S FIRST CALL FOR HELP
800-231-4377
Hours: M-F   8:00 a.m.-10:00 p.m.
This information and referral service provides resources based on a wide variety of needs. Information and Referral Specialists are trained to link people to resources such as child care, single parent support, family counseling, food, and emergency assistance.

BOSTON FAMILY LIFE

"No one should ever feel isolated in taking care of a child" are some of the wisest words we heard from any of the support agencies we spoke with. In fact, as Hillary Clinton is so oft quoted, "It takes a village to raise a child." The resources in this chapter offer support for every kind of family situation (although single parenting and teen parenting resources are listed in Boston Chapter 5), and can help you create your own village to foster the growth of a newborn into a toddler, as well as ease the stress and anxiety that the little wonder may provoke. There are agencies that place doulas or baby nurses to meet the family's immediate postpartum needs, resources for educating parents on a range of topics, and some of the best services anywhere in the country to treat postpartum depression. We have also gathered a selection of family activities for you to enjoy with your little ones. We encourage you to review these resources and create a network, a village if you will, where you can get the support you need to raise your child in a happy, healthy and safe environment.

Create a network where you can get the support you need to raise your child in a happy, healthy and safe environment.

PARENTING SUPPORT

The following groups and organizations offer many different services for new parents including, in many cases, parent education. Many also offer playgroups. We have included two subgroupings: Father Support and Gay and Lesbian Support. Organizations whose sole focus is parenting education are grouped separately in the following section.

■ BOSTON CHILDREN'S SERVICES
(617) 267-3700
271 Huntington Ave.
Boston, MA 02115
BCS, the oldest child welfare agency in the country, is a voluntary, nonprofit organization serving families in greater Boston, but concentrating on those who are low income or at risk. Its services include parent aides, respite aides, teen aides, mentors, support to parents with developmental disabilities, community outreach, counseling, and intensive family intervention.

■ CENTER FOR FAMILIES OF NORTH CAMBRIDGE
(617) 349-3002
The Fitzgerald School
70 Rindge Ave.
Cambridge, MA 02140

This center serves North Cambridge families and those with children attending the Fitzgerald School. They run an indoor playspace for parents of children up to 5 years of age with a climbing structure and developmentally appropriate toys for toddlers and preschoolers. The center has drop-in hours, scheduled programs, and on site staff. There are groups for parents, a newborn home visiting program and parent training.

■ CENTER FOR FAMILY DEVELOPMENT OF HEALTH AND EDUCATION SERVICES
(978) 921-1190
30 Tozer Rd.
Beverly, MA 01915

The Center for Family Development promotes the well-being and mental health of families on the North Shore. Their Family Outreach Program provides individual and family therapy to at-risk children and families. By visiting families in their homes, workers facilitate a safe home environment and help keep families intact and functioning.

■ CENTER FOR PARENT EDUCATION
(617) 964-2442
115 Pine Ridge Rd.
Waban, MA 02168

The Center for Parent Education is run by Dr. Burton White, author of The New First Three Years of Life and The Happy Unspoiled Child. The center offers counseling and support for parents with children from birth to 3 years of age. They can provide information on child development and evaluation of young children.

■ CHILDREN'S TRUST FUND
(DOTS PARTNER)
800-252-8403
(617) 727-8957
294 Washington St., Ste. 640
Boston, MA 02108

The Children's Trust Fund (CTF) was created to help communities strengthen and support families, so that children can grow up safely, free from abuse and neglect. Supported by public and private funds, CTF serves as an umbrella organization which funds, evaluates and promotes many programs across the state, such as parenting education and support, Healthy Families newborn home visiting, and Massachusetts Family Centers. CTF also offers free training and materials, has a lending library, and publishes a quarterly newsletter. Contact CTF to learn about programs in your community.

■ CONCORD FAMILY SERVICE
(978) 369-4909
Community Agencies Building
Concord, MA 01742

Concord Family Service, a division of Concord-Assabet Family and Adolescent Services, Inc., provides a range of services for families who live or work in Concord or the surrounding towns. They run support groups, provide consultations and counseling, maintain a Speakers Network, and offer educational workshops. Highlights include a first time mother's group, parenting support for couples, and a Young Parent Program for pregnant and parenting women under 25. Services are offered on a sliding scale fee.

■ CONNECTING THE DOTS FOR BOSTON TOTS
(DOTS PARTNER)
(617) 534-7091
c/o The Family Nurturing Center
One Boston Medical Center Pl., MAT 5
Boston, MA 02118
Connecting the Dots for Boston Tots (Dots) is a partnership of parents, providers and community leaders working together to ensure that the city's children get the best possible start in life. Dots unites city-wide efforts in creating a more nurturing city for families with young children. They are building a city-wide leadership that includes the Mayor's Office and is staffed by three lead organizations: The Family Nurturing Center, Parents United for Child Care, and Health Care for All. Through neighborhood-based "circles of caring" and a Public Policy Working group, Dots works to improve every family's access to quality health care, child care and family support services. Dots partners are also developing "welcome baby baskets" that include gifts for the new baby and his/her parents. These baskets will be delivered by teams of neighborhood visitors to congratulate the family on the arrival of the new baby and share with them information about neighborhood programs and services. There are over 50 groups in Boston that are Dots Collaborating Partners. Many of these groups are listed throughout this guide.

■ DORCHESTER CARES
(DOTS PARTNER)
(617) 474-1256
200 Bowdoin St.
Dorchester, MA 02122
This agency serves the community of Dorchester in providing a variety of family support activities. They offer pregnancy and parenting home visits to support women and their partners as well as parenting workshops, playgroups for children and a parent leadership group. Dorchester Cares also has nurturing programs for families. As part of their Welcome Baby Initiative, they deliver a basket of goods to the families of new babies as a way to reach out to new parents and to help link them to available services.

■ THE FAMILY NETWORK INC.
(978) 745-3326
(978) 468-1198
Through a grant from the Children's Trust Fund, the Family Network runs a weekly parent support group on the North Shore offered free of charge for parents with children 6 and under. Child care is provided for a small fee. They also offer consultations, workshops, and presentations. Workshops may include such topics as discipline, self esteem, understanding behavior, and communication. Presentations are given on a number of topics such as toddler behavior, development, and sibling issues.

■ THE FAMILY NURTURING CENTER (FNC) (DOTS PARTNER)
(617) 534-7091
One Boston Medical Center Pl., MAT 5
Boston, MA 02118
The mission of the Family Nurturing Center is to build nurturing communities where children are cherished, families are supported, and private and public policies promote healthy human development. The center provides training and education to spread their philosophy through Family Nurturing Programs, validated curricula developed to foster positive parenting attitudes and behavior. Through a series of weekly sessions, parents and children learn ways to get along better, communicate more, and feel closer to each other. The Center's Nurturing Network, developed out of these strategic efforts, continues to expand with the goals of increasing access to community Nurturing Programs and developing parent leadership skills. The FNC is a key partner in the Connecting the Dots for Boston Tots city-wide initiative.

■ F.E.M.A.L.E.
(508) 788-6293 Framingham
(781) 237-7951 Wellesley/Natick
(617) 484-6523 Metrowest Boston
F.E.M.A.L.E. (Formerly Employed Mothers at the Leading Edge) is a national nonprofit organization of women who have left the full-time paid work force to raise their children at home. It is an organization for all women dealing with transitions between paid employment and at-home motherhood. There are three local chapters in the greater Boston area. Each chapter has its own personality, but each offers bimonthly evening meetings with topical discussion groups, guest speakers and book discussions. F.E.M.A.L.E. also offers its members ($24 annually) local and national newsletters, playgroups, children's activities, couple's night out, and other family activities. The leaders for the three local chapters (Patricia Welsby – Framingham, Stacey Poritsky – Wellesley/Natick Chapter, and Sue Morris – Metrowest Boston) can be reached by calling the applicable number above.

■ FIRST CONNECTIONS
800-348-0221
(978) 287-0221
111 Old Rd. to Nine Acre Corner
Concord, MA 01701
First Connections is a parenting resource network for families with children birth through 3 in the towns surrounding Concord. Services include parenting education, home visiting, playgroups, and family programs at no cost. Residents of other towns may also participate by paying a low, annual fee. First Connections publishes a bimonthly newsletter, has a parenting resource library and publishes a Family Resource Guide of community service. They also sponsor parent associations in towns surrounding Concord which offer additional parenting supports such as baby-sitting cooperatives, playgroups, mom's nights out, etc. First Connections is a Massachusetts Family Network program and is supported locally by Concord Family Service and the C.A.S.E. Collaborative.

■ GOODSTART HEALTHY FAMILIES METRO REGION
800-884-8827
(508) 872-8827
Massachusetts Society for the Prevention of Cruelty to Children
63 Fountain St.
Framingham, MA 01702

The Goodstart program is a statewide home visiting program for expectant parents and parents with infants and children through 3 years of age. Professionals and parent volunteers make weekly visits to help establish effective parenting skills, a safe and healthy home, and to ensure that parents connect with existing community resources.

■ MALDEN/EVERETT FAMILY NETWORK
(781) 322-7007
347 Pleasant St.
Malden, MA 02148

This Family Network, funded by the Department of Education, serves parents with children from pre-birth through 3 years of age in Malden and Everett. Each center has a play area, conference space for meetings and classes, and a resource library containing print, audio and visual materials with multi-ethnic titles for both parents and children. Classes include parenting education and postpartum exercise. The Malden/Everett Family Network also has a home visiting program for newborns and their families. Programs are free to residents of Malden and Everett.

■ MEDFORD FAMILY NETWORK
(781) 393-2106
215 Harvard St.
Medford, MA 02155

The Medford Family Network has a variety of programs to support and educate Medford families. They sponsor a weekly home visiting program from pregnancy through baby's first year. Medford Family Network also holds workshops on every issue from discipline and sibling rivalry to CPR and first aid training. They have five Family Resource Centers throughout Medford that house resource libraries of books, videos and developmentally appropriate games and toys as well as space for parents and children to meet. There is a Baby and Me play-support group for parents of children from birth to 18 months. They also hold support groups for fathers, teens, grandparents, and parents in recovery. All programs are free to families in Medford. Child care and transportation are available upon request. The Medford Family Network is supported through a grant from the Massachusetts Department of Education.

■ MOM TO MOM
(508) 875-3100
Jewish Family Service of Metrowest
14 Vernon St.
Framingham, MA 01701

Mom to Mom, a nonsectarian program, offers three programs for mothers in the Metrowest area. Their free home visiting program links experienced moms and new mothers for weekly meetings. Mom to Mom also sponsors a New Moms' Group for a small fee. A social worker leads these weekly meetings that include a topic such as language development or infant massage. You can also join the Mother Toddler group for an eight-week session. Jewish Family Service offers counseling for individuals, couples and families.

■ M.O.R.E.S.
(781) 396-4833

This group, Moms Over 30 Resource, Education, and Support, offers support and friendship to moms who have left careers to stay home with their children or moms with older children who are experiencing new motherhood for the second time. It is sponsored by the Children's Trust Fund and the Medford School System and meets weekly on Monday mornings at Grace Church, 160 High St., Medford. Topics include child development, stress management, parenting styles, school choices, women's health issues, conflict resolution, and issues that surround going from two incomes to one. There is no fee and child care is provided free of charge. Advanced registration is required.

■ MOTHERS OFFERING MOTHERS SUPPORT (MOMS)
(978) 287-3176
Old Rd. to Nine Acre Corner
Concord, MA 01742

This program, run by Emerson Hospital, offers one-on-one support for new mothers. They provide telephone outreach, a list of resources such as playgroups and child care sources, and arrange home visits from experienced moms. MOMS also runs a free weekly new mothers' group. Leave a message and your call will be returned.

■ MOTHERS' MENTORS PROJECT
(617) 451-0049
The Medical Foundation
95 Berkeley St.
Boston, MA 02116

The Mothers' Mentor Project brings together mothers who are willing to share their positive pregnancy, parenting, and life experiences with other women and their families in the Dorchester, Mattapan, and Roxbury communities. By linking mothers together, the project helps provide the support that is needed during pregnancy and the critical first years of parenting. Mentors assist new or young mothers in understanding how to nurture themselves and their families, accessing community health and family support services, and increasing their parenting skills. Mothers' Mentors is a project of the Massachusetts Prevention Center at the Medical Foundation.

■ PARENT TO PARENT
(781) 729-7945
24 Oneida Rd.
Winchester, MA 01890
Parent to Parent runs a monthly drop-in support group the first Monday of each month for parents of young children. They also offer free educational workshops for parents. Past topics have included gender and sibling issues and dealing with oppositional behavior.

■ PLAYSPACE FOR YOUNG CHILDREN AND CAREGIVERS
(617) 332-0302
Newton Highlands
This private organization brings together parents for a combination playgroup and support group in a renovated carriage house. Groups are organized around themes such as combining career and parenting, single or divorced parents, at home moms, and moms with postpartum depression. Each session begins with a period of spontaneous play and interaction between children and parents. Then parents take part in a facilitated discussion while the children play in an adjacent area with an early childhood development teacher. Groups meet for 12 sessions at $20 per session and a $25 registration fee.

■ SOMERVILLE COUNCIL FOR CHILDREN
(617) 625-6600, ext. 2400
167 Holland St.
Somerville, MA 02144
The Somerville Council for Children has programs to support and educate parents and to promote advocacy. Supper Hour Workshops for parents are held once a month. Past topics have included building your child's self-esteem, setting limits, sleep problems and racism. Workshops include a free, family style supper. The Parents Count Project organizes and facilitates parent support groups. Groups meet weekly, biweekly, or monthly and include single parents, fathers, Latino parents, parents of special needs children and groups organized by neighborhood. Free child care is provided for both programs.

■ SOMERVILLE FAMILY NETWORK (SFN)
(617) 629-2948
c/o The Powderhouse Community School
1060 Broadway
Somerville, MA 02144
SFN is a coalition of Somerville public schools, community organizations, social service agencies, family support centers, and health care providers. Their goal is to support parents and caregivers as they raise, nurture and educate their children. SFN serves Somerville families with children ages 0-3. Services include information and referrals, parent-child play groups, parent classes, parent support groups, a lending library with books and videos for children and adults, family activities, museum passes and ESL classes. English, Spanish, Portuguese and Haitian-Creole are spoken by SFN staff. Services are free for Somerville families.

■ THE VISITING MOMS PROGRAM (DOTS PARTNER)
(617) 558-1278
Jewish Family and Children's Service
1340 Centre St.
Newton, MA 02159
This nonsectarian free program offers home visiting support for pregnant women and new mothers as well as drop-in groups for mothers and babies. They also offer parent workshops, consultations and telephone support. Call the above number for programs in Newton and Medford. For Canton, Sharon and Brockton, call (781) 821-4990.

■ WARMLINES PARENT RESOURCES
Baby Pages
(617) 244-INFO (4636)
206 Waltham St.
W. Newton, MA 02165
Web site: www.warmlines.org
In addition to child care referral service, WarmLines offers many programs that provide information and support to parents. These programs are available free of charge to Corporate Alliance employees and to individual members (you can join for $75) or at a discounted fee. Several programs are also available to non-members on a fee for service basis. WarmLines offers New Babies/New Moms support groups which are facilitated by a trained counselor. Through its matching members program, moms, dads, single parents, parents of twins, adoptive parents, and caregivers can meet others with similar profiles. WarmLines also sponsors weekly Drop-in Playgroups in four locations: Watertown, Newton, Brookline, and Needham. Its Speaker Series covers topics of interest to many parents. WarmLines also publishes "Sitter Solutions," a booklet listing area baby-sitting resources and helpful hints for obtaining a baby-sitter, and *InfoLines*, a bimonthly magazine featuring children's book reviews, ideas for outings, parenting advice, and events listings.

"Stay-at-Home Dad"

A Life Experience by Andrew Brandt

Tell people you are a stay-at-home father, and the one thing you won't be astonished to hear is, "Oh, I think it's wonderful that you're doing that." People blurt this out unreflectingly, and they mean it to be complimentary. Nevertheless, it is one of those conventionalized utterances (such as another thing I often hear, "Your baby has such beautiful blond hair") that evokes an ambiguous response in me. "Wonderful," in the context of their phrase, is probably meant as "admirable," but with undertones of "freakish." Historically, of course, stay-at-home fatherhood is freakish, but today it should not be regarded as particularly admirable or particularly exceptional.

For my wife and me, the choice was easy—we could afford to lose my salary, but not hers. And while my wife may feel ambivalent about continuing to work, I feel unambivalent about staying home. Without talking about practical problems, like diapering and other dirty subjects, the chief problem I confront socially is the idea that there must be something different about the father, as opposed to the mother, watching the kids. But for me there is no difference. Why should there be, after all? The physical acts of "mothering" are easy to learn. As for the other part, what comes under the heading of "nurturing," I don't believe men are as incompetent on that score as they are made out to be.

Of course there are people out there who deplore the notion that the woman should work just because she makes more money. These people are right to the extent that being able to afford a minivan should not be regarded as the highest aspiration of family life; but we should completely reject the prejudice—whatever its source—that says that watching the baby is women's work.

I have noticed, however, that if traditional society regards baby watching as women's work, then taking the kids to the playground is the traditional male contribution. Just the *other day at the playground, a guy—there with his three kids—asked me, "Did your wife make you take them out?" Well, that's what I get for going to the playground after 5:00. If I take the kids in the morning, I look merely unemployed. But that too depends on* where *I take the kids. In Harvard Square, a stay-at-home father can pass. In certain parts of Somerville, he's a fish out of water. These differences reflect differences in political attitudes; but for the economic reasons that seem irresistible in our society, the stay-at-home father is becoming more a fixture, and less a freak.*

Politically speaking, couples should feel free to decide, for the reasons that suit them best, who watches the baby—mother, father, granny, sitter, or whoever. The only enemy is the feeling that still on some level pervades society, that men lose status by staying home with the kids. My hope is that by bucking thousands of years of tradition, stay-at-home fathers can raise not just their own status, but the status of parenting in general—for all the wrong reasons, let us admit. But the result would still be one worth hoping for.

ant
FATHERS' SUPPORT RESOURCES

■ FATHER'S AND FAMILY NETWORK
800-252-8403
(617) 727-8957
The Children's Trust Fund (CTF)
294 Washington St., Suite 640
Boston, MA 02108
CTF convenes a monthly meeting for providers who share an interest in working with fathers in group settings. The meetings' key components are information sharing, networking opportunities, training development, and presentations by program leaders and experts with a guided discussion following. You can be added to the mailing list upon request and will receive more detailed information about these meetings.

■ FATHERS' GROUP
(978) 879-4585 Framingham
(617) 357-4832 Metro Boston
(781) 892-6117 Arlington
The Father's Group is a nonprofit organization of single and divorced fathers. Groups meet monthly to provide support for fathers and to work on advocacy. The statewide lobbying arm works to pass legislation supporting the rights of fathers in the father-child relationship. Local meetings include a discussion of legislative and business issues and allow time for fathers to discuss experiences and concerns in an informal setting.

■ NETWORK OF DADS
(617) 354-6471
The Network of Dads runs two playgroups for fathers in the greater Boston area. The playgroups meet at a different member's house each week. You can also call for a referral for a playgroup in your area. Richard Colbath-Hess, a licensed social worker, runs this service in addition to his private practice to help couples and fathers with issues of transition regarding family and parenting.

■ THE PARENTING PROJECT AND YOUNG PARENTS PROGRAM
(617) 355-7718
Children's Hospital
300 Longwood Ave.
Boston, MA 02115
This project is open to all expectant or current fathers or partners of teenage mothers. Services include medical care for infants and toddlers, referrals for medical care, advocacy, a young fathers' club, help with school and job plans, support, education, and referrals to community resources. Transportation is provided. Many staff speak Spanish.

■ YOUNG FATHERS PROGRAM
(781) 593-2312
Catholic Charities North
55 Lynn Shore Dr.
Lynn, MA 01902
The Young Fathers Program focuses on offering outreach and support to fathers on the North Shore. The outreach arm, geared to Lynn residents, works to link young fathers with existing resources, such as employment assistance, and help them develop good parenting skills. The program also runs a free support group open to all fathers of any age. The group meets one night a week in 12-week cycles to provide support and guidance for fathers.

GAY AND LESBIAN PARENTING SUPPORT

■ ALTERNATIVE FAMILY MATTERS
(617) 576-6788
P.O. Box 390618
Cambridge, MA 02139
E-mail: altfammat@aol.com
Alternative Family Matters (AFM) is a comprehensive and compassionate resource for lesbians and gay men who have or want to have children. AFM's Conception Connection is a network and counseling service for lesbians and gay men who want to have children biologically with a known person of the opposite sex under one of any number of mutually agreed upon arrangements. AFM advises community based organizations and programs which serve lesbian and gay parents and develops materials and community-building projects for lesbian and gay parents and their children.

■ COLAGE
(617) 267-0900, ext. 446
P.O. Box 441942
Somerville, MA 02144
COLAGE (Children of Lesbians and Gays Everywhere) is an international organization run for and by children of lesbian/gay/bisexual and transgendered (l/g/b/t) parents. It provides support and community for daughters and sons of l/g/b/t parents; advocates for their rights and those of their families; and promotes acceptance and awareness in society that love makes a family. The Boston Chapter runs monthly meetings and groups for children (7-11 years old), adolescents (12-17 years old), and young adults (18 years old and up) who have l/g/b/t parents, offering these children a safe environment where they are encouraged to discuss their feelings and thoughts about having l/g/b/t parents.

■ GAY FATHERS OF GREATER BOSTON (GFGB)
(617) 742-7897
P.O. Box 1373
Boston, MA 02205
Web site: www.outspace.com/gayfathers
E-mail: GFGB2info@aol.com
For more than 15 years this organization has been providing support to gay fathers. It holds drop-in meetings the first and third Tuesday of each month from 8:00 to 10:00 p.m. in the Boston Room at the Boston Lindemanm Center at 25 Staniford Street. Meetings range from informal discussions to formal presentations by speakers. GFGB's monthly newsletter can be mailed or held for you at their office. GFGB sponsors social activities for gay fathers and for fathers with children. There is an optional $20 membership fee. They will be happy to refer you to gay parenting groups in communities outside of Boston.

■ GAY & LESBIAN ADVOCATES & DEFENDERS (GLAD)
800-455-GLAD (4523)
(617) 426-1350
P.O. Box 218
Boston, MA 02112
Founded in 1978, GLAD is New England's leading legal rights organization for lesbians, gay men, bisexuals, and people with HIV. GLAD's mission is to achieve full equality and justice for all individuals in these groups, primarily through litigation and education. GLAD

litigates impact cases, including custody, adoption, and parental rights matters. Services are free and there are no financial eligibility requirements. For referrals, call weekdays 1:30 p.m.-4:30 p.m. There is a Spanish-speaking advocate available on Tuesdays and Thursdays.

■ LESBIAN/GAY FAMILY AND PARENTING SERVICES
(617) 267-7766, ext. 569
Fenway Community Health Center
7 Haviland St.
Boston, MA 02115
Web site: www.fchc.org
E-mail: lcoolidge@fchc.org
Fenway Community Health Center provides medical and mental health care and services that are sensitive to the needs of lesbians, gay men, and bisexuals. Services include a support network, education, and advocacy for lesbian/gay/bisexual/transgender prospective parents, parents, and children, as well as medical alternatives for achieving conception through the Alternative Insemination Program.

PARENTING EDUCATION AND INFORMATION

■ BOSTON WOMEN'S HEALTH BOOK COLLECTIVE
(617) 625-0271
240 A Elm St., 3rd Floor
Somerville, MA 02144
E-mail: bwhbc@igc.apc.org
The Boston Women's Health Book Collective (BWHBC) has written and published, among other titles, the now classic Our Bodies Ourselves, a book by and for women about health, sexuality and understanding our bodies, including an entire chapter devoted to pregnancy. Among other women's health care policy projects, the BWHBC works with community organizations, such as the Massachusetts Friends of Midwives, to promote options for midwifery care in the home, birth centers, and hospitals. The BWHBC's Women's Health Information Center is an extensive library filled with materials from a range of hard-to-find sources. Their collection of women's health materials includes information on AIDS and women, birth control, cancers, childbearing, health policy, lesbians, mid-life and older women, and sexuality. As of this writing the library is not available for general public use, but hopes to re-open in the Spring of 1998.

■ **CHILD CARE PROJECT**
(DOTS PARTNER)
(617) 825-6554
1485 Dorchester Ave., Room 203
P.O. Box 503
Dorchester, MA 02122
This child care referral program offers workshops for parents and child care providers on issues such as child development, curriculum, and child care advocacy. Most are offered in both Spanish and English. Continuing education and college credits are available. A current listing of workshops, times and fees is available upon request.

■ **CHILDREN'S MUSEUM PARENTS' RESOURCE ROOM**
(DOTS PARTNER)
(617) 426-8855, ext. 386
The Children's Museum
300 Congress St.
Boston, MA 02210
Located in a comfortable room in the Playspace, the Parents' Resource Room has a wonderfully informative collection of parenting materials. The room is open to the public with the cost of admission. You will find lots of books on child development, parenting issues, special concerns, creative activities for children, and children's titles. The Resource Room also has numerous binders of articles, clipped from various periodicals, organized by topic. This is the place to look for everything from information on developmental and social topics to birthdays and family health care. Resources do not circulate but copying is available at 10 cents per page. Don't forget to check out the Resource Exchange binders. These binders, while somewhat underused, have pages for parents and others to list resources they can provide or want to request. Topics include babysitting, nursery schools, and educational resources.

■ **DIANNE DEVANNA CENTER FOR THE PREVENTION OF CHILD ABUSE AND NEGLECT, INC.**
(781) 843-7010
1599 Washington St., Suite 1B
Braintree, MA 02184
This organization offers an eight-week series of workshops titled Parenting the Very Young Child. Topics include development, self esteem, discipline and stress management. Classes are free and child care is available. Preregistration is required.

■ **EFFECTIVE BLACK PARENTING PROGRAM**
(617) 445-2056
G.C. Unlimited
56 Dale St.
Roxbury, MA 02119
The Effective Black Parenting Program is a 13-week curriculum for African American parents run by Gloria Coney. The program, offered free through a grant from the Children's Trust Fund, has a culturally based curriculum. Gloria Coney works to bring together ideas about parenting from a western perspective and the cultural background of African Americans. Subjects such as slavery, heroes and the Bible are integrated into discussions of parenting styles and philosophies.

■ FAMILIES FIRST PARENTING PROGRAM
(617) 868-7687
99 Bishop Allen Dr.
Cambridge, MA 02139
Families First offers parenting education workshops at various sites in the greater Boston area. Past workshops have included "Keeping up with your Toddler," "Positive Approaches to Discipline," and "Parenting in the First Year." Workshop leaders have backgrounds in early childhood development and experience delivering programs for adults. Cost is generally $60 for a four session series; however, some programs are subsidized and offered for a nominal fee. Families First also offers some individual, short-term counseling.

■ INSIGHT EDUCATION CENTER FOR PARENTS AND TEACHERS
(781) 829-0080
1130 Washington St.
Hanover, MA 02339
This private organization provides education and support for parents. Insight Education Center runs workshops on the South Shore and in greater Boston that help teachers and parents understand children's behavior and develop effective strategies. Cost is $20 for a two-hour workshop, $30 for a co-parenting couple, and $15 per person if you have a group of four or more people. Ask to be placed on their mailing list for a complete list of workshops held each month. Individual parenting consultations are also available.

■ MIT FAMILY RESOURCE CENTER
(617) 253-1592
77 Massachusetts Ave., Room 4-144
Cambridge, MA 02139
The MIT Family Resource Center runs free noontime seminars, covering a variety of parenting topics, that are open to the MIT community as well as the general public. Past seminars have included "Enhancing Children's Self-Esteem" and "New Expectations of Fatherhood."

■ PARENT CHILD CENTER OF NEW ENGLAND
(617) 566-6555
384 Harvard St.
Brookline, MA 02146
The Parent Child Center (PCC) runs an educational program for parents of children from birth to 4 years. Small groups of parents and children meet two hours each week for eight weeks. Mothers and their children gather for social interaction and play. For a portion of the time, child specialists observe and interact with the children as the mothers gather nearby for coffee and a discussion of infant and child development. At the end of the eight weeks, parents are offered a meeting time to discuss their child's development. PCC faculty are available for off-site seminars and lectures to community groups.

CHILD CARE REFERRAL NETWORK

The following members of the Massachusetts Child Care Resource and Referral Network offer trainings and workshops for child care providers. Most also open these workshops to interested parents. Topics vary but you will usually find workshops on infant/toddler development, behavior and curriculum. Some of the agencies also have resource libraries. For more information about child care referral and the individual agencies, see Boston Chapter 2. Call 800-345-0131 to find out which agency serves your community.

- **CHILD CARE CHOICES OF BOSTON**
(617) 542-5437, ext. 475
105 Chauncy Street, 2nd Floor
Boston, MA 02111
Child Care Choices of Boston offers workshops, college courses and CEU series. You can visit their library, by appointment, on Tuesday, Wednesday, and Friday. They lend materials, videos and children's books to licensed child care providers.

- **CHILD CARE CIRCUIT**
(978) 686-4288
190 Hampshire St
Lawrence, MA 01840

(978) 921-1631
196 R Cabot St.
Beverly, MA 01915
Child Care Circuit offers training opportunities, starting at $15 for a two-hour workshop. For $5 per year, you can receive information on all trainings and workshops. Parents who are members of the Child Care Circuit referral service receive a discount. Parents can also join the Resource Room to gain access to books, videos, curriculum kits and other early childhood resources.

- **CHILD CARE RESOURCE CENTER**
(617) 547-1063, ext. 231 or 228
130 Bishop Allen Dr.
Cambridge, MA 02139
A brochure, which lists times, locations and cost of workshops, is available upon request. Workshop prices generally range from $20-$40.

- **CHILD CARE SEARCH**
800-455-8326 or (978) 263-7744
43 Nagog Park
Acton, MA 01720
Their newsletter, sent upon request, lists upcoming workshops. A two-hour workshop costs $12. Their resource library is open weekdays until 5:00 p.m. and until 8:00 p.m. the first Tuesday of each month. An individual membership is $15 per year.

- **COMMUNITY CARE FOR KIDS**
800-637-2011 or (617) 471-6473
1509 Hancock St.
Quincy, MA 02169
Community Care for Kids publishes a newsletter, which lists topics, times and locations of parent and child care provider workshops. Workshops generally last two hours at a cost of $15.

■ PARENT LINE
(617) 624-8020
This computerized information line, sponsored by the United Way of Massachusetts Bay Success by Six Program, has prerecorded messages on a wide variety of topics. Each topic has a helpful four- to five-minute message. There are over 30 topics under the headings of parenting, child development and child behavior. Messages are available in both English and Spanish. You can also speak to a Parent Line Specialist for additional support and information or to request a card with a complete list of topics.

■ PARENTING RESOURCE ASSOCIATES, INC.
(781) 862-4446
76 Bedford St., Suite 16
Lexington, MA 02173
Parenting Resource Associates, Inc. provides education, support and counseling for parents—individually and in groups—as well as consultations and professional development workshops for early childhood teachers, educators, and mental health professionals. These programs are offered at their offices in Lexington and on-site in many community settings. Workshops focus on child development stages and common parenting concerns. Ongoing workshops are offered for parents of challenging children and mothers who are survivors of child sexual abuse. Some services are covered by insurance.

■ PEOPLE DEVELOPMENT
(781) 431-2288
201 Bristol Rd.
Wellesley, MA 02181
This private organization runs parent workshops on children and parent's personality styles (based on the Myers-Briggs Type Indicator) and how they impact personal and family development. Workshops such as "Myths of Mothering" and "Dad's Workshop" affirm the fact that everyone can promote a positive family relationship. Workshops are $150 per hour for nonprofit organizations. A private consultation, which includes taking the indicator and helpful booklets, costs $100.

■ POSITIVE PARENTING
(781) 235-7112
237 Weston Rd.
Wellesley, MA 02181
This organization holds parenting workshops in Quincy and other areas. In the past, they have offered a series of eight workshops at a cost of $10. They give participants written materials at each session and cover topics such as ways a healthy family system disciplines and sets limits, balancing work and family, and understanding the behavior and development of children. Positive Parenting workshops are based on STEP, Systematic Training for Effective Parenting. Individual and family counseling is available.

- **PROGRAM FOR THE ENHANCEMENT OF PARENT-CHILD RELATIONSHIPS**
(617) 724-9309
MGH Charlestown HealthCare Center
73 High St.
Charlestown, MA 02129
This free program, funded by the Children's Trust Fund, serves Charlestown and surrounding communities. It is a ten-week series for parents and their infants and toddlers. Each week, parents and children interact in play. Facilitators and guest speakers also lead discussions relating to parenting issues and give presentations on such topics as health issues and child development. Facilitators also teach stress reduction with relaxation techniques. Child care for older children is available. To preregister, call the above number and leave a message.

- **STEP PARENTING PROGRAM**
(617) 846-9360
R.E.W. Home Health Care Agency, Inc.
217 Lincoln St.
Winthrop, MA 02152
This home health care agency provides parent training based on STEP (Systematic Training for Effective Parenting) principles. They offer an eight-week course twice each year. Weekly sessions are an hour long and focus on topics such as effective discipline, behavior, and parenting expectations. R.E.W. Home Health Care serves the commu-

---

PARENT ORGANIZATIONS

Many towns around Boston have well established family organizations. These groups are often started by a few families looking for activities for their young children and a way to connect with other families. Many times they have grown into organizations of a few hundred families with several committees planning lots of different activities throughout the year. Usually you pay a fee of under $25 to join for the year. Most of the groups are based in a specific town but accept families from neighboring communities. The benefits to joining such a community group usually include an indoor playspace, a newsletter, outings and activities throughout the year, educational seminars and workshops, community resource guides, and of course, the chance to become involved with other families in your community. Here are a few of the parent organizations located around Boston.

- **BEDFORD FAMILY CONNECTION**, Bedford, (781) 271-0736
- **FAMILY ACTION NETWORK OF WINCHESTER**, Winchester, (781) 721-7613
- **FIRST FRIENDS**, Wilmington, (978) 657-8123
- **MOTHER TO MOTHER**, Burlington, (978) 933-5239
- **PARENT TALK** (affiliated with Deaconess-Glover Hospital), Needham, (781) 444-5600, ext. 1150

nities of Chelsea, East Boston, Revere and Winthrop. The program is free.

■ WOMEN'S HEALTH RESOURCE CENTER
(617) 732-5763
Brigham and Women's Hospital
850 Boylston St.
Chestnut Hill, MA 02167
Hours: 11:00 a.m.-5:00 p.m. most days, call ahead to confirm.
The Women's Health Resource Center has an extensive library of books, magazines, and articles related to every aspect of women's health. A large part of their collection deals with pregnancy, birth, postpartum, and parenting. Books may be taken out for one week periods. Educational programs addressing different topics on women's health are frequently held. The Women's Health Resource Center is open to the general public.

POSTPARTUM DEPRESSION

■ DEPRESSION AFTER DELIVERY (DAD)
(781) 843-2734
(781) 837-4242
This Massachusettts chapter of Depression after Delivery is an excellent place to start when looking for education and support around postpartum mood disorders. They help women with everything from "baby blues" after delivery to diagnosed postpartum psychosis or depression. These disorders can be treated, and the sooner the better. DAD can help you find the medical help you may need from professionals experienced in caring for women with postpartum depression. DAD also holds support meetings, once or twice a month, for new mothers experiencing depression.

■ THE CENTER FOR WOMEN'S DEVELOPMENT
Arbour-HRI Hospital
(617) 731-3200, ext. 194
227 Babcock St.
Brookline, MA 02146
The Center for Women's Development has three specialty mental health programs for women: for trauma survivors, eating disorders, and postpartum psychiatric disorders. The postpartum program offers outpatient consultations and treatment, partial hospitalization, and inpatient treatment for women suffering from a postpartum psychiatric disorder such as depression, anxiety or psychosis. Arbour-HRI's inpatient treatment is unique in the United States; as in many European psychiatric hospitals, a woman is often allowed to keep her baby with her. Private rooms and a nursery as well as a trained staff are available to facilitate this. Treatment can include individual, family, and group therapy and medication. Arbour-HRI will soon begin home-based evaluation as well. They also make referrals for women needing a less intensive level of treatment and can refer you to parenting support groups. For more information and referrals during business hours call Program Coordinator Paula Koren, LICSW, at extension 194. After business hours, call the main number and ask for the intake office.

POSTPARTUM HELP AND SUPPORT

Doulas, also called postpartum caregivers, give nonmedical support and hands-on help to the new mother and her family. Doulas are trained in breastfeeding, baby care, and recognizing postpartum depression symptoms. They cook, do laundry, and help with older children. The National Association of Postpartum Care Services Inc. is the licensing organization for postpartum doulas. All members are fully trained in infant CPR as well as postpartum care.

■ BROCKWELL AGENCY
(781) 235-5823
P.O. Box 812246
Wellesley, MA 02181
In business since 1964, this agency provides temporary part-time and full-time care as well as maternity care. Long term care may also be available. Their carefully screened caregivers provide services according to your family's needs. They will assist with duties such as night feedings and sibling care. Fees vary according to duties and number of other children.

■ CECILY SOSTEK INC.
(617) 244-1370
1647 Beacon St., Suite 5
Newton Upper Falls
Newton, MA 02168
Cecily Sostek Inc. has been providing new baby care for families in Boston and beyond for over 40 years. They will listen to your family's needs and then find a baby nurse who will be a good match. Cecily Sostek's baby nurses provide physical and emotional support for healthy new babies and their families. They will also make referrals for breastfeeding support or other needs when necessary. Fees vary.

■ JUST HOME
(781) 849-1717
100 Bay State Dr.
Braintree, MA 02185
This home care service provides nursing visits for moms who choose to be discharged early from the hospital or are willing to pay privately. Their skilled nurses will examine mom and baby, help with breastfeeding, and answer any questions new families have. Certified lactation consultants are also available to visit you in your home. Just Home provides child care aides who are especially trained to meet the emotional needs of siblings, as well as run errands, do laundry, or prepare meals so parents can focus on the new baby. Just Home serves 39 communities south of Boston.

■ MATERNAL OUTREACH, INC.
(781) 340-9101
63 Winter St.
Weymouth, MA 02188
This unique home health agency specializes in perinatal home care, concentrating on the needs of women during their pregnancy and early postpartum period. Their experienced nurses and mothers' helpers provide services at your home. For the postpartum women these services include: postpartum visits (available seven days a week, 24 hours a day) encompassing instruction in newborn care, support, doctor-ordered management of complications, and review of nutritional requirements for mom and baby; light housekeeping; sibling care; and 24-hour phone consultation to answer those unexpected questions.

MOTHERCARE SERVICES, INC.
Baby Pages
888-MY-DOULA (693-6852)
MotherCare Services, Inc., New England's first postpartum care service, provides educational, emotional, and practical support to the whole family in the greater Boston area. They will arrange a prenatal visit with a trained provider (doula) to assess your needs following the homecoming of your baby. Once the baby arrives, the doula comes to your home to provide guidance and help with newborn/mother care, breastfeeding support, parenting information, sibling care, nutritional information, meal preparation, household/nursery organization, errands, and household assistance. You will also receive a useful resource directory. Fees vary.

NEWBORN AND FAMILY CARE
(781) 444-2198
75 Bird St.
Needham, MA 02192
Newborn and Family Care, in business since 1984, provides postpartum short term as well as long term care. Their live-in and live-out caregivers have experience with nursing mothers. They can also provide sibling care, and help with general household chores such as meal preparation, laundry service, food shopping and errands. Fees vary according to needs of the family and duties performed.

NEWBORN NECESSITIES
(781) 449-5612
109 Noanett Rd.
Needham, MA 02194
Newborn Necessities offers postpartum care for newborns and their families as well as educating parents on the care of the newborn and breastfeeding management. In addition, a shopping service is provided during difficult pregnancies. Newborn Necessities can coordinate the planning of the traditional briss and remain through the celebration.

PARENTS IN A PINCH
(617) 739-5437
45 Bartlett Crescent
Brookline, MA 02146
In addition to back-up child care and nanny placement services, this agency also provides new baby care. Parents in a Pinch has a flexible program that will fill the specific needs of your family. Their trained caregivers provide newborn care, sibling care, and household duties. The agency fee is $50 per day for a four-hour minimum. The provider then receives an additional minimum of $10 per hour.

- **VNA CARE NETWORK, INC.**
800-728-1VNA (1862)
245 Winter St.
Waltham, MA 02154
The VNA Care Network offers home health and community care for 130 communities in eastern Massachusetts and southern New Hampshire. Postpartum services include assessment of mother's health, breastfeeding support, review of infant care and behavior, and referrals for postpartum complications or depression if needed. VNA also provides newborn assessment, skilled care for infants with complex health needs, parenting support and family support services. Many services are covered by insurance plans. The above central intake number can refer you to the VNA in your area.

- **FERTILITY AWARENESS SERVICES**
(508) 660-1126
52 Cedar St.
Walpole, MA 02081
Fertility Awareness Services provides education and support around fertility issues. This organization can help you understand postpartum fertility, avoid the use of hormones while breastfeeding, space or avoid pregnancy by natural methods, and prepare for a healthy pregnancy. They charge a $30 resource fee which includes printed materials, use of the resource center and access to its referral network. Private consultations are $40 for two to three hours. They also run community workshops and professional seminars.

FAMILY ACTIVITIES

The greater Boston area is a wonderful place to raise children. There are lots of interesting things to do, as we are surrounded by some of the best academic institutions in the world, and our history is rich and colorful. Listed below are some of the museums and other attractions that are particularly good for infants and toddlers. Your youngster may only want to stay an hour or less at these places, and you may not want to pay full admission. Plan ahead and take advantage of your public library's free passes to many of our selections. You will also find other appropriate events and places to visit listed in the calendar section of the *Boston Globe* and the *Boston Parents' Paper*. Don't forget to check out:

- Public libraries for sing-alongs as well as crafts, play times, story hours.

- Local Y's and recreation departments for classes and drop-in toddler gyms.

- South Station to see trains and have a snack.

- Your local fire station. Fire fighters are usually happy to let little ones check out the fire engines.

- Playgroups, often advertised on bulletin boards such as the children's room of your local library, in community newspapers and the *Boston Parent's Paper*. Many of the organizations listed in the Parent Support section of this chapter offer playgroups as well.

- Your own neighborhood for walks, a closer look at nature, and all the little things that as adults we often overlook but that are fascinating for children.

■ BLUE HILLS RESERVATION AND TRAILSIDE MUSEUM
(617) 333-0690
1904 Canton Avenue
Milton, MA 02186
Hours: T-Sun. 10:00 a.m.-5:00 p.m. (and some Monday holidays)

At the foot of the Blue Hills you and your family may visit the wildlife native to this gorgeous region we call home. You'll find animals that were and are local to the area, such as fox, turkey, deer, duck, hawk, bobcat, and otter—all living in outdoor cages displayed within their habitat. Admission to the outdoor exhibit and trails is free. The Trailside Museum features exhibits describing the animals' sleeping and eating habits. Enjoy a walk among the serene 6,500 acres that ramble only a hop, skip and a jump from bustling Boston. Admission to the Museum costs $3 for adults, $2 for senior citizens, kids 3-15 are $1.50, under 2 and Audubon members are free.

■ THE CHILDREN'S MUSEUM
(DOTS PARTNER)
(617) 426-8855
300 Congress St.
Boston, MA 02210
Hours vary by season.
Adults $7, children 2-15 and seniors $6, 1-year-old children $2. 5:00-9:00 p.m. on Fridays everyone pays $1.

This museum has something of interest for children of all ages. You can play dress-up, work at a construction site, or visit the many other interactive exhibits. For the youngest children, the museum offers the Playspace. This special room has books, a train set, a car to ride and a large structure to climb and explore. A hands-on activity, coordinated by a museum employee, is usually set up. There is also a wonderful Parents' Resource Room located off the Playspace. The museum is a ten-minute walk from South Station on the Red Line.

■ DECORDOVA MUSEUM AND SCULPTURE PARK
(781) 259-8355
51 Sandy Pond Road
Lincoln, MA 01773
Hours: T-Sun. Noon-5:00 p.m.
Adults $6, children 6-12, students and seniors $4, children under 6 free

The DeCordova Museum houses contemporary art with a focus on New England artists. Even if your infant or child is not going to allow you to leisurely stroll through an art museum, this is still a wonderful outing. The sculpture park is free and contemporary outdoor art enhances the landscape of these magical 35 acres. Your child will love to be outside and you will enjoy some fantastic artwork.

■ DRUMLIN FARM EDUCATION AND WILDLIFE SANCTUARY
(781) 259-9807
South Great Rd., Route 117
Lincoln, MA 01773
Hours vary by season
Adults $6; children 3-12 and seniors $4; under 3, Mass Audubon members free.

Drumlin Farm is a working farm run by the Massachusetts Audubon Society. It is a stimulating place to bring your children to see both farm animals and a selection of wild animals found in New England. When I visited, my son got to see a cow milked by hand. Older children were even allowed to try themselves. Drumlin Farm also offers hay rides in addition to special demonstrations, located in closely-spaced barns. Paths are stroller accessible. A visit in the spring is a special treat since you will have a chance to see many baby animals.

■ **FRANKLIN PARK ZOO**
(617) 442-2002
1 Franklin Park Rd.
Boston, MA 02121
Hours: April-Oct.
        M-F   10:00 a.m.-5:00 p.m.
        Sat., Sun., holidays:
               10:00 a.m.-6:00 p.m.
Adults $6, seniors $5, children 2-15 $3, under 2 free. Free the first Saturday of each month 10:00 a.m.-noon.
The Franklin Park Zoo is an often overlooked attraction in Boston. The highlight of the African Tropical Forest is the gorilla exhibit. The zoo also features a lion exhibit, camels, zebras, and a bird aviary and flight cage. Visit the Children's Zoo where kids can see and pet farm animals.

■ **MUSEUM OF SCIENCE**
(617) 723-2500
Science Park
Boston, MA 02114
Hours: M-Sun. 9:00 a.m.-5:00 p.m.
        F   9:00 a.m.-9:00 p.m.*
        *and holidays except Christmas and Thanksgiving
Adults $9, seniors and children $7, under 3 free.
The Museum of Science has many fascinating exhibits appropriate for all ages, including infants and toddlers. The Discovery Room is a special room designed for children under 4 with lots of discovery activities. A special area for infants to roll and crawl has developmentally appropriate toys. A large molded water table, complete with waterproof smocks and hand dryers when you are finished playing, is a favorite. There is also a ball pit, a magnet corner and a two-story structure to play and hide in. A handful of glass cages are home to small animals such as turtles and elephant shrews. Diaper changing facilities are located throughout the museum.

■ **NEW ENGLAND AQUARIUM**
(617) 973-5200
Central Wharf
Boston, MA 02110
Call ahead as hours and prices vary by day, season. Kids under 3 always free.
The Aquarium, one of the best spots in Boston, is often quite busy during weekends and throughout the summer. The best time to arrive is as soon as doors open. The highlight is the three story giant ocean tank brimming with ocean life such as sharks, sea turtles, and more fish than is possible to list. You will also find sea otters, penguins, and several tanks featuring aquatic life of salt marshes, fresh water, tropical water and more. The New England Aquarium also has sea lion presentations, whale watches and harbor cruises.

BOSTON'S BEST BABY BARGAINS

- **Franklin Park Zoo:** 10:00 am - 12:00 p.m., 1st Saturday of every month is free.
- **Natural History Museum at Harvard:** Free every Saturday before noon.
- **The Children's Museum:** Fridays 5:00 p.m.-9:00 p.m only cost $1.
- **The Tot Stop:** Babies under 6 months and parents are always free. *Baby Pages*
- **Free Indoor Playspaces** at the Arsenal Mall, the Atrium, and the Meadow Glen Mall.
- **MBTA:** Kids under 5 ride the T for free, everyday!
- **The Mapparium** at the Christian Science Center: Open all year round Mon. - Sat 9:30 a.m. - 4:00 p.m. (617) 450-3790 Walk inside a giant globe. The brilliant colors are heightened by several hundred electric lights. Even very young children will be impressed. Free!
- **Blue Hills Reservation and Trailside Museum:** Their outdoor exhibit of native animals is free.
- **Logan Airport:** Kidport at Terminal C has giant car, plane, train and rocket with a view of planes outside. Free!

■ MUSEUM OF CULTURAL AND NATURAL HISTORY
Harvard University
(617) 495-3045
11 Divinity Ave.
Cambridge, MA 02138
Hours: M-Sat. 9:00 a.m.-5:00 p.m.
Sun. 1:00 p.m.-5:00 p.m.
Adults $5; students, seniors $4; 3-13 $3
There are four museums located in the University Museum building. While you may be interested in the glass flower exhibit, the minerals, or the well-considered Native American displays, it may not be of great interest to your toddler or infant. However, The Museum of Comparative Zoology is a wonderful place, especially on a rainy Saturday morning (when the museum is free). If you enter at 11 Divinity Ave., rather than 26 Oxford St, you will be closer to the elevator and can walk through the other exhibits on your way to the animals. This museum has room after room of animal specimens grouped by category. Small children love to see the smallest mouse as well as the large whales.

■ SWAN BOATS
(617) 522-1966
Boston Public Gardens
Adults $1.75, kids under 13, 95 cents
A favorite among tourists, the Swan Boats should not be overlooked by those of us lucky enough to live near Boston. Open mid-April to mid-September, it is an inexpensive, relaxing activity that most kids love (bring bread to feed the ducks). Check out the duck sculptures based on the Robert McCloskey book, *Make Way*

for Ducklings, located near the corner of Beacon and Charles streets. It is also worthwhile to visit the nearby Frog Pond Pavillion on the Boston Common. It is a huge wading pool with fountains in the summer and an ice skating rink in the winter (with a system that allows ice skating even in warmer winter weather). Take the Greenline to Park Street or Arlington, or drive and park under the Common.

ACTIVITY CLASSES

If you are looking for activities that hold your child's attention and stimulate his/her mind, there are many options open to you in Boston. The following organizations provide music, dance, art and movement instruction for infants and toddlers (along with their parents). Remember to look into local Y's, Boy's and Girl's Clubs, and recreation departments for additional classes.

BEST FAMILY OUTINGS

Here are new-parent-approved places to go that will please parents and give baby some air and new stimulation. See our listings for more details on many of these activities.

- **Singing Beach, Manchester-by-the-Sea:** This picturesque beach, complete with bath houses and snack bar, is filled with families in the summer season and with town residents walking their dogs the rest of the year. Parking at the beach is restricted to residents, but you can easily park in town near the train station (or dispense with your car altogether and take the commuter rail) and walk. (978) 526-2040. Beach admission is $1.
- **Drumlin Farm, Lincoln:** A wonderfully bucolic place to wander. Infants love all the kids, the toddlers will love all the animals.
- **Wilson's Farm, Lexington:** Get your fruit and vegetable shopping done and visit the animals in the barn. (781) 862-3900.
- **DeCordova Museum and Sculpture Park, Lincoln:** Meander through the outdoor sculpture park, bring a picnic and maybe take a nap.
- **Castle Island, South Boston:** This unique park reminds us we live right near the ocean. Walk along the paths, let your tots play on their wonderful playground. Bring a picnic. Breathe the sea air and relax. (617) 727-7676.
- **Arnold Arboretum, Jamaica Plain:** Wander the 265 acres of this free tree museum in any season! Babies will love the walk, and you will marvel at nature's never ending show of variety. (617) 524-1717.

■ THE CHILDREN'S MUSIC WORKSHOP, INC.
(508) 435-6198 (Registration)
349 Boston Post Rd.
Weston, MA 02193
Cheryl Melody offers age-appropriate creative movement classes for newborns through age 2 (as well as for older children) that include chanting, circle games, rhythm instrument and finger play. Parents participate with their child. A six-week session costs $90.

■ CREATIVE MOVEMENT & ARTS CENTER
(781) 449-2707
145 Rosemary St.
Needham, MA 02192
Operating since 1980, the Creative Movement and Arts Center offers fitness oriented programs for babies 3-18 months (as well as older tots and children) and their parents. Baby Dance, a class with phases for newborns, crawlers and walkers, offers developmentally appropriate activities including music and movement, fingerplays and motor development that encourage muscle strengthening, coordination and balance. All classes are set to original music. The longest session is 16 weeks and costs $235; shorter sessions are adjusted accordingly.

■ GYMBOREE / KINDERMUSIK
(617) 437-1191
(781) 647-3371
(978) 531-5420
Locations also in Boston, Braintree, Framingham, Newton, Peabody, Watertown, Wellesley, West Roxbury, and Waltham.
Each 45-minute weekly Gymboree class combines individual and group activities offering games, stimulation and equipment for each stage of development. Classes are designed for children, aged newborn through 4 years old, with a stimulating blend of activities from touch, language, and motor skills to socialization and play. The classes offer a nice way to socialize with other parents. Kindermusik often operates out of

---

BABY FRIENDLY RESTAURANTS

- **Bertucci's, all over Metro Boston:** Kids get fun stuff!
- **Doyle's, Jamaica Plain:** Secluded booths for nursing. (617) 524-2345.
- **Full Moon, Cambridge:** Excellent food; kids' play area! (617) 354-6699.
- **Johnny's Luncheonette, Newton Centre:** Lots of other families, fun decor, and good kids' menu. (617) 527-3223.
- **Papa Gino's, all over Metro Boston:** Good kids' menu and fun stuff!
- **S & S Deli, Cambridge:** Plenty of high chairs and super friendly staff. (617) 354-0777.
- **Watch City Brewing Co., Waltham:** Good kids' menu, fun stuff and kids eat free on Sundays! (781) 647-7000

INFANT STUDY CENTERS

Several graduate schools' programs research the growth and development of infants and toddlers, and are always looking for babies to participate in their studies. Studies often start early in infancy. The parent or caregiver remains with the child through the visit, which generally lasts 20-40 minutes. Your child will be exposed to different situations, depending on the research topic, and his or her reactions will be observed and recorded. Often they reimburse you for parking and can arrange child care for other children during the visit.

- **Boston University Infant Study Center**, Boston (617) 353-5449

- **M.I.T. Infant Cognition Lab**, Kendall Square, Cambridge (617) 253-3415

- **Tufts University Infant Development Laboratory**, Somerville (617) 627-3057

the same location as Gymboree, and offers music and movement classes for children 18 months to 7 years old, plus special infant/parent classes.

■ GYMFIT
(508) 651-3838
148 E. Central Street
Natick, MA 01760

GYMFIT provides movement and gymnastics programs to the families of the western suburbs. Each week you and your toddler, age 12 to 39 months, will explore the possibilities of body awareness and coordination through the use of tumbling and climbing equipment, hoops, balls, balance beams, rings and trampoline. Classes are divided into three age-based sections. Fall, winter, and spring sessions are 15 classes for $202.50, $5.00 for drop in.

■ MUSIC TOGETHER
Boston: (617) 783-9818
Locations also in Brookline, Dedham, Framingham, Newton, Watertown, Wellesley

Cambridge: (617) 868-2375
Locations also in W. Medford

Lexington and Concord:
(718) 861-6397

Parents and children, newborn through preschool, participate together in classes providing informal instruction through appropriate musical activities: song, dance, chant and finger and instrument play. Children may or may not participate as they choose, and they do so at their own developmental level. Parental involvement and listening to cassettes of class activities at home stimulate learning through the medium of play. Ten weekly 45-minute sessions cost $145, siblings are discounted to $110; siblings up to eight months attend free of charge.

■ POWERS MUSIC SCHOOL
(781) 484-4696
380 Concord Avenue
Belmont, MA 02178

In operation since 1962, this popular institution teaches music to adults as well as very young children. As early as 18 months and until he is 3 your child can enjoy a class called "Making Music Together" where parents and children explore songs, games and movement activities that stimulate the imagination while encouraging musical exploration. Fifteen classes cost $193. The school also offers Suzuki method instruction as well as a variety of musical lessons.

■ ROOM FOR CHILDREN
(617) 437-7997
105 Newbury Street
Boston, MA 02116

Room For Children offers a range of courses in movement, music and dance for children three months to 5 years. Toddler classes are grouped according to age. This two-year sequence of classes begins with early spatial awareness, moves into exploration of music and movement, continues with singing, and concludes with activities involving listening and language, motor skills and peer/social skills. They also offer Kindermusik classes. Twelve-week classes cost $229.

■ SUPERSTARTS
(781) 444-5496
46 Brentwood Circle
Needham, MA 02192

This program is devoted to introducing young children to the fine arts. In a warm and nurturing group setting parent and toddler (18 to 24 months) share age-appropriate art activities in a course called "ART Start," intended to involve your child's awareness of the world around him/her. Projects include many different stimulating materials and are designed to help your child develop his/her basic skills. Twelve week, 45-minute sessions cost $204, materials included.

INDOOR PLAYSPACES

Once your baby starts to crawl around and explore the world, entertaining activities can become more of a challenge, especially on days when the weather doesn't allow for an outside excursion. While the spaces differ, almost all provide ball pits, slides, tunnels, ramps, climbing structures, bright colors, music, and mirrors. Some have computer rooms and make-believe areas with play kitchens and dress up. Most have a separate area for infants and toddlers and comfortable seating for parents. All have changing facilities in the restrooms. Prices range from $3.50-$5.99 per child per day, with parents and non walkers usually admitted free. Annual passes range from $49-$100 per child. Concession-type food is available at snack bars. Hours vary by season.

- **Discovery Zone**, South Shore Plaza, Braintree, (781) 843-0700
- **Discovery Zone**, Route 1 South, Danvers, (978) 750-4141
- **Discovery Zone**, Sherwood Plaza, Route 9 East, Natick, (508) 651-0142
- **Kid's Playground**, 15 Normac Rd., Woburn, (781) 935-2300
- **Kids In Space**, 411 Waverly Oaks Rd., Waltham (781) 894-7012
- **Tot Stop**, 41 Foster St., Arlington, (781) 643-TOTS (8687), *Baby Pages* Web site: www.totstop.com

INDEX

A
Activity Classes (Boston)   418
Addiction   252
AIDS (Boston)   372, 375
Anencephaly   159
At-Risk Resources   252
Autism
   Boston Resources   371, 372
Au Pair Agencies   69, 284

B
Baby Carriers   105
Baby Food   148
Baby Products   80
   Reference Numbers   82
Bedrest   192
   Support Groups   211
Bereavement Resources   378
Birth Announcements   338
Birth Centers   26, 260, 262
Book Stores   330
Boston Family Life   393
Bottle Feeding   148
Bottles and Accessories   112
Breastfeeding   133, 257, 348
   Breast Pumps   349
   Life Experience   139
   Nursing Products   108
   Resources   137, 349

C
Caffeine Chart   21
Car Safety   357
Car Seats   83
   Tethers   84
Cerebral Palsy   375
Cesarean Births Q&A   51
Cesarean Section, Hints for Avoiding   49
Cesarean Support   271
Child Abuse   201
   Prevention Resources   392
Child Care   67, 275
   Choosing   66
   In-Home Agencies   281
   Licensing   69, 278
   Referral Agencies   277
   Resources   68, 289
   Tax Information   284
   Temporary and Sick   286
Child Care Resource and Referral
   Network   277, 286
Child Safety   150, 357
   Resources   153
Child Support Services   347
Childbirth Education   36
   Resources   38, 267
Childproofing Companies   354
Children's Clothing Stores   313
Children's Trust Fund   369, 385, 386, 394, 403
Circumcision
   Life Experience   341
   Resources   340
Classes   267
Cleft Palate, Cleft Lip   159, 373
Clubfoot   159
Colic   223
Community Health Centers   246
Connecting the Dots for Boston
   Tots   395
Consignment Stores   325
Cord Blood Options   272
Cost of College   291
CPR and First Aid Training   359
Cribs   89
   Crib Safety   91
   Portable Cribs   94
   Special Cribs   92
Crying   223
Cystic Fibrosis   159

D
Day Care (see Child Care)   70
Deafness, Congenital   159
Deliver, Where To   255
Department and Discount Stores   303
Development   222
Diapers and Diapering   115, 336
Diapers To Dormitories   291
Directory of Birthing Resources   245, 250, 265, 348
Disclosure Law   255
Doula, Finding a   250
Doula Life Experience   247

Doulas, Labor 16
Doulas, Postpartum 412
Down Syndrome 159, 374

E

Early Intervention Services 367, 385
Ensuring Your Baby's Health 19, 250
   At-Risk Resources 252
   Chemicals Which May Affect the Fetus 20
Exercise 33, 265

F

Family Activities 414
   Baby Friendly Restaurants 419
   Best Family Outings 418
   Boston's Best Baby Bargains 417
   Indoor Playspaces 422
Family and Medical Leave Act 60
Family Physician 11, 124, 240
Family Resource Center 367
Family Ties 368
Fathers' Support Resources 403
Federation for Children With Special Needs 368
Feeding Baby 147, 353
   Foods to Avoid 149
   Resources 353
Fetal Alcohol Syndrome 252, 372
Financial Assistance 352
FIRSTLink 346
FIRSTSteps 369
Food Stamp Benefits, Boston 353
Formula 147
Furnishings and Equipment 295

G

General Practitioner 11
Getting To Know Your Baby 222
Gift Ideas 119, 300
Goodstart Healthy Families 397
Grief, Coping With 173
   Boston Support Groups 378
   Miscarriage 175, 380
   Resources 178, 378
Growing Up Healthy 351

H

HBV Immunization 128, 344
Health Care For All 254, 346
Health Care Provider, Your Child's 122
   Checklist 123
Health Coverage 254, 346
Healthy Baby/Healthy Child 252
Healthy Families 386
Healthy Start 245, 250, 254, 347
Heart Defects 158
HIB Immunization 128, 344
High Chairs 102
Home Activities 222
Home Birth in Massachusetts 262
Homemade Baby Food 148
Hospital Choices 24, 255
Hospital Comparison Chart 258, 260
Hospital Stay 263
   48-Hour Law 263
   Self-Insured Plans 264
Hospital Stay, One Day or More? 30
Hospitals
   Cesarean Deliveries 25, 257
   Fetal Monitoring 25
   LDR 26, 256
   Security Precautions 27
   Short Stay 30
Hotlines 245, 253, 254, 347, 357, 358, 392
Hypospadias 159

I

Immunizations 127, 344
   Resources 130, 345
In-Home Child Care
   Tax Implications 69
Infant Massage 227
Infant Study Centers 420
Infertility 169
   Boston Infertility Programs 377
   Life Experience 166
   Resources 172, 376
Insurance 22
Internet
   Parenting Sites 213
IVF 166

Index

J
Jaundice 223

L
Labor Doulas 16
Labor Pain Relief 40
   Coping With Back Labor 42
Lactation Consultants 136, 348
Lead Poisoning Prevention 252, 355
Life Experiences
   Alicia 156
   Bedrest Blues . . . and Triumphs 189
   Birth, From A Doula's View 247
   Birth of a Book 235
   Camaraderie Makes the Difference 206
   Choosing to Stay Home 74
   In Remembrance of Sara 176
   Letter From A Dad, With Love 4
   Life as a Teen Parent 197
   Measure of Love, A 131
   More Than Blues 220
   My Baby's Premature Birth 182
   My Cesarean Birth 46
   Pacifier Pointers 145
   Perfect Baby, The 365
   Real Life With Baby 214
   Single Mother's Story, A 388
   Souvenir Pregnancy 28
   Stay-at-Home Dad 401
   Working at Home 65
   Yes, I'm Pregnant 166
   You Are My Sunshine 193
   You Can Work and Breastfeed 139
   Zen and the Art of Mothering 229
Lighter Side of Pregnancy 56
Local Products and Artists 334
Loss (see Grief)

M
Massachusetts Friends of Midwives 245, 246
Massachusetts Midwives Alliance 246, 262
MassHealth 254
Maternal Age Factors 7, 199
   "Older Mom," The 199, 398
   Teen Mothers 199
Maternal Health Coverage 254
Maternity Leave 60, 273
   Resources 62, 274, 345
Maternity Leave (Boston) 273
Maternity Leave Q&A 63
Maternity Statistics 255
Maternity Stores 300
Medical Pain Relief in Childbirth 43
   Epidurals 43
   General Anesthesia 44
Mental Retardation 158, 371, 373
Midwives 12, 243, 245, 246, 256
MMR Immunization 128
Multiple Birth Resources 196, 344
Multiple Birth Resources 194, 383

N
Nanny 69
   Agencies 71
Naturopathic Physicians 13
Newborn Home visiting 386
Newborn Screening Program, Massachusetts 340
NICU: Parent Support 378, 381
Nurse Practitioner 12
Nursing (see Breastfeeding) 137, 348
Nursing Products 108
Nutrition, Pregnancy 9, 250-251

O
Obstetrician 12, 240
Online Support 212
Ovulation Disorders 170

P
Pacifier Pros and Cons 144
Parent Organizations 410
Parenthood
   Vast Advantages of 231
Parenting Education 405
Parenting Support 393
   Fathers' Support 403
   Gay and Lesbian Support 404
Paternity Acknowledgment Program 390
Pediatrician
   Choosing 124, 339
   First Visit 126
   Interview Q&A 124
Perinatologist 12

Photographers   334
Physician's Assistant   12
Poisons   151
Portable Cribs   94
Postpartum Depression
   Life Experience   220
   Q&A   216
   Resources   219, 411
   Tips for Coping   217
Postpartum Help   412
Postpartum Planning   58
Practitioner
   Interviewing   13
   Resources   14, 239
Preconceptional Health Assessment   6
Pregnancy Discrimination Act   61
Pregnancy Nutrition   9, 250-251
Premature Infants   381
   Hospital Facilities   381
Premature Infants Q&A   184
Prenatal Health   250
Products, Local   334
Provider, Choosing Your   239
Provider Referrals   244
Provider Resources   245
Publications Offering Support   210
Pyloric Stenosis   159

R
Relationships
   Keeping Them Alive   204
Resale and Consignment Stores   325

S
Safety   150
   Bottle Feeding   148
   Resources   153, 357
Shop, Where to   293
   Malls   294
Shopping
   Children's Clothing Stores   313
   Department and Discount Stores   303
   Furnishings and Equipment   295
   Maternity Stores   300
   Resale and Consignment Stores   331
   Specialty Stores   331
   Toy and Book Stores   330
Shopping Smart for Your New Baby   78

SIDS   178, 378
SIDS Prevention Strategies   179
Single Parenting Life Experience   388
Single Parenting Resources   390
Sleep: Getting a Full Night's Rest
   Q&A   142
Special Concerns   363
Special Needs   156
   Child Care   368
   Diagnosis-Specific Resources   371
   Public Benefits   370, 371
   Resources   160, 367
Spina Bifida   159, 374
Staying In Shape   33, 265
Stores (see Shopping)
Strollers   98
Substance Abuse   252-254
Support Groups   208, 378, 393
Survival Strategies   361
Swings   96

T
Teen Mothers   199
Teen Pregnancy and Parenting
   Life Experience   197
   Resources   384
   Teen Living Programs   384
Temperament, Infant   220
Toy Stores   330
Twins
   Life Experience   193
   Resources   196, 383

W
WarmLines   280, 290, 400
WIC   251, 351, 353

THE BABY PAGES

- *Consumer information for the greater Boston area.*
- *Coupons are perforated for ease of area.*
- *Don't forget to let merchants know you found them through the Baby Resource Guide.*

The Baby Pages are separate from the editorial portion of this book. I'm Expecting was not paid for its editorial content of the book by participants in the Baby Pages. Nor does I'm Expecting endorse any of the merchants in this section.

PROTECT YOUR NANNY*™

Special Low Cost Health Insurance Program Now Available To Individuals Or Organizations To Offer Their Clients

The Official Insurance Representative of the International Nanny Association
*We also protect non-nannies

Call 617-964-4849 • 800-777-5765

Richard A. Eisenberg Associates
1340 Centre St., Suite 203, Newton, MA 02159

Nanny Taxes...

Nanitax, the payroll tax service preferred by more tax professionals. Client-friendly tax compliance and preparation services. Call today for service options.

1-800-NANITAX
Free On-Line Tax Calculations

http://www.4nannytaxes.com
Home/Work Solutions Inc., Sterling, VA 20165

European live-in child care

Experience the benefits of flexible, intercultural child care!

- English speaking au pairs with legal U.S visas
- Carefully screened and trained
- Just $230 per week, regardless of the number of children

For more information call:

1-800-333-6056

www.ef.com

EF AuPair
One Memorial Drive
Cambridge, MA 02142
email: aupair@ef.com

A goverment designated non-profit organization

CHARLES RIVER CHILDREN'S CENTER
508-653-6300
▲ Infant ▲ Toddler ▲ Preschool

SOUTH NATICK CHILDREN'S CENTER
508-655-6645
▲ Preschool

WESTWOOD CHILDREN'S CENTER
781-329-7766
▲ Infant ▲ Toddler ▲ Preschool

Afterschool, Inc.
Before/after school care, Kindergarten through 5th/6th grade. Open early release days, school vacation & snow days all year, 7 a.m.-6:15 p.m.

- ❖ Theatre, Sports, Art
- ❖ Computer Specialists
- ❖ Transportation Provided
- ❖ Optional Classes
- ❖ 7:00 a.m.-6:15 p.m.
- ❖ Summer Program

Framingham	508-872-6282
South Natick	508-650-1561
Sudbury	978-443-0074
Westwood	781-329-7775
Needham	781-444-5444

VISIT OFTEN — OUR INVENTORY CHANGES WEEKLY!

For Beautiful Bargains on Breastfeeding Fashions

Visit our Factory Outlet and save on fashionable dresses, shirts, and nursing bras designed for easy and discreet breastfeeding.

We carry first quality, irregular, and discontinued items — all at great prices.

NEW! Maternity clothes at bargain prices!

Motherwear's
FACTORY OUTLET

In the courtyard of the Cutlery Building
320 Riverside Drive • Northampton, MA
Call for directions: **(413) 586-2175**

OPEN THURS: 12-8, FRI & SAT: 10-4

A Country Inn For Families

Remember how wonderful it was going to a Country Inn before you had children! Now there is a Country Inn that has all the warm memories of yesteryear, but is also set up to host your whole family.

This 22 room inn, with 10 family suites, is located on over 500 acres and is only 3 hours from Boston.

In 1997 the Inn was acclaimed by Yankee Mag. as one of the best family inns in New England.

The Wildflower Inn

Darling Hill Road • Lyndonville, Vermont 05851 • 1-800-627-8314
Email : Wldflwrinn@aol.com • Web : www.pbpub.com/wldflwr.htm

THE BABY PLACE
FURNITURE & ACCESSORIES

FREE INNERSPRING MATTRESS WITH EVERY CRIB

The Complete Baby Store
Layette and Infants Clothing
50 Worcester Road (Route 9), Natick
on the Natick/Wellesley line

PHONES: (508) 653-0959 & (508) 655-5305
http://www.thebabyplace.com
OPEN: Monday through Saturday, 10:00-5:30
Wednesday & Thursday Eves 'til 8:30
Sunday, 12:00-5:00

WE LOVE BABIES WE LOVE BABIES WE LOVE BABIES

THREE LITTLE MONKEYS

Reading & Playing

The Mall at Chestnut Hill
199 Boylston Street
Chestnut Hill, MA 02167
617.558.8001

Hughes Photography
Needham, Ma.
(718) 444-9814
e-mail:HughesFoto@aol.com
Color
Black & White
Hand Coloring

"Specializing in Children"

WarmLines Parent Resources

A private, not-for-profit organization founded in 1978.

Connecting parents to each other and the information they need.

617-244-INFO

Community Services

- Child Care Referrals
- Drop-in Playgroups
- Preschool Guide
- Day Camp Referrals
- Matching Members
- New Moms Groups
- Speaker Series
- InfoLines Magazine
- Sitter Solutions
- Special Events

Corporate Services

- Child Care Resource and Referral Program
- Elder Care Resource and Referral Program
- Workplace Seminars on Work/Life Issues

Visit our Web Site: www.warmlines.org

Our breastpumps come with four women attached.

Sure, Dot, Sandra, Mary and Barbara rent and sell the best Medela equipment. But as board certified lactation consultants, they also stay with you every step of the way, from training to support. So, call when you need the very best care.

Lactation Care, inc.

MEDELA BREASTPUMP RENTALS • SALES
ALSO, CLASSES & CONSULTATION

♥ (617) 244-5593 ♥

Boston Baby Pages™   **431**

Your Newborn has a Precious Resource. Consider Banking It.™

Your newborn's umbilical cord blood is precious. Expectant parents around the country are choosing to save their newborn's cord blood as a type of "biological insurance" for their family's future. You have one opportunity to collect and preserve your baby's cord blood — at the time of birth. If preserved, cord blood may be used as an alternative to bone marrow in treating a variety of diseases and disorders.

Recognized as the leader in cord blood banking, Viacord provides the highest quality service and the most comprehensive care for families who choose to preserve their newborn's cord blood.

For additional information to help you evaluate this option for your family, call Viacord at **800-998-4226**.

VIACORD
The Premier Cord Blood Banking Service for Your Family's Future™

800-998-4226

Maternal Outreach, Inc.

Helping with the transition...

- *Private childbirth education classes*
- *Breastfeeding classes*
- *Lactation consultants*
- *Supplies for pregnant moms*
- *Breastpump rental and sales*
- *Essential breastfeeding supplies*
- *Nursing bras*
- *Baby Shower Registry*
- *Gift certificates*

*Home Care of Expectant Mom's, New Moms & Their Infants
Provided by RN's & Mother's Helpers*

Call or Visit us at... **Maternal Outreach, Inc.
(781) 340-9101**

63 Winter Street ❖ Weymouth, MA 02188

Curious George® Goes to WORDSWORTH

Books & Gifts for Children of All Ages

Every book discounted
(except textbooks)
open late
worldwide shipping

One JFK St., Cambridge, MA
617.498.0062 / fax 617.354.4064
www.wordsworth.com

Pregnant ??

Dress for Success...

Change your office attire monthly to fit your professional needs. Consider renting...
For the cost of a 2pc suit.....
...rent 5 suits...

Going Out...

Rent a dress for the weekend !

Newly purchased, stylish, quality, conservative apparel

Sarah Julian Maternity
1381 Washington Street
West Newton, MA 02165
(617) 558-1280 (Call for hours)

Nothing tastes as good as fresh milk from a glass bottle.

Nothing preserves the taste...nothing holds the cold quite like glass. And only Crescent Ridge delivers delicious milk — straight from our dairy to your door — in refillable, very chillable glass bottles.

And eggs...and cheeses...and ice cream...and breads...and bagels ...and frozen meats...and fresh-squeezed orange juice...and home-baked pies...and even Town Spa pizza... and much more.

So farm-fresh you'll swear you can hear the rooster crowing.

Delicious Crescent Ridge home-delivered dairy and other fine products. For over 65 years, fresh from the Parrish family to yours.

- **Fresh milk in returnable glass bottles!**
- **Variety of taste-tested foods!**
- **Home delivery saves you time and effort!**

Since 1932...
The Parrish Family
Crescent Ridge Dairy

Our cows are never given growth hormones.

Fresh...from the Parrish family to yours
In Massachusetts
1-800-660-2740

NANNY POPPINS INC.

A Full Service Nanny & Babysitting Agency

- Full & Part-time Nannies
- Babysitters on Call

- **Beverly**
  978 • 927 •1811
- **Boston**
  617 • 227 •KIDS
- **Marblehead**
  617 • 639 •0237

100 CUMMINGS CENTER, SUITE 311h
BEVERLY, MA 01915 • (978) 927-1811

BABY SPECIALTIES SUPER STORES

NEW ENGLAND'S LARGEST SELECTION OF BABY FURNITURE & ACCESSORIES!

Teen & Juvenile Furniture ■ Bunk Beds ■ Gifts

Complete lines of:
- RAGAZZI, PALI, SIMMONS
- CHILDCRAFT, VERMONT PRECISION
- PEREGO, COMBI, DUTAILIER
- CRIB 4 LIFE

Layaways and Delivery Available

DISCOUNT PRICES!
SUPER STORE SELECTION!
SPECIALITY STORE SERVICE!

(508) 653-2229
Rte. 9, SherwoodPlaza
Natick
Across from Natick Mall
Hours:
Mon. Tues. & Sat. 10-6,
Wed.-Fri .10-9, Sun. 12-5.

(508) 791-2599
700 Southbridge Street
Worcester
Exit 11 off I290
Hours:
Mon. & Tue. 10-6,
Wed.-Fri. 10-9, Sat.
10-5 Sun 12-5.

THE CHILDREN'S VILLAGE INC.

- Ages 10 weeks to 5 years
- Open Monday-Friday, 8 a.m.- 6 p.m.
- Qualified and experienced staff
- Developmentally appropriate curriculum
- Nutritious, warm lunches and snacks
- Large outdoor play area

Our staff believes in the individuality of each child.

Please call, Just Holm, Director
or Regina Mee, Assistant Director,
to arrange a tour, or for more information.
NAEYC - Accredited

The Children's Village Inc.
55 Wheeler Street *(near Fresh Pond Circle)*
Cambridge, MA 02138
(617) 492-1990

A PLACE TO GROW
"We take care of families"

- ♥ Infants
- ♥ Toddlers
- ♥ Pre-school
- ♥ After school

Hudson
(978) 562-4428
127 Forest Ave.

Stratton School
Arlington
(781) 646-6021
180 Mountain Ave.

Bedford
(781) 271-9847
402 Concord Rd.

Belmont
(617) 489-4240
259 Beech St.

Concord
(978) 371-9660
235 Sudbury Rd.

Arlington
(781) 646-7689
118 Pleasant St.

AM-PM Medical Supplies

featuring

QUALITY PRE & POSTPARTUM PRODUCTS

- ❖ Fine Maternity Lingerie & Support Stockings
- ❖ Breast Pumps—Medela & Ameda Egnell
- ❖ Special Back Supports for Pregnancy
- ❖ Baby Carriers
- ❖ Thermometer Pacifiers, Vaporizers, and European Baby Products

VISIT OUR CONVENIENT LOCATIONS:

BRIGHTON—*1577 Commonwealth Avenue,* (617) 562-4400
LYNN—*110 Broad Street,* (781) 593-8300
FRAMINGHAM—*20-22 Union Street,* (508) 620-8811

We'll Do The Homework So You Can Afford College Costs.

We Can Help You Achieve Your Financial Goal.

It takes more than a summer job to cover college costs — it requires careful planning. At American Express Financial Advisors, we have the tools and the experience to help your family's dreams a reality. No matter what your financial goal is, we can help. To get started, give us a call today.

Financial Advisors

American Express Financial Advisors Inc.
Paul Derbyshire
Personal Financial Advisor / Registered Representative
American Express Financial Advisors Inc.
25 Braintree Hill Park, Suite 301
P.O. Box 9154
Braintree, MA 02184
Tel: **(617) 849-0980 ext. 151**
Fax: **(617) 848-3617**

© 1996 American Express Financial Corporation

Yes. I would like to meet with an American Express financial advisor for a free consultation.

Name _____

Address _____

City _____ State _____ Zip _____

Phone _____

Mail to: **American Express Financial Advisors Inc.**
P.O. Box 9154
Braintree, MA 02184

WHEN YOU'RE PREGNANT
CONNECT
1 (800) 531-BABY
(2229)

YOUR BABY
DESERVES
A HEALTHY
START

BABIES COUNT IN BOSTON

THE BOSTON HEALTHY START INITIATIVE

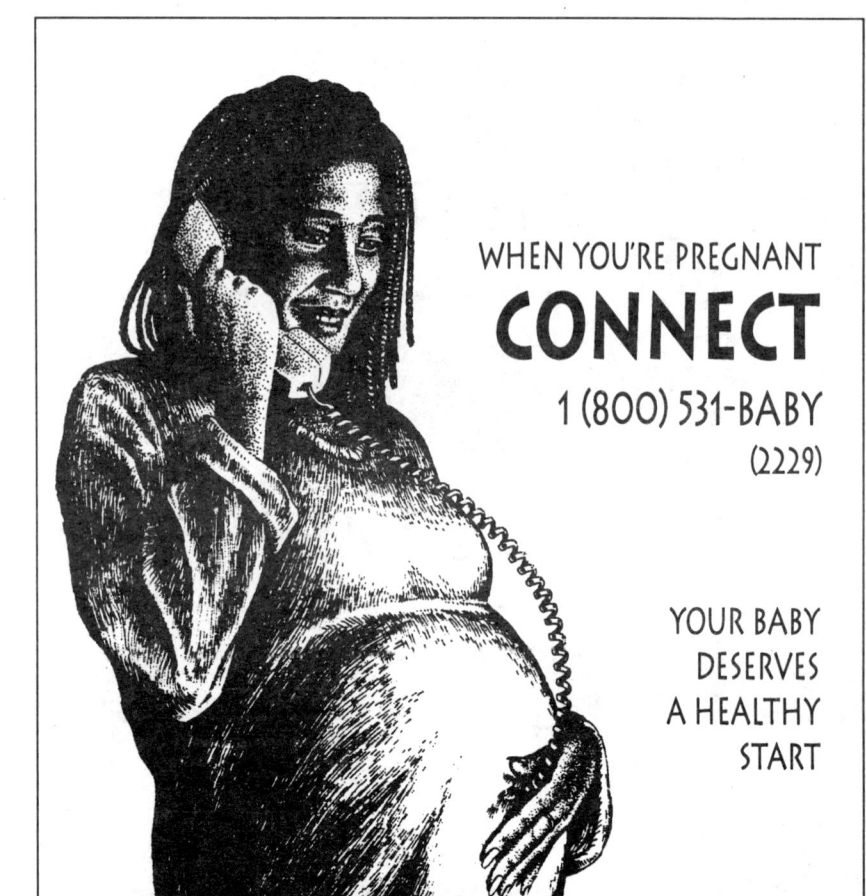

In Partnership with the

Boston Public Health Commission

MOUNT AUBURN MIDWIFERY ASSOCIATES- THE BEST OF BOTH WORLDS.

**Skilled Care.
Personal Attention.**
*Get The Best Of Both Worlds
During Your Pregnancy,
Labor And Childbirth.*

Our board-certified nurse-midwives offer a family-centered experience that is supportive of your individual needs and preferences. Working with Mount Auburn Hospital obstetricians and gynecologists, our midwives offer a full range of services, including:

- *Prenatal and Postpartum Care,*
- *Individualized Birthing Options at the BirthPlace at Mount Auburn Hospital,*
- *Childbirth Classes,*
- *Routine Gynecologic Care, including Breast Exams and Pap Tests,*
- *Family Planning Services.*

Get the skilled care and personal attention that you need from Mount Auburn Midwifery Associates. For a free, informative visit, call us at **(617) 499-5141**. For your convenience, we accept most major forms of insurance.

MOUNT AUBURN HOSPITAL
A founding hospital of CAREGROUP

Phyllis Gorman, C.N.M.
Director of Midwifery Services

Marcia Snyder, C.N.M.

Pam Faulkner, C.N.M.

Patricia Callahan, C.N.M.

Laura Emmons, C.N.M.

MOUNT AUBURN MIDWIFERY ASSOCIATES
330 Mount Auburn Street, Cambridge, MA 02138 (617) 499-5141
Other office locations in Arlington, Cambridge, Lexington, and Somerville.

Boston's Biggest Baby Faire

Presented by **TOYS "R" US**
April 4 & 5, 1998
Saturday 9 am-5 pm
Sunday 10 am-5 pm
Bayside Expo Center

ALL THE BIGGEST NAMES IN BABY AND TODDLER CARE UNDER ONE ROOF!

NEW PRODUCT DEBUTS

FREE AMERICAN BABY GROUP WELCOME BAGS FOR EVERY FAMILY

FREE PRODUCT SAMPLES

PLAY AREAS AND DAY-LONG ENTERTAINMENT FOR KIDS

Adults $7 • Children FREE (with an adult)

$2 DISCOUNT COUPONS AVAILABLE AT ALL AREA **TOYS "R" US** STORES
For information call (781) 395-KISS (Press ext. BABY)
For 1999 Boston Baby Faire dates, please call (781) 729-4500

Raising a child is a big job. Let us help.

Software for new and expectant parents offers just the help you need.

We can't change diapers for you, but if you have a personal computer, you now have access to a wealth of help and advice on pregnancy, child-raising, and more.

5,123 Baby Names and Baby Bits, Jr. are just two of the 20 parenting titles you can choose from.

Find us at Baby Stores Nationwide

To locate the store nearest you, call 1-888-449-8084. Or visit our web site at www.daxinnovations.com

DAX is proud to support the SIDS (Sudden Infant Death Syndrome) Alliance.

DAX INNOVATIONS
www.daxinnovations.com

BOSTON BABY HAS THE MOST COMPLETE SELECTION OF BABY & TEEN FURNITURE IN NEW ENGLAND!

- VERMONT TUBBS
- Emmaljunga
- Silver Cross
- VERMONT PRECISION WOODWORKS
- Aprica
- Morigeau
- SIMMONS Juvenile Products Company, Inc.
- LEGACY
- COMBI
- child craft
- Peg Perego

NOBODY HAS INVENTORY LIKE BOSTON BABY!

DON'T FORGET ABOUT UNCLE MIKEY'S BABY DATE CONTEST! YOUR BABY COULD WIN YOU $500!

OVER 1,000 CRIBS IN STOCK FOR IMMEDIATE DELIVERY!

Uncle Mikey

At Boston Baby... "Little Things Count The Most!"

BOSTON BABY SUPERSTORES
Beds n' Bunks too!

NEWTON
30 Tower Rd.
(617) 332-1400

HINGHAM
Hingham Plaza
(781) 749-5770

AVON
Christmas Tree Plaza
(508) 559-1400

DANVERS
Danvers Crossing,
Behind Circuit City
(978) 777-1414

(Avon & Danvers Open Sunday 12-5)

Fun for the whole family!

Call 800-241-1848 for a free brochure!

BABY JOGGER
www.babyjogger.com
P.O. Box 2189
Yakima, WA 98907

Ask about our safe Bumpa Bed crib mattress!

New!

INTRODUCING...
www.thebabyguide.com

THE WEBSITE CREATED FOR PARENTS-TO-BE!

- For continuous updates of the latest 'Baby' information.
- For local and national resources...as they become available.
- To find out where to purchase Baby Guides for other areas.

THE BABY RESOURCE GUIDE
http://www.thebabyguide.com

Diaper Genie® puts an end to diaper odor.

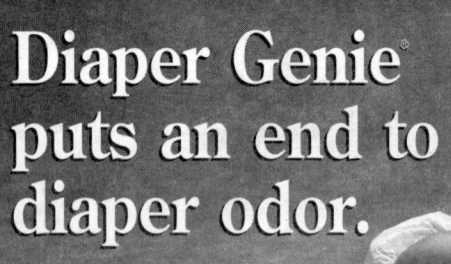

Easy as A, B, C...

Diaper Genie® makes it easy to individually seal away diapers for maximum odor control. The wide opening handles the largest diapers, and the convenient size means it now holds up to 25 diapers at a time. And it's so easy. Just put in a diaper, turn the twist rim to seal, and close the lid. Diaper Genie works only with the wide, **blue** Diaper Genie refills, which wrap up to 180 newborn diapers each.

A
Convenient
Holds up to 25 diapers

B
Wide Opening
Handles the largest diapers

C
Easy
Operates with one hand

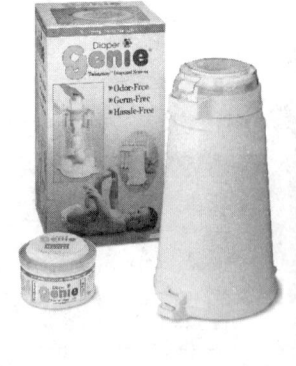

Full Lifetime Warranty

© 1998 Mondial Industries, Limited   Streetsboro, Ohio, USA

Diaper Genie®

Odor-Free. Germ-Free. Hassle-Free.

Chinook Outdoor Adventure
(617) 776-8616
93 Holland Street
Davis Square
Somerville, MA 02144
Hours:
- M-F 11-7
- Sat. 10-6
- Sun. 12-5

Clothing, gifts and gear for little adventurers—and their parents too!

CHINOOK
Outdoor Adventure

15% Off any In-Stock Chinook Fleece Products

Specializing in custom fleece products for babies, kids, & adults...

BOSTON BABY PAGES™

The Baby Place
(508) 653-0959 or (508) 655-5305
50 Worcester Rd. (Rt. 9)
Natick on the Natick Wellesley line
http://www.thebabyplace.com

- Baby Registry & Gift Certificates, Layaway
- All Cribs Include Free Innerspring Matress

The Complete Baby Store

10% OFF CRIB BEDDING
with crib purchase

THE BABY PLACE
FURNITURE & ACCESSORIES

The Largest Selection of Crib Bedding in New England

- Baby Registry
- Gift Certificates
- Layaway

BOSTON BABY PAGES™

Nature Springs Water Co.
800-649-5972 or (781) 449-5972

Nature's purest drinking water from the deep mountain springs of Vermont.

PURE WATER FOR... YOU & YOUR BABY!

VERMONT PURE NATURAL SPRING WATER

NATURE SPRINGS WATER CO.

Receive a..... FREE*

▲ 2 Five Gallon Bottles
▲ One Month Cooler Rental
▲ Delivery *($25.00 Value)*

CALL **800-649-5972** TODAY!
*FREE with 1 year contract, or $25 service fee applies

BOSTON BABY PAGES™

CHINOOK
Outdoor Adventure

15% Off any In-Stock Chinook Fleece Products

Specializing in custom fleece products for babies, kids, & adults...

Not good with any other offer. One coupon per customer.

Chinook Outdoor Adventure
(617) 776-8616
93 Holland Street
Davis Square
Somerville, MA 02144
Hours:
  M-F 11-7
  Sat. 10-6
  Sun. 12-5

Clothing, gifts and gear for little adventurers— and their parents too!

10% OFF CRIB BEDDING
with crib purchase

Valid thru 11-1-98

coupon must be presented at the time of purchase.
Only one coupon per customer
Coupon not valid on Sale Bedding or Custom Bedding.

Not good with any other offer. One coupon per customer.

The Baby Place
(508) 653-0959 or
(508) 655-5305
50 Worcester Rd. (Rt. 9)
Natick on the Natick Wellesley line
http://www.thebabyplace.com

- Baby Registry & Gift Certificates, Layaway
- All Cribs Include Free Innerspring Matress

The Complete Baby Store

PURE WATER FOR... YOU & YOUR BABY!

VERMONT PURE NATURAL SPRING WATER

NATURE SPRINGS WATER CO.

- ▲ Sodium Free
- ▲ 100% Bacteria Free
- ▲ No Additives
- ▲ No Purifiers
- ▲ No Filtering

Not good with any other offer. One coupon per customer.

Nature Springs Water Co.
800-649-5972
or (781) 449-5972

Nature's purest drinking water from the deep mountain springs of Vermont.

New England Cord Blood Bank, Inc.
888-700-CORD (2673)
or (617) 262-5612
665 Beacon Street
Suite 302
Boston, MA 02215-3202
Hours:
  M-F 8 a.m.-5 p.m.

See the section on Umbilical Cord Blood Banking to find out more about New England Cord Blood Bank, Inc.

New England Cord Blood Bank

$50 Off
Laboratory Processing Fee

Cord Blood Banking: A Life-Saving Choice℠

1 888 700-CORD (2673)
Offer Valid Without Coupon

BOSTON BABY PAGES™

WarmLines Parent Resources
(617) 244-INFO
206 Waltham Street
West Newton, MA 02165
http://www.warmlines.org

Connecting parents to each other and the information they need.
🍃 *See Chapter 2, Child Care Referral Agencies, and Chapter 6, Parenting Support Groups, to learn more about WarmLines.*

WarmLines
PARENT RESOURCES

A private, not-for-profit organization founded in 1978

10% off new membership
(617) 244-INFO

BOSTON BABY PAGES™

Tot Stop
(781) 643-8687
41 Foster Street
Arlington, MA
Hours: Mon.-Sat.,
    9:30 a.m.-5:30 p.m.
    Friday until 8:00 p.m.
▲ *"1998 Parents' Paper Family Favorite Award"*
▲ *Best infant toddler area*
▲ *Indoor beach*
▲ *Best place in Boston for "under 6" birthday parties*
▲ *http://www.totstop.com*

YOUR CHILD'S FIRST PLAYGROUND

Tot Stop — Where The Little Kids Play!

Meet New Parents

Always... FREE Admission for Babies Under 6 Months
Good for—ONE FREE ADMISSION

BOSTON BABY PAGES™

NECBB, Inc. Facts:

> Laboratory established in 1982
> Based in Boston
> Bank is company owned and operated
> Stem cells prepared and stored
> Affordable

New England Cord Blood Bank, Inc., provides a quality, accessible banking service for those families interested in long-term storage of umbilical cord blood stem cells. Umbilical cord blood stem cells can be used in treating life-threatening diseases.

Not good with any other offer. One coupon per customer.

New England Cord Blood Bank, Inc.
888-700-CORD (2673)
or (617) 262-5612
665 Beacon Street
Suite 302
Boston, MA 02215-3202
Hours:
    M-F 8 a.m.-5 p.m.

See the section on Umbilical Cord Blood Banking to find out more about New England Cord Blood Bank, Inc.

WarmLines
PARENT RESOURCES

A private, not-for-profit organization founded in 1978

10% off new membership
(617) 244-INFO

Not good with any other offer. One coupon per customer.

WarmLines Parent Resources
(617) 244-INFO
206 Waltham Street
West Newton, MA 02165
http://www.warmlines.org

Connecting parents to each other and the information they need.
See Chapter 2, Child Care Referral Agencies, and Chapter 6, Parenting Support Groups, to learn more about WarmLines.

YOUR CHILD'S FIRST PLAYGROUND

Tot Stop
Where The Little Kids Play!

COME VISIT US
41 Foster Street
Arlington, MA
(781) 643-8687
http://www.totstop.com

Good for—ONE FREE ADMISSION

Not good with any other offer. One coupon per customer.

Tot Stop
(781) 643-8687
41 Foster Street
Arlington, MA
Hours: Mon.-Sat.,
    9:30 a.m.-5:30 p.m.
    Friday until 8:00 p.m.
▲ *"1998 Parents' Paper Family Favorite Award"*
▲ *Best infant toddler area*
▲ *Indoor beach*
▲ *Best place in Boston for "under 6" birthday parties*
▲ *http://www.totstop.com*

CHILDREN'S ORCHARD
(888) 5-RESALE
for the location nearest you or franchise information

🐦 *14 stores in MA over 70 nationwide*

New and gently used clothing, toys, books, baby equipment, furniture and accessories.

$3 Off Small Stuff.

We carry loads of new and gently used kids' stuff for infants through size 8, but our prices only go from teeny tiny to extra small

(888) 5-RESALE
for the location nearest you

on purchase over $10. Not valid with any other offer. Please present this coupon with purchase.

CHILDREN'S ORCHARD
We Pay Cash for Gently Used Kids Stuff

Streamline Inc.
(781) 320-1900
27 Dartmouth Street
Westwood, MA 02090

Hours:
Mon. - Thurs. 8 a.m-midnight
Fri. 8 a.m.-5 p.m.
Sun. 3:30 p.m.-midnight

See the business reply card on the last page for more information

---

streamline®

Home Shopping & Delivery

$30.00 Off

Your First Week's Order

MAKING LIFE A LITTLE SIMPLER

BOSTON BABY PAGES™

Animal, Vegetable, Mineral
(617) 547-2404
2400 Massachusetts Ave.
Cambridge, MA 02140

Hours:
Mon. & Tue. 10:15-5:30
Wed.-Sat. 10:15-6:00
Sun. 12:00-4:00

Gifts for all ages... and, the BEST source for creative toys.

ANIMAL VEGETABLE • MINERAL

2400 Massachusetts Ave. Cambridge, MA 02140
(617) 547-2404

★ **$5.00 OFF** ★
$10 or more

NATURE & WHIMSEY FOR MOM & BABY

- Infant Toys and Mobiles
- Folkmanis Puppets
- Polar Fleece
- Handmade Soaps
- Camille Beckman Lotions
- Aromatherapy Candles

BOSTON BABY PAGES™

$3 Off Small Stuff.

We carry loads of new and gently used kids stuff for infants through size 8, but our prices only go from teeny tiny to extra small

(888) 5-RESALE
for the location nearest you

on purchase over $10. Not valid with any other offer. Please present this coupon with purchase.

CHILDREN'S ORCHARD
We Pay Cash for Gently Used Kids Stuff

CHILDREN'S ORCHARD
(888) 5-RESALE
for the location nearest you or franchise information

🌿 *14 stores in MA over 70 nationwide*

New and gently used clothing, toys, books, baby equipment, furniture and accessories.

---

streamline®

Home Shopping & Delivery

$30⁰⁰ Off

Your First Week's Order

Making Life a Little Simpler

Not good with any other offer. One coupon per customer.

Streamline Inc.
(781) 320-1900
27 Dartmouth Street
Westwood, MA 02090

Hours:
Mon. - Thurs. 8 a.m-midnight
Fri. 8 a.m.-5 p.m.
Sun. 3:30 p.m.-midnight

See the business reply card on the last page for more information

---

ANIMAL VEGETABLE • MINERAL

2400 Massachusetts Ave. Cambridge, MA 02140
(617) 547-2404

★ **$5.00 OFF** ★
$10 or more

Nature & Whimsey For Mom & Baby

- Infant Toys and Mobiles
- Folkmanis Puppets
- Polar Fleece
- Handmade Soaps
- Camille Beckman Lotions
- Aromatherapy Candles

Not good with any other offer. One coupon per customer.

Animal, Vegetable, Mineral
(617) 547-2404
2400 Massachusetts Ave.
Cambridge, MA 02140

Hours:
Mon. & Tue. 10:15-5:30
Wed.-Sat. 10:15-6:00
Sun. 12:00-4:00

Gifts for all ages... and, the BEST source for creative toys.

Susan Van Meter
(978) 975-2489
4 Arlitt Court
Lawrence, MA 01841

A Birth Doula to warmly guide you and your family through the childbearing process.

ΔΟΥΛΑΣ
DOULAS

For Professional Labor Support

Susan Van Meter
Birth Doula   978/975-2489

Save 10% off fee with this coupon

BOSTON BABY PAGES™

VIACORD
800-998-4226
551 Boylston Street
Suite 40
Boston, MA 02116

VIACORD—The Leader in Cord Blood Banking Service ™

VIACORD

Receive Your First Year Annual Storage Fee — FREE

800-998-4226

BOSTON BABY PAGES™

Lambert's Rainbow Fruit
Dorchester
  777 Morrissey Blvd.
  (617) 436-2997
Westwood
  220 Providence Hwy.
  (781) 326-5047
Brockton
  826 Crescent St.
  (508) 580-2736

Hours:
  Mon.-Sat. 7 a.m.-9 p.m.
  Sun. 7 a.m.-6 p.m.

Preferred 10% Off Customer

LAMBERT'S RAINBOW·FRUIT

■ Dorchester
777 Morrissey Blvd.
(617) 436-2997 / (617) 436-3091

■ Westwood
220 Providence Hwy.
(781) 326-5047
(781) 329-7400

■ Brockton
826 Crescent St.
(508) 580-2736
(508) 588-4099

Receive discount each time you shop ❖ Please present card before order is rung-up ❖ Offer excludes speciality, sale, and reduced items

BOSTON BABY PAGES™

ΔΟΥΛΑΣ DOULAS
For Professional Labor Support

Two prenatal visits; two postpartum visits, labor support in your home (if desired), flat fee regardless of length of labor, experienced La Leche League Leader, certified doula (NACA).

Contact me today for additional information!

978/975-2489

e-mail jodyvm@ix.netcom.com

Not good with any other offer. One coupon per customer.

Susan Van Meter
(978) 975-2489
4 Arlitt Court
Lawrence, MA 01841

A Birth Doula to warmly guide you and your family through the childbearing process.

VIACORD

Receive Your First Year Annual Storage Fee — FREE

800-998-4226

Not good with any other offer. One coupon per customer.

VIACORD
800-998-4226
551 Boylston Street
Suite 40
Boston, MA 02116

VIACORD—The Leader in Cord Blood Banking Service ™

LAMBERT'S RAINBOW • FRUIT

Not good with any other offer. One coupon per customer.

Lambert's Rainbow Fruit
Dorchester
  777 Morrissey Blvd.
  (617) 436-2997
Westwood
  220 Providence Hwy.
  (781) 326-5047
Brockton
  826 Crescent St.
  (508) 580-2736

Hours:
  Mon.-Sat. 7 a.m.-9 p.m.
  Sun. 7 a.m.-6 p.m.

Boston Baby Pages™   449

Stork Time
(617) 969-5930
1015 Boylston Street
Route 9
Newton, MA 02161

Hours:
   Mon.-Sat. 10 a.m.-5 p.m

See the store section to read more about this unique, discounted maternity store.

STORK TIME
Discounted Brand Name Maternity

1015 Boylston Street, Route 9, Newton

Receive a Complimentary Dress Clip with any $25.00 purchase!

(617) 969-5930

BOSTON BABY PAGES™

Maternal Outreach, Inc.
(781) 340-9101
63 Winter Street
Weymouth, MA 02188

- *Boutique Hours:*
Mon.-Fri. 9 a.m.-5 p.m.
Sat. 10 a.m.-1 p.m.
- *Office Hours:*
Mon.-Fri. 9 a.m.-5 p.m.
Sat. 10 a.m.-1 p.m.

Helping with the transition.

Maternal Outreach, Inc.

Supplies and services for pregnant and new moms

- Breastpump rental and sales
- Breastfeeding supplies
- Supplies for pregnant moms

10% OFF ...any item in the boutique

One FREE hour of mothers' helper service with the purchase of four hours or more

BOSTON BABY PAGES™

Debbie Bermudes, OTR/L, CIMI
(781) 646-4797
22 Linwood Street
Arlington, MA 02174-6622

Infant Massage benefits your baby, and you...

~Infant Massage~

a parent education program that empowers parents and fosters respect for children

10% off
regular course fee

See Reverse Side for Benefits

BOSTON BABY PAGES™

Stork Time
(617) 969-5930
1015 Boylston Street
Route 9
Newton, MA 02161

Hours:
　Mon.-Sat. 10 a.m.-5 p.m.

See the store section to read more about this unique, discounted maternity store.

STORK TIME
Discounted Brand Name Maternity

1015 Boylston Street, Route 9, Newton

Receive a Complimentary Dress Clip with any $25⁰⁰ purchase!

(617) 969-5930

Not good with any other offer. One coupon per customer.

Maternal Outreach, Inc.
(781) 340-9101
63 Winter Street
Weymouth, MA 02188

- Boutique Hours:
  Mon.-Fri. 9 a.m.-5 p.m.
  Sat. 10 a.m.-1 p.m.
- Office Hours:
  Mon.-Fri. 9 a.m.-5 p.m.
  Sat. 10 a.m.-1 p.m.

Helping with the transition.

Maternal Outreach, Inc.
Supplies and services for pregnant and new moms
- ❖ Breastpump rental and sales
- ❖ Breastfeeding supplies
- ❖ Supplies for pregnant moms

10% OFF...any item in the boutique

One FREE hour of mothers' helper service with the purchase of four hours or more

Not good with any other offer. One coupon per customer.

Debbie Bermudes, OTR/L, CIMI
(781) 646-4797
22 Linwood Street
Arlington, MA 02174-6622

Infant Massage benefits your baby, and you...

Infant Massage benefits both your baby *and* you by.......

...promoting communication and bonding;

...helping to relieve symptoms of gas and colic;

...contributing to deeper, more restful sleep.

10% off
regular course fee

Debbie Bermudes OTR/L, CIMI

Not good with any other offer. One coupon per customer.

Mount Auburn Midwifery Associates
(617) 499-5141
330 Mount Auburn St.
Cambridge, MA 02138

☞ *Other office locations in Arlington, Cambridge, Lexington, and Somerville*

MOUNT AUBURN MIDWIFERY ASSOCIATES

330 Mount Auburn Street • Cambridge, MA 02138

For a free, informative visit, please call us at

(617) 499-5141

Other office locations in Arlington, Cambridge, Lexington, and Somerville.

MOUNT AUBURN HOSPITAL
A founding hospital of CAREGROUP

BOSTON BABY PAGES™

Music Together of Boston, Inc.
(617) 783-9818
5 Bigelow Street
Brighton, MA 02135

Hours:
Classes Mon. through Sat. mornings & afternoons

Locations in Boston, Brookline, Dedham, Framingham, Newton, Watertown & Wellesley

MUSIC & MOVEMENT CLASSES

$10 OFF TUITION

Infants, Toddlers & Preschoolers Enjoy Song & Rhythm with the Participation of Parents, Grandparents or Caregivers

BOSTON BABY PAGES™

Baby Specialties Super Stores

☞ **Worcester**
(508) 791-2599
700 Southbridge Street
Hours: Mon. & Tue. 10-6,
Wed.-Fri. 10-9
Sat. 10-5, Sun 12-5.

☞ **Natick**
(508) 653-BABY (2229)
1276 Worcester Road
Rt. 9 East
Hours: Mon., Tue. & Sat. 10-6
Wed.-Fri.10-9, Sun. 12-5

SAVE $20.00

ON MATCHING OTTOMAN WITH PURCHASE OF GLIDER
OVER 50 FABRIC SELECTIONS AVAILABLE

BABY SPECIALTIES SUPER STORES

Not valid with any other offers—with coupon only
Layaway not available on sale items
Please present coupon at time of purchase—one coupon per item

BOSTON BABY PAGES™

MOUNT AUBURN MIDWIFERY ASSOCIATES

330 Mount Auburn Street • Cambridge, MA 02138

For a free, informative visit, please call us at

(617) 499-5141

Other office locations in Arlington, Cambridge, Lexington, and Somerville.

MOUNT AUBURN HOSPITAL
A founding hospital of CAREGROUP

Not good with any other offer. One coupon per customer.

Mount Auburn Midwifery Associates
(617) 499-5141
330 Mount Auburn St.
Cambridge, MA 02138

Other office locations in Arlington, Cambridge, Lexington, and Somerville

---

Music & Movement

For Newborns—4 year-olds and their parents or Caregivers.

SONGS! INSTRUMENT PLAY! DANCING & MOVEMENT! FINGER PLAYS! CASSETTE & SONGBOOK! PARENT EDUCATION!

Regardless of your own musical ability you can help nuture the musical growth of your child. Experience MUSIC TOGETHER and see how much fun your role can be!

Not good with any other offer. One coupon per customer.

Music Together of Boston, Inc.
(617) 783-9818
5 Bigelow Street
Brighton, MA 02135

Hours:
Classes Mon. through Sat. mornings & afternoons

Locations in Boston, Brookline, Dedham, Framingham, Newton, Watertown & Wellesley

---

$50.00 OFF
DUTAILIER GLIDER WITH $1000.00 NURSERY PURCHASE
(MUST BE DONE AT TIME OF FURNITURE PURCHASE)

BABY SPECIALTIES SUPER STORES

Not valid with any other offers—with coupon only
Layaway not available on sale items
Please present coupon at time of purchase—
one coupon per item

Not good with any other offer. One coupon per customer.

Baby Specialties Super Stores

Worcester
(508) 791-2599
700 Southbridge Street
Hours: Mon. & Tue. 10-6,
Wed.-Fri. 10-9
Sat. 10-5, Sun 12-5.

Natick
(508) 653-BABY (2229)
1276 Worcester Road
Rt. 9 East
Hours: Mon., Tue. & Sat. 10-6
Wed.-Fri. 10-9, Sun. 12-5

Boston Baby Pages™   453

MotherCare Services, Inc.
888-MY-DOULA
(693-6852) or
(617) 545-1500
15 Bayberry Road
Scituate, MA 02066

New England's first postpartum home care service. Specializing in the practical care and well being of the entire family.
Gives your family time to count the sheep.

NEW BABIES & THEIR PARENTS NEED ATTENTION...

...LOVE & LOTS OF SLEEP

$25 OFF — One Weeks Services
Call Toll Free...888-MY-DOULA

BOSTON BABY PAGES™

Gymboree Play Program
(978) 531-5420
Melrose, Peabody
(781) 647-3371
Newton, Framingham, Watertown, West Roxbury, Wellesley

Weekday and Saturday classes. See the family activities section to learn more about Gymboree!

GYMBOREE
PLAY PROGRAMS

2 FREE introductory classes for parents and their infants
for families new to Gymboree
a $20.00 value
The internationally renowned developmental play program since 1976

BOSTON BABY PAGES™

Material Things
(508) 829-4637
1 Moscow Road
Holden, MA 01522
Hours:
   Mon.-Fri. 10 a.m.-5 p.m.

Home of Kangaroo Pouches™ Originally designed and created by Material Things. See our local products section for more information.
Make your child's room different from any other!

KANGAROO POUCHES™
ready made & custom orders available

by MATERIAL THINGS
Children's Window Treatments and Accessories

20% OFF all custom orders

BOSTON BABY PAGES™

MotherCare Service Provides

- *A prenatal visit between you and your caregiver*
- *Guidance as you adjust to becoming new parents*
- *Mother and Newborn care instruction*
- *Breastfeeding support*
- *Special care for siblings*
- *Grocery shopping and meal preparation*
- *Laundry and household assistance*
- *A FREE postpartum resource directory*

Not good with any other offer. One coupon per customer.

MotherCare Services, Inc.
888-MY-DOULA
(693-6852) or
(617) 545-1500
15 Bayberry Road
Scituate, MA 02066

New England's first postpartum home care service. Specializing in the practical care and well being of the entire family.
Gives your family time to count the sheep.

CradleGym: birth to four months
- Support, camaraderie and resources to help you cope with the demands of a newborn.
- Gentle music, movement and age-appropriate games that make it easy for you and your baby to bond through play.

BabyGym: three to twelve months
- Lively parent discussion offers valuable insights and information on a wide range of parenting topics.
- Exciting equipment, musical "Baby Boogies" and games that inspire a love of music and play while building coordination, motor and balance skills.

Not good with any other offer. One coupon per customer.

Gymboree Play Program
(978) 531-5420
Melrose, Peabody
(781) 647-3371
Newton, Framingham, Watertown, West Roxbury, Wellesley

Weekday and Saturday classes. See the family activities section to learn more about Gymboree!

20% OFF all custom orders

Not good with any other offer. One coupon per customer.

Material Things
(508) 829-4637
1 Moscow Road
Holden, MA 01522
Hours:
  Mon.-Fri. 10 a.m.-5 p.m.

Home of Kangaroo Pouches™. Originally designed and created by Material Things. See our local products section for more information.
Make your child's room different from any other!

Boston Baby Pages™ 455

Beach 'N' Sport Caddie™
(617) 332-8382
S.T.A.R. Enterprises, Inc.
Newton, MA

🍃 *to order*
 1-800-378-7198

🍃 *The Ultimate Recreation Cart.*

Beach 'n' **Sport** Caddie™

New!

Only $99.00
Special Order Price

FREE! Beach Bag
with every Caddie purchase
when you mention this coupon!

- Transports items easily
- Converts into a table top
- Fits into car trunk
- Rugged construction
- All terrain
- Proudly made in the USA

To Order: 1-800-378-7198
Free Brochure: 617-332-8382
Visit our web site at: www.channel1.com/users/timeink/bc.html

---

Lactation Care, Inc.
(617) 244-5593
25 Fisher Avenue
Newton, MA 02161

Hours:
  Mon.-Fri. 9-5:30
  Saturday 9-1
  (*urgent care available evenings*)

See our advertisement for additional information.

Lactation Care, inc.

will assist you with all your breastfeeding needs.

- Prenatal breastfeeding classes • Private consultations with board-certified lactation consultants • Medela breastpump rentals and sales with telephone support
- Breastfeeding pillows
- Return-to-work classes

$5 off any purchase over $20

Mon to Fri, 9 - 5:30 & Sat 9 - 1
Urgent care available evenings.

617 244-5593

Mother Child Center For Fitness & Wellbeing Jenkyns Physical Therapy
(617) 864-4225
Mailing address:
121 Reed Street
Cambridge, MA 02140

🍃 *Classes are held in Arlington, MA. Call for more information on times and class locations.*

MOTHER CHILD CENTER FOR FITNESS & WELLBEING
JENKYNS PHYSICAL THERAPY

PRENATAL EXERCISE
POST PARTUM EXERCISE

20% Discount
on 6 week session

BOSTON BABY PAGES™

Beach 'N' Sport Caddie™

Beach 'n' Sport Caddie™

The Ultimate Recreation Cart *New!*

Perfect for outdoor recreational activities: beach, camping, picnics, fishing, gardening, sporting events... *A great gift!*

Shown folded down into table top.

To Order: 1-800-378-7198
Free Brochure: 617-332-8382
Visit our web site at: www.channel1.com/users/timeink/bc.html

Beach 'N' Sport Caddie™
(617) 332-8382
S.T.A.R. Enterprises, Inc.
Newton, MA

🍃 *to order*
1-800-378-7198

🍃 *The Ultimate Recreation Cart.*

Our breastpumps come with four women attached.

Dot Norcross, IBCLC
Sandra Corsetti, IBCLC
Mary Bell
Barbara Popper, IBCLC

MEDELA BREASTPUMP RENTALS & SALES
ALSO, CLASSES & CONSULTATION

Lactation Care, inc.
617 244-5593

Lactation Care, Inc.
(617) 244-5593
25 Fisher Avenue
Newton, MA 02161

Hours:
Mon.-Fri. 9-5:30
Saturday 9-1
(*urgent care available evenings*)

See our advertisement for additional information.

MOTHER CHILD CENTER FOR FITNESS & WELLBEING
JENKYNS PHYSICAL THERAPY

▲ *Creative* ▲ *Fun* ▲ *Empowering*

CLASSES

Time to tune into your body, your baby, and gather insight and information about your pregnancy, childbirth, and new motherhood.

Not good with any other offer. One coupon per customer.

Mother Child Center
For Fitness & Wellbeing
Jenkyns Physical Therapy
(617) 864-4225
Mailing address:
121 Reed Street
Cambridge, MA 02140

🍃 *Classes are held in Arlington, MA. Call for more information on times and class locations.*

Our Customers Are Proud Of Their Deliveries.

If you're like most Streamline customers, you'd rather spend time making your 'new delivery' happy than fighting the lines at the supermarket. Let Streamline relieve you of the weekly chores that come between you and your family time – like grocery shopping, video rentals, dry cleaning, film processing, and parcel shipping.

To find out more about Streamline's home shopping and delivery service, fill out the reply card below or call us at 781.320.1900. And use our coupon from this book. You'll do your family proud.

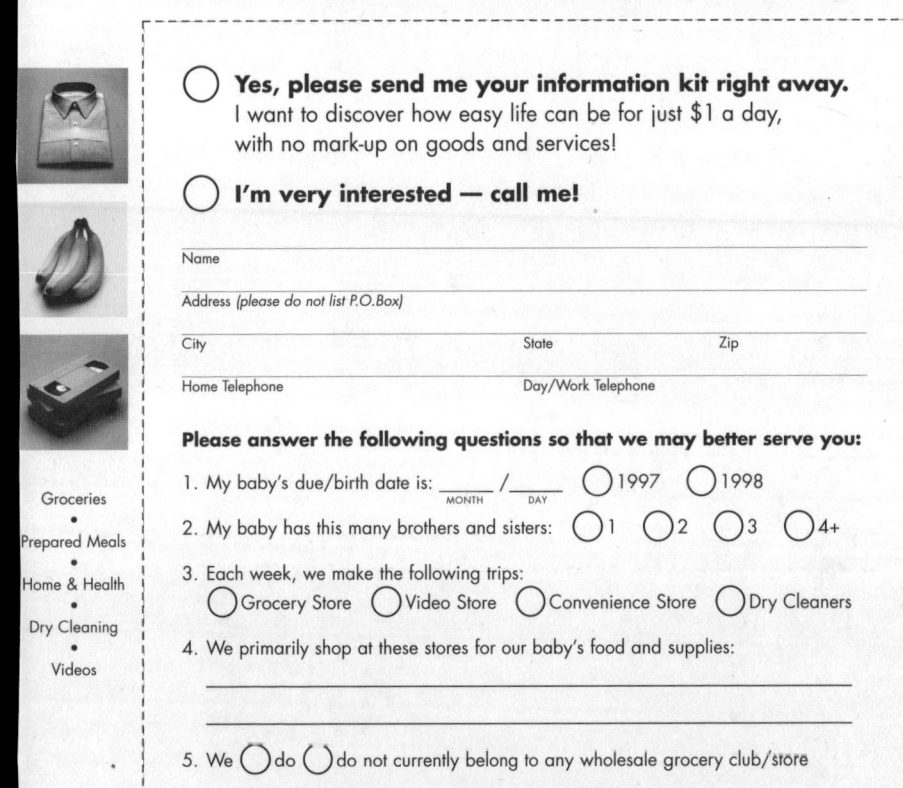

○ **Yes, please send me your information kit right away.**
I want to discover how easy life can be for just $1 a day, with no mark-up on goods and services!

○ **I'm very interested — call me!**

Name _____

Address *(please do not list P.O.Box)* _____

City _____ State _____ Zip _____

Home Telephone _____ Day/Work Telephone _____

Please answer the following questions so that we may better serve you:

1. My baby's due/birth date is: ____/____ ○ 1997 ○ 1998
   MONTH DAY

2. My baby has this many brothers and sisters: ○ 1 ○ 2 ○ 3 ○ 4+

3. Each week, we make the following trips:
   ○ Grocery Store   ○ Video Store   ○ Convenience Store   ○ Dry Cleaners

4. We primarily shop at these stores for our baby's food and supplies:
   _____
   _____

5. We ○ do ○ do not currently belong to any wholesale grocery club/store

**Call us at 781.320.1900 to speak with our representatives.
Or, visit us on the web at www.streamline.com**
Streamline service is subject to availability and geographic location.

Groceries
•
Prepared Meals
•
Home & Health
•
Dry Cleaning
•
Videos

call
781
.
320
.
1900

DETACH AND MAIL

streamline®
Where shopping is going.™

27 Dartmouth Street   Westwood, MA 02090

streamline®
Where shopping is going.™

Groceries • Prepared Meals • Home & Health • Dry Cleaning • Videos
27 Dartmouth Street   Westwood, MA 02090

NO POSTAGE
NECESSARY
IF MAILED
IN THE
UNITED STATES

BUSINESS REPLY MAIL
FIRST CLASS MAIL   PERMIT NO. 755   NORWOOD, MA

POSTAGE WILL BE PAID BY ADDRESSEE

STREAMLINE
27 DARTMOUTH STREET
WESTWOOD MA 02090-9808

Mail this card or call:

**781
•
320
•
1900**